AN INTRODUCTORY GRAMMAR OF
RABBINIC HEBREW

FCB 4/11/15

AN INTRODUCTORY GRAMMAR OF RABBINIC HEBREW

BY

MIGUEL PÉREZ FERNÁNDEZ

TRANSLATED BY

JOHN ELWOLDE

BRILL
LEIDEN · BOSTON · KÖLN
1999

Published with financial support from the Dirección General del Libro y Bibliotecas del Ministerio de Cultura, Spain.

Originally published in 1992 as *La Lengua de los sabios*, I. Morfosintaxis, by Editorial Verbo Divino, Estella, Spain. © Copyright of the Spanish edition: Editorial Verbo Divino, 1992 and Institución San Jerónimo, 1992.

This book is printed on acid-free paper.

Die Deutsche Bibliothek - CIP-Einheitsaufnahme

Pérez Fernández, Miguel:
An introductory grammar of rabbinic Hebrew / by Miguel Pérez Fernández. Transl. by John Elwolde. - Leiden ; Boston ; Köln : Brill, 1999
Einheitssacht.: La lengua de los sabios <dt.>
Text teilw. engl., teilw. hebr.
ISBN 90-04-10904-8

Library of Congress Cataloging-in-Publication Data
is also available

ISBN 90 04 10904 8

PRINTED IN THE NETHERLANDS

FOREWORD

This practical teaching grammar for students who already have a reasonable knowledge of Biblical Hebrew was initially developed over the period 1990 to 1992 as a handbook for courses in Rabbinic Hebrew at the University of Granada. Each unit concludes with vocabulary and twenty exercise texts relating to the grammatical point at issue in the unit. The exercises are generally drawn from tannaitic literature, and the student should find everything required to deal with them in the book. Many of the early exercises come from Abot, which, although not typical of the Mishnah, is more accessible to the beginner in rabbinic language and thought.

Each unit is divided into six sections: Introductory text, Morphology (including a presentation of diachronic matters), Grammar and usage, Phraseology, Vocabulary, and Exercises. The introductory texts and short explanations are designed to introduce the student to the language and concepts of the *tannaim*. Each introductory text exhibits the linguistic feature covered by the unit, although it serves primarily as a starting-point for discussion of literary, theological, historical, and methodological issues.

Overall, the work is divided into four parts: Nouns (including pronouns and adjectives), Verbs, Particles (including prepositions, conjunctions, and adverbs), and Clauses. The part dealing with clauses includes sentence syntax and the use of the conjunctions, but excludes the syntax of the noun and of the verb, which are dealt with in the first two parts.

The Introduction gives an account of the present state of Rabbinic Hebrew research, including a discussion of (1) the relationships of early—or tannaitic—Rabbinic Hebrew to its later—or amoraic—variety, to classical and later Biblical Hebrew, and to the Hebrew of the Dead Sea Scrolls, and (2) the nature of Rabbinic Hebrew as a spoken language in the light of modern studies in phonetics, vocabulary, and dialect. The Bibliography at the close of the book should be helpful to readers wishing to pursue particular issues further, although it is not exhaustive.

It is not only the pedagogical orientation of this book that clearly sets it apart from M.H. Segal's *A Grammar of Mishnaic Hebrew* (Oxford, 1927), but also its use of manuscripts—rather than printed editions—of the Mishnah (notably Codex Kaufmann), its general avoidance of later—amoraic—Rabbinic Hebrew, and its inclusion of texts from the early *midrashim*.

Texts from the Mishnah follow either C. Albeck's edition or, if preceded by 'K', Codex Kaufmann. For the Tosefta, the editions of M.S. Zuckermandel and S. Lieberman are followed, and for the Mekhilta, Sifra, Sifre to Numbers, and Sifre to Deuteronomy, those of J.S Lauterbach, I.H. Weiss, H.S. Horovitz, and L. Finkelstein, respectively.

ACKNOWLEDGEMENTS

I owe a large debt of gratitude to everyone who helped me during the two years I spent preparing the original volume, in particular to Professor Günter Stemberger of the University of Vienna and Professor Luis Girón, of the Complutensian University, Madrid, who read and annotated the first draft in detail, to my colleagues José Ramón Ayaso and Lola Ferre, who helped me with the indices, and to my niece, Esther, for her assistance in computing matters.

Dr J.F. Elwolde of the Dept. of Biblical Studies, University of Sheffield, brought the Spanish original to the attention of scholars through his review in *The Society for Old Testament Study Book List* of 1993. His English version incorporates many minor additions and corrections as well as an improved bibliography and a greatly expanded set of indices. We are extremely grateful to Anne Lee, a student in Dr Elwolde's department, who entered the vast bulk of the exercises into the computer, and who, with Rosemarie Kossov, a graduate student, helped with the proofreading; thanks are due as well to Martin F.J. Baasten of the University of Leiden, for his help with the passage from Contini on p. 186, and Kate Dove Davis, a colleague of Dr Elwolde, who helped with the production of the camera-ready copy. We should also like to record our thanks to the publishers, E.J. Brill, especially in the persons of Hans van der Meij, who oversaw the commissioning and progress of the translation, and Anne Folkertsma and her successor, Mattie Kuiper, for their helpfulness at the beginning and end of the publishing process. The publication has been funded in large measure by a grant to the publishers from the Dirección General del Libro y Bibliotecas of the Ministerio de Cultura in Madrid and was undertaken as part of a research project, *Lengua y Literatura del Judaismo Clásico*, sponsored by the Ministerio de Educación y Ciencia (PB93/1161).

Miguel Pérez Fernández
Granada, March 1997

CONTENTS

1. The language of the Torah by itself, the language of the
wise by itself. **2.** Tannaitic Hebrew (RH1) and Amoraic
Hebrew (RH2). **3.** RH1, a spoken language. **4.** Foreign influence in vocabulary and the legacy of Biblical Hebrew
(BH). **5.** BH and RH1—two different languages. **6.** RH1,
LBH (Late Biblical Hebrew), and the Hebrew of the Dead
Sea Scrolls. **7.** Influence of BH on RH1. **8.** Differences between manuscripts and printed editions. **9.** Rabbinic Hebrew (RH) phonetics. **10.** Traditions and dialects of RH1.
11. Conclusion.

Part I   Nouns

1–2. Abot 1.1: transmission of the Torah. **3.** BH and RH
personal pronouns. **4.** The variations ‏אנחנו/אנו, אנכ/אני‎/
‏הן/הם, את/אתם, אתה/את, נחנו‎. **5.** Suffixed pronouns; use of
‏את־‎. **6.** Suffixed pronouns with ‏אין‎. **7.** Emphatic function of
pronouns. **8.** Pronoun as copula in nominal clause. **9.** Proleptic pronoun before subject. **10.** Demonstrative usage
(‏הַהוּא‎, etc.). **11.** Proleptic pronoun before object. **12.** ‏הוּא‎
‏הָיָה אוֹמֵר‎. **13.** ‏וְכֵן הוּא אוֹמֵר‎. **14.** ‏הֲרֵי אַתָּה דָן‎.

1–2. SNm 84.2: fulfilment and harmonization of Scripture.
3. BH and RH demonstratives. **4.** Strengthened forms. **5.**
Pronominal and adjectival uses. **6.** Repetition of demonstrative to express movement or reciprocity. **7.** Deictic
function of ‏אֶת־‎. **8.** ‏עֶצֶם‎ as demonstrative. **9.** ‏כָּל־עַצְם־‎. **10.**
Demonstrative use of personal pronoun (‏הַהוּא‎, etc.). **11.**
‏כָּל עַצְם־‎. **12.** ‏לְעוֹלָם הַבָּא, בָּעוֹלָם הַזֶּה‎.

CONTENTS

1. Naz 3.6: *maʿaśiyyot* in the Mishnah. **2.** RH differences from BH in the perfect: קָטְלָה for קָטְלָה, קָטַלְתְּ for קָטַלְתְּ, קְטַלְתֶּן for קְטַלְתֶּם. **3.** *Qal* perfect forms קָטֵל, קָטֹל; קָטַל absent; יָכוֹל. **4.** *Ayin-waw* and *-yod* verbs. **A.** *Qal*: קָם, מֵת, בּוֹשׁ; *Nifʿal*: נִדּוֹן/נָדוֹן. **B.** *Piʿel* (etc.): כִּיֵּון, מְיֵּיל, נִתְגַּיֵּיר, קִיֵּים; שֵׁיֵּיר (< שׁאר). **C.** *Poʿlel*: עוֹרֵר; *Pilpel*: זִגְזֵג. **5.** *Lamed-alef* and *-he* verbs. **A.** *Lamed-alef* verbs inflected like *lamed-he*: מָצִינוּ, קָרִינוּ, קָרִיתִי. **B.** Third person feminine singular *Qal* in ת-ָ: שָׁתָת, הָיָת. **C.** Third person feminine singular *Nifʿal*: נִמְצֵאת, נִגְלֵית. **D.** Suffixed forms of *lamed-he* verbs inflected like *lamed-alef*: עֲשָׂאָן, עֲשָׂאוּהוּ. **6–7.** Perfect expresses action that took place at specific point in past; distinguished from general or atemporal statements; effect of disappearance of וַיִּקְטֹל construction; use of perfect to begin *meshalim*. **8.** Perfect with pluperfect significance; in combination with הָיָה + participle/noun. **9.** Perfect with present reference. **A.** In dialogues and colloquial speech: בָּאחֶם לְשָׁלוֹם, לֹא זָכִיתִי מִן הַדִּין, אָמַרְתָּ. **B.** Expressing a state or condition that arose in past but persists in present הִכְשַׁרְתִּי אֶת נִזְקוֹ. **10.** Perfect in declarations of general validity: נִכְנַס יַיִן, יָצָא סוֹד. **11–12.** Perfect in protasis of conditional/temporal sentence, in halakhic formulations and narrative; distinguished from liturgical atemporal present. **13.** Future perfect, expressing future event regarded as already having taken place. **14.** אִם-עָשִׂיתִי עָשִׂיתִי, מַה-שֶּׁעָשָׂה עָשָׂה expressing irreversibility. **15.** אָמַרְתָּ. **16.** לֹא זָכִיתִי מִן הַדִּין. **17.** [לֹא] יָצָא.

1. SDt 355: development of oral law sanctioned by Moses. **2.** Disappearance of infinitive absolute in RH; infinitive construct with -ל, מִל-; negated by שֶׁלֹּא; development of negative form of infinitive in BH, LBH, etc. **3.** *Qal* infinitive based on imperfect; table of forms; occasional retention of BH structures. **4.** Assimilation of *lamed-alef* to *lamed-he* forms of infinitive: לְמַלֹּאות, לִקְרוֹת. **5–6.** Elision of preformative -ה in *Nif'al* and *Hif'il* infinitive: לִיכָּנֵס, לַרְבּוֹת, לִינָּשֵׂא, לֵיעָשׂוֹת, לִיכָּרֵת, לִיבָּטֵל. **7.** RH infinitive with -ל only accepts object suffixes. **8.** Abandonment of BH כְּצֵאתוֹ, בְּצֵאתוֹ constructions. **9.** Functions of infinitive: as subject or object (complement) of verb; expressing purpose; used attributively, modifying noun; used modally, as

Part IV Clauses

ABBREVIATIONS

Mishnah tractates

Abot	Abot	Naz	Nazir
Arakh	'Arakhin	Ned	Nedarim
AZ	'Abodah Zarah	Neg	Nega'im
BB	Baba Batra	Nid	Niddah
Ber	Berakhot	Ohol	Oholot
Beṣ	Beṣah	Orl	'Orlah
Bekh	Bekhorot	Par	Parah
Bik	Bikkurim	Pea	Pe'ah
BM	Baba Meṣi'a	Pes	Pesaḥim
BQ	Baba Qama	Qid	Qiddushin
Dem	Dema'i	Qin	Qinnim
Eduy	'Eduyyot	RS	Rosh ha-Shanah
Erub	'Erubin	Sanh	Sanhedrin
Giṭ	Giṭṭin	Shab	Shabbat
Ḥag	Ḥagigah	Shebi	Shebi'it
Ḥal	Ḥallah	Shebu	Shebu'ot
Hor	Horayot	Sheq	Sheqalim
Ḥul	Ḥullin	Soṭ	Soṭah
Kel	Kelim	Suk	Sukkah
Ker	Keritot	Taa	Ta'anit
Ket	Ketubot	Tam	Tamid
Kil	Kil'aim	Ṭeb	Ṭebul Yom
Ma'aśrot	Ma'aśrot	Tem	Temurah
Mak	Makkot	Ter	Terumot
Makhsh	Makhshirin	Ṭoh	Ṭohorot
Meg	Megillah	Uqṣ	'Uqṣin
Mei	Me'illah	Yad	Yadaim
Men	Menaḥot	Yeb	Yebamot
Mid	Middot	Yom	Yoma
Miqw	Miqwa'ot	Zab	Zabim
MQ	Mo'ed Qaṭan	Zeb	Zebaḥim
MS	Ma'aśer Sheni		

Other rabbinic texts

ARN	Abot de Rabbi Nathan, 'A' text, numbered according to the 1987 translation of Mª Angeles Navarro Peiró
F	L. Finkelstein's 1939 edition of Sifre to Deuteronomy
H	H.S. Horovitz's 1917 edition of Sifre to Numbers
K	Codex Kaufmann of the Mishnah
L	J.Z. Lauterbach's 1933–35 edition of Mekhilta
Mek	Mekhilta de Rabbi Ishmael (followed by Exodus chapter and verse reference)
PesR	Pesiqta Rabbati
PRE	Pirqe de Rabbi Eliezer, numbered according to the 1984 translation of M. Pérez Fernández
S	S. Schechter's 1887 edition of Abot de Rabbi Nathan
SDt	Sifre to Deuteronomy
SLv	Sifra (followed by Leviticus chapter and verse reference)
SNm	Sifre to Numbers
j	Talmud Jerushalmi (Jerusalem, or Palestinian, Talmud)
Tos	Tosefta (according to MSS Erfurt and Vienna)
W	I.H. Weiss's 1862 edition of Sifra

Books of the Bible

Gn Ex Lv Nm Dt Jos Jg 1 S 2 S 1 K 2 K Is Jr Ezk Ho Jl Am Ob Jon Mc Na Hb Zp Hg Zc Ml Ps Jb Pr Ru Ca Ec Lm Est Dn Ezr Ne 1 C 2 C

Mt Mk Lk Jn Act Rm 1 Co 2 Co Gal Eph Ph Col 1 T 2 T Tit Phlm Hbr Jm 1 P 1 J 2 J 3 J Ju Rv

Other abbreviations (see also Bibliography)

AH	Archaic Hebrew (of early biblical poetry and of inscriptions)
BH	('Classical') Biblical Hebrew (especially of pre-exilic prose)
LBH	Late Biblical Hebrew
RH	Rabbinic Hebrew
RH1	Rabbinic Hebrew of the *tannaim* ('Mishnaic Hebrew')
RH2	Rabbinic Hebrew of the *amoraim*

INTRODUCTION

1. *The language of the Torah by itself, the language of the wise by itself*

The student who reads a Rabbinic Hebrew text for the first time will usually be surprised and somewhat disconcerted by a series of striking differences from the grammar of Biblical Hebrew, among them the following:

> Merger of final *mem* and *nun*, with masculine plurals usually ending in *nun*;
> Relative particle -שֶׁ instead of אֲשֶׁר;
> Genitive particle שֶׁל 'of', partially replacing the construct chain of classical Biblical Hebrew;
> Very frequent use of הָיָה 'be' with participle;
> Complete disappearance of the *waw*-consecutive;
> Loss of the infinitive absolute and of special forms for the cohortative and jussive.

Nowadays, Rabbinic Hebrew is generally treated as an historically distinct phase of the Hebrew language, and the saying attributed to Rabbi Joḥanan in AZ 58b—the language of the Torah by itself, the language of the wise by itself—reflects early awareness of its distinctiveness.

In the development of Hebrew, four major periods are discernible: BH (Biblical Hebrew), RH (Rabbinic Hebrew), MH (Mediaeval Hebrew), and IH (Israeli, or Modern, Hebrew). This wide-ranging classification allows for further subdivision and transitional phases. Thus, BH can be subdivided into Archaic Hebrew (AH), the Hebrew of archaic poetry; Biblical Hebrew (BH) proper, the standard language of pre-exilic prose writings; and post-exilic, or Late Biblical, Hebrew (LBH), whereas RH naturally divides into Early Rabbinic Hebrew (RH1), the language of the *tannaim*; and Late Rabbinic Hebrew (RH2), the language of the *amoraim*. This study will focus on RH1.

2. *Tannaitic Hebrew (RH1) and Amoraic Hebrew (RH2)*

In political terms, the tannaitic period is that of the 'restoration' of Judaism after the disasters of 70 and 135 CE; from a literary and theological perspective, this period witnesses the compilation, classification, and editing of an immense corpus of oral law, which is presented, and defended, as being a logical development of the written law of the Bible. The vast literature that emerged over this period (from 70 CE until halfway through the third century) is evidence of the enormous labour and exceptional ability of the tannaitic teachers who developed the Mishnah, Tosefta, halakhic *midrashim* (Mekhilta de Rabbi Ishmael, Mekhilta de Rabbi Shimeon ben Yoḥai, Sifra to Leviticus, Sifre to Numbers and to Deuteronomy, Sifre Zuṭṭa, etc.), as well as non-halakhic works such as Seder Olam Rabbah.

The language of these works clearly differs from BH, as is evident from the most cursory examination, and also has features that distinguish it from the Hebrew of the *amoraim* (RH2), who, from the fourth century, compiled the Jerusalem Talmud, early haggadic and homiletic *midrashim* (Genesis Rabbah, Leviticus Rabbah, Pesiqta de Rab Kahana), and the Babylonian Talmud. The main difference is that in the RH2 period Hebrew began to die out as a spoken language, being replaced in this rôle by Aramaic. Other features include the enormous Aramaic influence on RH2 in morphology, vocabulary, and grammar, the large number of Graecisms, and a return to biblical vocabulary and constructions. Indeed, the dictum of Rabbi Joḥanan given earlier occurs in connection with the claim of a Babylonian *amora* that the plural form רְחֵלִים 'sheep', attested in the Bible, was more correct than רְחֵלוֹת. E.Y. Kutscher (1972b, 57) makes the important point that if a BH or Aramaic form is not found in the *tannaim* but 'reappears' in RH2, it was probably never employed by the *tannaim* at all but is an amoraic innovation

M. Bar-Asher (1990a, 208) lists three characteristic features of RH2 (see also Sokoloff 1969): the demonstrative הַלָּלוּ, first person singular imperfect with initial *nun* (reflecting Aramaic influence), and the expression מַשֶּׁהוּ 'something' used in the sense of כָּל־שֶׁהוּ 'a little'. While some RH2 texts can give the appearance of a linguistic mosaic, other amoraic compositions, such as Midrash Rabbah to Song of Songs (see Girón 1988–89; 1990), employ the language and style of the *tannaim*.

3. RH1, a spoken language

Given the highly technical nature of tannaitic literature (legal, halakhic, exegetical), we have to specify what is meant when we say that RH1 was a spoken language. It could have been spoken just in academic circles, for teaching or in court—in the same way that Latin was used in mediaeval scholarship and, until quite recently, in the Roman Catholic church—but not in everyday life. We know, in any case, that the early rabbinic texts in the form they are preserved in the Mishnah postdate any original spoken version of such material by a considerable period, during which the writing down of the oral law was prohibited (see Rabin 1976, 1008; Stemberger 1996, 31–44)—although there were a few incomplete collections of written *halakhot*, systematic editing of such works is assumed not to have begun until around 300 CE.

Even so, these considerations do not mean that RH1 should not be regarded as a popular, spoken language. Indeed, it is generally believed that the

Dead Sea Scrolls, specifically the Copper Scroll and also the Bar-Kokhba letters, have furnished clear evidence of the popular character of MH. Moreover, the faithfulness and care with which oral traditions can be transmitted is well known. For example, in the Mishnah (Eduy 1.3) it is stated that 'each person has to speak in the language of his teacher'; however this is to be understood exactly, it clearly functions as a guarantee of fidelity of transmission of rabbinic statements, and in the light of this it comes as no surprise that the Mishnah itself records sayings of Hillel in Aramaic (Abot 1.13), doubtless because they were originally formulated in that language. Finally, without denying the technical nature of most tannaitic literature, the language of which would clearly have differed from the daily vernacular, within the tannaitic corpus itself there are also popular sayings and parables (*meshalim*), *exempla* (*ma'asiyyot*), testimonies, and descriptive narratives relating to, for example, the royal liturgy in Sot 7.8 or the festival of first fruits in Bik 3.2–8, which display a more lucid and popular style.

In terms of dialect geography, at the time of the *tannaim* Palestine could be divided into the Aramaic-speaking regions of Galilee and Samaria and a smaller area, in Judaea, in which Rabbinic Hebrew was used among the descendants of returning exiles. To the south of Palestine, North Arabian dialects would have been spoken, while in the north there were probably a few isolated areas where Phoenician was still spoken. Greek would have been predominant in Hellenistic cities and, along with Latin, was employed as the language of Roman administration, used in official documents and inscriptions as well as in politics and commerce. There would also have been languages spoken by Jews in the diaspora, as well as Biblical Hebrew with its prestigious and insistent presence in the temple cult and synagogue liturgy. It is not simply that at this time there were many languages spoken in Palestine but that the same person would speak a variety of languages. To be more precise, the following three situations are possible (following Rabin 1976).

1. Bilingualism/multilingualism, typical, for example, of exiles who returned speaking both Hebrew and Aramaic or of the children of marriages of Hebrew- and Aramaic-speakers;

2. Lingua franca, used by speakers of different native languages who would adopt it as a common 'second' language for communication among themselves in, for example, the realms of administration, commerce, or liturgy—such a language does not require perfect fluency, and, for commercial purposes, for example, an elementary knowledge suffices;

3. Diglossia, or the use, as determined by social convention, of a native language at two levels, popular and literary, is found to some extent in all languages (it is particularly striking in the differences between spoken and literary Arabic), and it is noticeable that switching between levels is not easy for all speakers.

It is obvious, then, that all three situations would have been commonly found, and it is against this background that the use by the same writer of Hebrew and Aramaic or the abundant production at this time of Jewish literature in Greek—the New Testament, apocrypha, pseudepigrapha, etc.—is to be explained.

As a lingua franca, Greek was doubtless employed in a myriad different day-to-day situations, and BH would have served a similar function in liturgical contexts.

Given the different stages and styles of RH, we may conclude that Hebrew-speakers could have found themselves in a situation of diglossia, with the language of the Mishnah and *midrashim* belonging to a level that required a relatively high degree of education in order to understand its grammar and terminology.

Bearing in mind the small area in which it took root—post-exilic Judaea—it is generally accepted that the decisive factor in the extinction of RH1 in Palestine was the suppression of the Bar-Kokhba revolt in 135, with the consequent ravaging of the land, deportations, and an exodus to Galilee.

Although we know that even in the fourth century Hebrew was still used in Palestine for conversation (עִבְרִי לְדִבּוּר), along with Greek, Latin, and Aramaic (see Mishor 1989), its linguistic isolation and the transfer of Judaean intellectuals to Galilee caused RH to lose its literary character and the ability to develop. In Aramaic-speaking Galilee, the descendants of Judaean exiles found it increasingly difficult to maintain RH1 as a living language, with the result that Aramaic became dominant and a new scholarly language, RH2, emerged (see Kutscher 1972b, 57ff.).

4. *Foreign influence in vocabulary*

Given the sociolinguistic facts as described, it is hardly surprising that we find incorporated in RH1 many features of vocabulary and grammar from the surrounding languages. Recent studies suggest that about half the vocabulary of RH1 coincides with that of BH, while of the remainder, a large proportion is shared with Aramaic, with a significant number of Greek—and to a lesser extent Latin—loanwords, as well as words of Akkadian or Persian origin.

4.1 *The legacy of Hebrew*

We begin with an obvious fact, namely, that the Bible does not include all the Hebrew vocabulary spoken in biblical times. In the light of this, it is quite possible that RH has conserved a number of ancient—but non-biblical—Hebrew words. Among those recognized as falling into this category are חָזַר 'return', סָמָךְ 'harvest olives', עָצַר 'uproot', צָרִיךְ 'necessary', and טְחוֹל 'spleen'.

For some words, early forms, not found in BH, have been preserved, for example, the singular לֵילִי 'night' (Nid 4.4) as against BH לֵיל, לַיְלָה, and לֵיל; whereas לַיִל and לֵיל are secondary forms resulting from the *loss* of the second diphthong, לַיְלָה results from the *reduction* of this diphthong (*laylay > laylā, with the final *he* as *mater lectionis*), and it is only in RH that the shape of the original form of the word has persisted (see Bar-Asher 1990a, 204).

As might be expected, BH words commonly undergo semantic development in RH, for example מָעָה 'grain' > 'money', מְזוּזָה 'doorpost' > '*mezuzah* (attached to doorpost)', עוֹלָם 'eternity' > 'world', גָּזַר 'cut' > 'decree', לָקַח 'take' > 'buy', and מַעֲשֶׂה 'deed' > 'event'.

A word that has thus acquired a new meaning will sometimes undergo a change in its morphological shape (see Unit 9) or in its gender or number (see Unit 10); note, for example, the forms, אֲכִילָה 'food', הֲלִיכָה 'walk', כָּבוּד 'honour', הלך *Qal* 'go', *Pi'el* 'walk about'.

4.2 The influence of Aramaic

Perhaps as a reaction to earlier scholarship, which had viewed Mishnaic Hebrew as an artificial language—either Hebraized Aramaic or Aramaized Hebrew—M.H. Segal understated the influence of Aramaic on RH. In fact, without detracting from the independent status of RH1, the presence of Aramaic is obvious, not simply in loanwords and loan-translations but also in the basic grammatical structure of the language, in the inflection of nouns and verbs, as the following examples demonstrate.

1. Pronominal suffixes of the second person singular masculine and feminine in ךְ- or ךְ- (see Unit 4.4).

2. The imperatives הֱוִי 'be' (singular) and הֱווֹ 'be' (plural), alongside the corresponding Hebrew forms הֱוֵי and הֱווּ (see Unit 21.5).

3. The second person singular masculine pronoun אָתּ, perhaps an archaic dialect form (see Nm 11.15) that has re-emerged under Aramaic influence (see Unit 1.4B).

4. M. Moreshet (1980a) registered 210 RH1 verbs derived from Aramaic as against 241 from BH.

5. Common words like אַבָּא 'father', אִמָּא 'mother', שָׁעָה 'hour', and מָמוֹן '*mammon*, wealth' are Aramaic loanwords.

6. New nouns are frequently patterned according to the Aramaic morphological patterns קַטָּלָה and הַקְטָלָה (see Unit 9.5–6). Aramaic vocalization can also displace what would be expected in Hebrew, for example כְּלָל 'general rule, generalization' for כָּלוֹל.

7. Aramaic influence is also visible in the addition to קְטִילָה-type nouns of the suffix וּת-, expressing verbal action (see Unit 9.10), for example גְּמִילוּת 'fulfilment, act of fulfilling', נְשִׂיאוּת 'elevation, act of raising up'.

8. Aramaic has been instrumental in changes of gender in certain words—for example, כּוֹס 'cup' is feminine in BH, with the feminine plural כּוֹסוֹת attested in RH (Pes 10.1), but in the singular it is treated as masculine for the purpose of agreement with adjectives: כּוֹס רִאשׁוֹן 'first cup' (Pes 10.2).

9. Numerous Aramaic particles have entered RH1, for example לָאו 'not', generally used in disjunctives or as an alternative—negative—condition ('and if not'; see Units 23.11B; 28.7C). The adversative אֶלָּא 'but rather' is simply a contracted form of Aramaic אֵן לָא—the BH equivalent is אִם לֹא.

10. Although the relative particle שֶׁל is a native Hebrew form, the extent of its use has been influenced by the Aramaic relative דִי.

However, it has been emphasized that not all the Aramaisms of RH are necessarily of recent origin, with some deriving from a common Semitic substratum, and others reflecting a reverse influence, of RH on Aramaic. Statements about the correspondence of the two languages in other areas, such as the syntax of the verb, likewise have to be formulated with care.

4.3 *Greek and Latin loanwords*

See Unit 12. Although there is an abundance of Greek words in RH1, which became even more pronounced in RH2 (however, it is not always clear when a form entered the language), Greek has not had any significant effect on the morphological or syntactic structure of Hebrew, but has simply enriched the lexicon of RH. The following are a few of the more obvious examples.

1. Loan-translations (calques), translated verbatim from Greek into Hebrew, include יָפֶה אָמַרְתָּ 'you have spoken well (literally, 'beautifully')' (καλῶς εἶπας) and מִכָּל־מָקוֹם 'in every case (literally, 'from every place')' (ἐκ παντὸς τρόπου).

2. Greek words ending in -η usually have a Hebrew plural in -*a'ot*, which recalls to some degree the plurals -αι and -*ae* of Greek and Latin (see Units 10.6; 12.5C). Some native Hebrew words have also adopted this feature in their plurals, for example מְקְוָאוֹת from מִקְוֶה 'ritual bath'.

3. Various Greek words compounded with ἀρχί- ('chief') have passed into RH, for example אַרְכּיּוֹדִיקִי 'chief judge' (ἀρχίiudex) (Genesis Rabbah 50.2). In Abot 1.8, there is a striking example, in which this Greek prefix has been placed before a native Hebrew word, yielding the sequence אַרְכִי דִינִים, found in Codex Kaufmann and later rather clumsily erased in order to Hebraize ἀρχί- as עוֹרְכֵי 'arrangers of' (see Sznol 1990).

4. Only a few verbs are taken from Greek (Moreshet 1980a lists just thirty from Greek and Latin), of which some are native Hebrew denominalizations of loanwords, for example בִּסֵּם 'base' (from βάσις 'base'), זִוֵּג 'join' (from זוּג/ζεῦγος 'yoke'), לִסְטֵם 'assault' (from ληστής 'robber').

The extensive Greek vocabulary of the *meshalim* (see Unit 12.7) shows the influence of Greek in the popular language and the high degree to which it had been integrated within RH at all levels.

4.4 *Akkadian and Persian*

Akkadian vocabulary has come via Aramaic, as, for example, with תַּרְנְגוֹל 'cock', גֵּט 'document (of divorce)', תַּרְגּוּם *'targum*, translation'. The Persian administration of Palestine also left its mark in a few words like וֶרֶד 'rose'.

5. *BH and RH1—two different languages*

Nowadays the status of RH1 as a popular, spoken, language is no longer in question, and the linguistic debate has a different focus, namely, whether RH1 should be regarded as the last stage of BH, that is, as representative of BH as it developed in the post-exilic period, or, instead, as a dialect that was already in existence before the exile, which had carried on evolving alongside BH as the language of a particular group or area and which—for whatever reason—emerged as a literary idiom in the rabbinic period.

In support of the first position, it is clear that every language develops over time, and in the case of RH, there are several clear examples of such development.

1. New conjugations, such as the *Nitpa'al* and *Nuf'al*, have to be understood as the result of popular desire to find a more expressive way of stating reflexive and passive verbal relationships. Both examples mentioned result from a merger with the *Nif'al*—of the *Hitpa'el* on the one hand and of the *Pu'al* on the other (see Units 15.3C; 15.4D).

2. The same tendency is seen in the conjugation of stative verbs, like יָרֵא 'fear', as reflexives or intensives, thus: מִתְיָרֵא.

3. In vocabulary, semantic changes and the incorporation of new words, especially from Greek and Latin, imply diachronic development. Aramaic vocabulary in particular requires detailed study in this respect (see above, at the end of §4.2).

4. The first person plural pronoun, אָנוּ 'we', has been constructed by analogy with אֲנִי 'I' and with the first person plural object suffix, exemplified in שְׁמָרָנוּ 'he has kept us'. Similarly, the demonstrative אֵלּוּ 'these' has supplanted biblical אֵלֶּה in an attempt to express more clearly the demonstrative's plural reference, employing the וּ- ending of the third person plural of the verb in the perfect.

On the other hand, it is also clear that RH witnesses to a very early form of the Hebrew language, as seen in the following examples.

1. אֲנִי 'I', widespread in BH and reflected in Ugaritic 'an, is used in RH to the exclusion of the alternative BH form, אָנֹכִי.

2. While Aramaic influence might be responsible for the widespread use of אַתְּ 'you' as a masculine pronoun, it is also found in the Bible at Nm 11.15.

3. The feminine demonstrative זֹו/זֹה 'this', which replaces BH זֹאת, seems to have come from a northern dialect of Hebrew (see 2 K 6.19; Ezk 40.45; Ho 7.16; Ps 132.12).

4. The relative particle -שֶׁ 'that, which' (not a development from אֲשֶׁר) is found in Akkadian and Phoenician as well as in some of the earliest biblical texts (Jg 5–8; see Unit 8.3–4).

5. The extent to which the use of final *nun* in place of *mem* became widespread is perhaps due to Aramaic influence, but the phenomenon itself probably reflects a dialect feature of nasalization found at a very early stage of the language, as evidenced by the Mesha stela (in Moabite) and by Jg 5.10. The use of *nun* is not limited to plurals, in K BB 6.6 we find דֶּרֶךְ בְּנֵי אָדָן 'the way of the sons of humankind', although in the printed editions the form אָדָן has been systematically 'corrected' to BH אָדָם.

6. The RH1 second person singular masculine perfect ending in ־תָּה, alongside standard BH ־תָּ, is also found in early BH, for example Ps 8.4,7; 68.10; see Unit 16.4A).

7. The archaic third person singular feminine perfect termination in ־ת instead of ־ה reappears in *lamed-he* (*lamed-alef*) and *lamed-yod* verbs in RH. The form is also attested in the Siloam tunnel inscription (הית 'it was') and sporadically in the Bible (see Units 16.4B; 17.5B).

8. The plural יְמוֹת 'days' for יָמִים may be due to the influence of Aramaic יוֹמָת, although it is also attested at Dt 32.7 (see Unit 10.11).

9. In the use of the tenses there are also archaic features, for example עַל קַן צִפּוֹר יַגִּיעַ רַחֲמֶיךָ 'even unto the nest of a bird your mercy reaches' (Meg 4.9), where the durative function of the imperfect is evidenced (see Unit 18.12).

These examples show clearly that RH may be regarded neither as an artificial creation nor simply as the result of evolution from BH. Certain phenomena are best explained by assuming that RH was a living dialect even before the exile and that it developed alongside—but not out of—BH. That is the conclusion of M. Bar-Asher (1990a, 205): 'We have to recognize that it is not a matter of two successive stages of the language, but of two different synchronic systems, reflecting two different dialects. In other words, RH is not the direct result of BH, but rather a related dialect'.

It is not difficult to imagine where and by whom this language was spoken. For C. Rabin (1976, 1015), it was the language used by the inhabitants of the area known in post-exilic times as Judaea; for E.Y. Kutscher (1972b, 57ff.), this area was more precisely that of Jerusalem and its environs, to which the exiles from Babylonia returned. It is clear that RH was the language of the Pharisees, in which their literature was composed and in which it was for so long faithfully transmitted; it was the language of the oral law, scandalizing the (priestly?) Qumran sectarians, who called it a 'blasphemous, uncircumcised language' (see *Hodayot* 2.18–19; 4.16–17; Damascus Document 5.11–12, cited in Rabin 1976, 1018). What we seem to have in RH is a further sign of the Pharisaic revolution and one of the keys to its success—the ascent of the common people and their language to the realm of religious discourse and debate. There is an obvious analogy here with similar phenomena in the western world, where the introduction of vernacular languages into the Roman Catholic liturgy has marked the conclusion of a centuries-long struggle.

6. RH1, LBH, and the Hebrew of the Dead Sea Scrolls

The eruption of this dialect into literary expression had begun centuries before in various contexts, as demonstrated by the presence of RH syntax and vocabulary in the Hebrew of the later books of the Bible (LBH) and of the Dead Sea Scrolls. The following are a few examples (others may be found in Qimron 1986, 98–104).

1. The BH *Hif'il* participle is formed according to the pattern מַקְטִיל (masculine), מַקְטִילָה (feminine). RH, as ever seeking greater expressivity, adds the feminine marker ת- to the second form, hence, מַקְטֶלֶת, on the analogy of the *Qal* participle, for example, הָאִשָּׁה אֵין מֵדֶּרֶת אֶת־בְּנָהּ 'the woman cannot impose a vow on her son' (Soṭ 3.8). But the same pattern is already found in Esther: אֵין אֶסְתֵּר מַגֶּדֶת 'Esther did not tell' (Est 2.20; see Unit 19.7A).

2. בִּזָּיוֹן 'scorn, shame, opprobrium' is a technical term in tannaitic literature (see SNm 35 [H 39]; 116.1 [H 130]) that had already appeared in Esther (1.18).

3. The RH genitive particle שֶׁל 'of' appears in Ca 3.7 (along with the characteristically RH phenomenon of proleptic possessive suffix on the preceding noun): הִנֵּה מִטָּתוֹ שֶׁלִּשְׁלֹמֹה 'behold the couch (literally, 'his couch') of Solomon'. שֶׁל also occurs in the Temple Scroll and Copper Scroll from Qumran and in the Bar-Kokhba letters.

4. The Book of Jonah makes an obvious effort to imitate classical BH. But even here, in the space of two verses (Jon 1.7–8), we find, first, RH בְּשֶׁלְּמִי 'on whose account?', followed by an attempt to recast this expression in a more classical mould: בַּאֲשֶׁר לְמִי.

7. The influence of BH on RH1

RH1 should not be regarded as a homogenous body of literature. Some tannaitic literature displays a relatively high level of influence—much of it inevitable—from BH, and we find that biblical structures and meanings have not yielded to their rabbinic counterparts. Three examples, drawn from the work of M. Bar-Asher, are as follows: jussives, although virtually obsolete in RH1, are retained in Abot (1.8; 2.4, etc.; see Unit 18.4–5); the denominative form הִתְחִיל 'he began' (from תְּחִילָה 'beginning'), found throughout RH1, gives way to the standard BH *Hif'il* form הֵחֵל (root חלל) in Tam 2.2–3; the verb לָקַח, which in RH1 gradually develops the meaning of 'buy' (Meg 3.1), is still found at RS 1.9 and elsewhere in the biblical sense of 'take'.

Analysis and evaluation of textual sources is required in such instances, to ascertain whether they represent an earlier stage of literary RH or, instead, a later revision. But in any case, the prestige of the biblical language was such as to maintain certain BH forms in the face of a popular tendency to replace them, for example, the infinitives לָלֶכֶת 'to go', לָתֵת 'to give', and לֶאֱכֹל 'to eat', which were used alongside their rabbinic counterparts לֵילֵךְ, לִיתֵּן, and לוֹכַל (see Unit 20.3). E.Y. Kutscher claimed that such remnants of BH 'were not part and parcel of M[ishnaic] H[ebrew]' (Kutscher 1972b), but that one should not draw wider conclusions from this.

8. Differences between manuscripts and printed editions

A superficial comparison of printed texts of the Mishnah with texts found in the earliest manuscripts reveals a large number of linguistic and even literary differences. Evaluating them is of the essence in attempting to uncover spoken RH. The following are some of the differences between C. Albeck's edition of the Mishnah (Jerusalem, 1952) and Codex Kaufmann (K), dated between the eleventh and thirteenth centuries and unanimously agreed to be the best witness to the language of the Mishnah.

1. In Abot 4.20, Albeck reads אֱלִישָׁע בֶּן אֲבוּיָה 'Elisha ben Abuiah' and רַבִּי יוֹסֵי 'Rabbi Jose', while K has אֱלִישָׁע בֶּן אֲבִיָּיה 'Elisha ben Abijah' and ר יוֹסֶה 'R. Joseh'. Which of the two better reflects the original orthography and pronunciation?

In the same text, Albeck reads four times הַלּוֹמֵד 'the one who learns', while K has הַלָּמֵד in the same sense. The first is an active participle, the second an intransitive, stative, participle. Are we to believe that over time active forms replaced earlier statives (see Unit 19.3A)?

Also in Abot 4.20, Albeck reads לְאוֹכֵל עֲנָבִים 'for him who eats grapes' and K reads לְאוֹכֵל עֲנָבִים, where it is clear that the vocalization does not correspond to the consonantal text. Given the existence of a *Pa'ol* participle, should K's reading be regarded as more consistent with the spoken language?

2. In Abot 5.2, Albeck reads הָיוּ מַכְעִיסִין וּבָאִין 'they were *continually* provoking'. וּבָאִין (literally, 'and coming') is a characteristic participial usage of RH, indicating modality—of movement, progression, etc. (similarly, וְהוֹלֵךְ 'and going', וְיוֹרֵד 'and going down', etc.; see Unit 19.14). Yet it is precisely וּבָאִין that is lacking in K and in other good manuscripts.

3. In Sheq 2.5, Albeck reads כָּל שֶׁהוּא בָא לְשֵׁם חַטָּאת וּלְשֵׁם אַשְׁמָה 'whatever he might offer *in the name of* a sin offering or *in the name of* a guilt offering'. K reads מְשׁוּם instead of לְשֵׁם and other manuscripts have מְשֵׁם. Is לְשֵׁם the earlier form, or מְשׁוּם, and if it is the latter, does מְשׁוּם or מְשֵׁם better reflect Palestinian pronunciation (see Unit 22.19–20)?

4. In Naz 2.7, Albeck reads הֲרֵינִי נָזִיר לִכְשֶׁיִּהְיֶה לִי בֵן 'I shall be a Nazirite *(for) when* I have a son'. K has כְּשֶׁ 'when' instead of לִכְשֶׁ. The same phenomenon is frequently found in respect of other texts, leading us to ask whether the longer form לִכְשֶׁ is a later development (see Unit 27.8). A similar question arises in connection with the conjunction כְּדֵי-לְ 'in order to' followed by the infinitive, and כְּדֵי-שֶׁ 'in order that' followed by the imperfect (see Unit 30.8), for which K sometimes just has the infinitive or imperfect, as, for example, at Ber 1.1; 2.2.

5. The differences sometimes go beyond the purely linguistic, as, for example, at Pes 10.5 (introductory text in Unit 29), where K lacks completely the citation of Ex 13.8. Similarly, at Abot 3.17 (introductory text in Unit 8), K does not cite Jr 17.6, 8. This seems to reflect a midrashic tendency over time to introduce biblical passages in justification of halakhic statements.

9. *RH phonetics*

In order to evaluate the differences described in the preceding section and to place them in a sociolinguistic context, a close consideration of the various phonetic phenomena of RH is required, for it is clear that phonetic developments have not always been consistently represented in orthographic practice.

1. There has been a weakening, though not a complete disappearance, of the gutturals, as shown by the Greek transcriptions of Aquila, Theodotion, and Symmachus. Usually, this is a purely phonetic phenomenon with no consequences for orthography. In Meg 24b, there is an explicit testimony regarding the inhabitants of various Galilaean villages, who did not distinguish *alef* and *ayin* or *he* and *het*. Doubtless it is this phonetic confusion that helps explain the change from ארכי to עוֹרְכֵי at Abot 1.8 (see above, §4.3.3).

2. There are some instances in which a different pronunciation has had morphological repercussions and created a new word, as, for example, at Taa 3.8, עָג עוּגָה 'he made a circle' instead of the expected חָג חוּגָה (we find a similar phenomenon at Ben Sira 37.29, where two mediaeval manuscripts have

the form אֵל־תִּתְחַנַּג, apparently for BH אַל־תִּתְעַנַּג 'do not enjoy yourself'). Elision of intervocalic *he* in *Hif'il* and *Nif'al* infinitives is attested in numerous verbs, for example לְהָכְנֵס, לִיכָּנֵס 'to enter' > לְהָכָּרֵת, לִיכָּרֵת 'to be cut off' > לְהִפָּרֵע, לִיפָּרֵע 'to uncover oneself' > לְהַרְבּוֹת, and לְרַבּוֹת 'to multiply' > לְרַבּוֹת (see Units 9.5C; 15.4A, E). A few instances of the same phenomenon are already attested in BH, for example לְבִיא 'to bring' < לְהָבִיא (Jr 39.7; 2 C 31.10) and בִּכָּשְׁלוֹ 'in his stumbling' < בְּהִכָּשְׁלוֹ (Pr 24.17).

3. *Alef* at the beginning or end of a word may lose its consonantal value and function simply as a *mater lectionis*. For example, the verb שׁאר 'remain' has given rise in RH to a *Pi'el* form שִׁיֵּר 'he abandoned', which uses the same pattern that is found in the *Pi'el* of קוּם 'arise', namely, קִיֵּם 'he established'. Continuing the analogy with קוּם, we may surmise that the *Qal* form of שׁאר was pronounced not שָׁאַר 'he left', but without the *alef*, as שָׁר, just like קָם 'he arose' (see Units 15.4B; 17.4B).

We also find that original *lamed-alef* verbs can be treated as though they were *lamed-he*—giving rise to such forms as קָרָאנוּ and קָרִינוּ 'we called' and מָצָאנוּ and מָצִינוּ 'we found' (see Unit 17.5A)—and vice-versa—thus, some *lamed-he* verbs take an *alef* when suffixes are attached, for example עֲשָׂאָן 'he prepared them' (Par 3.5) and עֲשָׂאוּהוּ 'they prepared him' (Ṭoh 1.5).

Similarly, at the beginning of a word *alef* can alternate with *he*, and we cannot be sure whether the written forms אֵיכָן and הֵיכָן 'where?' or אַגָּדָה and הַגָּדָה '*haggadah*, legend'—in which the first form in each pair corresponds to the Palestinian tradition and the second to the Babylonian—reflect different pronunciations in which Aramaic influence has had an effect on the weakening/confusion of the gutturals.

4. There is clear evidence that *het* continued to receive a guttural pronunciation. Even in the amoraic era, the Greek word κλεπσύδρα 'bowl' was transcribed as חֲלַף סְדְרָא (Genesis Rabbah 49), and in Miqw 9.4 *het* is confused with fricative *kaf*: לִכְלוּכֵי 'soilings of' < לְחִלּוּחֵי.

5. In respect of the *bgdkpt* consonants, RH has clearly taken part in a general process of spirantization evident in Hebrew and Aramaic dialects of the period, and we find Greek *chi* regularly transcribed as *kaf*, for example הַפַּרְכְיָא 'prefecture' (ἐπαρχία) and פּוֹלִימַרְכוֹס 'general' (πολέμαρχος) in SNm 131.1 (H 170). But the interchange of *bet* and *pe* in, for example, קֵפֵּחַ for BH גִּבֵּחַ 'bald' (Bekh 7.6) or לְהַבְקִיעַ for לְהַפְקִיעַ 'to break up' (Taa 2.9), shows that a plosive realization of these consonants was still maintained (this interchange is also attested in very early Hebrew sources; for example, Arad ostracon 24 reads והבקידם for BH וְהִפְקִידָם 'and appoint them'). Spirantization of *bet* is evident in its interchange with *waw* or *waw-waw*, as in the case of יוונה and יבנה 'Jabneh, Jamnia' or אביר and אוויר 'air'.

6. To judge from the Greek transcriptions, there were just two sibilants, with *zeta* representing *zayin* and *sigma* representing *samekh, ṣade, sin, and shin*, although this might simply reflect the inability of one language to represent the phonemes of another. However, RH orthography has retained

all five sibilants, although some interchange of *samekh* and *sin*—for example BH שָׂרַף, RH סָרַף 'burn', BH פָּשַׂע, RH פָּסַע 'step'—and *zayin* and *samekh*—for example BH מָסַך, RH מָזַג 'mix'—indicates that in pronunciation they tended not to be distinguished.

7. The alternation of final *mem* and *nun* is a characteristically RH phenomenon, reflecting an old dialect feature (see Unit 10.5A), in which Aramaic has had a considerable influence.

8. Assimilation of consonants occurs as in BH, although in the *Hitpa'el* and *Nitpa'al* conjugations, the *taw* of the prefix has a greater tendency to be assimilated in RH (see Unit 15.4D).

Instances of dissimilation are common in transcription of Greek words, for example מַרְגָּלִית 'pearl' (μαργαρίτης) at Kel 26.2 and פְּלַטְרִין 'praetorium' (πραιτώριον) at SNm 134.5 (H 180). Metathesis of consonants is also found, as in the case of Greek λιμήν 'port', transcribed in the Babylonian tradition as נְמִיל—compare the *textus receptus* of Erub 4.2, פַּעַם אַחַת לֹא נִכְנְסוּ לַנָּמֵל 'on one occasion they did not enter the port', with the version in K, פַּעַם אַחַת לֹא נִכְנְסוּ לַלְמָן.

9. Prosthetic *alef* is frequent in the transcription of Greek words beginning with a double consonant, for example אִזְמֵל < σμίλη 'razor, scalpel', אַכְסַנְיָא < ξένος 'foreigner', אִצְטְלִית < στολή 'garment' (see Unit 12.4). Prosthetic *alef* can also be found in native Semitic words, such as אֲגוּדָל 'thumb' (Yom 2.1) and אֵבִיתְ 'in, within, where' (see Unit 22.6A).

The reverse phenomenon, loss of initial *alef*, especially in proper names, for example אֶלְעָזָר < לְעָזָר 'Eleazar' or אֱלִיעֶזֶר < לִיעֶזֶר 'Eliezer', is another feature attested in inscriptions and the presence of which in Palestine is evidenced by the Gospels in the name Lazarus (Jn 11.1, etc.).

10. As already noted, differences in pronunciation from one dialect to another are evident in the manuscript tradition. To the examples already cited may be added the proper name 'Hillel', thus vocalized (הִלֵּל) in the printed editions but rendered as הֶלֵּל in K and other western manuscripts, reflecting Ἑλλήλ in the Septuagint, and demonstrating the existence of different dialects in Palestine.

Other examples from K include לִבְלָר (Latin *libellarius, librarius*) 'scribe', for לַבְלָר, סָפְסָל, סַפְסָל (Latin *subsellium*) 'bench' for חוֹצְפָּה 'arrogance' for חוּצְפָּה, and שֶׁמָּא 'in case' for שְׁמָא. In the first two instances, K has retained the original Latin vowel, while חוֹצְפָּה exemplifies a tendency to replace original short *u* by an *o*-vowel.

11. The shift of *-em* to *-um* in, for example, שׁוּם < שֵׁם 'name' probably results from labial assimilation. Assimilation also occurs with *r*, as in קַרְדּוֹם > קוֹרְדּוֹם 'spade' יַרְדֵּן > Ἰορδάνης 'Jordan'.

12. Vowel dissimilation occurs in the vocalization נִימוֹס for Greek νόμος 'law'.

10. *The traditions and dialects of RH1*

M. Bar-Asher has attempted to classify and evaluate the written and oral traditions of the Mishnah and place them in a sociolinguistic context. For the
Mishnah, Bar-Asher distinguishes a Palestinian and a Babylonian branch,
with the Palestinian variety represented by manuscripts of the Mishnah
alone, that is, without the *Gemara* of the Babylonian Talmud, whereas the
Babylonian branch is represented by the text of the Mishnah incorporated
within manuscripts of the Babylonian Talmud as a whole. The differences
between them are easily noticed by any reader of rabbinic texts. Some of the
more obvious are as follows.

1. Orthography. Word-final diphthong *-ay*: Palestinian י- or יי- (e.g. שמיֹ/
'Shammai', יני 'Yannai'), Babylonian אי- (ינאי, שמאי); final syllable *-a*:
Palestinian ה- (e.g. עקיבה 'Akiba'), Babylonian א- (עקיבא); interconsonantal
-a-: not represented in Palestinian (e.g. כן 'here'), Babylonian א- (כאן); final
-e: Palestinian ה- (e.g. יוסה 'Jose'), Babylonian י- (יוסי).

2. Pronunciation. Palestinian מְשֵׁם 'because of, in the name of', הוֹרָיָה
'instruction', חֲזִיר 'pig'; Babylonian מְשׁוּם, הוֹרָאָה, חוֹזִיר.

3. Morphology. Plural of nouns in וּת- (see Unit 10.6B): Palestinian יוֹת-ָ
(e.g. מַלְכְיוֹת 'kingdoms), Babylonian וּיוֹת- (מַלְכֻיוֹת); preposition מִן 'from'
with third person singular suffixes (see Unit 22.6C; 22.14): Palestinian מִמֶנּוּ
'from him' and מִמֶנָּה 'from her', Babylonian הֵימֶנּוּ and הֵימֶנָּה; *Pu'al* participle
(see Units 15.4C; 19.5B): Palestinian מְמוּעָט 'reduced', Babylonian מוּעָט.

4. Syntax. Palestininian: relative -שׁ followed by pronoun and participle
(e.g. K Abot 5.2: שֶׁהֵן מְאַבְּדִין 'which they destroy', שֶׁהֵן מְקִימִין 'which they
establish'), Babylonian: relative -שׁ followed by participle (printed editions:
שֶׁמְקִימִין, שֶׁמְאַבְּדִין).

The 'Babylonian' forms do not have to be generally or originally due to
the influence of Babylonian Aramaic in the Babylonian Talmud, but might
instead be genuinely Palestinian, as indicated by the use of הֵימֶנּוּ and הֵימֶנָּה,
מַלְכֻיוֹת, and מוּעָט in the Dead Sea Scrolls; Babylonian -שׁ followed by participle (without an intermediate pronoun) is also found in LBH (Ec 9.12;
10.5; Ps 133.2–3). There is an interesting re-evaluation of 'Palestinian' and
'Babylonian' characteristics in Friedman 1995.

Within the Palestinian branch, Bar-Asher further distinguishes two traditions
of pronouncing the same consonantal text, a western tradition represented by
manuscripts from the area of Italy (MSS Kaufmann, Parma A, Cambridge,
Paris, Florence), and an eastern tradition, represented by MSS Parma B and
Antonin 262. To give but one example, the western nominal type קַטְלָן (e.g.
גַּזְלָן 'robber') is read in the east as קֹטְלָן (גּוֹזְלָן). Again it has to be said that
the western forms are no less Palestinian than the eastern ones, as indicated
by numerous Greek transcriptions and the oral tradition of different communities.

In conclusion, both textual and pronunciation differences signal the existence of dialect variants within the spoken Hebrew of tannaitic Palestine and the need for further detailed analysis of texts in order to advance our understanding of this subject.

11. *Conclusion*

In the face of the complex issues raised concerning the texts and traditions of tannaitic literature, the words of M. Bar-Asher (1987, 12), especially those of his final sentence, are encouraging, and provide a rationale for the present work: 'These distinctive features, be they early or be they individual scribal peculiarities, are an integral part of any linguistic description. They must be noted, investigated, and clarified. They must not, however, distract the student of mishnaic Hebrew from the main task at hand, namely, finding and collecting features common to all manuscripts and describing the language according to all its branches and traditions'.

PART I

NOUNS

PERSONAL PRONOUNS

I *Introductory text* (Abot 1.1)

מֹשֶׁה קִבֵּל תּוֹרָה מִסִּנַי וּמְסָרָהּ לִיהוֹשֻׁעַ וִיהוֹשֻׁעַ לִזְקֵנִים וּזְקֵנִים לִנְבִיאִים
וּנְבִיאִים מְסָרוּהָ לְאַנְשֵׁי כְנֶסֶת הַגְּדוֹלָה. הֵם אָמְרוּ שְׁלֹשָׁה דְבָרִים.

Moses received the Torah from Sinai and transmitted it to Joshua, Joshua to
the elders, the elders to the prophets, and the prophets to the men of the Great
Assembly. They are the ones who made the three statements.

1. The concept of tradition is absolutely basic to Judaism. The word-pair
קִבֵּל–מָסַר (cf. English *masorah* and *kabbalah*) expresses the reception and
transmission of the Torah in an uninterrupted chain of tradition, 'Moses received the Torah and transmitted it'. The terminology is reflected in New
Testament passages (παραδίδωμι, παραλαμβάνω) that emphasize the faithfulness of the process of gospel transmission—I transmitted to you first that
which I in turn had received (1 Co 15.3; cf. 11.23).

The Torah from—or received at—Sinai is not simply the Bible, which is
a material copy of the Torah, but also its interpretation or spirit, which
Judaism labels as the oral Torah (תּוֹרָה שֶׁבְּעַל־פֶּה). In the naïve representation
of Moses receiving the written law and the oral law at Sinai, there is an obvious implication, namely that the text of the Bible has to be read and transmitted within the tradition of Israel (see Pea 2.6; Eduy 8.7). מִקְרָא 'Scripture,
reading' and מִשְׁנָה 'Mishnah, repetition' are two other terms that express the
Torah in its double aspect.

2. The Great Assembly or Synagogue refers in Pharisaic tradition to the
assembly of the people, who, on returning from exile, congregated around
Ezra to hear the law (Ne 8). Although it is unlikely that the Great Assembly
ever became a regular institution, it is around the time of the return from exile that the resurgence of Judaism and the special place in it of the Torah is to
be placed.

II *Morphology*

3. The following is a comparative table of RH and BH pronouns.

Person	RH form	BH form
1cs	אֲנִי	אֲנִי, אָנֹכִי
2ms	אַתְּ, אַתָּה	אַתָּה
2fs	אַתְּ	אַתְּ
3ms	הוּא	הוּא
3fs	הִיא	הִיא
1cpl	אָנוּ	נַחְנוּ, אֲנַחְנוּ
2mpl	אַתֶּם/ן	אַתֶּם
2fpl	אַתֶּם/ן	אַתֵּן, אַתֵּנָה
3mpl	הֵם/ן	הֵמָּה, הֵם
3fpl	הֵן/ם	הֵן, הֵנָּה

4. Observations.

A. The form אָנֹכִי 'I' has disappeared in RH except in solemn liturgy and, of course, in citations of biblical texts, being replaced by אֲנִי, a popular form already found in BH that has almost entirely supplanted אָנֹכִי in the literary idiom of LBH—Chronicles systematically replaces אָנֹכִי in Samuel and Kings by אֲנִי; at Jon 1.9 both are found together (in Ugaritic the form *'an* is attested).

B. אַתְּ 'you', undeniably influenced by Aramaic, is frequently used for the masculine, for example אַתְּ מכרית זרע עמלק 'you will destroy the descendants of Amalek' (SDt 67 [F 132]) and אִם אֵין אַתְּ בָּא 'if you do not come' (K Ned 8.7). It is also found at Qumran and three times in LBH (Jb 1.10; Ec 7.22; Ne 9.6), where the Masoretes have vocalized according to the *qere*—אַתָּה. Such 'corrections' are commonplace in printed editions and manuscripts of the Mishnah. But bearing in mind that the reading אַתְּ with masculine reference also exists in BH (e.g. Nm 11.15), it is possible that here we have an archaic, dialect, form, which, under pressure from Aramaic, only rose to the literary surface in the final phase of BH and during the rabbinic period.

C. In the first person plural, RH אָנוּ 'we' has completely replaced the BH forms אֲנַחְנוּ and נַחְנוּ, the result of internal development in Hebrew, whereby the first person plural suffix in forms like שְׁמָרָנוּ 'he has kept us' is used to form a plural pronoun corresponding to that of the singular, אֲנִי. אָנוּ is attested at Qumran and as a *ketiv* at Jr 42.6. When occasionally אֲנַחְנוּ re-emerges, it is due to copyists, who, perhaps unconsciously, have reinstated the biblical form.

D. In the second and third persons plural, RH has simplified the various BH forms (a similar phenomenon is the suppression of forms like תִּקְטֹלְנָה), resulting in the merger of masculine and feminine pronouns. Aramaic influence and the characteristic alternation of final *mem* and *nun* are both seen here.

5. As in BH, personal object pronouns are suffixed to עַל, אֶל, בְּ-, לְ-, אֵת, etc. or directly to finite and infinitive forms of the verb. It is only the plural active participle that always takes the object-marker אֶת before an object pronoun.

6. The negative particle אֵין 'there is not' takes personal suffixes without epenthetic *nun*, thus אֵינִי 'I am not' (for אֵינֶנִּי), אֵינָךְ 'you are not', אֵינוֹ 'he is not' (for אֵינֶנּוּ), אֵינָהּ 'she is not' (for אֵינֶנָּה), אֵינָן 'they are not', etc.

III *Grammar and usage*

7. RH uses the personal pronouns rather less than BH. They tend to be employed for purposes of emphasis, a function that is especially obvious when pronouns are preceded by or follow verbs, which already include reference to a subject in their affixes. Frequently, an even greater emphasis is provided by an associated particle with adverbial or adjectival force, for example, אַף 'also, indeed', גַּם 'also', עַצְמוֹ 'himself', עַצְמִי 'myself', etc.

8. Just as in BH, the third person pronoun, singular or plural, can be used as a copula in noun clauses, as in לֹא הַמִּדְרָשׁ הוּא הָעִקָּר 'study is not the most important thing' (Abot 1.17) or אִם אֲנִי הוּא הַטָּמֵא/הַטָּהוֹר 'if I am impure/pure' (Naz 8.1). For greater emphasis, the pronoun may come at the end of a phrase, as in הַקָּדוֹשׁ בָּרוּךְ הוּא 'the holy one, blessed be he' or כל מה שאתה רואה שלך הוא 'everything you see is yours' (SDt 19 [F 31]).

9. A particular way of emphasizing the subject is to anticipate it with its corresponding pronoun. The expression עוֹמֵד הַטָּהוֹר 'the one who is purified may stand up' is made more emphatic in Par 5.5: עוֹמֵד הוּא הַטָּהוֹר 'that one, the one who is purified, is the one who may stand up'.

10. The previous example indicates the demonstrative use of the personal pronouns, found also in constructions like בַּיּוֹם הַהוּא 'that day', frequent in BH, in which the pronoun, preceded by the article, functions as an adjective with demonstrative value, 'that, those', alongside the other demonstratives, זֶה 'this' (masculine), זוֹ 'this' (feminine), אֵלּוּ 'these'.

11. A characteristic feature of RH is the placing of the pronoun proleptically before an object, as in מה מהנה להם לישראל 'What use was it to them—to the Israelites' (Mek 17.11 [L 2.144]), אין מקרבין לו לאדם 'they do not come near to him—to the man' (Abot 2.3), or אין עומדין לו לאדם 'they do not stand by him—by the man' (Abot 2.3); however, K tends not to use the proleptic pronoun—at Abot 2.3 the לו is omitted both times and at Abot 1.17 K reads היו לרבן 'they were to our rabbi' as against היו לו לרבן in printed editions.

IV *Phraseology*

12. הוּא הָיָה אוֹמֵר 'he used to say' is a common formula used to introduce a saying of an authority who has just been cited. The construction הָיָה plus participle conveys continuity and iteration, as a rhetorical device to signal the correctness or permanent validity of what is being said. The pronoun, which is not strictly necessary, adds a special emphasis that can be conveyed by a rendering such as 'this is what he used to say'.

13. וְכֵן הוּא אוֹמֵר 'and in the same sense it says' is frequent in the tannaitic *midrashim*, with הוּא always having reference to a biblical text, and is employed to introduce new texts intended to confirm a particular exegesis.

14. הֲרֵי אַתָּה דָן 'behold, you can argue the case yourself' is used in the tannaitic *midrashim* to introduce an analogical, or *gezerah shawah*, argument.

V *Vocabulary*

אֶלָּא 'but rather' (adversative particle)
אֵלוּ 'these' (demonstrative)
אוֹהֵב 'friend'
הִתִּיר–אָסַר (הִתִּיר from the root נתר) 'bind–loose, prohibit–permit' (cf. Mt 16.19; 19.18)
בָּזוֹז 'robber'
בִּוּזָא 'pillage, robbery'
דָּן 'judge, deduce logically'
הֲרֵי 'behold' (contrast BH הִנֵּה)
חָבִיב 'beloved'
חַזָּן '(synagogue) cantor'
טַבְלָה (Latin *tabula, tabella*) '(writing) tablet'
מִדְרָשׁ 'study, investigation, exegetical or homiletic commentary'
סוֹטָה '(suspected) adulteress'
עִקָּר 'root, principle, essence'
פָּנָס (φανός) 'torch, lantern'
פָּרָשָׁה 'pericope, section (of the Bible)' (e.g. פָּרָשַׁת סוֹטָה 'the section concerning the suspected adulteress' [Nm 5.12–31])
קָפַח 'withdraw'
-שֶׁ 'that, which' (relative pronoun corresponding to BH אֲשֶׁר)
שָׂכָר 'prize, recompense'

VI *Exercises*

1. אַנְטִיגְנוֹס אִישׁ סוֹכוֹ קִבֵּל מִשִּׁמְעוֹן הַצַּדִּיק. הוּא הָיָה אוֹמֵר, אַל תִּהְיוּ כַּעֲבָדִים.
2. לֹא הַמִּדְרָשׁ הוּא הָעִקָּר אֶלָּא הַמַּעֲשֶׂה.
3. חֲמִשָּׁה תַלְמִידִים הָיוּ לוֹ לְרַבָּן יוֹחָנָן בֶּן זַכַּאי וְאֵלוּ הֵן.
4. וְנֶאֱמָן הוּא בַּעַל מְלַאכְתָּךְ שֶׁיְשַׁלֶּם־לָךְ שְׂכַר פְּעוּלָתָךְ.
5. לִפְנֵי מֶלֶךְ מַלְכֵי הַמְּלָכִים הַקָּדוֹשׁ בָּרוּךְ הוּא.

6. הוּא אֵל הוּא הַיּוֹצֵר הוּא הַבּוֹרֵא הוּא הַמֵּבִין, הוּא הַדַּיָּין הוּא עֵד.

7. וְאָמַר לוֹ, מְכוֹר לִי חֲמוֹרְךָ זֶה ... [מְכוֹר לִין חֲמוֹרְךָ הוּא.

8. הַפֶּה שֶׁאָסַר הוּא הַפֶּה שֶׁהִתִּיר.

9. שֶׁלָּנוּ הוּא הַפֶּסַח.

10. הֶחָזָן רוֹאֶה ... אֲבָל הוּא לֹא יִקְרָא.

11. וְאַף הִיא עָשְׂתָה טַבְלָה שֶׁל זָהָב שֶׁפָּרָשַׁת סוֹטָה כְּתוּבָה עָלֶיהָ.

12. גדולי מלכות קרובין אצלו ואומרים לו, אנו נוטלין את הפנס ונאיר לפני בניך. והוא אמר להן, לא.

13. מפני מה אתה בורח? אמר לו, לא מפניך אני בורח אלא מפני המלך.

14. אביהן אמר ... אף אני לא אקפח שכרכם.

15. חביבים הם ישראל.

16. הרי אתה דן.

17. אין נזירה בכל מקום אלא פרישה, וכן הוא אומר, וינזרו מקדשי בני ישראל [ויקרא כב׳ ב׳].

18. והלך לו הבן ההוא אצל אוהבו של מלך.

19. אם אתה מבקש אנו נותנים לך כל מה שתבקש ... והוא לא היה מבקש.

20. אתה הוא הלל.

Sources. 1. Abot 1.3. 2. Abot 1.17. 3. Abot 2.8. 4. Abot 2.14, 16. 5. Abot 3.1. 6. Abot 4.22. 7. BB 5.2. 8. Dem 6.11. 9. Pes 9.10. 10. Shab 1.3. 11. Yom 3.10. 12. Mek 13.21 (L 1.185). 13. Mek 14.21 (L 1.228). 14. Mek 14.2 (L 1.233). 15. SNm 1.10 (H 4). 16. SNm 22.4 (H 25) *et passim*. 17. SNm 23.3 (H 28). 18. SNm 86.1 (H 85). 19. PesR 14. 20. Shab 31a.

UNIT TWO

DEMONSTRATIVES

I *Introductory text* (SNm 84.2 [H80])

ויאמר משה קומה ה׳ [במדבר י׳ להי], וכתוב אחד אומר, על פי ה׳ יחנו ועל פי ה׳ יסעו [במדבר ט׳ כג׳]. כיצד יתקיימו שני כתובים הללו?

Moses exclaimed, Arise, O Y. [Nm 10.35]. But a scripture says, At the voice of Y. they encamped and at the voice of Y. they decamped [Nm 9.23]. How can these two scriptures be fulfilled?

1. A typically rabbinic form of exegesis is to put somewhat contradictory texts alongside each other in an attempt to harmonize them. The text above endeavours to resolve the contradiction between Nm 10.35, according to which Moses used to give the command to decamp, and Nm

9.20–23, according to which it was God himself who gave the command. How can both texts be fulfilled? How can they both be valid?

2. The rabbinic expression 'fulfilment of scriptures' extends beyond the fulfilment of prophecy to the truth or verification of the Bible as a whole, and is typically associated with the verb קוּם in the *Pi'el*, 'establish', and *Nitpa'al* or *Hitpa'el*, 'be established'.

II *Morphology*

3. The RH demonstratives listed below display a number of differences with respect to their BH counterparts. Some, like אֵלּוּ, result from developments within RH itself, while others, like זוֹ or זֹה, appear to derive from an early dialect of BH.

Meaning	RH form	BH form
'this' (masc.)	זֶה	זֶה
'this' (fem.)	זוֹ	זוֹ, זֹה, זֹאת
'these' (common)	אֵלּוּ	אֵלֶּה

זֹאת tends to be replaced in RH by זוֹ or, less often, זֹה, apparently a northern dialect form (see 2 K 6.19; Ezk 40.45; Ho 7.16; Ps 132.12), which reappeared in LBH. זֹה and זוֹ are probably older forms, cognate with Aramaic דָּא, while זֹאת is a secondary form, with ת- suffixed to emphasize its grammatically feminine character. The replacement of אֵלֶּה by אֵלּוּ is to be understood as resulting from an internal development within RH, whereby the plural reference of the particle is made more explicit by replacing the ה- of אֵלֶּה with the וּ- of the third person plural of the perfect.

4. RH, especially in the amoraic period, also uses the following longer forms of the demonstratives.

Meaning	RH form	BH form
'this' (common)	הַלָּז	הַלָּז, הַלָּזֶה
'this' (common)	הַלָּה	—
'this' (fem.)	הַלֵּזוּ	הַלָּז, הַלָּזֶה
'these' (common)	הַלָּלוּ	—

הַלָּה is an abbreviated form (הַלָּזֶה > הַלָּז > הַלָּה > הַלֵּזוּ), while הַלָּלוּ is a contraction of הַלָּה and אֵלּוּ, and a form typical of the Palestinian *amoraim*, although already common in both SNm and SDt. In our introductory text, הללו is lacking in MS Vatican 32.

III *Grammar and usage*

5. Apart from הַלָּה, which is only employed as a pronoun, the demonstratives are used both as pronouns, for example זֶה אוֹמֵר 'this one says' or זֶה בָּא 'this one comes', and as adjectives, for example בָּעוֹלָם הַזֶּה 'in this world', כְּתוּבִים הַלָּלוּ 'these writings', and כָּל הנסין האלו 'all these miracles'. As adjectives, they usually follow the noun, for example פָּרָשָׁה זוֹ 'this passage', but sometimes precede it, for example זֶה מִדְרָשׁ 'this interpretation' (Ket 4.6) or זוֹ עֵדוּת 'this testimony' (Naz 3.2), perhaps due to the stylistic influence of Aramaic. The BH noun clause construction, exemplified by זֶה פִּתְרֹנוֹ 'this is its interpretation' (Gn 29.12), is also found in RH, for example

זו עדות סתירה ... זו עדות טומאה

It is the testimony concerning concealment ... it is the testimony concerning impurity (TosSot 1.2).

6. In listing a number of items, repetition of a demonstrative expresses succession, movement, or reciprocity (see Unit 7.7A), as in the following texts: זה בא וחרש וישב לו וזה בא וחרש וישב לו 'one after another, they were coming, ploughing, and resting' (SLv 26.13 [W 111b]), וְשָׁוִין אֵלּוּ וָאֵלּוּ 'these and the others [i.e. the followers of Hillel and Shammai] agree' (Shab 1.9); זו למעלה לזו 'one on top of the other' (SDt 10 [F 18]).

7. The particle אֵת strengthens its originally determinative or deictic force.

A. With third person suffix attached, it has a demonstrative and sometimes emphatic function, as in אוֹתוֹ הַיּוֹם 'this very day' or

ונכנס אותו הפועל עמהם. אמר לו למלך לאותו הפועל

That worker entered with them. The king said to that worker (SLv 26.9 [W 111a]).

B. It is used to emphasize a subject (as sometimes in BH, e.g. Jg 20.46, and especially in LBH) or, in the form שֶׁ-אֶת, a clause functioning as subject, for example אֶת שֶׁהוּא נִרְאָה עִמּוֹ אָסוּר 'the one that appears alongside it is forbidden' (AZ 4.1). The subject of a passive sentence may also be introduced by אֵת (as also, for example, at Gn 27.42).

C. אֵת as object-marker is employed less often than in BH, and RH maintains the preference found at Qumran for object pronouns attached directly to the verb.

8. In BH, the use of עֶצֶם, literally 'bone', in the sense of 'the same' is attested, in phrases like בְּעֶצֶם הַיּוֹם הַזֶּה 'on this very day' (Gn 7.13, etc.). This usage is continued and developed in RH, so that (a) עֶצֶם can also apply to persons and (b) עֶצֶם with suffix is used as a demonstrative particle with intensive or reflexive value (see also Unit 7.4), as in

הָאִשָּׁה עַצְמָהּ מְבִיאָה אֶת־גִּיטָּהּ

The woman herself is to bring her document of divorce (Git 2.7).

9. The locution כָּל עֶצֶם- means 'absolutely, totally', for example:

כל עצמן של שני כתרים הללו

These two crowns [of priesthood and kingship], in their totality
(SNm 119.3 [H 144]);

כל עצמם אביהם ליסטים היה

All their ancestors, without exception, were robbers (SDt 343 [F
396]).

10. For the demonstrative use of the article followed by third person
pronoun, see Unit 1.10.

IV *Phraseology*

11. לְעוֹלָם הַבָּא–בָּעוֹלָם הַזֶּה 'in this world–in the world to come'; עוֹלָם is
a word that has undergone a clear semantic development in RH, from
'eternity' to 'world', employed in eschatological contexts in constructions
that contrast the present and future worlds.

12. כָּל עַצְם- 'all of it, absolutely, without exception' (see above, §9; for
other examples, see Soṭ 2.3, SNm 70.2 [H 67], and SDt 1 [F 343]).

V *Vocabulary*

הֵיאַךְ 'how?'
טַעַם 'sense, cause, reason'
יַבְנֶה 'Yavneh, Jamnia' (near to modern-day Jaffa)
לֵץ 'cynical, wicked'
מִדָּה 'rule, norm, quality'
פָּטַר 'permit, exempt'
מָעָה '(Tyrian) coin', plural מָעוֹת 'money'
מִשּׁוּם 'in the name of, in the capacity of, in virtue of'
עָסַק 'occupy oneself with'
פְּרוֹזְדוֹר (πρόθυρον) 'vestibule'
תַּלְמוּד 'study'
תַּלְמִיד 'pupil, disciple'

VI *Exercises*

1. שְׁנַיִם שֶׁיּוֹשְׁבִים וְאֵין בֵּינֵיהֶן דִּבְרֵי תוֹרָה הֲרֵי זֶה מוֹשַׁב לֵצִים.
2. הָעוֹלָם הַזֶּה דּוֹמֶה לִפְרוֹזְדוֹר בִּפְנֵי הָעוֹלָם הַבָּא.
3. יָפָה שָׁעָה אַחַת בִּתְשׁוּבָה וּמַעֲשִׂים טוֹבִים בָּעוֹלָם הַזֶּה מִכָּל חַיֵּי הָעוֹלָם הַבָּא.
4. כָּל מִי שֶׁיֵּשׁ בְּיָדוֹ שְׁלֹשָׁה דְבָרִים הַלָּלוּ, מִתַּלְמִידָיו שֶׁלְאַבְרָהָם אָבִינוּ.
5. וְכָל מִי שֶׁעוֹסֵק בְּתַלְמוּד תּוֹרָה הֲרֵי זֶה מִתְעַלֶּה.
6. אֶת-שֶׁלִּפְנֵי הַמִּטָּה וְאֶת-שֶׁלְאַחַר הַמִּטָּה ... פְּטוּרִין ... אֵלּוּ וְאֵלּוּ פְּטוּרִין.

מִן הַתְּפִילָה.

7. אֶת שֶׁהָעֵדִים נִקְרִין עִמּוֹ כָּשֵׁר.

8. זֶה מִדְרָשׁ דָּרַשׁ רִבִּי אֶלְעָזָר בֶּן עֲזַרְיָה לִפְנֵי הַחֲכָמִים בַּכֶּרֶם בְּיַבְנֶה.

9. נִמְצָא זֶה אוֹכֵל פֵּירוֹתָיו בְּטָהֳרָה וְהַלָּה עוֹשֶׂה צָרְכּוֹ בְּמָעוֹתָיו.

10. וְהָצֵא הַלָּזוּ מִשּׁוּם אֲחוֹת אִשָּׁה.

11. גדולה מדה זו.

12. זה אחת משלשה דברים.

13. זו מדה בתורה.

14. והיה לאותו האיש עשרה בנים, זה בא וחרש וישב לו וזה בא וחרש וישב לו.

15. נכנסו כל הפרות ואותה הפרה לא נכנסה.

16. למה משה דומה באותה שעה?

17. הכרת תכרת הנפש ההיא [במדבר טו׳ לא׳], הכרת, בעולם הזה, תכרת, בעולם הבא. דברי ר׳ עקיבא.

18. אלו מביאים טעם לדבריהם ואלו מביאים טעם לדבריהם.

19. מה עשה אותו הרשע? אומר לני אחד חבירו, בא וראה היאך אני משחק ביהודים הללו.

20. אותו הפה שאמר, אני משחק בהם, התחיל אומר, ברוך שבחר באומה הזו.

Sources. 1. Abot 3.2. 2. Abot 4.16. 3. Abot 4.17. 4. Abot 5.19. 5. Abot 6.2. 6. Ber 3.1. 7. Giṭ 9.5. 8. Ket 4.6. 9. MS 3.3. 10. Yeb 13.7. 11. ARN 1 (S 1). 12. Mek 12.2 (L 1.15–16). 13. Mek 12.5 (L 1.32). 14. SLv 26.13 (W 111a). 15. SLv 26.13 (W 111a). 16. SNm 93 (H 94). 17. SNm 112.4 (H 121). 18. Genesis Rabbah 1.15. 19. PesR 14. 20. PesR 14.

UNIT THREE

ARTICLE

I *Introductory text* (Abot 1.17)

לֹא הַמִּדְרָשׁ הוּא הָעִקָּר, אֶלָּא הַמַּעֲשֶׂה.

The important thing is action, not words.

1. In rabbinic usage, מִדְרָשׁ (from the root דָּרַשׁ ‘seek’) refers to the investigation and study of Scripture, and is in this sense broadly synonymous with תַּלְמוּד ‘study’. מִדְרָשׁ can also denote the exposition and clarification of Scripture, with one of its two plurals, מִדְרָשׁוֹת, meaning ‘interpretations’ and the other, מִדְרָשִׁים, employed for rabbinic commentaries of an exegetical or

homiletic character (although this form never appears in the tannaitic literature).

Although Judaism gave a special place to the study of the Torah
(תַּלְמוּד תּוֹרָה) as the activity for which humankind had been created (Abot
2.8), the saying quoted above, attributed to Simeon ben Gamaliel, demonstrates awareness of the tension that could exist between study and practice
(מַעֲשֶׂה).

II *Morphology*

2. In Abot 1.17, each of the three nouns is preceded by the article:
הַמִּדְרָשׁ, הָעִקָּר, הַמַּעֲשֶׂה. The definite article as prefixed *ha-* (accompanied by
strengthening of the following consonant where possible, or, where not, by
alteration of the length or quality of the vowel of the article itself) entered
West Semitic relatively late (see Meyer 1992, §32.1) and, although uncommon in AH poetry, remained in this form in BH and throughout the subsequent stages of Hebrew.

III *Grammar and usage*

3. In origin, the article functioned as a demonstrative with deictic function. It is used less widely in RH than in BH.

4. As in BH, the article can be used as a vocative, as in הַמֶּלֶךְ 'O king',
and this usage has given rise to certain expressions that have survived as interjections, for example הָאֱלֹהִים 'by God', הַשָּׁמַיִם 'by heaven', הָעֲבוֹדָה 'by
the service (of the temple)', and הַמָּעוֹן הַזֶּה 'by this abode' (i.e. the temple).

5. Adjectives and participles used as nouns can also take the article:
הַיָּבֵשׁ 'that which is dry', הַיּוֹרְדִים 'those who go down', הַקּוֹרִין 'the readers'.

6. As a general rule, the article is repeated before an attributive adjective
accompanying a definite noun, as in BH, for example הָאִישׁ הַזֶּה 'this man',
הַיָּם הַגָּדוֹל 'the great sea' (i.e. Mediterranean). Very often, though, an indefinite noun is followed by an adjective with article, the purpose of which is to
emphasize the importance of the attribute (expressed by the adjective) for the
noun or relative to other, indefinite, adjectives. For example, in Mek 13.2 (L
1.133), we find

צָרוֹת הָאַחֲרוֹנוֹת מַשְׁכְּחוֹת הָרִאשׁוֹנוֹת

The latter tribulations erase the memory of the former
and at TosSoṭ 1.2

אֵי זוֹ הִיא עֵדוּת הָרִאשׁוֹנָה

Which one is the first testimony?

In both instances, the use of the article seems to emphasize the adjective: the
last of the tribulations (in contrast to all the earlier ones), the *first* of the tes-

timonies (as more important than any subsequent ones).

7. As well as such semantically significant usages of the article with adjective, there are also many set phrases or technical terms where the article is attached to the adjective alone. Such expressions include כְּנֶסֶת הַגְּדוֹלָה 'the great synagogue', אָדָם הָרִאשׁוֹן 'the first human being', נָחָשׁ הָרָשָׁע 'the wicked serpent', שׁוֹר הַנִּסְקָל 'the ox to be stoned', and שַׁעַר הָעֶלְיוֹן 'the upper gate'. The construction is also occasionally evidenced in BH, at least according to the Masoretic pointing, for example לָאִישׁ הֶעָשִׁיר 'to that rich man' (2 S 12.4).

8. In the reverse situation, where only the noun has the article, the adjective is sometimes to be understood as forming a circumstantial clause:

נֶאֱמָנִים עַל הַיָּרָק חַי וְאֵין נֶאֱמָנִים עַל הַמְּבוּשָׁל

They are to be trusted concerning vegetables when they are raw but they are not to be trusted concerning cooked (vegetables) (Pea 8.4).

In other words, הַיָּרָק חַי functions at a certain level of grammatical analysis as a noun clause: 'the vegetables are raw'. In adjectival constructions of this kind, the absence of the article may be attributable to such factors as scribal error and vernacular usage for which we lack the evidence to analyse systematically.

9. Various other expressions, especially construct chains, are regarded as intrinsically definite and, therefore, regularly omit the article. Examples include תַּלְמוּד תּוֹרָה 'the study of the law', עֹל תּוֹרָה 'the yoke of the law', כֶּתֶר תּוֹרָה 'the crown of the law', כֹּהֵן גָּדוֹל 'the high priest', בַּעַל מוּם 'person/beast with defect', חֲכָמִים אָמְרוּ 'the sages have said', דֶּרֶךְ אֶרֶץ 'courtesy, work', and גְּמִילוּת חֲסָדִים 'deeds of mercy'. Probably in the alternation of יֵצֶר טוֹב 'the impulse of goodness' and יֵצֶר רַע 'the impulse of wickedness' with יֵצֶר הַטּוֹב and יֵצֶר הָרַע the article has a euphonic purpose, avoiding two consecutive stressed syllables (Waldman 1989, 133).

10. In proverbs and aphorisms, the absence of the article points to a general or universal significance, as in

מַרְבֶּה תוֹרָה מַרְבֶּה חַיִּים

One who increases Torah, increases life (Abot 2.7),

with which we might compare

יִרְאַת יְ׳ רֵאשִׁית דֵּעַת

The fear of Y. is the beginning of wisdom (Pr 1.7),

עִוֵּר וּפִסֵּחַ לֹא יָבוֹא אֶל־הַבָּיִת

The blind and the lame will not enter the temple (2 S 5.8),

and

בְּרֹב חָכְמָה רָב־כָּעַס

With great wisdom comes great vexation (Ec 1.18).

Here again, though, there is little consistency, and N.M. Waldman (1989, 132) rightly contrasts Mak 2.3 הָאָב גּוֹלֶה עַל יְדֵי הַבֵּן 'the parents are exiled because of the children', with Ml 1.6, בֵּן יְכַבֵּד אָב וְעֶבֶד אֲדֹנָיו 'sons honour fathers and servants, their masters' (although here it also has to be borne in mind that in BH poetry, following the example of AH, the article is often lacking in situations where in prose we would expect to find it).

11. The article is not employed before a noun introduced by שֶׁל 'of' if the noun is referred to proleptically by a suffix attached to the preceding noun (see Unit 4.14), for example יָדוֹ שֶׁל עָנִי 'the hand of the poor' (Shab 1.1) and שְׁלוּחוֹ שֶׁל אָדָם כְּמוֹתוֹ 'a person's agent is like the person themself' (Mek 12.3, 6 [L 1.33, 40]). In such cases, the second noun is regarded as already definite due to the construction in which it occurs.

IV *Phraseology*

12. בָּא הַכָּתוּב וְלִמֵּד עַל 'this text is there to teach about', in reference to the teaching expressed by a particular verse or longer text that has just been cited. Because of that, the article should be rendered as a demonstrative, 'this', and כָּתוּב, literally 'written', as '(scriptural) passage, text', thus, 'this text', 'the verse in question', etc.

V *Vocabulary*

גָּרַם 'cause, be the cause of, bring about'
הוֹכִיחַ (hi. of יכח) 'respond, admonish, argue against'
הִרְבָּה (hi. of רבה) 'increase, multiply'
יְשִׁיבָה 'class, school, rest'
מִכָּאן 'from here'
נִתְקַיֵּים (ntp. of קום) 'be fulfilled, continue, endure'
סְיָג 'fence, hedge, protection'
שִׂיחָה 'conversation'
שְׁיָר (BH שְׁאָר) 'survivor, remnant'
שְׁכִינָה 'abode, divine presence' (used as a substitute for the divine name)

VI *Exercises*

1. שִׁמְעוֹן הַצַּדִּיק הָיָה מִשְׁיָרֵי כְנֶסֶת הַגְּדוֹלָה. הוּא הָיָה אוֹמֵר, עַל שְׁלֹשָׁה דְבָרִים הָעוֹלָם עוֹמֵד, עַל הַתּוֹרָה, וְעַל הָעֲבוֹדָה, וְעַל גְּמִילוּת חֲסָדִים.
2. מִכָּאן אָמְרוּ חֲכָמִים, כָּל זְמָן שֶׁאָדָם מַרְבֶּה שִׂיחָה עִם הָאִשָּׁה, גּוֹרֵם רָעָה לְעַצְמוֹ.
3. וְתִגְלוּ לִמְקוֹם מַיִם הָרָעִים, וְיִשְׁתּוּ הַתַּלְמִידִים הַבָּאִים אַחֲרֵיכֶם וְיָמוּתוּ.
4. יָפֶה תַלְמוּד תּוֹרָה עִם דֶּרֶךְ אֶרֶץ.
5. מַרְבֶּה תוֹרָה, מַרְבֶּה חַיִּים, מַרְבֶּה יְשִׁיבָה, מַרְבֶּה חָכְמָה.
6. קָנָה לוֹ דִבְרֵי תוֹרָה, קָנָה לוֹ חַיֵּי הָעוֹלָם הַבָּא.
7. שְׁנַיִם שֶׁיּוֹשְׁבִים וְיֵשׁ בֵּינֵיהֶם דִּבְרֵי תוֹרָה, שְׁכִינָה בֵּינֵיהֶם.
8. כָּל הַמְקַבֵּל עָלָיו עֹל תּוֹרָה, מַעֲבִירִין מִמֶּנּוּ עֹל מַלְכוּת וְעֹל דֶּרֶךְ אֶרֶץ.

9. אִם אֵין קֶמַח, אֵין תּוֹרָה, אִם אֵין תּוֹרָה, אֵין קֶמַח.

10. אֵין לְךָ אָדָם שֶׁאֵין לוֹ שָׁעָה וְאֵין לְךָ דָּבָר שֶׁאֵין לוֹ מָקוֹם.

11. אָמַר רַבָּן שִׁמְעוֹן בֶּן גַּמְלִיאֵל, הַמָּעוֹן הַזֶּה, לֹא אָלִין הַלַּיְלָה.

12. אדם הראשון עשה סייג לדבריו.

13. באותה שעה היה נחש הרשע נוטל עצה בלבו.

14. אמר לו, השמים אם עשיתי כן.

15. בא הכתוב ללמדך.

16. צרות האחרונות משכחות הראשונות.

17. ולֹא יקרא עוד את שמך אברם, וגו׳ [בראשית י״ז ה׳], עבר שם הראשון
    ונתקיים שם השני.

18. ושרף את הפרה לעיניו [במדבר י״ט ה׳], לא פרים הנשרפים.

19. והשורף אותה יכבס בגדיו [במדבר י״ט ה׳], ולא השורף בגדים המנוגעים.

20. אמר ר׳ טרפון, העבורה אם יש בדור הזה מי שיכול להוכיח.

Sources. 1. Abot 1.2. 2. Abot 1.5. 3. Abot 1.11. 4. Abot 2.2. 5. Abot 2.7.
6. Abot 2.7. 7. Abot 3.2. 8. Abot 3.5. 9. Abot 3.17. 10. Abot 4.3. 11. Ker
1.7. 12. ARN 1 (S 3). 13. ARN 1 (S 4). 14. ARN 38 (S 114). 15. Mek 12.3
(L 1.26) *et passim*. 16. Mek 13.2 (L 1.133). 17. Mek 13.2 (L 1.134). 18.
SNm 124.2 (H 155). 19. SNm 124.12 (H 157). 20. SDt 1 (F 3).

UNIT FOUR

POSSESSIVE PRONOUNS AND THE GENITIVE PARTICLE *SHEL*

I Introductory text (SNm 78.4 [H 76])

אם לבן ביתו של בשר ודם מטיבים לו
קל וחומר לבן ביתו של מי שאמר והיה עולם.

If they treat the son of a human family well, how much more the son of the
family of the-one-that-spoke-and-the-world-was.

1. This is a comment on Nm 10.29: Moses said to Jobab son of Reuel the
Midianite ..., Come with us and we shall treat you well. Jobab is representa-
tive of the proselyte, a person who is not by birth a member of the people of
Israel, but who incorporates himself into it.

2. The text contrasts the son of a human family (literally, 'son of the
house of flesh and blood'), that is, a proselyte, with the son of the divine
family (literally, 'son of the house of the-one-that-spoke-and-the-world-
was'), that is, a native Israelite. The collocation 'flesh and blood' in rabbinic
literature emphasizes the fragility of human beings compared to the power of

the creator (the one who by a mere word calls the world into existence).

3. קַל וָחוֹמֶר (also written קול וחומר in some of the best manuscripts, for example MS Vatican 66) is a stereotype phrase (literally, 'light and heavy'), here used to introduce the second term of an *a fortiori* comparison (if … how much more!). Argument by קַלוָחוֹמֶר is the first of Hillel's rules for the interpretation of Scripture (see Unit 26.8C).

II *Morphology*

4. The RH possessive suffixes coincide with those of BH, except for the second person singular masculine (ךְ-) and feminine (ךְ-), in which the influence of Aramaic can be seen and which are reflected to some degree in the Greek transcriptions of Hebrew in the second column (*Secunda*) of Origen's Hexapla (third century CE). These characteristic RH forms were retained in good manuscripts and in the Sefardi and Yemenite oral traditions, although in printed editions they have been 'corrected' and assimilated to their BH counterparts. In the second and third persons plural, BH final ם- is frequently replaced by ן- and vice-versa.

Person	RH form	BH form
1cs	דְּבָרִי	דְּבָרִי
2ms	דְּבָרָךְ	דְּבָרְךָ
2fs	דְּבָרִיךְ	דְּבָרֵךְ
3ms	דְּבָרוֹ	דְּבָרוֹ
3fs	דְּבָרָה	דְּבָרָהּ
1cpl	דְּבָרֵנוּ	דְּבָרֵנוּ
2mpl	דְּבָרְכֶן/ם	דְּבָרְכֶם
2fpl	דְּבַרְכֶן/ם	דְּבַרְכֶן
3mpl	דְּבָרָן/ם	דְּבָרָם
3fpl	דְּבָרָן/ם	דְּבָרָם

(It should also be noted that as well as the endings ם- and ן- there is another possessive suffix, ־ֹי, which has generally been 'corrected' in manuscripts and printed editions.)

5. In addition to the possessive suffixes. RH has developed an independent possessive pronoun, which consists of the particle שֶׁל followed by pronominal suffix (with strengthening of the connecting ל, thus שֶׁלִּי, etc., as seen in the table at §7, below).

6. שֶׁל is made up of the relative -שֶׁ 'that, which, who' (see Unit 8) and the preposition -לְ 'to, of', and corresponds to the BH formula of possession אֲשֶׁר לְ- (1 S 21.8; 1 K 4.2, etc.), literally 'which is to', that is, 'belonging to, of'.

Although printed editions normally write שֶׁל as a separate word, good manuscripts show that it was originally prefixed to the following noun, with assimilation of the -ה of the article if necessary), for example שֶׁלַּזְּבָחִים 'of the sacrifices' and שֶׁלַּמֶּלֶךְ 'of the king'. The structure is already found in LBH at Ca 3.7 (הִנֵּה מִטָּתוֹ שֶׁלִּשְׁלֹמֹה 'behold, the couch of Solomon') and also in the Temple Scroll from Qumran (6.1: שלנחושת 'of bronze'); the construction שלרבי 'of Rabbi (Gamaliel, etc.)' occurs twice in late second-century CE and twelve times in mid third-century CE tomb inscriptions from Beth Shearim. Thus, it would seem that שֶׁל as a separate word was a mediaeval scribal creation. On the other hand, the discovery of the same form in a fragment of a letter from Bar-Kokhba (5/6ḤevEp 5: שהיו של הגואין 'which were of the gentiles') means that we can no longer regard it as a purely mediaeval phenomenon. It also shows, as E.Y. Kutscher (1971, 1602) points out, 'that the dialect of the Bar-Kokhba letters is not identical with MH as it is known today', and, more generally, that we should be aware of dialect differences within RH, as strikingly reflected in the use of שֶׁל.

7. Corresponding to the BH structures אֲשֶׁר לָךְ, אֲשֶׁר לְךָ, אֲשֶׁר לִי, etc. we have, then, the following series of forms based on שֶׁל.

Person	With *shel*	Meaning
1cs	שֶׁלִּי	my, mine
2ms	שֶׁלְּךָ	your(s)
2fs	שֶׁלִּיךְ	your(s)
3ms	שֶׁלּוֹ	his
3fs	שֶׁלָּהּ	her(s)
1cpl	שֶׁלָּנוּ	our(s)
2mpl	שֶׁלָּכֶן/ם	your(s)
2fpl	שֶׁלָּכֶן/ם	your(s)
3mpl	שֶׁלָּהֶן/ם	their(s)
3fpl	שֶׁלָּהֶן/ם	their(s)

8. M.H. Segal (1927, §385) rightly notes that the genitive construction with שֶׁל is a genuinely Hebrew development, not an adaptation of Aramaic דִּי or -דְּ.

III *Grammar and usage*

9. As we can see from the translations in §7, the independent possessive pronoun (i.e. שֶׁל + suffix) may be used like a noun (e.g. שֶׁלְּךָ שֶׁלִּי 'what's yours is mine') or simply as a replacement for a pronominal suffix (e.g. דָּבָר שֶׁלִּי in place of דְּבָרִי 'my word'). The latter usage is standard in connection with loanwords that fit uneasily into normal patterns of Hebrew word formation, or when a suffixed pronoun would have to be added to each of a series of nouns or to an expression consisting of several words. But in the

majority of cases, שֶׁל, like BH לְ־אֲשֶׁר, is used instead of the construct relationship for stylistic variety or for the sake of emphasis.

10. In RH, as in BH, the genitive relationship is also commonly conveyed by means of a construct chain, where two or more nouns are linked together in such a way that the first noun 'belongs to' the second, and the second to the third, etc. The final noun, or *nomen rectum*, remains in its
'absolute' state, that is, it undergoes no changes in the position of its accent
(that is, where it is stressed) or, consequently, in its vowels. Any preceding
noun, or *nomen regens*, however, is converted into a 'construct' form, that is,
a form which usually does undergo such changes, and, in any case, does not
bear the accent of the construct chain as a whole; that is borne by the *nomen
rectum* (See Unit 11).

11. However, in RH the use of שֶׁל becomes ever more frequent, and, like
the construct chain, it expresses not only relationships of possession but also
other close associations that might exist between two nouns. In such cases,
שֶׁל may more accurately be rendered by 'made from', 'consisting of', etc.,
for example טַבְלָה שֶׁל זָהָב 'tablet of gold' (Yom 3.10) and שֶׁבַע כִּתּוֹת שֶׁל
צַדִּיקִים 'seven classes of just ones' (SDt 10 [F 18]).

12. As a general rule, שֶׁל is employed when a construct chain would be
unwieldy or unclear, if, for example, there is more than one *nomen regens*
and/or the *nomen regens* or *nomen rectum* consists of more than one word, or
if the *nomen regens* is a loanword for which no special construct form exists,
or if, for any reason, a construct chain might be difficult to interpret.

13. Given that there is often no clear motive for the use of שֶׁל rather than
the construct chain, it is also possible that the use (and abuse) of שֶׁל has been
affected by Aramaic practice.

14. A typically RH device (already seen in Unit 3.11) is to anticipate the
word to be introduced by שֶׁל by means of a suffix attached to a *nomen regens*, as in שְׁלוּחוֹ שֶׁל אָדָם כְּמוֹתוֹ 'a person's agent is like the person themself'
(Mek 12.3, 6 [L 1.33, 40]). The construction also occurs in LBH, at Ca 3.7
(see above, §6); in RH it is especially common when the noun following שֶׁל
is a personal name.

IV *Phraseology*

15. מְשֶׁלְּךָ, מְשֶׁלִּי 'of mine, of yours': the forms שֶׁלִּי, שֶׁלְּךָ, etc., which
originated as relative clauses ('which is to me', 'which is to you'), can
function as possessive pronouns ('my', 'your') or as nominalized relative
clauses ('that which is to me, mine', 'that which is to you, yours'), which can
also be employed predicatively ('what's mine is yours', etc.). By means of
such forms, we find at Abot 3.7 concise and alliterative expression of a
fundamental doctrine of Judaism, namely, that a human being is a creation of
God and can give nothing to God which does not in fact already belong to

God: תֵּן לוֹ מִשֶּׁלוֹ, שֶׁאַתָּה וְשֶׁלָּךְ שֶׁלּוֹ 'Give him of (that which is) yours, for you and yours are his'.

V *Vocabulary*

בִּימָה (βῆμα) 'platform'
בֵּינוֹנִי 'central, halfway, average, common'
הַפַּרְכוֹס (ὕπαρχος) 'governor'
חָבִית 'jug, flask'
חִיצוֹן 'outer'
מַלְכוּת 'kingdom' (especially in reference to the Roman empire)
מָקוֹם 'place' (also in metonymic reference to God as omnipresent)
מוֹצָא 'exit'; מוֹצָאֵי שַׁבָּת/חַג 'the outgoings of (i.e. evening after) the sabbath/a festival'
פַּלְטֵרִין (πραιτώριον) 'palace'

VI *Exercises*

1. הִלֵּל אוֹמֵר, הֱוֵי מִתַּלְמִידָיו שֶׁלְאַהֲרוֹן, אוֹהֵב שָׁלוֹם וְרוֹדֵף שָׁלוֹם.
2. אֵין אַתָּה יוֹדֵעַ מַתַּן שְׂכָרָן שֶׁלַּמִּצְווֹת.
3. רַבָּן גַּמְלִיאֵל בְּנוֹ שֶׁלְרַבִּי יְהוּדָה הַנָּשִׂי.
4. רַבִּי אֱלִיעֶזֶר אוֹמֵר, יְהִי כְבוֹד חֲבֵרְךָ חָבִיב עָלֶיךָ כְּשֶׁלָּךְ.
5. רַבִּי חֲנִנְיָה סְגַן הַכֹּהֲנִים אוֹמֵר, הֱוֵי מִתְפַּלֵּל בִּשְׁלוֹמָהּ שֶׁלַּמַּלְכוּת.
6. רַבִּי דוֹסָא בֶּן הַרְכִּינָס אוֹמֵר, שֵׁנָה שֶׁלְשַׁחֲרִית, וְיַיִן שֶׁלְצָהֳרַיִם, וְשִׂיחַת הַיְלָדִים, וִישִׁיבַת בָּתֵּי כְנֵסִיּוֹת שֶׁלְעַמֵּי הָאָרֶץ, מוֹצִיאִים אֶת הָאָדָם מִן הָעוֹלָם.
7. אַרְבַּע מִדּוֹת בָּאָדָם, הָאוֹמֵר, שֶׁלִּי שֶׁלִּי וְשֶׁלְּךָ שֶׁלָּךְ, זוֹ מִדָּה בֵּינוֹנִית ... שֶׁלִּי שֶׁלְּךָ וְשֶׁלְּךָ שֶׁלִּי, עַם הָאָרֶץ, שֶׁלִּי שֶׁלְּךָ וְשֶׁלְּךָ שֶׁלָּךְ, חָסִיד. שֶׁלִּי שֶׁלִּי וְשֶׁלְּךָ שֶׁלִּי, רָשָׁע.
8. וּשְׁיָרֵי הַדָּם הָיָה שׁוֹפֵךְ עַל יְסוֹד מַעֲרָבִי שֶׁלַּמִּזְבֵּחַ הַחִיצוֹן.
9. חָבִית שֶׁל זָהָב.
10. בְּמוֹצָאֵי יוֹם טוֹב הָרִאשׁוֹן שֶׁל חַג.
11. כֹּל אֶחָד וְאֶחָד מַכִּיר אֶת שֶׁלּוֹ.
12. לֹא הָיְתָה שִׂמְחָה לְפָנָיו בַּמָּרוֹם עַל אָבְדָן שֶׁל רְשָׁעִים.
13. כְּשֶׁיִּשְׂרָאֵל עוֹשִׂין רְצוֹנוֹ שֶׁל מָקוֹם.
14. אַף חוּלְדָה הַנְּבִיאָה הָיְתָה מִבְּנֵי בָנָיו שֶׁל רָחָב הַזּוֹנָה.
15. לִפְתֹּחַ פַּלְטֵרִין שֶׁלּוֹ.
16. ר' אֱלִיעֶזֶר אוֹמֵר, נָתַן כֹּחַ בְּעֵינָיו שֶׁל מֹשֶׁה וְרָאָה מִסּוֹף הָעוֹלָם וְעַד סוֹפוֹ.
17. אָמַר לָהֶם הַפַּרְכוֹס שֶׁלּוֹ.
18. מֶלֶךְ בָּשָׂר וָדָם יוֹשֵׁב עַל בִּימָה שֶׁלּוֹ.
19. שֶׁבַע כָּתּוֹת שֶׁל צַדִּיקִים בְּגַן עֵדֶן.
20. לְשֶׁבַע שְׂמָחוֹת פְּנֵיהֶם שֶׁל צַדִּיקִים דּוֹמִים.

Sources. 1. Abot 1.12. 2. Abot 2.1. 3. Abot 2.2. 4. Abot 2.10. 5. Abot 3.2.

6. Abot 3.10. 7. Abot 5.10. 8. Yom 5.6. 9. Suk 4.10. 10. Suk 5.2. 11. ARN 2 (S 14). 12. Mek 15.1 (L 2.6). 13. Mek 15.1 (L 2.19). 14. SNm 78.1 (H 74). 15. SNm 134.5 (H 180). 16. SNm 136 (H182). 17. SDt 3 (F 11). 18. SDt 9 (F 17). 19. SDt 10 (F 18). 20. SDt 10 (F 18).

UNIT FIVE

INTERROGATIVES

I *Introductory text* (ARN 4 [S 21])

פעם אחת היה רבן יוחנן בן זכאי יוצא מירושלים והיה ר' יהושע הולך אחריו
וראה בית המקדש חרב. אמר ר' יהושע, אוי לנו על זה שהוא חרב מקום
שמכפרים בו עונותיהם של ישראל. א"ל, בני אל ירע לך, יש לנו כפרה אחת
שהיא כמותה. ואיזה, זה גמילות חסדים, שנאמר, כי חסד חפצתי ולא
זבח [הושע ו' ו'].

Once, Rabban Johanan b. Zakkai was leaving Jerusalem and R. Joshua, who was coming behind him, saw the temple in ruins. He exclaimed, Woe to us, for the place where the sins of Israel used to be expiated lies in ruins. He replied, My son, do not torment yourself, for we have a form of expiation that is as (effective as) that. What is it, then? Deeds of mercy; as it was said, For I desire mercy and not sacrifice [Ho 6.6].

1. The destruction of the temple at Jerusalem by the Romans in 70 CE was of enormous consequence throughout the Jewish world, not simply because of national pride but also, and perhaps more profoundly, for religious reasons. Without the temple, and, therefore, without the opportunity to offer atoning sacrifices, the people would remain with their sins before God for ever. From this abject situation, the rabbis were able to point to the prophetic tradition: love for one's neighbour and acts of mercy can take the place of sacrifices.

גְּמִילוּת חֲסָדִים, literally 'fulfilment of mercies', is the technical term for acts of kindness. Lists of such acts are to be found in Soṭ 14a, Ecclesiastes Rabbah 7.1–3, Targum Neofiti to Gn 35.9, Targum pseudo-Jonathan to Ex 18.20 and Dt 34.6, and, in the New Testament, Mt 25.35–40. Jewish tradition gave particular emphasis to attending weddings and congratulating newly-weds and to burying the dead and consoling the bereaved as acts of kindness (see PRE 16–17).

II *Morphology*

2. RH shares with BH the interrogative pronouns מִי 'who?' and מָה 'what?'. מִי is used with both masculine and feminine nouns, generally in reference to persons, rarely, to things, whereas מָה usually refers to things rather than persons. As in BH, the vocalization of מָה varies, although it usually behaves like the article in that it strengthens the first consonant of the word that follows. In this respect, the pointing מֶה רָּאִיתָ 'what did you see?', instead of מָה רָאִיתָ, at K Eduy 6.3 is noteworthy, as here K treats *resh* as a non-guttural consonant, strengthening it with *dagesh* rather than compensating for lack of strengthening by increasing the vowel length of the interrogative. (In fact, *resh* with *dagesh* is typical of the eastern tradition of Hebrew and only rarely appears in K; see Unit 8.2 and Bar-Asher 1987, 13–14.)

3. RH has also developed another interrogative structure:

Meaning	RH form
which (one)? (masc.)	אֵיזֶה, אֵיזֶהוּ
which (one)? (fem.)	אֵיזוֹ, אֵיזוֹהִי
which ones? (common)	אֵי־זֵלוּ

The forms אֵיזֶה, אֵיזוֹ, and אֵילוּ are composed of the old interrogative particle אֵי and the demonstrative pronouns זֶה, זוֹ, and אֵלוּ. In both manuscripts and printed editions, אֵילוּ, the proper form of the plural interrogative, is often written like the demonstrative אֵלוּ.

The form אֵי־זֶה, in the sense 'whither?, where is?, which?', is found seventeen times in the Bible. In RH, the singular אֵיזֹה sometimes, as in our introductory text, has feminine reference and is to be pointed not אֵיזֶה but אֵיזֹה.

In LBH, at least as represented by Ecclesiastes, the feminine demonstrative זוֹ came to prominence as a phonetic variant of זֶה, although it is also found, always in the company of זֶה, in earlier texts (Jg 18.4; 2 S 11.25; 1 K 14.5; 2 K 6.19), as well as in Ezekiel (40.45), regarded as transitional between classical BH and LBH; eventually, in RH, the זוֹ form became lexicalized as זוֹ (which also appears twice in the Bible, at Ho 7.16 and Ps 132.12).

אֵיזֶהוּ and אֵיזוֹהִי are evidently composed of the interrogative and demonstrative particles followed by a suffixed pronoun; in important early manuscripts like K, these forms are also written as separate words: אֵי זֶה הוּא and אֵי זוֹ הִיא.

4. M.H. Segal (1927, §82) claimed that the semantic development of the RH interrogative can be traced clearly within BH. Thus, at 1 S 9.18, אֵי־זֶה בֵּית הָרֹאֶה, the זֶה does little more than emphasize אֵי as an independent interrogative, 'where?' (hence, 'where is the house of the seer?'), whereas at 2 K 3.8, אֵי־זֶה הַדֶּרֶךְ נַעֲלֶה, the emphasis has passed to the demonstrative particle, so that the sense is not so much 'where?' as 'which?' (hence, 'which way shall we go up'?); this second usage is the one that survived, and is clearly seen in texts like Ec 11.6, אֵי זֶה יִכְשַׁר הֲזֶה אוֹ־זֶה 'which one will be successful, this one or this one?', where there is no trace of the locational sense found in the Samuel passage. To Segal's observations, we might add that the later, non-locational, meaning of אֵיזֶה is also seen in the early post-biblical book of Ben Sira (30.40), according to Segal's own reconstruction: באיזה דרך תבקשנו 'by which way will you seek him?'.

III *Grammar and usage*

5. מִי is only used as a pronoun, whereas מָה can function as a pronoun or as an adjective. Both forms may be preceded by a preposition, for example, בְּמָה 'by what?', בְּמִי 'by whom?', לְמָה 'to what?', לְמִי 'to whom?', אֶת־מִי 'with whom?', 'by what?', etc.

6. In exegetical literature, the contraction מָהוּ is commonly used for מָה הוּא 'what is he?, what is it?' when asking about the meaning of a biblical text. Thus, at Mek 17.8 (L 2.138), רפידים מהו, literally, '*Refidim*, what is it?', means 'How is one to interpret *refidim*?' In the Tosefta and various *midrashim*, particularly Sifre to Deuteronomy, the expression מָהוּ אוֹמֵר, literally 'what is it saying?', is also frequently employed to introduce one of a series of biblical citations and means 'what does this text add?' (here, as in the for-mula וְכֵן הוּא אוֹמֵר 'and in the same sense it says', already encountered at Unit 1.13, הוּא always refers to a biblical text).

7. Although the combinations מִי שֶׁ- and מָה שֶׁ- may represent indefinite pronouns, 'whoever, whatever' (see Unit 6.7), this is not always so. For example, they are used with very definite reference in the divine 'name' מִי שֶׁאָמַר וְהָיָה עוֹלָם 'the-one-that-spoke-and-the-world-was' (see the introductory text of Unit 4) and in the saying recorded at Abot 2.14:

דע מה שתשיב לאפיקורוס

Know what you have to reply to a heretic.

Sometimes, as in the Bible (e.g. 1 S 20.4 and Est 9.26), the relative particle (-שֶׁ) is omitted, for example אֵין לוֹ מִי יַתִּירֶנּוּ 'it has no-one to make it permissible' (Men 4.3) and אֵין לִי מָה אָשִׁיב 'I have nothing to reply' (Kel 13.7).

8. מָה can also be used to introduce the first term in a comparison: מָה ... אַף 'like this ... also that', מָה אִם ... אֵינוֹ דִין/דִּין הוּא 'if this is so ... is it not correct?/it is correct', מָה אִם ... קַל וָחוֹמֶר 'if it is true for this ... it is even more true for that'. Such formulations are common in rabbinic arguments that employ *gezerah shawah* or *a fortiori* deductions (see Unit 26.8; there are numerous examples in the tannaitic *midrashim*). M.H. Segal's interpretation (1927, §§463; 499–500) of the מָה here as exclamatory, 'what!' is debatable; whatever its origins, in RH it simply functions as part of a lexicalized expression introducing the first term in a comparison.

9. מָה in particular is also found as part of numerous adverbial expressions, for example כַּמָּה 'how much?', בְּכַמָּה 'for how much?', עַד כַּמָּה 'how far?', לָמָה 'why?', מִפְּנֵי מָה 'for what reason?', and בִּשְׁבִיל מָה 'on account of what?'.

Frequently, a preposition is attached to an interrogative, as in

משלמי היו הבהמות

Whose were the cattle? (Mek 14.7 [L 1.201]).

Compare Jon 1.7:

בְּשֶׁלְּמִי הָרָעָה הַזֹּאת לָנוּ

On whose account has this misfortune come to us?

10. Although אֵיזֶהוּ and אֵיזוֹהִי only function as pronouns, אֵיזוֹ, אֵיזֶה, and אֵילוּ may be used as pronouns or as adjectives, for example

וְרוֹאִים אֵלּוּ הָאֲבָנִים הָרְאוּיוֹת לְהִשְׁתַּבֵּר

And they examine which stones are likely to break (BM 10.1)

and

וְאֵין יָדוּעַ אֵלּוּ שֶׁהָפְכוּ וְאֵלּוּ שֶׁקָּדְמוּ

And it is not known who have changed and who have progressed (TosNeg 2.7).

11. אֵיזֶה, אֵיזוֹ, and אֵילוּ imply a choice, as in

עַל אֵלּוּ הַטֻּמְאוֹת הַנָּזִיר מְגַלֵּחַ

For which contaminations does the Nazirite have to shave? (Naz 7.1)

and

וְאֵינִי יוֹדֵעַ אֵיזֶה מִכֶּם

And I do not know which of you two (Naz 8.1).

Followed by the relative -שֶׁ, they are employed demonstratively to specify one of a group of items, for example יָבִיא אֵיזוֹ שֶׁיִּרְצֶה 'he will bring that which he wishes (from among the offerings promised)' (Men 13.7).

IV *Phraseology*

12. לְמָה הַדָּבָר דּוֹמֶה 'what is this like?'—parables (or narrative *meshalim*) are usually constructed around a series of rigidly defined formulas:

A. מָשָׁל 'a parable' or מָשְׁלוּ מָשָׁל 'they recounted a parable';

B. לְמָה הַדָּבָר דּוֹמֶה 'what is this like?, to what might it be compared?';

C. -לְ 'to a(n)';

D. at the end, the parable's relevance to the lives of the audience or to biblical interpretation is usually stated, with such statements generally introduced by כָּךְ וְכֵן, לְכָךְ, כָּךְ, etc., 'therefore, in the same way'.

These narrative formulas are found not only in the rabbinic *meshalim* but also in the parables of the New Testament.

13. מָה רָאִיתָ, מָה רָאוּ, מָה רָאָה 'what did he/they/you see?', a lexicalized expression meaning 'what is the reason why he/they/you?, what is his/their/your basis for?', for example:

אָמְרוּ לוֹ לְרַבִּי נְחוּנְיָא, מָה רָאִיתָ לַחֲלוֹק מִדּוֹתֶיךָ

They said to R. Neḥunia, What is your basis for distinguishing your norms (i.e. for establishing new rules) (Eduy 6.3).

It is commonly used in exegetical literature, for example מה ראו חכמים לומר 'On what basis do the sages interpret?' (SNm 77.4 [H 71]) and

מה ראית לומר עולה בעולה

What is your reason for saying one holocaust (may be offered) for another? (SLv 1.3 [W 5c]).

V *Vocabulary*

אִילָן 'tree'
בַּקָּשָׁה 'request'
הֶכְשִׁיר 'permit, make suitable or *kosher*'
הֶנָּה 'make use of, benefit from'
הֲנָיָה 'advantage'
חָלַץ 'take off sandal (etc.), perform the ritual of *ḥaliṣah* (Dt 25.5–10)'
חַמִּים 'thermal waters'
טבריה 'Tiberias'
יִבֵּם 'fulfil the law of levirate marriage, marry the widow of a deceased childless brother' (Dt 25.5–10)
כַּפָּרָה 'expiation, atonement'
כְּשֶׁ- 'when' (contrast BH כַּאֲשֶׁר)
מֻתָּר 'permitted' (from the root נתר)
נָאֶה 'beautiful'
עֲבֵרָה 'transgression, sin'
עָשִׁיר 'rich'

VI *Exercises*

1. אִם אֵין אֲנִי לִי מִי לִי, וּכְשֶׁאֲנִי לְעַצְמִי מָה אֲנִי?
2. דַּע מַה לְמַעְלָה מִמָּךְ.
3. צְאוּ וּרְאוּ אֵי זוֹ הִיא דֶרֶךְ טוֹבָה.
4. דַּע מַה שֶׁתָּשִׁיב לְאֶפִּיקוֹרוֹס וְדַע לִפְנֵי מִי אַתָּה עָמֵל.
5. מַה־נָּאֶה אִילָן זֶה, וּמַה־נָּאֶה נִיר זֶה.
6. בֶּן זוֹמָא אוֹמֵר אֵי זֶה הוּא חָכָם? הַלּוֹמֵד מִכָּל אָדָם ... אֵיזֶה הוּא גִּבּוֹר? הַכּוֹבֵשׁ אֶת־יִצְרוֹ ... אֵיזֶהוּ עָשִׁיר? הַשָּׂמֵחַ בְּחֶלְקוֹ.
7. הַלּוֹמֵד [הַלָּמֵד K] יֶלֶד לְמָה הוּא דוֹמֶה? ... הַלּוֹמֵד [הַלָּמֵד K] זָקֵן לְמָה הוּא דוֹמֶה? ... הַלּוֹמֵד [הַלָּמֵד K] מִן הַקְּטַנִּים לְמָה הוּא דוֹמֶה? ... הַלּוֹמֵד [הַלָּמֵד K] מִן הַזְּקֵנִים לְמָה הוּא דוֹמֶה?
8. חֲכָמִים אוֹמְרִים עַל אֵיזֶה מֵהֶן שֶׁיִּרְצֶה, מְבָרֵךְ.
9. רַבִּי שִׁמְעוֹן אוֹמֵר, מְיַבֵּם לְאֵיזוֹ מֵהֶן שֶׁיִּרְצֶה אוֹ חוֹלֵץ לְאֵיזוֹ מֵהֶן שֶׁיִּרְצֶה.

‏10. מה ראו ישראל לפדות פטרי חמורים ולא פטרי סוסים וגמלים?‏

‏11. מה הדם מהנה למלאך או מה מהנה להם לישראל?‏

‏12. מה ראית להשחית שער נאה?‏

‏13. מפני מה המן משתנה להם לכל דבר שהיו רוצים?‏

‏14. מפני מה לא ברא המקום חמים בירושלים כחמי טבריה?‏

‏15. ראה משה בעיניו מה שלא הלך יהושע ברגליו.‏

‏16. ראו איזו עבירה עברתי וכמה בקשות בקשתי.‏

‏17. נאמר כאן שמחה ונאמר להלן שמחה מה שמחה האמורה להלן שלמים
אף שמחה האמורה כאן שלמים.‏

‏18. שלש מצוות ... איני יודע איזה יקדום.‏

‏19. במה הכתוב מדבר?‏

‏20. מה מים מותרים בהניה אף דם מותר בהניה, מה מים מכשירים את
זרעים אף דם מכשיר את הזרעים.‏

Sources. 1. Abot 1.14. 2. Abot 2.1. 3. K Abot 2.9. 4. Abot 2.14. 5. Abot
3.7. 6. K Abot 4.1. 7. Abot 4.20. 8. Ber 6.4. 9. Yeb 2.2. 10. Mek 17.8 (L
2.138). 11. Mek 17.11 (L 2.144). 12. SNm 22.6 (H 26). 13. SNm 87.2 (H
86). 14. SNm 89.5 (H 90). 15. SNm 136 (H 183). 16. SNm 136 (H 183).
17. SDt 64 (F 130.1). 18. SDt 67 (F 132). 19. SDt 71 (F 134) *et passim*. 20.
SDt 71 (F 136).

UNIT SIX

INDEFINITE EXPRESSIONS

I *Introductory text* (Abot 3.9)

‏רַבִּי חֲנִינָה בֶּן דּוֹסָא אוֹמֵר, כָּל־שֶׁיִּרְאַת חֶטְאוֹ קוֹדֶמֶת לְחָכְמָתוֹ, חָכְמָתוֹ
מִתְקַיֶּמֶת, וְכָל־שֶׁחָכְמָתוֹ קוֹדֶמֶת לְיִרְאַת חֶטְאוֹ, אֵין חָכְמָתוֹ מִתְקַיֶּמֶת.
הוּא הָיָה אוֹמֵר, כָּל־שֶׁמַּעֲשָׂיו מְרֻבִּין מֵחָכְמָתוֹ, חָכְמָתוֹ מִתְקַיֶּמֶת,
וְכָל־שֶׁחָכְמָתוֹ מְרֻבָּה מִמַּעֲשָׂיו, אֵין חָכְמָתוֹ מִתְקַיֶּמֶת.‏

Rabbi Ḥaninah ben Dosa says, All whose fear of sin exceeds their wisdom,
their wisdom will endure, but all whose wisdom exceeds their fear of sin,
their wisdom will not endure. He also used to say, All whose deeds are
greater than their wisdom, their wisdom will endure, but all whose wisdom is
greater than their deeds, their wisdom will not endure.

1. Ḥaninah ben Dosa was a charismatic miracle-worker from Galilee.
Some authors have compared him to another Galilaean, Jesus of Nazareth.
Ḥaninah's declaration emphasizes the tension that exists between study and

practice. The dialectic contrast in which the statement is couched is typical of
Semitic rhetoric. But Ḥaninah does not claim that the one excludes the other,
as if wisdom and practice/piety were incompatible. Set against the isolated
wisdom of the scholar, which can lead to pride, he affirms the superiority of
charity and humble piety, which form the basis of a pure and enduring wisdom.

II *Morphology*

2. RH's only indefinite pronoun is כְּלוּם '(not) anything, nothing', which,
according to M.H. Segal (1927, §437) probably has its origins in כָּל־מְאוּמָה
(literally, 'all something', i.e. 'everything, anything').

3. Other terms that function as part of indefinite expressions, in RH as in
BH, include:

    A. the interrogatives מִי 'who?' and מָה 'what?';

    B. various nouns of generalized reference, such as אָדָם and אִישׁ
'person', פְּלוֹנִי 'someone', כָּל 'all', and דָּבָר 'thing';

    C. a number of grammatical constructions.

III *Grammar and usage*

4. The indefinite function of אָדָם 'person, (some)one', כָּל־אָדָם 'everyone, anyone', and אֵין אָדָם 'no-one', of דָּבָר '(some)thing', כָּל־דָּבָר 'everything, anything', and of אֵין דָּבָר 'nothing' can be seen at Abot 4.3:

אַל תְּהִי בָז לְכָל אָדָם וְאַל תְּהִי מַפְלִיג לְכָל דָּבָר, שֶׁאֵין לְךָ אָדָם
שֶׁאֵין לוֹ שָׁעָה וְאֵין לְךָ דָּבָר שֶׁאֵין לוֹ מָקוֹם

Do not despise anyone and do not allow anything to seem impossible to you, for you will find no-one for whom there is not a time and
nothing for which there is not a place.

In fact, this usage is presaged in the Bible, where we find at Ec 9.15 the
following:

וְאָדָם לֹא זָכַר אֶת־הָאִישׁ הַמִּסְכֵּן הַהוּא

And nobody had mentioned that poor man.

כָּל may be used as an adjective with any noun, giving that noun a general or indefinite sense, as in

כָּל תּוֹרָה שֶׁאֵין עִמָּהּ מְלָאכָה

Any (study of the) Torah that is not accompanied by work (Abot
2.2),

כָּל כְּנֵסִיָה שֶׁהִיא לְשֵׁם שָׁמַיִם

Any assembly that gathers in the name of heaven (Abot 4.11),

and

כָּל כִּתְבֵי הַקֹּדֶשׁ ... וְאַף עַל פִּי שֶׁכְּתוּבִים בְּכָל לָשׁוֹן

Any holy writings ... in whatever language they are written (Shab 16.1).

In addition, the formula מִכָּל־מָקוֹם 'in every case, whatever the circumstance' is used to confirm the overall validity of a conclusion.

5. The expressions כָּל־שֶׁהִיא, [כָּל־שֶׁהוּא], and כָּל־שֶׁהֵן are employed as adjectives or pronouns and convey the sense of 'whatever it (e.g. quantity, character, etc.) might be', for example בְּפֶחָמִין כָּל שֶׁהוּא 'with coals in whatever quantity' (Shab 1.11), אֵלּוּ אֲסוּרִין וְאוֹסְרִין בְּכָל שֶׁהֵן 'these things, whatever their quantity, are prohibited and cause prohibition' (AZ 5.9).

6. Statements of universal validity usually begin with כָּל־ followed by participle (see the exercises at the end of the unit), as in several *mishnayot* from Abot, for example כָּל הַמְחַלֵּל אֶת שֵׁם שָׁמַיִם 'anyone who profanes the heavenly name' (4.4).

כָּל־שֶׁ- 'whoever' is used in the same way, for example כָּל שֶׁאֵינוֹ יָכוֹל 'whoever is not able' (Ḥag 1.1).

7. The interrogatives מִי and מָה can also have indefinite significance, particularly in the sequence מִי/מָה שֶׁ- 'whoever, whatever' (see Unit 5.7) and especially when preceded and reinforced by כָּל־, as in מַאֲכִיל לְכָל מִי שֶׁיִּרְצֶה 'feeding whomsoever' (BB 8.7). In the earliest stages of Hebrew, מִן appears to have had a similar function, as at Dt 33.11: מִן־יְקוּמוּן 'whoever rises up'.

8. The terms [מַשֶּׁהוּא], מַשֶּׁהִיא, and מַשֶּׁהֵן have the sense of 'something, any amount, the smallest quantity' and are usually employed with adverbial force, for example אדם טועה משהו 'whoever is wrong in the smallest matter' (Pes 11b), הברזל ממית במשהו 'iron kills, whatever its size' (SNm 160.5 [H 217]). In AZ 5.8, מַשֶּׁהוּא is found alongside כָּל־שֶׁהוּא in the same sense; M. Bar-Asher (1990a, 208) claims that in Babylonian amoraic literature the first form eventually replaced the second.

9. כְּלוּם is usually found in negative sentences of the type לֹא עָשָׂה כְלוּם 'he didn't do anything', for example הַשְּׁלִשִׁית וְהָרְבִיעִית אֵין לָהֶם כְּלוּם 'the third and the fourth don't have anything' (Qin 2.3), although it can function as a negative word in its own right, as in כלום יש לו עלינו אלא גשמים 'he has nothing for us except rain' (MS Erfurt TosSoṭ 3.7, the import of which is clearer in MS Vienna: 'he only inconveniences himself for us to the extent of giving us a couple of drops of rain').

10. מִקְצָת '(a) part (of), some (of)' (derived from מִן קָצָה 'from the end of') has a partitive function and usually governs a genitive, for example

מִקְצָתָן רְעֵבִים וּמִקְצָתָן שְׂבֵעִים

Some of them were hungry and some of them were sated/
While some were hungry, others were sated (Abot 5.8).

11. An indefinite structure is also formed by partitive מִן 'some (of)', as at Mek 15.18 (L 2.80): תפש מהם, הרג מהם, צלב מהם 'some he seized, others he slaughtered, others he crucified' (see also Unit 22.14).

12. [פְּלוֹנִית] 'so-and-so, such-and-such' can be used pronominally or adjectivally with reference to both persons and things, as at Yeb 16.6:

אִישׁ פְּלוֹנִי בֶּן אִישׁ פְּלוֹנִי מִמָּקוֹם פְּלוֹנִי מֵת

Such-and-such a person, the son of such-and-such a person, from
such-and-such a place, is dead.

13. Statements of general application, in which the subject is not specified (with a second or third person form of the verb or a participle [see Unit
19.11]), comprise a further class of indefinite expressions. An example is

אִם לָמַדְתָּ תוֹרָה הַרְבֵּה נוֹתְנִים לְךָ שָׂכָר הַרְבֵּה

If one has studied (literally, 'you have studied') much Torah, one
will be given (literally, 'giving to you') an abundant reward (Abot
2.16).

To this category belongs the standard formulation of conditional sentences in legal and sapiential contexts (see Units 17.10–12; 19.19; 28.4–5),
for example קָרָא וְלֹא דִקְדֵּק בְּאוֹתִיּוֹתֶיהָ ... יָצָא 'if one reads, albeit without
clearly enunciating the letters, one has fulfilled one's obligation' (Ber 2.3)
and הַכּוֹתֵב נְכָסָיו לְבָנָיו צָרִיךְ שֶׁיִּכְתֹּב 'if a person assigns their property to their
children, that person must write it down' (BB 8.7).

IV *Phraseology*

14. וְיֵשׁ אוֹמְרִים 'there are those who say', a formula employed to introduce divergent opinions.

15. מִכָּל־מָקוֹם 'in every case, whatever the circumstance' (see above,
§4). This appears to be a loan-translation from Greek ἐκ παντὸς τρόπου:

תלמוד לומר , קדוש יהיה [במדבר ו' ה'], מכל מקום

The text says, It will be holy [Nm 6.5]—whatever the circumstance!
(SNm 25.5 [H 31]).

V *Vocabulary*

בָּזָה 'despise'

בַּצֹּרֶת 'drought'

בָּרַר 'clarify, select, choose'

גּוּף 'body, essence' (as in שִׁבְעָה גוּפֵי עֲבֵרָה 'the seven basic transgressions, the
seven capital sins')

הֵבִיא 'bring' (hi. of בוא); in liturgical language, 'offer'; in exegetical texts,
'include, cite, expound'

טָעַן 'load, carry, demand, require', טְעוּנִין גְּנִיזָה 'requiring safekeeping'

יָצָא 'go out'; in legal parlance, 'fulfil an obligation'

לִסְטֵס (plural לִסְטִים; λῃστής) 'robber'

מוֹעֲדוֹת (plural of מוֹעֵד 'appointed time') 'days on which festivals are held,
holidays'

מָמוֹן 'money, wealth'

מַתֶּכֶת 'metal'

סֵבֶר 'hope'; סֵבֶר פָּנִים 'cordiality'

עִשֵּׂר 'give/take tithe'

פִּלְפֵּל 'pepper'

פּוּרְעָנוּת (plural פּוּרְעָנִיּוֹת) 'punishment, retribution'

מָעַט–רָבָה 'increase–decrease', מְרוּבָּה–מוּעָט[מְ] (pu. participles employed as adjectives) 'much–little'

שׁוֹאֵבָה 'drawing of water', בֵּית הַשּׁוֹאֵבָה 'house from where water is drawn' (in reference to the temple fountain in the court of the women, from where water was carried in procession for libations during the festival of Succoth)

שַׁחֲרִית 'dawn, morning, morning prayer (in synagogue)'

VI *Exercises*

1. וֶהֱוֵי מְקַבֵּל אֶת כָּל הָאָדָם בְּסֵבֶר פָּנִים יָפוֹת.
2. כָּל הַמַּרְבֶּה דְבָרִים מֵבִיא חֵטְא.
3. אֵיזוֹהִי דֶרֶךְ יְשָׁרָה שֶׁיָּבֹר לוֹ הָאָדָם? כָּל שֶׁהִיא תִפְאֶרֶת לְעוֹשָׂהּ וְתִפְאֶרֶת לוֹ מִן הָאָדָם.
4. מַרְבֶּה צְדָקָה, מַרְבֶּה שָׁלוֹם. קָנָה שֵׁם טוֹב, קָנָה לְעַצְמוֹ.
5. כָּל הַפּוֹרֵק מִמֶּנּוּ עֹל תּוֹרָה, נוֹתְנִין עָלָיו עֹל מַלְכוּת וְעֹל דֶרֶךְ אֶרֶץ.
6. הַמְחַלֵּל אֶת הַקֳּדָשִׁים וְהַמְבַזֶּה אֶת הַמּוֹעֲדוֹת ... אֵין לוֹ חֵלֶק לָעוֹלָם הַבָּא.
7. אֵיזֶהוּ חָכָם? הַלּוֹמֵד מִכָּל אָדָם.
8. וֶהֱוֵי שְׁפַל רוּחַ בִּפְנֵי כָל אָדָם.
9. שִׁבְעָה מִינֵי פוּרְעָנוּיּוֹת בָּאִין לָעוֹלָם עַל שִׁבְעָה גוּפֵי עֲבֵרָה, מִקְצָתָן מְעַשְּׂרִין וּמִקְצָתָן אֵינָן מְעַשְּׂרִין, רָעָב שֶׁלְבַצֹּרֶת בָּא, מִקְצָתָן רְעֵבִים וּמִקְצָתָן שְׂבֵעִים.
10. הַקּוֹרֵא אֶת שְׁמַע וְלֹא הִשְׁמִיעַ לְאָזְנוֹ, יָצָא.
11. אֵיזֶהוּ קָטָן? כָּל שֶׁאֵינוֹ יָכוֹל לִרְכּוֹב עַל כְּתֵפָיו שֶׁל אָבִיו.
12. מִי שֶׁיֶּשׁ לוֹ אוֹכְלִים מְרוּבִּים וּנְכָסִים מוּעָטִים [מְמוּעָטִים K], מֵבִיא שְׁלָמִים מְרוּבִּים וְעוֹלוֹת מוּעָטוֹת [מְמוּעָטוֹת K].
13. פִּלְפֶּלֶת כָּל שֶׁהִיא ... מִינֵי בְשָׂמִים וּמִינֵי מַתָּכוֹת כָּל שֶׁהֵן.
14. כָּל מִי שֶׁלֹא רָאָה שִׂמְחַת בֵּית הַשּׁוֹאֵבָה לֹא רָאָה שִׂמְחָה מִיָּמָיו.
15. אַף אדם הראשון לא טעם כלום עד שעשה מלאכה.
16. שמעו לסטים ובאו ... נטלו ממנו כל ממונו, לשחרית אין לו כלום.
17. משביע אני עליך, לֹא ראית לפלוני יוצא מתוך ביתי טעון כלים?
18. למה הדבר דומה? למי שאמר לו רבו.
19. למה נאמר, כי יפליא [במדבר ו' ב']? להביא את מי שיודע להפלות.
20. גלוי היה לפני הקב"ה שהברזל ממית במשהוא.

Sources. 1. Abot 1.15. 2. Abot 1.17. 3. Abot 2.1. 4. Abot 2.7. 5. Abot 3.5. 6. Abot 3.11. 7. Abot 4.1. 8. Abot 4.10. 9. Abot 5.8. 10. Ber 2.3. 11. Ḥag 1.1. 12. Ḥag 1.5. 13. Shab 9.6. 14. Suk 5.1. 15. ARN 11 (S 45). 16. ARN 11 (S 47). 17. Mek 22.3 (L 3.107). 18. SLv 1.2 (W 4c). 19. SNm 22.3 (H 25). 20. SNm 160.5 (H 217).

UNIT SEVEN

REFLEXIVE AND RECIPROCAL STRUCTURES

I *Introductory text* (Pea 1.1)

אֵלּוּ דְבָרִים שֶׁאָדָם אוֹכֵל פֵּירוֹתֵיהֶם בָּעוֹלָם הַזֶּה וְהַקֶּרֶן קַיֶּמֶת לוֹ לָעוֹלָם הַבָּא,
כִּבּוּד אָב וָאֵם וּגְמִילוּת חֲסָדִים וַהֲבָאַת שָׁלוֹם בֵּין אָדָם לַחֲבֵרוֹ, וְתַלְמוּד תּוֹרָה
כְּנֶגֶד כֻּלָּם.

These are the things whose fruits one enjoys in this world and whose capital
remains for one in the world to come: honouring one's father and mother,
acts of kindness, and making peace among people. But the study of the Torah
takes in all of them.

1. Judaism holds that any action, good or bad, must have its recompense;
if that has already come in this life it must not be expected again in the next.
However, certain deeds, such as those mentioned in this text, endure for ever,
and reward for them is obtained not only in the present world but throughout
eternity. The belief in heavenly reward/punishment also underlies numerous
New Testament texts, such as Lk 6.20–38 (the beatitudes), 14.12–14, and
18.28–30 (a further instance of a double reward, both on earth and in
heaven).

In the final clause, the expression כְּנֶגֶד conveys the idea of 'correspondence' (see Unit 26.6A), and we might translate more literally as 'the study
of the Torah corresponds to all of them'. תַּלְמוּד תּוֹרָה 'study of the Torah' has
to be understood in an extended sense that encapsulates both study and
practice: the Torah tells us exactly how to carry out good deeds and prevents
us from claiming ignorance of them.

Note that in the first line K reads מִתְקַיֶּמֶת 'is raised' for קַיֶּמֶת 'stands (i.e.
'remains')', employing the *Hitpa'el* in its 'middle' sense (see Unit 15.10D).

II *Morphology*

2. RH lacks specific reflexive or reciprocal pronouns ('myself', etc.), making
use instead of:
    A. -לְ followed by a suffixed pronominal object (לִי, לְךָ, לוֹ, etc.);
    B. the *Nif'al* and *Hitpa'el/Nitpa'al* conjugations of the verb;

C. various expressions based on nouns such as נֶפֶשׁ 'soul', חַיִּים 'life', גּוּף 'body', לֵב 'heart', and, most importantly, עֶצֶם 'bone'.

III *Grammar and usage*

3. -לְ followed by pronominal suffix.

A. The construction is commonly used to express the reflexive, as in BH, for example וַיִּקַּח־לוֹ לֶמֶךְ שְׁתֵּי נָשִׁים 'and Lamech took two wives for himself' (Gn 4.19), with which Abot 2.7 might be compared:

קָנָה לוֹ דִבְרֵי תוֹרָה קָנָה לוֹ חַיֵּי עוֹלָם

If one acquires for oneself the words of the Torah, one acquires for oneself the life of the world to come.

However, K omits לוֹ both times, indicating that it is a kind of 'superfluous dative', which adds little to the meaning of the text; for a similar phenomenon in K, see Unit 1.11.

B. Especially with verbs of motion, the construction can carry instead a 'middle' or 'ingressive' sense, as at AZ 5.4, הָלַךְ לוֹ 'he betook himself, he went away', Mek 12.1 (L 1.7–8), אֶבְרַח לִי ... אֵלֵךְ לִי 'I shall run away ... I shall go away', or Hor 1.2, יָשַׁב לוֹ בְתוֹךְ בֵּיתוֹ ... הָלַךְ לוֹ לִמְדִינַת הַיָּם 'he kept himself at home ... he betook himself to a distant land'.

C. Ambiguity is often inevitable and only the context can show whether, for example, אָמַר לוֹ means 'he said to another' or 'he said to himself, he thought'.

4. עֶצֶם.

A. With pronominal suffixes attached, עֶצֶם 'bone, essence' forms not only an emphatic demonstrative ('this very'; see Unit 2.8–9) but also an authentic reflexive pronoun, as in קָנָה שֵׁם טוֹב קָנָה לְעַצְמוֹ 'whoever gains repute, gains it for himself' (Abot 2.7).

B. Apart from לְעַצְמוֹ, the forms בְּעַצְמוֹ and מֵעַצְמוֹ also occur. Their precise meaning can only be resolved in context: 'by oneself', 'separately', 'on one's own initiative', 'with one's own abilities', 'without coercion', etc. At Shab 19.2, יָנֵתַן זֶה בְּעַצְמוֹ וְזֶה בְּעַצְמוֹ, the sense is 'each one is applied separately'; similarly, AZ 58b, לשׁון תורה לעצמה ולשׁון חכמים לעצמה, appears to mean that BH and RH are autonomous languages (see Introduction); at Ber 1.3, וְסִכַּנְתִּי בְּעַצְמִי מִפְּנֵי הַלִּסְטִים, the sense is 'I myself was in danger because of the thieves'. At SLv 1.15 (W 9a), to indicate that in the burnt offering of birds the head and the body are burnt separately, we find הראשׁ לעצמו והגוף לעצמו 'the head by itself and the body by itself'. A variant of מֵעַצְמוֹ is מֵאֵלָיו 'of itself', as at BM 7.9: בִּזְמָן שֶׁבָּאוּ מֵאֲלֵיהֶן 'when they come of their own accord'.

C. בֵּינוֹ לְבֵין עַצְמוֹ, בֵּינָן לְבֵין עַצְמָן, literally, 'between himself and himself', 'between them and themselves', etc., implies 'on his/their own, in private, in a hushed voice', and so on. At Bik 1.4, private prayer (בֵּינוֹ לְבֵין עַצְמוֹ) is distinguished from that of the synagogue:

וּכְשֶׁהוּא מִתְפַּלֵּל בֵּינוֹ לְבֵין עַצְמוֹ, אוֹמֵר ... וּכְשֶׁהוּא בְּבֵית הַכְּנֶסֶת, אוֹמֵר

And when he prays on his own, he says ... and when he is in the
synagogue, he says.

5. Expressions using חַיִּים, נֶפֶשׁ, and גּוּף.

A. The following example (Abot 4.5) shows how the reflexive is expressed in the first half by the *Nif'al* and in the second by חַיִּים:

כָּל הַנֶּהֱנֶה מִדִּבְרֵי תוֹרָה נוֹטֵל חַיָּיו מִן הָעוֹלָם

All who gain themselves (financial, etc.) advantage from the words
of the Torah are taking themselves (literally, 'his life') away from
the world (i.e. they are working towards their own destruction).

B. נֶפֶשׁ is commonly used with reflexive significance in BH, for example
Jos 23.11: וְנִשְׁמַרְתֶּם מְאֹד לְנַפְשֹׁתֵיכֶם 'and watch yourselves closely'. The same
usage continues, although less frequently, in RH, as, for example, at SNm
131.1 (H 169): אבדת את נפשך ואבדת את ממונך, literally, 'you have lost your
soul and you have lost your money'.

C. גּוּף only rarely occurs in reflexive structures, for example:

וְלֹא מָצָאתִי לַגּוּף טוֹב אֶלָּא שְׁתִיקָה

And I have found nothing better for myself than silence (Abot 1.17);

כָּל הַמְכַבֵּד אֶת הַתּוֹרָה, גּוּפוֹ מְכֻבָּד עַל הַבְּרִיּוֹת

Everyone that honours the Torah is honoured themselves (literally,
'his body') by humankind (Abot 4.6);

עדות שבגופה

Testimony concerning oneself (TosKet 1.6).

6. The common formula קִבֵּל עַל followed by a suffixed pronoun
referring to the subject has the reflexive value of 'take upon oneself, accept,
commit oneself', as in הַמְקַבֵּל עָלָיו לִהְיוֹת חָבֵר 'one who commits himself to
be a member of a group'.

7. Just as RH has no specifically reflexive pronoun, neither does it have
one that expresses reciprocity ('one another', etc.). Instead, it employs the
following devices.

A. Repetition of the demonstrative, as in BH, for example:

שִׁחְרְרוּ זֶה אֶת זֶה

They freed one another (Yeb 11.5);

בִּזְמַן שֶׁהֵן מְעִידוֹת זוֹ אֶת זוֹ

When each testifies concerning the other (Ket 2.6).

B. The BH collocation אִישׁ ... רֵעַ 'one ... one's companion' (e.g. Gn
11.3), as in כְּדֵי שֶׁלֹּא יַכּוּ אִישׁ אֶת־רְעֵהוּ 'so that they do not injure one another'
(Pea 4.4);

C. חָבֵר 'colleague, companion' followed by a suffix that refers to the accompanying noun, especially in the construction בֵּין ... לַחֲבֵרוֹ, literally,
'between (a person/thing) ... and their colleague', that is, 'some with others',
'between these and those', 'reciprocally', etc.; examples include:

הֲבָאַת שָׁלוֹם בֵּין אָדָם לַחֲבֵרוֹ

Making peace between one person and another (Pea 1.1, quoted in the introductory text);

אִם אֵין בֵּין קָנֶה לַחֲבֵרוֹ שְׁלֹשָׁה טְפָחִים

If from one reed to another there is not a gap of three palms (Kil 4.4, illustrating how חָבֵר can be used of things as well as persons and animals).

D. The *Nif'al* form נֶחְלְקוּ 'they were divided', expressing discrepancy (see Unit 15.7C).

IV *Phraseology*

8. מִתְחַיֵּב בְּנַפְשׁוֹ 'being responsible for one's (loss of) life, condemning oneself, placing oneself under sentence of death', for example

כָּל הַמִּתְחַיֵּב בְּנַפְשׁוֹ אֵינוֹ מְשַׁלֵּם מָמוֹן

No-one sentenced to death pays a fine (Ket 3.2; see also BQ 3.10; Abot 3.4, 7–8; Ḥul 1.1).

9. בֵּינוֹ לְבֵין עַצְמוֹ 'privately, on one's own' (see above, §4C).

10. קִבֵּל עָלָיו 'take upon oneself, commit oneself' (see above, §6).

11. לֹא יֹאמַר אָדָם לַחֲבֵרוֹ 'let no-one say to their neighbour, let nobody say to anyone'; for example

וְלֹא יֹאמַר אָדָם לַחֲבֵרוֹ בִּירוּשָׁלַיִם, הֵילָךְ יַיִן וְתֵן לִי שֶׁמֶן

In Jerusalem let no-one say to their neighbour, Drink wine and give me oil (MS 1.1; see also Shab 23.3; BM 5.9; Sanh 4.5; Abot 5.5).

V *Vocabulary*

בַּטָּלָה 'vanity, emptiness, annulment, uselessness'

בֶּן־חֹרִין 'free (person)'

בְּרִיָּה 'creature, human being' (plural בְּרִיּוֹת 'humankind')

הֲבָאָה 'bringing, taking'

הֵילָךְ (i.e. הֵי 'behold' and לָךְ 'to you') 'here you are'

זָהִיר 'cautious, prudent'

חַיָּב 'guilty, condemned', הִתְחַיֵּב 'be guilty, condemned', חַיָּב–פָּטוּר 'exempt– under obligation'

טָבַע 'mint'

יִתְרוֹ 'Jethro' (Moses' father-in-law)

כְּדֵי־שֶׁ- 'in order that, so that'

כְּנֶגֶד 'corresponding to, opposite'

לַח וְיָבֵשׁ 'wet and dry, liquid and dry food' (expressing totality)

מַטְבֵּעַ 'coin'

פְּרִי (plural פֵּרוֹת) 'fruit'

צִעֵר 'deprive oneself, abstain'

צֹרֶךְ 'necessity'

ק״ו, abbreviation of קַל וָחֹמֶר 'light and heavy', in the sense of 'how much more!', מָה אִם ... ק״ו ל- 'if this is so ... how much more the other!'

קֶרֶן 'horn, principal, initial investment'

יֵין מִצְוָה ... יֵין רְשׁוּת 'power, authority, government, liberty, permission', רְשׁוּת 'wine that it is prescribed to drink ... wine that one is free to drink'

שְׁתִיקָה 'silence'

VI *Exercises*

1. וּכְשֶׁאֲנִי לְעַצְמִי, מָה אֲנִי?
2. כָּל יָמַי גָּדַלְתִּי בֵּין הַחֲכָמִים, וְלֹא מָצָאתִי לַגּוּף אֶלָּא טוֹב אֶלָּא שְׁתִיקָה.
3. אַל תַּאֲמֵן בְּעַצְמָךְ עַד יוֹם מוֹתָךְ.
4. הֱווּ זְהִירִין בָּרְשׁוּת, שֶׁאֵין מְקָרְבִין לוֹ לָאָדָם אֶלָּא לְצֹרֶךְ עַצְמָן.
5. הַמְפַנֶּה לִבּוֹ לְבַטָּלָה, הֲרֵי זֶה מִתְחַיֵּב בְּנַפְשׁוֹ.
6. יֵשׁ חַיָּב עַל מַעֲשֵׂה שׁוֹרוֹ וּפָטוּר עַל מַעֲשֵׂה עַצְמוֹ.
7. הַמְקַבֵּל עָלָיו לִהְיוֹת חָבֵר אֵינוֹ מוֹכֵר לְעַם הָאָרֶץ לַח וְיָבֵשׁ.
8. מִי שֶׁחֶצְיוֹ עֶבֶד וְחֶצְיוֹ בֶּן חֹרִין עוֹבֵד אֶת רַבּוֹ יוֹם אֶחָד וְאֶת עַצְמוֹ יוֹם אֶחָד.
9. אִם נִטְמְאוּ יָדָיו, נִטְמָא גּוּפוֹ.
10. אִם אֵין בֵּין שׁוּרָה לַחֲבֵרְתָּהּ שֵׁשׁ עֶשְׂרֵה אַמָּה, לֹא יָבִיא זֶרַע לְשָׁם.
11. לֹא יִשְׂכֹּר אָדָם פּוֹעֲלִים בַּשַּׁבָּת, וְלֹא יֹאמַר אָדָם לַחֲבֵרוֹ לִשְׂכֹּר לוֹ פּוֹעֲלִים.
12. אָדָם טוֹבֵעַ כַּמָּה מַטְבְּעוֹת בְּחוֹתָם אֶחָד, וְכֻלָּן דּוֹמִין זֶה לָזֶה אֶת זֶה, וּמֶלֶךְ מַלְכֵי הַמְּלָכִים הַקָּדוֹשׁ בָּרוּךְ הוּא טָבַע כָּל הָאָדָם בְּחוֹתָמוֹ שֶׁלְּאָדָם הָרִאשׁוֹן, וְאֵין אֶחָד מֵהֶן דּוֹמֶה לַחֲבֵרוֹ.
13. לֹא יַנִּיחַ אדם עטרה מעצמו בראשו, אבל אחרים יניחו לו.
14. ומה אם המצער נפשו מן היין צריך כפרה, ק״ו למצער נפשו על כל דבר.
15. ישמור את נפשך בשעת המיתה.
16. אם יתרו חותנו של מלך לא קיבל עליו, ק״ו לשאר בני אדם.
17. כדי שלא יאמר אדם לחבירו, נלך ונעלה לירושלים.
18. וישמע י׳ [במדבר י״ב ב׳], מלמד שלא היתה שם בריה, אלא בינו לבין עצמן דברו בי
19. אבדת את נפשך ואבדת את ממונך ... אבדת את עצמך ואבדת את כבודך.
20. אמר להם, לא מעצמי אני אומר לכם, אלא מפי הקדש אני אומר לכם.

Sources. 1. Abot 1.14. 2. Abot 1.17. 3. Abot 2.4. 4. Abot 2.3. 5. Abot 3.4. 6. BQ 3.10. 7. Dem 2.3. 8. Eduy 1.13. 9. Eduy 3.2. 10. Kil 4.8. 11. Shab 23.3. 12. Sanh 4.5. 13. ARN 11 (S 46). 14. SNm 30.2 (H 36). 15. SNm 40 (H 44). 16. SNm 80.1 (H 76). 17. SNm 89.5 (H 90). 18. SNm 100 (H 99). 19. SNm 131.1 (H 169). 20. SDt 5 (F 13).

UNIT EIGHT

THE RELATIVE PRONOUN *SHE-*

1 *Introductory text* (Abot 3.17)

כָּל שֶׁחָכְמָתוֹ מְרֻבָּה מִמַּעֲשָׂיו, לְמָה הוּא דוֹמֶה? לְאִילָן שֶׁעֲנָפָיו מְרֻבִּין
וְשָׁרָשָׁיו מוּעָטִין, וְהָרוּחַ בָּאָה וְעוֹקַרְתּוּ וְהוֹפַכְתּוּ עַל פָּנָיו, שֶׁנֶּאֱמַר, וְהָיָה
כְּעַרְעָר בָּעֲרָבָה וְלֹא יִרְאֶה כִּי־יָבוֹא טוֹב וְשָׁכַן חֲרֵרִים בַּמִּדְבָּר אֶרֶץ
מְלֵחָה וְלֹא תֵשֵׁב [ירמיה יז ו]. אֲבָל כָּל שֶׁמַּעֲשָׂיו מְרֻבִּין מֵחָכְמָתוֹ,
לְמָה הוּא דוֹמֶה? לְאִילָן שֶׁעֲנָפָיו מוּעָטִין וְשָׁרָשָׁיו מְרֻבִּין, שֶׁאֲפִלּוּ כָל
הָרוּחוֹת שֶׁבָּעוֹלָם בָּאוֹת וְנוֹשְׁבוֹת בּוֹ אֵין מְזִיזוֹת אוֹתוֹ מִמְּקוֹמוֹ, שֶׁנֶּאֱמַר,
וְהָיָה כְּעֵץ שָׁתוּל עַל־מַיִם וְעַל־יוּבַל יְשַׁלַּח שָׁרָשָׁיו וְלֹא יִרְאֶה כִּי־יָבֹא חֹם
וְהָיָה עָלֵהוּ רַעֲנָן וּבִשְׁנַת בַּצֹּרֶת לֹא יִדְאָג וְלֹא יָמִישׁ מֵעֲשׂוֹת פֶּרִי [ירמיה יז ח].

Those whose wisdom exceeds their works, what are they like?: a tree whose
branches are abundant but whose roots are few, and when the wind blows, it
uproots it and knocks it over, as it was said, He will be as a tamarisk in the
steppe, and will not recognize good when it comes, for it inhabits a burning
desert, salty and inhospitable land [Jr 17.6]. However, those whose works
exceed their wisdom, what are they like?: a tree of few branches but
abundant roots; even if all the winds in the world were to come and blow
against it they could not move it from its place, as it was said, He will be as a
tree planted next to water, taking root alongside a stream; when the heat
comes it will not be afraid, its foliage will stay green; in a year of drought it
will not take fright, it will not cease yielding fruit [Jr 17.8].

1. The explanation and application of Scripture is the most typical function of *midrash*. In the passage above, two texts from the prophetic tradition
are adduced in settlement of the issue, possibly more theoretical than real, of
the pre-eminence of wisdom (study of Torah) or deeds (fulfilment of Torah).

The same question, couched in very similar terms, is found in the New
Testament, where, at Mt 7.24–25, we read of those who hear and practise
what they hear (wisdom with deeds) and of others, who hear but do not put
what they hear into practice.

In its version of the introductory text, K lacks the biblical quotations, so
the passage is also of significance for the study of the development of
midrash as a literary genre and how this influenced the textual transmission
of the Mishnah.

II *Morphology*

2. The BH relative pronoun אֲשֶׁר is almost completely replaced in RH by -שֶׁ, with אֲשֶׁר reserved only for biblical quotations and liturgical texts. Where possible, -שֶׁ is accompanied by strengthening of a following consonant, extending even to *resh* in the eastern tradition and occasionally in K, as at RS 1.7, 9: שֶׁרָאוּ, שֶׁרָאָה (see Unit 5.2).

3. -שֶׁ cannot be regarded as a shortened form of אֲשֶׁר that has developed over time, as it is also present at the earliest stage of Semitic in the form of Akkadian *ša*, as well as in Phoenician *'š* (with prosthetic *alef*) and Punic *š-*. In the Bible, it is attested in passages like Jg 6.17 (אוֹת שָׁאַתָּה מְדַבֵּר עִמִּי) 'the sign of which you spoke to me'), four more times in Jg 5–8, as well as in other early texts.

4. Probably because it was regarded as a northern colloquialism, -שֶׁ disappeared from the literary idiom of BH but re-emerged in the LBH period (in Ca, Ec, Ps, Jon, and Lm), where it alternates with אֲשֶׁר. -שֶׁ, then, appears to be a dialect form that was conserved in the vernacular language. E. Qimron (1986, 82–83) claims that while -שֶׁ was rejected at Qumran as inappropriate for literary composition, the many instances in the Scrolls of אֲשֶׁר לְ- 'which is to' (or simply לְ- 'of, to' on its own) echo RH usage of -שֶׁ (and more specifically שֶׁל). In the Copper Scroll and 4QMMT, שֶׁל is used extensively.

III *Grammar and usage*

5. -שֶׁ's origins as a demonstrative particle is reflected in its use both as a relative pronoun in relationship to an antecedent and as a conjunction in relationship to a following clause. A text such as

בָּרוּךְ י׳ שֶׁלֹּא נְתָנָנוּ טֶרֶף לְשִׁנֵּיהֶם

at Ps 124.6 may be interpreted in two, not always mutually exclusive, ways: 'blessed be Y., who did not/because he did not deliver us as prey to their teeth'. In many colloquial situations, -שֶׁ has a purely demonstrative rôle, for example פָּשַׁט ... וְנָתַן ... אוֹ שֶׁנָּטַל '(if) he stretched out ... and placed ..., or (even if) he took away' (Shab 1.1).

6. -שֶׁ as relative.

A. Like BH אֲשֶׁר, -שֶׁ is indeclinable and requires further grammatical specification through the use of suffixes referring to the antecedent, which are attached to verbs or prepositions. Retrospective determination of this kind is exemplified by

כָּל תּוֹרָה שֶׁאֵין עִמָּהּ מְלָאכָה

Any Torah with which there is not (literally, 'which there is not with her') work (Abot 2.2),

שָׂדֶה שֶׁקְּצָרוּהָ גוֹיִים

A field that gentiles harvested (literally, 'that harvested her') (Pea 2.7), and

זו שעה שנלכדה בה ירושלם

That is the hour at which Jerusalem was captured (literally, 'which was captured at her') (SLv 26.33 [W 112b]).

B. -שֶׁ can also be retrospectively determined by an adverb of place (שָׁם 'there', מִשָּׁם 'from there', and לְשָׁם 'to there', equivalent to מִמֶּנּוּ,בּוֹ, מִמֶּנָּה, and לוֹ/לָהּ) when the antecedent is מָקוֹם 'place' or has spatial reference, for example הַמָּקוֹם שֶׁהָלַךְ לְשָׁם 'the place to which he went' (Pea 4.1). The same usage is common in BH (e.g. 2 K 6.2).

C. Retrospective determination may be omitted when there is no question of ambiguity, as in וּבְמָקוֹם שֶׁאֵין אֲנָשִׁים הִשְׁתַּדֵּל לִהְיוֹת אִישׁ 'and in the place that (i.e. 'where') there are no men, make the effort to be a man' (Abot 2.5).

D. -שֶׁ's originally demonstrative function is especially clear when it has as antecedent מִי 'who?', מָה 'what?', or כָּל 'all', in structures like מִי שֶׁ- 'who(m)ever', מָה שֶׁ- or מָה שֶׁהוּא 'whatever', and כָּל־שֶׁהוּא 'all/anyone who(m)' (see Unit 6.5–8).

E. For the particle שֶׁל (i.e. -שֶׁ followed by לְ- 'to, of') and the independent possessive pronoun, see Unit 4.

F. Relative -שֶׁ is sometimes preceded by אֵת with no clear antecedent. The resulting construction, -שֶׁ אֵת 'that which' may function as an object or as a subject, but its primary rôle is to indicate a greater degree of determination, which is sometimes best expressed by rendering -שֶׁ אֵת as 'with regard to that which'. In BH, a similar formulation, אֵת אֲשֶׁר, occurs in structures incorrectly classified as independent relative clauses, which are in reality clauses introduced by determinative אֲשֶׁר (see Meyer 1992, §115.5B–C, where Gn 49.1 is cited; for the demonstrative function of אֵת, see Unit 2.7). Examples of -שֶׁ אֵת include:

אֵת שֶׁצָּרִיךְ כַּפָּרָה, יָצָא מֵת שֶׁכַּפָּרָה לוֹ נַפְשׁוֹ

With regard to that which requires expiation, the dead are excluded as their soul atones for them (SNm 4.5 [H 7]);

אֵת שֶׁדַּרְכּוֹ לְהַטְבִּיל, יַטְבִּיל

That which it is customary to immerse, let it be immersed (AZ 5.12);

אֵת שֶׁאָסוּר מִשּׁוּם נְבֵלָה, אָסוּר לְבַשֵּׁל בְּחָלָב

That which is prohibited because it is carrion, it is prohibited to cook in milk (Hul 8.4).

7. -שֶׁ as conjunction.

A. With the meaning 'that', -שֶׁ introduces an 'object clause' where BH would employ כִּי or אֲשֶׁר. In this sense it is also commonly used to introduce indirect speech, for example אַל תֹּאמַר שֶׁהִיא תָבוֹא אַחֲרֶיךָ 'do not say that it will come after you' (Abot 4.14). (In Ec 5.4 [LBH], we find אֲשֶׁר and -שֶׁ together: טוֹב אֲשֶׁר לֹא־תִדֹּר מִשֶּׁתִּדּוֹר וְלֹא תְשַׁלֵּם 'better is one who does not vow than one who vows and then does not fulfil the vow'.

B. Rarely, -שֶׁ also introduces direct speech, as in:

אמר לו בגזירה שתאכל את הדג

He strictly commanded him, Eat the fish (Mek 14.5 [L 1.195]);

הֵעִיד רַבִּי פַּפְּיָס ... שֶׁאִם גִּלַּח אֶת הָרִאשׁוֹנָה יוֹם שְׁלֹשִׁים

Rabbi Papias gave testimony ..., If one shaves for the first time on
the thirtieth day (Naz 3.2);

נאמן אדם לומר שאמר לי אבא

Deserving of credit is one who says, My father said to me' (TosKet
3.3).

Usually, though, direct speech is introduced by an oath formula of the
kind -אָמֵן שֶׁ, -שְׁבוּעָה שֶׁ, -קָרְבָּן שֶׁ, or -קוֹנָם שֶׁ, all of which mean 'most truly', 'I
swear', etc. The following example comes from SNm 15.2 (H 20):

ואמרה האשה אמן אמן [במדבר ה׳ כב׳], אמן שלא נטמיתי, אמן
שלא אטמא

And the woman will respond, Amen, amen [Nm 5.22]: Truly I have
not defiled myself, truly I shall not defile myself.

The formula -נִשְׁבַּע שֶׁ 'swear that' with personal subject is also used in
this context, for example

נִשְׁבָּע אֲנִי בְּשִׁמְךָ הַגָּדוֹל שֶׁאֵינִי זָז מִכָּאן עַד שֶׁתְּרַחֵם עַל בָּנֶיךָ

I swear by your great name, I shall not move from here until you
take pity on your children (Taa 3.8).

C. After a biblical quotation, -שֶׁ can have explanatory or exegetical
value, 'meaning/teaching/showing that', 'that is to say', etc., for example

ונזרעה זרע [במדבר ה׳ כח׳], שאם היתה עקרה, נפקדת

And she will have offspring [Nm 5.28], (which is to say) that if before she was barren, now she is visited (with children) (SNm 19.3
[H 23]).

A fuller version of the formula, -מְלַמֵּד שֶׁ 'teaching that' or -מַגִּיד שֶׁ 'declaring
that', is often found.

Frequently, though, 'exegetical' -שֶׁ has a final sense, 'in order that, so
that', as in the common formula שֶׁלֹא יֹאמַר '(this is written) so that one might
not say' (see also Unit 30.6).

D. Alone or in combination with a preposition, for example -עַד שֶׁ 'until,
before', -מִפְּנֵי שֶׁ 'because', -כְּשֶׁ 'when', or -מִשֶּׁ 'after', -שֶׁ introduces causal,
temporal, final, and consecutive clauses. Of special note is the use of causal
-שֶׁ in the meaning of 'if', as in הֲרֵינִי נָזִיר שֶׁזֶּה פְּלוֹנִי 'I shall become a Nazirite
because/if this is so-and-so' (Naz 5.5) or

אקפח את בני שזו הלכה מקפחת

May I bury my children if this is not a corrupt *halakhah* (Ohol
16.1).

8. The demonstrative function of -שֶׁ is especially striking in the
adverbial construction -שֶׁלֹא בְּ introducing a circumstantial clause, for
example הַהוֹרֵג נֶפֶשׁ שֶׁלֹא בְעֵדִים 'whoever kills without witnesses' (Sanh 9.5).
A similar construction, שֶׁלֹא עַל מְנָת, is found at Abot 1.3:

הַמְשַׁמְּשִׁים אֶת־הָרַב שֶׁלֹּא עַל מְנָת לְקַבֵּל פְּרָס

Who serve the master, not for the sake of receiving remuneration.

The structure -אֲשֶׁר לֹא בְ is found only once in the Bible (Dt 8.9), but is well-attested in the Manual of Discipline from Qumran.

The construction -בְ ... -שֶׁלֹּא is frequently employed to help express a totality by means of affirmation and denial, for example

אוֹכְלִין פֵּרוֹת שְׁבִיעִית בְּטוֹבָה שֶׁלֹּא בְטוֹבָה

The fruits of the seventh year can be eaten with thanks and without thanks (Eduy 5.1).

With -לְ for -בְ, the construction is found at, for example, Makhsh 6.8:

לְרָצוֹן ... שֶׁלֹּא לְרָצוֹן

Whether deliberately or not.

The following text exemplifies a structure often found in tannaitic exegetical literature:

כה תברכו את בני ישראל [במדבר ו׳ כג׳], בעמידה, אתה אומר
בעמידה, או אינו אלא בעמידה ושלא בעמידה?

Thus you are to bless the children of Israel [Nm 6.23]. Standing. Standing, you maintain, but is it not the same whether standing or not standing? (SNm 39.3 [H 42]).

9. The use of -אוֹ שֶׁ (see above, §5) gives an adversative character to the proposition that follows. The Mekhilta text already quoted (§7b) continues

או שתלקה מאה מכות או שתתן מאה מנה

(Eat the fish) or you will suffer a hundred strokes or you will pay a hundred minas (Mek 14.5 [L 195]).

Similar are גִּלַּח אוֹ שֶׁגִּלְּחוּהוּ לִסְטִים 'whether he shaved himself or robbers shaved him' (Naz 6.3) and אֲכָלַתּוּ חַיָּה אוֹ שֶׁיָּרְדוּ עָלָיו גְּשָׁמִים 'if a wild animal devours him or the rain falls upon him' (SNm 112.4 [H 122]). N.M. Waldman (1989, 134–35) repeats J. Blau's finding that a series of alternative propositions beginning with אוֹ requires the repetition of the conjunction that introduced the very first clause (i.e. 'if ... or if', not simply 'if ... or'); similarly, each alternative in a sequence of indirect questions may be preceded by אוֹ שֶׁ- (see Pes 9.9, quoted at Unit 25.9). In other structures expressing alternatives, the אוֹ may be omitted, for example

שְׁחָטוֹ שֶׁלֹּא לְאוֹכְלָיו וְשֶׁלֹּא לִמְנוּיָיו

If one slaughters (the lamb), but not for those who might eat it or are numberered (among those who might eat it) (Pes 6.6).

When expressing a contrast, the verb of the antithesis is often introduced by the formula -וְהוּא שֶׁ 'but, nonetheless, he', for example

הֵיכָן שׁוֹרִי. אָמַר לוֹ, מֵת, וְהוּא שֶׁנִּשְׁבַּר

Where is my ox? He answered him, It's dead, but in fact it was just lame (Shebu 8.2).

IV *Phraseology*

10. -לְ אֶת־שֶׁדַּרְכּוֹ 'that which is the custom of', where דֶּרֶךְ 'way' refers to something that occurs habitually; the formula as a whole is continued by an infinitive, for example

אֶת־שֶׁדַּרְכּוֹ לִישָּׂרֵף יִשָּׂרֵף וּמָה שֶׁדַּרְכּוֹ לִיקָּבֵר יִקָּבֵר

That which is normally burnt is burnt and that which is normally buried is buried (Tem 7.5; other examples include Dem 2.5; Shebi 8.3; Orl 3.7).

11. שֶׁנֶּאֱמַר, literally 'which was said', a frequent way of introducing a quotation from Scripture to back up or exemplify a statement, usually rendered by 'as it is said'.

12. -בְּ ... וְשֶׁלֹּא בְּ- 'with ... and without'. See above, §8, and Unit 26.10. A related expression is -שֶׁ וּבֵין ... -שֶׁ בֵּין 'whether ... or', for example

בֵּין שֶׁקּוֹרִין בָּהֶן ... וּבֵין שֶׁאֵין קוֹרִין בָּהֶן

Whether they read them ... or do not read them (Shab 16.1).

V *Vocabulary*

אֶלָּא אֵינוֹ אוֹ 'is it not rather?' (introducing an alternative interpretation)

אָגַד 'bind, unite, make a sheaf'

אֲפִילוּ (אַף אִילוּ) 'even if'

שֶׁ פִּי עַל אַף (אע״פ) 'although'

בַּיִת 'house', often with special reference to the temple: בִּפְנֵי הַבַּיִת 'in the presence of the temple' (i.e. before its destruction)

בֵּית דִּין 'tribunal'

גְּזֵירָה 'decree, law'

הֲרֵינִי (i.e. הֲרֵי אֲנִי) 'here I am' (BH הִנְנִי)

זָז 'move, depart'

כְּלָל 'totality, general rule, principle, or formula, generalization'

לָקָה 'receive strokes, be whipped'

מַשָּׂא 'transport', מַגָּע 'contact'; כְּלָל מַגָּע/מַשָּׂא 'the general principle applying to contact/transport' (case-law terms relating to the transmission of impurity)

מִנַּיִן (i.e. מִן אַיִן) 'from where?' (often used in exegetical literature to find out the biblical source-text of a particular conclusion)

נָהַג 'guide, be in use, be applicable, be practised'

נְשִׁיכָה 'bite'

נְשִׂיאוּת כַּפַּיִם 'raising of hands' (in blessing)

קָבַע 'fix, establish, determine'

שׁוּק 'market, town square'

תָּקַן 'prepare, correct'

VI *Exercises*

1. צְאוּ וּרְאוּ אֵיזוֹהִי דֶּרֶךְ יְשָׁרָה שֶׁיִּדְבַּק בָּה הָאָדָם ... צְאוּ וּרְאוּ אֵיזוֹהִי דֶּרֶךְ רָעָה שֶׁיִּתְרַחֵק מִמֶּנָּה הָאָדָם.

2. רוֹאֶה אֲנִי אֶת דִּבְרֵי אֶלְעָזָר בֶּן עֲרָךְ, שֶׁבִּכְלָל דְּבָרָיו דִּבְרֵיכֶם.

3. וֶהֱוֵי זָהִיר בְּנַחֲלָתָן שֶׁלֹּא תִכְוֶה, שֶׁנְּשִׁיכָתָן נְשִׁיכַת שׁוּעָל.

4. וְהַתְקֵן עַצְמְךָ לִלְמוֹד תּוֹרָה, שֶׁאֵינָהּ יְרוּשָׁה לָךְ.

5. מִנַּיִן שֶׁאֲפִילוּ אֶחָד שֶׁיּוֹשֵׁב וְעוֹסֵק בַּתּוֹרָה, שֶׁהַקָּדוֹשׁ בָּרוּךְ הוּא קוֹבֵעַ לוֹ שָׂכָר?

6. הַמְגַלֶּה פָנִים בַּתּוֹרָה שֶׁלֹּא כַהֲלָכָה, אַף עַל פִּי שֶׁיֵּשׁ בְּיָדוֹ תּוֹרָה וּמַעֲשִׂים טוֹבִים, אֵין לוֹ חֵלֶק בָּעוֹלָם הַבָּא.

7. אַל תְּהִי דָן יְחִידִי, שֶׁאֵין דָּן יְחִידִי אֶלָּא אֶחָד.

8. אֶת שֶׁנּוֹהֵג בּוֹ מִשּׁוּם [מִשֵּׁם K] אֱלוֹהַּ אָסוּר, וְאֶת שֶׁאֵינוֹ נוֹהֵג בּוֹ מִשּׁוּם [מִשֵּׁם K] אֱלוֹהַּ מֻתָּר.

9. אֶת שֶׁבָּא לִכְלָל מַגַּע בָּא לִכְלָל מַשָּׂא, לֹא בָא לִכְלָל מַגַּע לֹא בָא לִכְלָל מַשָּׂא.

10. בֵּית הִלֵּל אוֹמְרִין, אֶת שֶׁדַּרְכּוֹ לֵאָגוֹד בַּבַּיִת, אוֹגְדִין אוֹתוֹ בַּשּׁוּק.

11. שְׁבוּעָה שֶׁלֹּא אֹכַל, וְאָכַל כָּל שֶׁהוּא, חַיָּב.

12. אָמְרוּ לוֹ לְחוֹנִי הַמְעַגֵּל, הִתְפַּלֵּל שֶׁיֵּרְדוּ גְשָׁמִים.

13. בֵּית שַׁמַּאי אוֹמְרִים, בְּפָנָיו, וּבֵית הִלֵּל אוֹמְרִים, בְּפָנָיו וְשֶׁלֹּא בְּפָנָיו. בֵּית שַׁמַּאי אוֹמְרִים, בְּבֵית דִּין, וּבֵית הִלֵּל אוֹמְרִין, בְּבֵית דִּין וְשֶׁלֹּא בְּבֵית דִּין.

14. שְׁתֵּי יְבָמוֹת, זוֹ אוֹמֶרֶת, מֵת בַּעֲלִי, וְזוֹ אוֹמֶרֶת, מֵת בַּעֲלִי, זוֹ אֲסוּרָה מִפְּנֵי בַּעֲלָהּ שֶׁל זוֹ וְזוֹ אֲסוּרָה מִפְּנֵי בַּעֲלָהּ שֶׁל זוֹ. לְזוֹ עֵדִים וּלְזוֹ אֵין עֵדִים, אֶת שֶׁיֵּשׁ לָהּ עֵדִים אֲסוּרָה, וְאֶת שֶׁאֵין לָהּ עֵדִים מֻתֶּרֶת. לְזוֹ בָנִים וּלְזוֹ אֵין בָּנִים, אֶת שֶׁיֵּשׁ לָהּ בָּנִים מֻתֶּרֶת, וְאֶת שֶׁאֵין לָהּ בָּנִים אֲסוּרָה.

15. כה תברך את בני ישראל [במדבר ו' כג'], בנשיאות כפים. אתה אמר, בנשיאות כפים, או אינו אלא בנשיאות כפים ושלא בנשיאות כפים?

16. והזר הקרב יומת [במדבר יח' ז'], לעבודה. אתה אומר, לעבודה, או לעבודה ושלא לעבודה?

17. מה נחלה נוהגת בפני הבית ושלא בפני הבית, אף מעשר ראשון נוהג בפני הבית ושלא בפני הבית.

18. משלו משל, לעבד שהיה לכהן. אמר, אברח לי לבית הקברות, מקום שאין רבי יכול לבא אחרי. אמר לו רבו, יש לי עבדים כנענים כמותך. אמר יונה, אלך לי לחוצה לארץ, מקום שאין השכינה נגלית.

19. משל. למה הדבר דומה? לאחד שאמר לעבדו, צא והבא לי דג מן השוק. יצא והביא לו דג מן השוק מבאיש. אמר לו בגזירה, שתאבל את הדג או שתלקה מאה מכות או שתתן מאה מנה. אמר, הריני אוכל.

20. כשעלה האחרון שבישראל מן הים, ירד האחרון שבמצרים לתוכו.

Sources. 1. Abot 2.9. 2. Abot 2.9. 3. Abot 2.10. 4. Abot 2.12. 5. Abot 3.2. 6. Abot 3.11. 7. Abot 4.8. 8. AZ 3.4. 9. Ḥul 9.5. 10. Shebi 8.3. 11. Shebu 3.1. 12. Taa 3.8. 13. Yeb 13.1. 14. Yeb 16.2. 15. SNm 39.4 (H 42). 16. SNm 116.6 (H 134). 17. SNm 119.6 (H 146). 18. Mek 12.1 (L 1.7–8). 19. Mek 14.5 (L 1.195). 20. Mek 14.27 (L 1.245).

UNIT NINE

NOUN PATTERNS

I *Introductory text* (Ber 1.5)

מַזְכִּירִין יְצִיאַת מִצְרַיִם בַּלֵּילוֹת. אָמַר רַבִּי אֶלְעָזָר בֶּן עֲזַרְיָה, הֲרֵי אֲנִי כְּבֶן
שִׁבְעִים שָׁנָה וְלֹא זָכִיתִי שֶׁתֵּאָמֵר יְצִיאַת מִצְרַיִם בַּלֵּילוֹת, עַד שֶׁדְּרָשָׁהּ בֶּן
זוֹמָא, שֶׁנֶּאֱמַר, לְמַעַן תִּזְכֹּר אֶת־יוֹם צֵאתְךָ מֵאֶרֶץ מִצְרַיִם כֹּל יְמֵי חַיֶּיךָ [דְּבָרִים
טז' ג']. יְמֵי חַיֶּיךָ, הַיָּמִים, כֹּל יְמֵי חַיֶּיךָ, הַלֵּילוֹת. וַחֲכָמִים אוֹמְרִים, יְמֵי חַיֶּיךָ,
הָעוֹלָם הַזֶּה, כֹּל יְמֵי חַיֶּיךָ, לְהָבִיא לִימוֹת הַמָּשִׁיחַ.

During the night, one has to mention the exodus from Egypt. Rabbi Eleazar
ben Azariah said, I was already seventy years old and had still not been able
to prove that the exodus from Egypt was to be recited at night until Ben
Zoma explained it in accordance with what had been said: That you might
remember the day of your coming out from the land of Egypt all the days of
your life [Dt 16.3]: 'the days of your life' refers to the days, 'all the days of
your life' refers to the nights. However, (the) sages affirm: 'the days of your
life' refers to the present world, 'all the days of your life' includes the days
of the Messiah.

1. This is an example of the typical tannaitic enterprise of legitimizing
halakhah through Scripture. The prescription that governed the praying of
the *shema'* was that at night one did not have to recite the section about
phylacteries (Nm 15.37–41) except for the final verse, which mentions the
liberation from Egypt. What was the justification for this rule? Ben Zoma
saw the answer in the apparently unnecessary use of כֹּל 'all' at Dt 16.3,
which he understood as a particle of 'amplification' (רִיבּוּי), that extends the
meaning of 'the days of your life' to include the nights. It should be said,
though, that the value of this *halakhah* does not in any way derive from the
fact that it could be justified by Scripture but simply from its inclusion in the
halakhic tradition, for in fact the rabbis rejected Ben Zoma's exegesis.

As we noted in connection with the introductory text of Unit 8 (Abot
3.17), here too K dispenses with biblical quotations.

II *Morphology*

2. The vast majority of RH nouns and adjectives are also found in BH or
derive from old Hebrew roots. Even nouns taken from Aramaic are usually

found to have counterparts from the same root in Hebrew. In many cases, Aramaic influence is seen in RH's choice of noun pattern (see Introduction, §4.2.6–7), although these are also always found, albeit to a more limited extent, in BH.

3. RH displays a great capacity for exploiting the noun patterns of BH for generating new words. Particularly striking are the patterns קְטִילָה, הַקְטָלָה/הַקְטֵל/הֶקְטֵל, קְטָלָה/קְטוּל, which express the verbal action of, respectively, the *Qal*, *Pi'el*, and *Hif'il* conjugations, and קַטָּל, which is used to designate persons who work in particular fields or hold particular offices.

4. Nouns of type קְטִילָה.

A. Nouns of this pattern are created with ease by RH and greatly outnumber instances of the same model found in the Bible—שְׁרִיקוֹת 'hissings' (Jg 5.16) is one of the few examples found in AH and in classical BH the pattern is only attested in texts of northern origin (for example, perhaps גְּבִירָה in the sense of 'lordship' at 1 K 15.13.). However, in the Mishnah alone, the קְטִילָה pattern has given rise to 130 nouns, such as אֲכִילָה 'eating', נְשִׁיכָה 'bite', and שְׁתִיקָה 'silence'. In the following example, פְּרִישָׁה and נְזִירָה have been created by RH from the verbs נָזַר and פָּרַשׁ:

אין נזירה בכל מקום אלא פרישה

Abstinence always implies separation (SNm 23.3 [H 28]).

B. The קְטִילָה pattern can be realized in a variety of ways, so that we find, for example, most commonly עֲבֵירָה, then עֲבִירָה, and then עֲבֵרה 'transgression', but גְּזֵירָה, then גְּזֵרָה, and then גְּזִירָה 'law, decree'.

C. In *lamed-yod* and *lamed-alef* verbs, קְטִילָה takes the form exemplified by בְּרִיָּה (plural בְּרִיוֹת) 'creation, creature' (from the root ברא). The form קִירְיָיה 'reading, recitation', found at Abot 2.13 in K, is often modified to קְרָאָה/קְרָיָה (root קרא), perhaps to distinguish it clearly from קְרָיָה 'village'. In *ayin-yod* and *ayin-waw* verbs, the קְטִילָה pattern is illustrated by בִּיאָה 'entrance' (root בוא), קִימָה 'establishing' (root קום), בִּינָה 'understanding' (root בין), and מִיתָה 'death' (root מות), which generally replaces its BH counterpart מָוֶת.

5. Nouns of type קַטָּלָה/קַטּוּל.

A. Again, there are numerous examples of new nouns generated according to the קִטּוּל pattern, expressing the verbal action of the *Pi'el*, or intensive, conjugation, as in כִּבּוּד אָב וָאֵם 'honouring father and mother' (Pea 1.1), חִלּוּל הַשֵּׁם 'profaning the (divine) name' (Abot 4.4), מִעוּט–רִיבּוּי 'multiplication–diminution', דִּבּוּר 'speaking', etc. Often, new formations replace older words, for example צִיוּוּי, which is used instead of מִצְוָה 'commandment', as in ציווי זה אינו אלא לנו 'this commandment is only for us' (SDt 345 [F 402]), although originally a slight semantic distinction might have been intended (the process or act of commanding as against the commandment that results from this process or act; see below, §10).

B. The frequency of the קְטָלָה variant, also found in BH, is clearly due to Aramaic influence. Examples include קַבָּלָה 'reception', בַּטָּלָה 'annulment, emptiness', and כַּוָּנָה 'intention'.

C. The passive and reflexive conjugations (*Nif'al* and *Hitpa'el*) do not give rise to specific noun patterns; instead, nouns are formed from the corresponding active conjugations (*Qal* and *Pi'el*). Thus, for example, the verbal noun of the *Hitpa'el* הִתְוַדָּה 'confess' is the קָטוּל form וִידּוּי 'confession'. On the other hand, the noun כָּרֵת 'extermination', commonly found in the Mishnah, is simply a form of the *Nif'al* infinitive הִכָּרֵת (where the form with introductory -לְ 'to', i.e. לְהִכָּרֵת 'to be exterminated', has undergone elision of *he*, giving לִיכָּרֵת; after removal of the -לִ, now regarded as nothing more than the *lamed* of the infinitive, the nominal form כָּרֵת is the result; see Segal 1927, §§116–17).

6. Nouns of type הַקְטָלָה/הֶקְטֵל/הַקְטֵל.

A. Whereas the הַקְטָלָה pattern, exemplified by הַבְדָּלָה 'separation' and הַפְסָקָה 'interruption', is typical of Aramaic, הַקְטֵל and הֶקְטֵל, as in הֶפְסֵד 'loss', הֶיקֵשׁ 'comparison' (root נָקַשׁ), and הֶיכֵּר 'recognition' (root נָכַר), are nominalized forms of the *Hif'il* infinitive.

B. From *lamed-yod* verbs are derived nouns exemplified by the word for 'instruction' (from the verb יָרֵי): הוֹרָאָה in the Babylonian tradition, הוֹרָיָה in the Palestinian tradition. From *pe-yod* verbs come nouns like הוֹצָאָה 'extraction' (from יָצָא) and הוֹרָדָה 'descent' (from יָרַד). An example of a noun derived from an *ayin-waw* verb is הֲבָאָה 'bringing' (from בוֹא).

7. Nouns of type קַטָּל.

Many names of offices, professions, and verbal actions conform to this model, for example בַּקָּר 'cowhand', סַפָּן 'sailor', סַפָּר 'barber', דַּיָּין 'judge', חַיָּיב 'debtor', הָרָג 'murderer', and חַיָּיט 'tailor'. There is a striking concentration of such terms in Qid 4.14:

לֹא יְלַמֵּד אָדָם אֶת בְּנוֹ חַמָּר, גַּמָּל, סַפָּר, סַפָּן, רוֹעֶה וְחֶנְוָנִי,
שֶׁאֻמָּנוּתָן אֻמָּנוּת לִסְטִים

> Let no-one teach their child (the office of) ass-driver, camel-driver, barber, sailor, shepherd, or shopkeeper, for each is the office of robbers.

8. Nouns of type קַטְלָן/קוֹטְלָן.

This characteristically RH noun pattern, employed, like קַטָּל, for agents of actions, professions, and permanent attributes, is conserved in the eastern tradition as קוֹטְלָן. Thus, for example, at BQ 10.5, וְאִם מֵחֲמַת הַגַּזְלָן 'if it is on account of the robber', K reads הַגּוֹזְלָן.

III *Grammar and usage*

9. The extraordinarily widespread use of the patterns קָטוּל, קְטִילָה, and הַקְטָלָה in the creation of new words is explicable in terms of a corresponding decrease in the use of the infinitive construct, which had previously functioned as a genuine noun, even to the extent of taking pronominal suffixes

and being governed by prepositions, for example בִּהְיוֹתָם בְּמִצְרָיִם 'when they were (literally, 'in their being') in Egypt' (1 S 2.27). Already in LBH this kind of usage was beginning to give way to -כְּשֶׁ 'when' followed by finite verb and eventually to the use of a noun as such. Using the verb יָצָא 'go out', the process may be schematically represented thus: וַיְהִי בְּצֵאתוֹ 'and it was in his going out' > בְּצֵאתוֹ 'in his going out' > כְּשֶׁיָּצָא 'when he went out' > בְּיצִיאָתוֹ שֶׁלּוֹ 'in his exit'. In this chain of events, Qumran occupies an intermediate position (see Qimron 1986, 72–73).

10. In origin, such new nouns denoted the action of the verbs they derive from and are often incorrectly labelled 'abstract'. In fact, in many cases they have, over time, come to signify the result of an action rather than the action itself. Thus, for example, גְּזֵרָה, '(action of) decreeing' came to mean the decree itself or the law decreed by it and, similarly, צִוּוּי '(action of) commanding' ended up by denoting the 'commandment' itself, יְשִׁיבָה '(act of) sitting' came to mean 'session', 'settlement', or the place or type of meeting, and חֲתִיכָה '(action of) cutting' came to mean, first, 'cut, slash', and then, with a *dagesh* in the *kaf*, the 'piece' that had been cut off. (E.Y. Kutscher [1971, 1601] saw in חֲתִיכָה a vestige of RH's attempt to form a special pattern, קְטִילָה, to express the result of an action.)

In some cases, semantic development went even further. For example, שְׁכִינָה, literally 'habitation' (which, although frequent in the *midrashim* and *targumim*, occurs only twice in the Mishnah and not at all in the Bible), came to denote the divine presence and eventually was employed as a figure for God himself, as at SNm 161.3:

חביבים הם ישראל שאע״פ שהם טמאים שכינה ביניהם

How beloved are the Israelites, among whom, even when they are impure, the Shekhinah dwells.

In other instances, though, the original verbal action sense has remained, for example חִלּוּל–כִּבּוּד 'honouring–profaning' and הֲלִיכָה 'walking'.

11. Clearly under Aramaic influence, nouns of the type קְטִילָה can be made to re-express basic verbal action by addition of the old feminine abstract suffix וּת-, for example גְּמִילוּת חֲסָדִים 'performing deeds of love' and נְשִׂיאוּת כַּפַּיִם 'raising of hands'.

IV Phraseology

12. אִסּוּרָן אִסּוּר הֲנָאָה 'the prohibition on them is a prohibition on (deriving any) benefit (from them)' (AZ 2.3; see also AZ 2.4, 6, etc.), used in reference to unclean things from which no benefit may be derived in any way whatsoever, for example, by selling them to gentiles.

13. הֶפְסֵד מִצְוָה 'loss that comes from fulfilling a precept', הֶפְסֵד עֲבֵרָה 'loss that results from transgression'. The expression הֶפְסֵד מִצְוָה כְּנֶגֶד שְׂכָרָה (Abot 2.1) means something like 'what is lost by what is gained' (more liter-

ally, 'the loss [that comes through fulfilment] of a precept is in correspondence to its reward').

14. בְּדִבּוּר אֶחָד 'with just one word', a formula that concerns the miracu-
lous ability of God to say many things with a single utterance, exemplified by
the giving of the ten commandments, as presented at Mek 20.1 (L 2.22):

וידבר אלוהים את כל הדברים האלה [שמות כ׳ א׳], מלמד שאמר
המקום עשרת דברים בדיבור אחד, מה שאי אפשר לבשר ודם
לומר כן ... מלמד שאמר הקב״ה עשרת הדברות בדיבור אחד וחזר
ופרטן דיבור דיבור בפני עצמו

And God spoke all these words (Ex 20.1). This teaches that the omnipresent one spoke the ten commandments by means of only one
utterance, something impossible for flesh and blood .... It teaches
that the holy one, blessed be he, spoke the ten commandments by
means of only one utterance and afterwards specified them one by
one separately.

Other, more prosaic, examples can be found at SNm 102.2 (H 100) and SDt
233 (F 265).

15. מִפְּנֵי תִקּוּן הָעוֹלָם 'for the maintenance of the world, for the good
order of the world', for example Giṭ 4.6:

אֵין פּוֹדִין אֶת הַשְּׁבוּיִים יוֹתֵר עַל כְּדֵי דְמֵיהֶן, מִפְּנֵי תִקּוּן הָעוֹלָם. וְאֵין
מַבְרִיחִין אֶת הַשְּׁבוּיִין, מִפְּנֵי תִקּוּן הָעוֹלָם

Captives cannot be ransomed for more than their price, so as to
maintain the order of the world. Nor may one liberate captives, so as
to maintain the order of the world.

V *Vocabulary*

אִי/אַי (BH אֵין/אַיִן) 'no(t)', used in front of words beginning with *alef*, e.g.
אִי אֶפְשָׁר 'impossible'
אִסּוּר 'prohibition'
בְּטֵלָה 'empty, null' (participle/adjective from the stative verb בָּטֵל)
גָּרַר 'push, lead'
הֲלִיכָה 'walk'
הֲנָאָה 'advantage, use, enjoyment, usufruct'
הֶפְסֵד 'loss, disadvantage'
חָשַׁד 'suspect', חָשׁוּד 'suspected (of)'
חָסַךְ/חָשַׂךְ 'set apart, hold back'
יְגִיעָה 'weariness, work, effort'
לְחִישָׁה 'hiss'
עֲקִיצָה 'sting'
עַקְרָב 'scorpion'
פֻּנְדְּקָא (πανδοκεῖον) 'tavern, inn'
פְּרִישׁוּת 'separation, withdrawal'

רְבִיעָה 'bestiality'

שְׁפִיכָה 'spilling', as in שְׁפִיכַת דָּמִים 'bloodshed'

VI *Exercises*

1. הֱוֵי מִתַּלְמִידָיו שֶׁלְּאַהֲרֹן ... אוֹהֵב אֶת הַבְּרִיּוֹת וּמְקָרְבָן לַתּוֹרָה.

2. לֹא מָצָאתִי לַגּוּף טוֹב אֶלָּא שְׁתִיקָה.

3. וֶהֱוֵי מְחַשֵּׁב הֶפְסֵד מִצְוָה כְּנֶגֶד שְׂכָרָהּ וּשְׂכַר עֲבֵרָה כְּנֶגֶד הֶפְסֵדָהּ, וְהִסְתַּכֵּל בִּשְׁלֹשָׁה דְבָרִים, וְאִי אַתָּה בָא לִידֵי עֲבֵרָה.

4. יָפֶה תַלְמוּד תּוֹרָה עִם דֶּרֶךְ אֶרֶץ, שֶׁיְּגִיעַת שְׁנֵיהֶם מְשַׁכַּחַת עָוֹן. וְכָל תּוֹרָה שֶׁאֵין עִמָּהּ מְלָאכָה, סוֹפָהּ בְּטֵלָה וְגוֹרֶרֶת עָוֹן.

5. מַרְבֶּה יְשִׁיבָה, מַרְבֶּה חָכְמָה.

6. שׁוּב יוֹם אֶחָד לִפְנֵי מִיתָתְךָ.

7. וֶהֱוֵי מִתְחַמֵּם כְּנֶגֶד אוּרָן שֶׁלַּחֲכָמִים, וֶהֱוֵי זָהִיר בְּגַחַלְתָּן שֶׁלֹּא תִכָּוֶה, שֶׁנְּשִׁיכָתָן נְשִׁיכַת שׁוּעָל, וַעֲקִיצָתָן עֲקִיצַת עַקְרָב, וּלְחִישָׁתָן לְחִישַׁת שָׂרָף, וְכָל דִּבְרֵיהֶם כְּגַחֲלֵי אֵשׁ.

8. שְׁנֵי שֶׁיּוֹשְׁבִין וְיֵשׁ בֵּינֵהֶם דִּבְרֵי תוֹרָה, שְׁכִינָה בֵּינֵהֶם.

9. נְדָרִים סְיָג לַפְּרִישׁוּת, סְיָג לַחָכְמָה שְׁתִיקָה.

10. אִם אֵין בִּינָה, אֵין דַּעַת, אִם אֵין דַּעַת, אֵין בִּינָה.

11. מִצְוָה גּוֹרֶרֶת מִצְוָה וַעֲבֵרָה גּוֹרֶרֶת עֲבֵרָה, שֶׁשָּׂכַר מִצְוָה מִצְוָה וּשְׂכַר עֲבֵרָה עֲבֵרָה.

12. הַחוֹשֵׁךְ עַצְמוֹ מִן הַדִּין, פּוֹרֵק מִמֶּנּוּ אֵיבָה.

13. אַרְבַּע מִדּוֹת בְּתַלְמִידִים, מַהֵר לִשְׁמֹעַ וּמַהֵר לְאַבֵּד, יָצָא שְׂכָרוֹ בְהֶפְסֵדוֹ, קָשֶׁה לִשְׁמֹעַ וְקָשֶׁה לְאַבֵּד, יָצָא הֶפְסֵדוֹ בִשְׂכָרוֹ, מַהֵר לִשְׁמֹעַ וְקָשֶׁה לְאַבֵּד, חָכָם, קָשֶׁה לִשְׁמֹעַ וּמַהֵר לְאַבֵּד, זֶה חֵלֶק רַע.

14. אַרְבַּע מִדּוֹת בְּהוֹלְכֵי לְבֵית הַמִּדְרָשׁ, הוֹלֵךְ וְאֵינוֹ עוֹשֶׂה, שְׂכַר הֲלִיכָה בְיָדוֹ, עוֹשֶׂה וְאֵינוֹ הוֹלֵךְ, שְׂכַר מַעֲשֶׂה בְיָדוֹ, הוֹלֵךְ וְעוֹשֶׂה, חָסִיד, לֹא הוֹלֵךְ וְלֹא עוֹשֶׂה, רָשָׁע.

15. כָּל מִיתָה שֶׁיֵּשׁ בָּהּ שְׂרֵפָה יֵשׁ בָּהּ עֲבוֹדָה זָרָה.

16. אֵין מַעֲמִידִין בְּהֵמָה בְּפֻנְדְּקָאוֹת שֶׁלַּגּוֹיִם, מִפְּנֵי שֶׁחֲשׁוּדִין עַל הָרְבִיעָה ... וְלֹא יִתְיַחֵד אָדָם עִמָּהֶן, מִפְּנֵי שֶׁחֲשׁוּדִין עַל שְׁפִיכַת דָּמִים.

17. אֵלּוּ דְבָרִים שֶׁלַּגּוֹיִם אֲסוּרִין, וְאִסּוּרָן אִסּוּר הֲנָאָה.

18. חָתָן פָּטוּר מִקְּרִיאַת שְׁמַע בְּלַיְלָה הָרִאשׁוֹן עַד מוֹצָאֵי שַׁבָּת, אִם לֹא עָשָׂה מַעֲשֶׂה.

19. כשהיה הדבור יוצא מפי הקדוש ברוך הוא, היה יוצא דרך ימינו של הקדוש ברוך הוא לשמאל ישראל.

20. ואין ישיבה אלא אכילה ושתייה.

Sources. 1. Abot 1.12. 2. Abot 1.17. 3. Abot 2.1. 4. Abot 2.2. 5. Abot 2.7. 6. Abot 2.10. 7. Abot 2.10. 8. Abot 3.2. 9. Abot 3.13. 10. Abot 3.17. 11. Abot 4.2. 12. Abot 4.7. 13. Abot 5.12. 14. Abot 5.14. 15. AZ 1.3. 16. AZ 2.1. 17. AZ 2.3. 18. Ber 2.5. 19. SDt 343 (F 399). 20. TosSot 3.10.

UNIT TEN

GENDER AND NUMBER OF NOUNS

I *Introductory text* (SNm 112.4 [H 121])

הכרת תכרת הנפש ההיא [במדבר טו' לא'], הכרת בעוה״ז, תכרת לעוה״ב,
דברי ר' עקיבא. אמר לו ר' ישמעאל, לפי שהוא אומר, ונכרתה הנפש ההיא
[במדבר טו ל], שומע אני שלש כריתות בשלשה עולמות. מה ת״ל, תכרת
תכרת הנפש ההיא. דברה תורה כלשון בני אדם.

That person will be exterminated with extermination [Nm 15.31]: will be exterminated, in this world; with extermination, in the world to come as well—
words of R. Akiba. But R. Ishmael responded, Because it also says, And that
soul must be exterminated [Nm 15.30], do I have to understand that there are
three exterminations corresponding to three worlds? The Torah was speaking
in the idiom of human beings.

1. Here we see the clear difference of mood and method that distinguishes Akiba and Ishmael. For Akiba, the structure of finite verb followed
by its infinitive absolute alludes to the present and future worlds. But Ishmael
insists that such a form of expression is simply a matter of emphasis, typical
of the way in which human beings speak, which is also the way in which the
Bible itself communicates. Because of that, inferences of the type drawn by
Akiba are avoided by the school of Ishmael—the mention of the verb
'exterminate' in the preceding verse confirms the absurdity of exploiting this
kind of linguistic detail for exegetical ends.

Throughout the Mishnah and tannaitic *midrashim*, the plural עוֹלָמוֹת
'worlds' is found only here and at Uqs 3.12 (where the text may well not
be original; there is also a further example in a manuscript of the Tosefta),
and refers to a fantastic or impossible world (see below, §11).

II *Morphology*

2. From a morphological perspective, RH, like BH, recognizes just two
genders in the noun and adjective—masculine and feminine—and three
kinds of number—singular, plural, and dual.

3. There is no special marker for masculine singular nouns and adjectives.

4. Feminine singular.

A. A feminine singular noun is not always discernible as such from the viewpoint of morphology, because it does not necessarily result from the transformation of a corresponding masculine noun but can employ a completely different root (as in אָב–אֵם 'father–mother'). As a rule, in RH, as in BH, female creatures, parts of the body occurring in pairs, and countries and cities are all construed as feminine.

B. As in BH, the typical marker of feminine gender is the suffix ־ָה, which will usually convert masculine adjectives and, less often, nouns into feminine, for example צָרִיךְ/צְרִיכָה 'obliged', גָּדוֹל/גְּדוֹלָה 'great', נָבִיא/נְבִיאָה 'prophet/prophetess'.

C. Because of the ־ָה ending, therefore, all nouns of type קְטָלָה, קְטִילָה, and הַקְטָלָה (see Unit 9) are feminine.

D. The ancient Semitic feminine suffix *-(a)t* is retained in RH much more often than in BH, for example כֹּהֶנֶת 'priestess' (i.e. a female member of a priestly family). The *Nif'al* participle feminine is generally of the form נִקְטֶלֶת, not, as in BH, נִקְטָלָה; for example, from the verb קָרָא comes the common form נִקְרָאת 'called'. See further Units 16.6 and 19.2.

E. The use of ־א for ־ָה has to be understood as an Aramaism, dating back either to the original text or to copyists.

F. A characteristic feminine morpheme is the suffix ־ִית in adjectives and nouns, especially diminutives, for example טַלִּית '(prayer) shawl, mantle', אֲרָמִית 'Aramaic', כַּדִּידִית 'little jug', and also ־וּת, in abstracts and in nouns expressing the action of a verb (see Unit 9), for example עֲשִׁירוּת 'wealth' and פְּרִישׁוּת 'separation'.

5. Masculine plural.

A. The masculine plural marker ־ִים alternates with ־ִין, doubtless under the influence of Aramaic, although this is not to deny that the ending *-in* is a feature of the Semitic languages in general and appears in the Mesha stela and at Jg 5.10 (see Segal 1927, §281). E.Y. Kutscher (1982, 121–22) showed how final *-m* passed to *-n*, and not only in the plural, in the final phase of the biblical period. Thus, the pervasive use of final *nun* for *mem* probably relates to nasalization as a dialect feature that can be traced back to the very earliest stages in the development of Hebrew.

B. Some nouns change their morphological shape when pluralized, for example שָׁלִיחַ 'emissary' (of type קָטִיל), שְׁלוּחִין 'emissaries' (of type קָטוּל)—in this instance, the alternation is really between noun and participle, although the presence in good manuscripts of a *Qal* passive participle in קָטוּל, 'corrected' in printed editions (see Unit 19.3F), should also be noted.

On occasions, we also find morphological patterns employed for the plural that differ from those used by BH, for example צַד 'side', pluralized as צָדִים in BH but צְדָדִים in RH. (However the form שְׁוָרִים as the plural of שׁוֹר 'ox' is not unique to RH, as M.H. Segal [1927, §282] seems to imply, but is also found at Ho 12.2).

C. As in BH, there are many feminine nouns that take a masculine form in the plural, for example חִטָּה 'wheat' (חִטִּים) and שְׂעֹרָה 'barley' (שְׂעֹרִים).

6. Feminine plural.

A. The standard marker of the feminine plural is ־וֹת, as in BH.

B. However, nouns ending in ־וּת, which in BH would take a plural in ־וּיוֹת (e.g. מַלְכוּת 'kingdom', מַלְכוּיוֹת 'kingdoms'), take ־יוֹת in manuscripts reflecting the Palestinian tradition of RH (thus, מַלְכִיוֹת). There is a considerable increase in nouns of this kind in RH, for example נְזִירוּת (plural נְזִירִיוֹת) '(vow of) Naziritehood' (Naz 3.2). Manuscripts belonging to the Babylonian tradition of RH conserve the equally Palestinian form of the plural in ־וּיוֹת (see Introduction, §10.3).

C. Under the influence of the numerous Greek and Latin words that came into common usage, the ending ־אוֹת or ־יוֹת was introduced, not only for Hebraized loanwords but also, by analogy, for native words, for example מִקְוֶה (plural מִקְוָאוֹת) 'ritual bath' (see Unit 12.5B–C).

D. For אֵם 'mother', the plurals אִמּוֹת and אִמָּהוֹת are attested. As in BH, the plural of אָחוֹת 'sister' is אֲחָיוֹת.

E. Many masculine nouns take the feminine suffix in the plural, for example מִקְרָא 'reading' (plural מִקְרָאוֹת 'comments'), תִּינוֹק 'infant' (plural תִּינוֹקוֹת).

To this group belong the numerous nominalized infinitives of type הֶקְטֵל/הַקְטֵל (see Unit 9.3, 6), which form their plural in ־וֹת, according to the feminine pattern הַקְטָלָה, for example הֶקְדֵּשׁ 'consecrated property' (plural הַקְדֵּשׁוֹת). The same is true of כָּרֵת 'extermination', the nominalized *Nif'al* infinitive [הִ]כָּרֵת], which in the plural becomes כְּרִיתוֹת, as though from a singular form כְּרִיתָה.

7. The dual retains the same morphological marker that it has in BH: ־ַיִם.

III *Grammar and usage*

8. Because BH represents just a limited portion of the language used in the biblical period, it comes as no surprise that in the Bible certain words are only known in their singular or plural or masculine or feminine forms. The presence in RH of forms unattested in BH is important simply because they represent the way in which the Hebrew language underwent morphological and semantic developments. And, as N.H. Waldman (1989, 118) has noted, 'gender changes between Biblical and Mishnaic Hebrew are quite dramatic'.

9. RH can obtain an extended meaning for certain words merely by employing them in a different grammatical gender but without any overt morphological change, for example:

> כַּף feminine 'palm (of hand)', 'scale (for weights)', masculine 'spoon';
>
> סֶלַע feminine 'rock', masculine 'coin';

רֶגֶל feminine 'foot' (dual רַגְלַיִם 'feet'), masculine 'pilgrim festival' (plural רְגָלִים).

Sometimes, the gender change is due solely to Aramaic influence, as with כּוֹס 'cup', which is feminine in BH (Lm 4.21) but masculine in RH (for example כּוֹס רִאשׁוֹן 'first cup' at Pes 10.2 and כּוֹסוֹת מְשׁוּבָּחִין 'exquisite cups' at TosSoṭ 3.4), despite maintaining the plural in וֹת- (see also Pes 10.1).

10. When a noun develops masculine and feminine forms, these usually mean something subtly different, for example:

גַּן 'garden', גִּינָה/גִּנָּה 'vegetable garden';

דִּיר 'shed (for animals or logs)'; דִּירָה 'dwelling place (of humans)';

חוֹב 'debt, offence'; חוֹבָה 'obligation';

חוֹל 'sand'; חוֹלָה 'sand dune';

חֶרֶב 'sword'; חַרְבָּה 'knife'.

11. The development of two plural forms, one masculine, the other feminine, implies the addition of a special extended meaning, for example:

יוֹם 'day', יָמִים 'days', יְמוֹת 'epoch' (always in the construct), a collective sense employed in such phrases as בִּימוֹת הַמָּשִׁיחַ 'in the messianic age' or יְמוֹת הַגְּשָׁמִים-יְמוֹת הַחַמָּה 'dry season–rainy season' (here we have once again an archaic form that has reappeared in RH—it occurs at Dt 32.7 alongside שְׁנוֹת);

שָׁנָה 'year', שָׁנִים 'years', שָׁנוֹת 'age, era' (collective);

קֶבֶר 'grave', קְבָרִים 'graves', קְבָרוֹת 'graveyard';

רַב 'much', רַבִּים 'many', רַבּוֹת 'teachers' (always with pronominal suffix);

תְּפִלָּה 'prayer', תְּפִלּוֹת 'prayers', תְּפִלִּים 'phylacteries';

עוֹלָמִים/עוֹלָם 'world, eternity', עוֹלָמוֹת 'hypothetical worlds', a difference analogous to that of אֱלֹהִים 'God', אֱלֹהוֹת 'gods' (note also the tone of exaggeration conveyed by the use of the rare plural יֵינוֹת, from יַיִן 'wine', at TosSoṭ 3.4:

היא השקתו יינות משובחין בכוסות משובחין

She [the adulteress] gave him exquisite wines to drink from exquisite cups);

מִדְרָשׁ *midrash, study*, מִדְרָשִׁים 'midrashic texts' (although this is a mediaeval formation), מִדְרָשׁוֹת '(midrashic) interpretations'.

12. In its use of the dual, we can appreciate how RH has developed independently of both BH and Aramaic. For the dual, which had been widely used in the early Canaanite dialects but was much less common in BH and virtually unknown in Aramaic, returned in vigorous form to RH to indicate anything found in pairs, for example קַבַּיִם 'two kabs' or כּוֹרַיִם 'two cors'. RH also preserves dual forms, such as גַּבַּיִם 'backs' (singular גַּב) and קְרָבַיִם 'intestines' (singular קֶרֶב), which are only attested in the Bible in construct or with suffixes.

IV *Phraseology*

13. מִיָּמַי 'from my days', מִיָּמֶיךָ 'from your days', etc. signify, in negative constructions, 'never', as in:

לֹא רָאָה שִׂמְחָה מִיָּמָיו

He never saw happiness/He never knew what happiness was (Suk 5.1);

אֵיזוֹ הִיא בְתוּלָה? כָּל־שֶׁלֹּא רָאֲתָה דָּם מִיָּמֶיהָ, אַף עַל פִּי שֶׁנְּשׂוּאָה

Who is a maiden? Whoever has never menstruated even when married (Nid 1.4);

מִימֵיהֶם שֶׁלְּכֹהֲנִים לֹא נִמְנְעוּ

Ever since priests have existed, they have never abstained (Eduy 2.1).

The construction is found as well in questions, always in a negative context, for example

רָאִיתָ מִיָּמֶיךָ חַיָּה וְעוֹף שֶׁיֵּשׁ לָהֶם אֻמָּנוּת

Have you ever seen an animal or a bird that had a profession? (Qid 4.14).

14. דֶּרֶךְ הָרַבִּים–דֶּרֶךְ הַיָּחִיד 'private way–public way' (literally, 'the way of only one–the way of many'), a common formula for distinguishing public and private domains.

15. רַגְלַיִם לַדָּבָר, literally 'feet for the thing' or 'the thing has feet', meaning that something has a basis or is probable, that there is evidence to maintain it, for example

רַבִּי נְחֶמְיָה אוֹמֵר, פָּטוּר, שֶׁרַגְלַיִם לַדָּבָר

Rabbi Neḥemiah interprets, He is exempt (from responsibility), because there is a basis for it (Naz 9.4; see also 9.2–3).

V *Vocabulary*

בּוּר 'uncultivated land'

לְעוֹלָם הַבָּא, abbreviations of בָּעוֹלָם הַזֶּה 'in this world' and לְעוֹלָם הַבָּא 'in the future world'
'in the future world'

הִזִּיק (hi. of נזק) 'cause harm'

זָכָה בְּ- 'take possession of, acquire the right to'

זְכוּת 'benevolence'

כָּרָאוּי '(-כְּ 'as' plus רָאָה 'see') 'aptly, as it should be'

כָּתַשׁ 'strike' (in htp. 'fight')

מְגִלָּה 'scroll'; used specifically as a designation for the book of Esther

מִיָּד (מִן 'from' plus יָד 'hand') 'immediately'

מַלְכִיּוֹת (plural of מַלְכוּת) 'kingdoms', also in reference to biblical verses on the kingdom of God recited on new year's day (see RS 4.5, where שׁוֹפָרוֹת and זִכְרוֹנוֹת refer to verses about, respectively, memorials and sounding of the ram's horn)

מִשֶּׁ- (מִן 'from' plus -שֶׁ 'which') 'since, after'

עִנָּה 'postpone, delay'

עֲצֶרֶת 'conclusion', as a term for the Festival of Weeks (Pentecost)

פֵּאָה 'corner, angle', also the name of a Mishnah tractate concerned with the obligation to leave aside, without harvesting, a corner of the field to help the poor and the sojourner (see Lv 19.9; 23.22; Dt 24.19–22); לְהַפְסִיק לַפֵּאָה 'to interrupt for the corner' refers to the demarcation of fields in order to achieve for the poor as many corners as there are fields (see Pea 2.1).

פְּסֹלֶת 'refuse, unsellable stock, unfit item'

שְׁבִיל 'path'

שְׁלוּלִית 'channel, pool'

שְׁתִיָּה 'foundation, basis'

תַּרְקָב (תְּרֵי קַב 'two kabs'), a dry measure

VI *Exercises*

1. יְהוֹשֻׁעַ בֶּן פְּרַחְיָה אוֹמֵר, עֲשֵׂה לְךָ רַב, וּקְנֵה לְךָ חָבֵר, וֶהֱוֵי דָן אֶת כָּל הָאָדָם לְכַף זְכוּת.

2. אִם יִהְיוּ כָּל חַכְמֵי יִשְׂרָאֵל בְּכַף מֹאזְנַיִם, וֶאֱלִיעֶזֶר בֶּן הֻרְקְנוֹס בְּכַף שְׁנִיָּה, מַכְרִיעַ אֶת כֻּלָּם.

3. כַּמָּה יְהֵא בָעִיר וִיהֵא כְאַנְשֵׁי הָעִיר? שְׁנֵים עָשָׂר חֹדֶשׁ. קָנָה בָהּ בֵּית דִּירָה, הֲרֵי הוּא כְאַנְשֵׁי הָעִיר מִיָּד.

4. וַחֲכָמִים אוֹמְרִים, יְמֵי חַיֶּיךָ [דברים טז ג'], הָעוֹלָם הַזֶּה, כֹּל יְמֵי חַיֶּיךָ [שם], לְהָבִיא לִימוֹת הַמָּשִׁיחַ.

5. הַכּוֹנֵס צֹאן לַדִּיר וְנָעַל בְּפָנֶיהָ כָּרָאוּי, וְיָצְאָה וְהִזִּיקָה, פָּטוּר.

6. אָמַר רַבִּי חֲנַנְיָה סְגַן הַכֹּהֲנִים, מִיָּמַי לֹא רָאִיתִי עוֹר יוֹצֵא לְבֵית הַשְּׂרֵפָה.

7. הֵעִיד רַבִּי יְהוֹשֻׁעַ עַל עֲצָמוֹת שֶׁנִּמְצְאוּ בְדִיר הָעֵצִים.

8. מְגִלָּה נִקְרֵאת בְּאַחַד עָשָׂר ... כְּרַכִּין הַמֻּקָּפִין חוֹמָה מִימוֹת יְהוֹשֻׁעַ בֶּן נוּן, קוֹרִין בַּחֲמִשָּׁה עָשָׂר.

9. רַבִּי אֱלִיעֶזֶר אוֹמֵר, מִשֶּׁחָרַב בֵּית הַמִּקְדָּשׁ, עֲצֶרֶת כַּשַּׁבָּת. רַבָּן גַּמְלִיאֵל אוֹמֵר, רֹאשׁ הַשָּׁנָה וְיוֹם הַכִּפּוּרִים כָּרְגָלִים. וַחֲכָמִים אוֹמְרִים, לֹא כְדִבְרֵי זֶה וְלֹא כְדִבְרֵי זֶה, אֶלָּא עֲצֶרֶת כָּרְגָלִים, רֹאשׁ הַשָּׁנָה וְיוֹם הַכִּפּוּרִים כַּשַּׁבָּת.

10. וְאֵלּוּ מַפְסִיקִין לַפֵּאָה, הַנַּחַל, וְהַשְּׁלוּלִית, וְדֶרֶךְ הַיָּחִיד, וְדֶרֶךְ הָרַבִּים, וּשְׁבִיל הָרַבִּים, וּשְׁבִיל הַיָּחִיד הַקָּבוּעַ בִּימוֹת הַחַמָּה וּבִימוֹת הַגְּשָׁמִים, וְהַבּוּר, וְהַנִּיר, וְזֶרַע אַחֵר

11. אִם בָּאִים אָנוּ לָדוּן אַחַר בֵּית דִּינוֹ שֶׁלְּרַבָּן גַּמְלִיאֵל צְרִיכִין אָנוּ לָדוּן אַחַר כָּל בֵּית דִּין וּבֵית דִּין שֶׁעָמַד מִימוֹת מֹשֶׁה וְעַד עַכְשָׁיו.

12. אֵין מְמִיתִין אוֹתוֹ לֹא בְּבֵית דִּין שֶׁבְּעִירוֹ וְלֹא בְּבֵית דִּין שֶׁבְּיַבְנֶה, אֶלָּא מַעֲלִין אוֹתוֹ לְבֵית דִּין הַגָּדוֹל שֶׁבִּירוּשָׁלַיִם, וּמְשַׁמְּרִין אוֹתוֹ עַד הָרֶגֶל ... אֵין מְעַנִּין דִּינוֹ שֶׁלָּזֶה, אֶלָּא מְמִיתִין אוֹתוֹ מִיָּד, וְכוֹתְבִין וְשׁוֹלְחִים שְׁלוּחִים בְּכָל הַמְּקוֹמוֹת, אִישׁ פְּלוֹנִי בֶּן פְּלוֹנִי נִתְחַיַּב מִיתָה בְּבֵית דִּין.

13. מִי שֶׁזָּכָה בַקְּטֹרֶת הָיָה נוֹטֵל אֶת הַכַּף, וְהַכַּף דּוֹמֶה לְתַרְקָב נָּדוֹל שֶׁלְזָהָב.
14. עָתִיד הַקָּדוֹשׁ בָּרוּךְ הוּא לְהַנְחִיל לְכָל צַדִּיק וְצַדִּיק שְׁלֹשׁ מֵאוֹת וַעֲשָׂרָה
    עוֹלָמוֹת.
15. מִשֶּׁנִּטַּל הָאָרוֹן, אֶבֶן הָיְתָה שָׁם מִימוֹת הַנְּבִיאִים הָרִאשׁוֹנִים, וּשְׁתִיָּה הָיְתָה נִקְרֵאת
16. מה ראו חכמים לומר, מלכיות תחילה ואחר כך זכרונות ושופרות?
17. מימיהם לא עשו שלום זה עם זה ..., וכשבאו להלחם עם ישראל עשו שלום
    זה עם זה ונלחמו עם ישראל.
18. אם פסולת ערי ישראל ארבע מלכיות מתכנסות עליה, קל וחמר לשבחה
    של ארץ ישראל.
19. ארבע מלכיות מושלות בהם בישראל ואין בהם חכם ואין בהם נבון.
20. אלו שלשה דורות שלפני ימות המשיח.

Sources. 1. Abot 1.6. 2. Abot 2.8. 3. BB 1.5. 4. Ber 1.5. 5 BQ 6.1. 6. Eduy
2.2. 7. Eduy 8.5. 8. Meg 1.1. 9. MQ 3.6. 10. Pea 2.1. 11. RS 2.9. 12. Sanh
11.4. 13. Tam 5.4. 14. Uqs 3.12. 15. Yom 5.2. 16. SNm 77.4 (H 71). 17.
SNm 157.1 (H 209). 18. SDt 37 (F 72). 19. SDt 304 (F 323). 20. SDt 318
(F 363).

UNIT ELEVEN

ABSOLUTE AND CONSTRUCT

I *Introductory text* (Abot 6.2)

וְהַלֻּחֹת מַעֲשֵׂה אֱלֹהִים הֵמָּה וְהַמִּכְתָּב מִכְתַּב אֱלֹהִים הוּא חָרוּת עַל־הַלֻּחֹת
[שְׁמוֹת לב׳ טז]. אַל תִּקְרָא חָרוּת, אֶלָּא חֵרוּת, שֶׁאֵין לְךָ בֶּן חֹרִין אֶלָּא מִי
שֶׁעוֹסֵק בְּתַלְמוּד תּוֹרָה. וְכָל מִי שֶׁעוֹסֵק בַּתּוֹרָה תָּדִיר, הֲרֵי זֶה מִתְעַלֶּה.

The tablets were the work of God and the writing was the writing of God engraved on the tablets [Ex 33.16]. Do not read חָרוּת 'engraved' but חֵרוּת
'liberty', for you can find no free person who does not occupy themself in
studying the Torah. Anyone who is constantly occupied with the Torah will
be truly exalted.

1. In order to uncover the Bible's wealth of meanings (as the rabbinic
saying has it: יֵשׁ שִׁבְעִים פָּנִים לַמִּקְרָא 'there are seventy faces to Scripture'
[Numbers Rabbah 13.15–16]), the exegetical schools turned to different pro-
cedures or 'rules' (מִדּוֹת), one of which was that of אַל תִּקְרָא 'do not read',
that is, of changing the vocalization of the consonants in the biblical text. Of
course, this was employed to help justify accepted doctrines, never capri-

ciously or arbitrarily, and the use of such *middot* was governed by rabbinic tradition. Because of its clarity and the interesting nature of its contents, we have selected Abot 6.2 as an example (even though the whole of Abot 6 is a mediaeval addition), but the application of the *al tiqra* principle is also well-attested in the tannaitic tradition (see Unit 21.1).

II *Morphology*

2. As we have already indicated in Unit 4, RH continued to employ the typical BH system of expressing genitive relationships, whereby a single syntagmatic unit is formed out of the two related nouns, the first of them losing the accent (or retaining only a secondary accent) and being supported by the second noun, which bears the main accent. The first noun is designated נִסְמָךְ 'supported' and the second נִפְרָד 'separated'. In traditional western terms, the first noun is the '*(nomen) regens*', in the construct state, and the second is the '*(nomen) rectum*', in the absolute state. The phenomenon is also known by the Hebrew grammatical term סְמִיכוּת '*semikhut*, support'.

Because in *semikhut* the second element determines or specifies the value of the first, we have chosen to call the second element (absolute, *rectum*, נִפְרָד) the 'determinant' and the first element (construct, *regens*, נִסְמָךְ) the 'determined' noun.

3. The transformations that a word undergoes in the construct state are the same in RH as in BH: shortening, wherever possible, of vowels and conversion of the masculine plural suffix ־ִים to ־ֵי and of the feminine singular marker ־ָה to ־ַת. Sometimes, the only motive for the presence of the article before the determinant is in order to separate two accents that would otherwise be contiguous (see N.H. Waldman 1989, 133 and our earlier remarks at Unit 3.9).

III *Grammar and usage*

4. The nature of the determination or the kind of specification varies greatly and certainly cannot simply be mechanically rendered by 'of'.

A. When the determined word is a noun that expresses the action of a verb, the determinant is usually the object of the underlying verb, as can easily be seen in the construction כְּבוֹד אָב וָאֵם, which refers to the honour due to parents (as against כְּבוֹד אֵם 'honour of mother' and כְּבוֹד אָב 'honour of father' [Ker 6.9], which refers to the dignity parents possess just by being parents).

B. Often, it is only the theological, legal, or exegetical context that can provide the precise sense of a particular determinative relationship, for example:

מֵת מִצְוָה 'dead of precept' refers to a corpse that one must touch in order to carry out the 'act of kindness' of burying the dead, even though one will thereby become contaminated;

הֶפְסֵד מִצְוָה 'loss of precept' refers to the loss or inconvenience that occurs through fulfilling a commandment—the sense of the determinative relationship here is made clearer through its counterpart, שְׂכַר מִצְוָה 'recompense of precept';

טְבוּל יוֹם is the person who on a given day has been purified through ritual immersion;

חַיָּבֵי חַטָּאוֹת are those who are obliged to present an offering for sin;

בָּאֵי הָאָרֶץ are those who have come *to* the land of Israel and עוֹלֵי בָבֶל are not those that went up to Babylonia but the immigrants who came to Israel *from* Babylonia (see SDt 8 [F 16]).

Compare יוֹרְדֵי־בוֹר 'those who go down to the grave' (Is 38.18) and יוֹרְדֵי עָפָר 'those who go down to the dust' (Ps 22.30).

C. Passive participles are usually determined by their agent through *semikhut*, as at Yeb 11.1:

נוֹשֵׂא אָדָם אֲנוּסַת אָבִיו וּמְפֻתַּת אָבִיו, אֲנוּסַת בְּנוֹ וּמְפֻתַּת בְּנוֹ

A man may marry a woman raped by his father or seduced by his father or a woman raped by his son or seduced by his son.

In fact, every participle has both nominal and verbal characteristics (see Unit 19.8), which helps account for such phrases as עוֹלֵי בָבֶל and בָּאֵי הָאָרֶץ, mentioned above, as well as, for example, עוֹבְדֵי עֲבוֹדָה זָרָה 'adorers of idols' alongside עוֹבְדִין אֶת ע"ז 'adoring the idols'.

D. Determinative relationships with בֶּן 'son' and בַּעַל 'lord' specify a type of subject (not necessarily a person), for example בַּעַל תְּשׁוּבָה 'convert, penitent', בַּעַל מוּם 'defective (one)', בַּעַל בָּשָׂר 'fleshy one' (Shab 19.6, in reference to an incorrectly performed circumcision), בַּעַל חוֹב 'creditor', בַּעַל קְרִי 'one who has had an involuntary ejaculation', בֶּן־חוֹרִין 'free (person)', and בֶּן עִיר 'citizen'.

בֶּן and בַּת are often used to form diminutives; for example, in BB 7.4 a distinction is made between a חֲרִיץ, a ditch of six handbreadths, and a בֶּן־חֲרִיץ, a ditch of half that size.

5. As in BH, the general rule is that with plurals only the determined noun takes the plural marker, as with בְּנֵי־אָדָם 'people', בַּעֲלֵי תְשׁוּבָה 'penitents', etc.

However, in RH it is also common that both nouns, determined and determinant, are made plural, for example בַּעֲלֵי בָתִּים 'landlords, householders', בָּתֵּי מִדְרָשׁוֹת 'houses of study', and בַּעֲלֵי מוּמִים '(priests) who have physical defects' (SLv 1.5 [W 6b]). This phenomenon is seen already in LBH: אַנְשֵׁי שֵׁמוֹת 'famous people' (1 C 12.31), עֲצֵי אֲרָזִים 'cedar planks' (1 C 14.1), and חָרָשֵׁי עֵצִים 'carpenters' (1 C 14.1).

With בַּיִת 'house' as the determined noun, the plural marker is sometimes added only to the determinant, as the two words are perceived as a single unit, for example:

הַקְּמָחִים וְהַסְּלָתוֹת שֶׁלְּבֵית הַשְּׁוָקִים טְמֵאִין

Every kind of meal and flour that are in the markets is impure (Makhsh 6.2).

6. For the use of שֶׁל in place of *semikhut*, see Unit 4.11–14. The different constructions that arise can often diverge considerably in meaning. For example, the material from which something is made is usually determined by שֶׁל ('room [made] of wood'), whereas its purpose or nature tends to be expressed through *semikhut* ('room for wood'). See, for example, Mek 16.33 (L 2.125):

איני יודע של מה היא, אם של כסף או של זהב או של ברזל

I don't know what material it was made of, whether of silver or of gold or of iron.

7. Many prepositions are in origin nouns in the construct state: בֵּינִי, בֵּין, לִפְנֵי, אַחֲרֵי, תַּחַת, etc. Viewed in this light, conjunctions of the type -שֶׁ לִפְנֵי, אַחֲרֵי שֶׁ-, and עַד שֶׁ- may be seen as no more than prepositions in the construct state determined by a clause beginning with -שֶׁ.

In RH, there are also new conjunctions, including -כְּדֵי שֶׁ 'so that' (< 'as worthy to' < 'as sufficient for'; see Unit 30.8) and -בְּחֶזְקַת שֶׁ 'on the assumption that', in the sequences בְּחֶזְקַת שֶׁהוּא קַיָּם and בְּחֶזְקַת שֶׁהֶן קַיָּמִין 'on the assumption that he is/they are alive' at Gi ̣t 3.3, 7–8, which has developed out of the common non-conjunctional structure found in a phrase such as בְּחֶזְקַת טָהֳרָה 'with a presumption of purity' (Nid 2.4).

IV *Phraseology*

8. בֶּן־אָדָם 'son of humankind', בְּנֵי־אָדָם 'sons of humankind', the plural version, with reference to 'humankind' in general, being common in both the Mishnah and the tannaitic *midrashim*. Sometimes it is best translated as an adjective, 'human'. Examples include

דִּבְּרָה תוֹרָה בִּלְשׁוֹן בְּנֵי־אָדָם

The Torah spoke according to human language (SNm 112.4 [H 121]; see also SLv 20.2 in the exercises to this unit)

and

והיו מלאכי השרת תמהין לומר, בני אדם עובדי עבודה זרה מהלכין
ביבשה בתוך הים

The serving angels were full of wonder, saying, Some humans, idolaters, walking in the middle of the sea as if on dry land (Mek 14.29 [L 1.246]).

But the singular form, בֶּן־אָדָם is hardly used at all: it never appears in the Mishnah, not even in quotations, or in Sifra; it is found just once in SNm (103.4 [H 102]), in a quotation of Ezk 16.2, five times in Mek, always in quotations (Is 56.2; Ezk 2.1; 17.2; 26.2; 28.2), and eight times in SDt, of which six are quotations (Ezk 8.12; 17.2; 24.1–2; 33.7,24; 39.17; 44.5). Thus, in the whole of the Mishnah and the tannaitic *midrashim* there are just two original passages where בֶּן־אָדָם is employed. In those two texts, the meaning is generic or indefinite, 'one, someone, people':

לא תאמץ את לבבך [דברים ט''ו], יש בן אדם שמצטער
אם יתן אם לא יתן

Do not harden your heart [Dt 15.6]: there are people who worry thinking about whether to give or not to give (SDt 116 [F 175]);

ולא תקפוץ את ידך [דברים ט''ו], יש בן אדם שפוסט את ידו
וחוזר וקופצה

And do not close your hand [Dt 15.6]: there are people who stretch out their hand, but then close it again (SDt 116 [F 175]).

It is interesting to compare the Vienna manuscript version of TosSoṭ 3.12,

אין אנו צריכין שיבאו בני אדם עלינו

We do not require anyone to come to us,

with that of MS Erfurt,

אין אנו צריכין שיבא אדם אצלינו

(where the singular is expressed by אָדָם and not בֶּן־אָדָם).

The contrast with the extensive use of υἱὸς τοῦ ἀνθρώπου in the language of Jesus and the gospels is striking.

9. בַּת־קוֹל 'daughter of the voice', possibly with a somewhat diminutive or diminished sense, as it normally refers to a rumour, thunder, or voice, the source of which is uncertain and the authority of which is never accepted unequivocally in the rabbinic tradition, in clear contrast to the clarity of the word, דָּבָר, of Y. and the prophets (see Pes 114a and BM 59b, and, in the exercises, Abot 6.2, Yeb 16.6, Mek 18.27, and SDt 357).

10. דֶּרֶךְ בְּנֵי־אָדָם 'the habitual behaviour of human beings', כְּדֶרֶךְ בְּנֵי־אָדָם 'as is the custom':

מִי שֶׁיֵּשׁ לוֹ גִנָּה לִפְנִים מִגִּנָּתוֹ שֶׁלַחֲבֵרוֹ, נִכְנָס בְּשָׁעָה שֶׁדֶּרֶךְ בְּנֵי אָדָן
נִכְנָסִים, וְיוֹצֵא בְּשָׁעָה שֶׁדֶּרֶךְ בְּנֵי אָדָן יוֹצְאִין

Whoever has a vegetable garden within the vegetable garden of another may enter when it is the custom to enter and go out when it is the custom to go out (K BB 6.6; see also Ber 1.3, BQ 6.5, etc.).

V *Vocabulary*

אֲרִיכוּת 'prolongation', אֲרִיכוּת יָמִים 'longevity'

גְּנִיזָה 'safekeeping, store room'

דְּלֵקָה 'fire, conflagration'

דָּרַס 'rape'

הוֹאִיל וְ- 'because'

הַשְׁמָטָה 'cancellation'

הִכְרִיז 'announce, proclaim'

הִרְהֵר 'meditate, think'

הִשִּׂיא (hi. of נשא) 'give in marriage'

מְפוֹרָשׁ (pu. participle of פרשׁ) 'explained, explicit'

נָזַף 'reprove, excommunicate', נָזוּף 'reprobate'

עֶלְבּוֹן 'arrogance, insult, humiliation'

עָשָׂה ... כְּ- 'rank alongside, consider equal to'

קֶרִי 'accident', as euphemism for involuntary ejaculation

רְאָיָה 'proof, evidence'

VI *Exercises*

1. חַיָּה רָעָה בָּאָה לָעוֹלָם, עַל שְׁבוּעַת שָׁוְא וְעַל חִלּוּל הַשֵּׁם. גָּלוּת בָּא לָעוֹלָם, עַל עוֹבְדֵי עֲבוֹדָה זָרָה, וְעַל גִּלּוּי עֲרָיוֹת, וְעַל שְׁפִיכַת דָּמִים, וְעַל הַשְׁמָטַת הָאָרֶץ.

2. אָמַר רַבִּי יְהוֹשֻׁעַ בֶּן לֵוִי, בְּכָל יוֹם וְיוֹם בַּת קוֹל יוֹצֵאת מֵהַר חוֹרֵב וּמַכְרֶזֶת וְאוֹמֶרֶת, אוֹי לָהֶם לַבְּרִיּוֹת מֵעֶלְבּוֹנָהּ שֶׁלַּתּוֹרָה. שֶׁכָּל מִי שֶׁאֵינוֹ עוֹסֵק בַּתּוֹרָה נִקְרָא נָזוּף.

3. מִי שֶׁיֵּשׁ לוֹ בּוֹר לִפְנִים מִבֵּיתוֹ שֶׁלַּחֲבֵרוֹ, נִכְנָס בְּשָׁעָה שֶׁדֶּרֶךְ בְּנֵי אָדָם נִכְנָסִין, וְיוֹצֵא בְּשָׁעָה שֶׁדֶּרֶךְ בְּנֵי אָדָם יוֹצְאִין.

4. בַּעַל קֶרִי מְהַרְהֵר בְּלִבּוֹ וְאֵינוֹ מְבָרֵךְ.

5. אִם הָיָה בַעַל תְּשׁוּבָה, לֹא יֹאמַר לוֹ, זְכֹר מָה הָיוּ מַעֲשֶׂיךָ הָרִאשׁוֹנִים. וְאִם הָיָה בֶּן גֵּרִים, לֹא יֹאמַר לוֹ, זְכֹר מָה הָיוּ מַעֲשֵׂה אֲבוֹתֶיךָ.

6. וְרַבִּי יְהוֹשֻׁעַ אוֹמֵר, לֹא מִפִּיהָ אָנוּ חַיִּין. אֶלָּא הֲרֵי זוֹ בְּחֶזְקַת דְּרוּסַת אִישׁ, עַד שֶׁתָּבִיא רְאָיָה לִדְבָרֶיהָ.

7. אָמַר רַבִּי יְהוּדָה, בָּרִאשׁוֹנָה הָיוּ שׁוֹלְחִין אֵצֶל בַּעֲלֵי בָתִּים שֶׁבַּמְּדִינוֹת, מַהֲרוּ וְהַתְקִינוּ אֶת פָּרוֹתֵיכֶם.

8. כָּל הַנָּשִׁים בְּחֶזְקַת טַהֲרַת לְבַעֲלֵיהֶן. הַבָּאִין מִן הַדֶּרֶךְ, נְשֵׁיהֶן לָהֶן בְּחֶזְקַת טַהֲרָה.

9. שָׁחֲטוֹ וְנִמְצָא בַעַל מוּם, חַיָּב.

10. כָּל כִּתְבֵי הַקֹּדֶשׁ מַצִּילִין אוֹתָן מִפְּנֵי הַדְּלֵקָה, בֵּין שֶׁקּוֹרִין בָּהֶן וּבֵין שֶׁאֵין קוֹרִין בָּהֶן. וְאַף עַל פִּי שֶׁכְּתוּבִים בְּכָל לָשׁוֹן, טְעוּנִים גְּנִיזָה. וּמִפְּנֵי מָה אֵין קוֹרִין בָּהֶם? מִפְּנֵי בִּטּוּל בֵּית הַמִּדְרָשׁ.

11. מְעִידִין לְאוֹר הַנֵּר וּלְאוֹר הַלְּבָנָה. וּמַשִּׂיאִין עַל פִּי בַת קוֹל. מַעֲשֶׂה בְּאֶחָד שֶׁעָמַד עַל רֹאשׁ הָהָר וְאָמַר, אִישׁ פְּלוֹנִי בֶּן פְּלוֹנִי מִמָּקוֹם פְּלוֹנִי מֵת, הָלְכוּ וְלֹא מָצְאוּ שָׁם אָדָם, וְהִשִּׂיאוּ אֶת אִשְׁתּוֹ. וְשׁוּב מַעֲשֶׂה בְצַלְמוֹן בְּאֶחָד שֶׁאָמַר, אֲנִי, אִישׁ פְּלוֹנִי בֶּן אִישׁ פְּלוֹנִי, נְשָׁכַנִי נָחָשׁ, וַהֲרֵי אֲנִי מֵת, וְהָלְכוּ וְלֹא הִכִּירוּהוּ, וְהִשִּׂיאוּ אֶת אִשְׁתּוֹ.

12. מעשה באחד שאמר, קרבן מבני שותה מים היום. ויצאה בת קול מבית קדשי הקדשים ואמרה, מי שקיבל את קרבנותיהם במדבר, הוא יקבל את קרבנותיהם בשעה הזאת.

13. לא תעשו לכם [שמות כ׳ כג׳]. שלא תאמר, הואיל ונתנה תורה רשות לעשות [כרובים] בבית המקדש, הרי אני עושה בבתי כנסיות ובבתי מדרשות. ת״ל, לא תעשו לכם.

14. רבי יוסי אומר, דברה תורה כלשון בני אדם בלשונות הרבה וכולם

צריכין להידרש.

15. מיין ושכר יזיר חומץ יין וחומץ שכר לא ישתו [במדבר ו׳ ג׳], לעשות יין מצוה כיין רשות.

16. קדוש יהיה [במדבר ו׳ ה׳], זו קדושת שער, אתה אומר, זו קדושת שער, או אינו אלא קדושת הגוף?

17. על נפש מת לא יבא [במדבר ו׳ ו׳], שומע אני נפשות בהמה במשמע. ת״ל, לאביו ולאמו [במדבר ו׳ ז׳], במה ענין מדבר? בנפשות אדם

18. לאביו ולאמו אינו מטמא, אלא מטמא הוא למת מצוה.

19. ובדבר הזה תאריכו ימים [דברים לב׳ מז׳], זה אחד מן הדברים שעושה אותם אוכל פירותיהם בעולם הזה ואריכות ימים לעולם הבא. ומפורש כאן, בתלמוד תורה. בכבור אב ואם מנין? תלמוד לומר, כבד את אביך ואת אמך ... [שמות כ׳ יב׳].

20. רבי אליעזר אומר, בת קל יוצאת מתוך המחנה שנים עשר מיל על שנים עשר מיל והיתה מכרזת ואומרת, מת משה.

Sources. 1. Abot 5.9. 2. Abot 6.2. 3. BB 6.5. 4. Ber 6.4. 5. K BM 4.10. 6. Ket 1.7. 7. MS 8.7. 8. Nid 2.4. 9. Pes 6.6. 10. Shab 16.1. 11. Yeb 16.6. 12. Mek 18.27 (L 2.187). 13. Mek 20.23 (L 2.283). 14. SLv 20.2 (W 91b). 15. SNm 23.1 (H 26). 16. SNm 25.3 (H 31). 17. SNm 26.2 (H 32). 18. SNm 26.2 (H 32). 19. SDt 336 (F 386). 20. SDt 357 (F 428).

UNIT TWELVE

GREEK AND LATIN WORDS

I *Introductory text* (Mek 19.4 [L 2.203])

משל, לאחד שהיה מהלך בדרך והיה מנהג את בנו לפניו. ובאו לסטים לשבותו, נטלו מלפניו ונתנו לאחוריו. בא זאב לטרפו, נטלו מאחריו ונתנו לפניו. ליסטים מלפניו וזאב מאחריו, נטלו ונתנו על כתפיו, שנאמר, ובמדבר אשר ראית אשר נשאך י׳ אלהיך כאשר ישא איש את בנו [דברים א׳ לא׳].

A parable: It is like one who was going on a journey with his child in front of him. Bandits came to capture him; he took him from in front and put him behind. A wolf came to devour him; he took him from behind and put him in front. With robbers in front and the wolf behind, he took him and put him on his shoulders, as it is said, And in the desert, where you saw that Y. carried you like a man carries his child [Dt 1.31].

1. The parable attempts to explain Ex 19.4, I carried you *on* eagles' wings, bringing in Dt 1.31, where Y. appears as a father who carries his child on high (נָשָׂא): as the eagle bears its young upon its wings to protect them from the arrows, so Y. carries Israel upon his shoulders to protect them from their enemies. The midrashic function of the parable is the explanation of Scripture.

II *Morphology*

2. RH has a large stock of Greek and Latin words. In S. Krauss's dictionary (1898–1900), more than two thousand items are listed. Although over a third of them are doubtful and the timescale is large, the deep penetration of Greek into Hebrew cannot be denied.

Greek words started to enter vernacular Hebrew on a large scale after the conquests of Alexander the Great in the fourth century BCE, as part of the wider cultural phenomenon of Hellenization. Little by little, Palestine in the Hellenistic period became trilingual: Aramaic and Hebrew were spoken by the masses, with Greek as the language of administrators and the upper echelons of society (a situation somewhat analogous to the rôle of Hebrew, Arabic, and English in the State of Israel today; see Mussies 1976, 1051). However, almost everyone would have had a basic knowledge of Greek for day-to-day purposes.

Moreover, the Greek literary output of Palestine (deutero-canonical and apocryphal works, the New Testament, and so on) makes Jerusalem, and indeed all Palestine, of the intertestamental period a very important centre for the use and the study of Greek (see Introduction, §§3, 4.3).

Latin entered the arena with the Roman presence from the first century BCE onward. Its impact was less than that of Greek, although significant in military vocabulary.

3. The difficulties we face today in deciding whether to write '*midrashim*' or 'midrashes', '*curricula*' or 'curriculums', etc. help us to understand the inconsistencies in RH transcription and inflection of Greek and Latin words.

4. There is no uniform way of adapting these words.

A. Some are made to conform to genuine Hebrew or Aramaic noun patterns, for example אִצְטְלִית (στολή) 'clothes', מַרְגָּלִית (μαργαρίτης) 'pearl', and אַכְסַנְיָא (ξένος) 'stranger, hostel'.

B. Others are simply given a rough phonetic transcription, which displays little standardization, for example אוֹקְיָנוֹס (ὠκεανός) 'ocean' or פִּילֵי (πύλαι) 'city gates', though there are some recurrent features, such as the use of prefixed *alef* when transcribing Greek or Latin words beginning with two consonants, for example אִזְמֵל (σμίλη) 'knife', or the use of *ṣade* to represent *sigma* within a word, for example פַּרְצוּף (πρόσοπον) 'face, front'. It is noticeable that Palestinian and Babylonian sources differ in their transcriptions, with the latter displaying less knowledge of Greek.

C. However, many words were not clearly understood and have suffered in the process of textual transmission to the extent that they are scarcely recognizable today.

5. Not surprisingly, the inflection of foreign words posed problems and was avoided wherever possible.

A. Genitive structures with שֶׁל are preferred to construct chains. However, by the time of the *amoraim*, we have the striking case of ὄχλος 'crowd' used in a construct plural form:

שמא כשהית יושב ודורש בהר הבית והיו כל אוכלוסי ישראל
יושבין לפניך

Perhaps when you were sitting down to expound on the Temple Mount and all the multitudes of Israel were seated before you (ARN 38 [S 114]; cf. jBer 9.13c).

B. Plurals are formed regularly, with the suffixes -ִים and -וֹת, although if a word ends in אָ- or הָ- the suffix is normally -אוֹת rather than -וֹת, for example טַבְלָא (Latin *tabula*) 'tablet, table', טַבְלָאוֹת (not טַבְלוֹת).

C. This termination became a distinctive feature of foreign words and is commonly found in plurals of Greek words ending in -η and transcribed as -ִי, for example דייתיקי (διαθήκη) 'covenant', דייתקאות.

This success of the -אוֹת ending on foreign words was due in part to its similarity to the characteristic -αι and -*ae* terminations of first declension Greek and Latin nouns. Under the influence of these items, other native Hebrew words sometimes formed their plurals in the same way (see Unit 10.6).

III *Grammar and usage*

6. Greek and Latin vocabulary is found in every area of life, especially in administrative and legal spheres, commerce, industry, and military life. A short but illustrative list can be seen in Schürer 1979, 53ff.

7. However, so great was the impact of Greek and Latin words that they abound even in the most popular forms of literature. The following examples appear in the *meshalim* of Sifre to Numbers:

אנטיקיסר (ἀντίκαισαρ) 'pro-Caesar, pro-consul' (82.2 [H 78]);

הפרכיא (ἐπαρχία) 'prefecture' (131.1 [H 170]);

דינר (*denarius*) 'denarius' (131.1 [H 169]);

טריקלין (*triclinium*) 'refectory' (134.5 [H 180]);

סנדל (σανδάλιον) 'sandal' (115.5 [H 127]);

ספקלטור (*speculator*) 'inspector, executioner' (91.2 [H 91]);

ערכיין (ἀρχεῖον) 'archives, register' (117.1 [H 135]);

פידגוג (παιδαγωγός) 'tutor' (87.2 [H 87]; 105.1 [H 103]);

פולימרכוס (πολέμαρχος) 'general' (131.1 [H 170]);

פלומפילון (*primipilus*) 'chief centurion' (131.1 [H 169]);

פְּלַטְרִין (πραιτώριον) 'praetorium, praetor's residence' (134.5 [H 180]), sometimes also mistakenly used instead of פְּלָטִין (palatium) 'palace';

קִיטוֹן (κοιτών) 'bedroom' (134.5 [H 180]);

קִיטְרוֹן (centurio) 'centurion' (131.1 [H 169]).

8. The extraordinary number of Greek and Latin loanwords in RH is well-illustrated in the following two narratives devised by E.Y. Kutscher (1982, 139):

A. The judge יוֹדִיקִי [iudex] or the chief judge אַרְכִּיוֹדִיקִי [ἀρχιiudex], sitting on the podium בֵּימָה [βῆμα], questioned the defendant who was standing on a small platform גְּרְדוֹן [gradus]. Having heard the prosecutor קַטֵּיגוֹר [κατήγορ] and the defense attorney פַּרְקְלִיט [παράκλητος], they either discharged the defendant by giving him דִּימוֹס [dimissio] or convicted him by giving אֲפוֹפְסִיס [ἀπόφασις] and turned him over to the executioner סְפֶּקְלָטוֹר [speculator].

B. A stranger אַכְסְנָיי [ξένος] who travels the ocean אוֹקְיָנוֹס [ὠκεανός] in a ship לִיבּוּרְנִי [liburnus] trusted that his skipper קָבֶּרְנִיט [κυβερνήτης] would be able to avoid the pirates' פִּירָאטִי [πειρατής] ships and arrive safely in port לְמֵן [λιμήν]. From there he travelled sitting in the [carriage] קָרוֹן [carrus] of the highway אַסְטְרָטָה [strata] which was guarded by the watch-towers בּוּרְגָנִין [πύργος/burgi]. When he arrived at the metropolis מֶטְרוֹפוֹלִין [μετρόπολις] he had to enter it through the city gates פִּילֵי [πύλαι]. If the stranger was an important personality, e.g., the Caesar קִיסָר, the inhabitants would greet him with shouts of קָלוֹס [καλῶς]. He might arrive at the city square פְּלָטְיָה [πλατεῖα] and enter a building through the פְּרוֹזְדוֹר [πρόθυρον] and sit down in the inner room טְרִיקְלִין [triclinium] on a ... chair קָתֶדְרָה [καθέδρα].

9. The general lack of RH verbs deriving from Greek and Latin is reflected in their absence from Kutscher's two stories. However, various denominative verbs were created from loaned nouns, notably בָּסֵס 'base' (from βάσις 'base'), זִוֵּג 'couple' (from זוּג/ζεῦγος 'yoke', קָטְרֵג (κατηγορέω) 'accuse' (from קַטֵּיגוֹר [κατήγορος] 'prosecutor', with metathesis), and לִסְטֵם 'attack, assault' (from λῃστής 'bandit, highwayman').

Nevertheless, in spite of the vast size of the Greek and Latin vocabulary of RH, the structure of the language remained unaltered, as the loanwords had virtually no syntactic effect.

IV Phraseology

10. יָפֶה אָמַרְתָּ (καλῶς εἶπας) 'you have spoken well', a typically Greek turn of phrase; see Naz 7.4 (also Mek 12.31; 18.15; 19.24; SLv 13.3, etc.):

וכשבאתי והרציתי את הדברים לפני רבי יהושע, אמר לי, יפה אמרת

When I came and explained these things before Rabbi Joshua, he said to me, You have spoken very well.

11. כֹּהֵן הֶדְיוֹט 'the normal, or regular, priest' as against the כֹּהֵן הַגָּדוֹל 'high priest'; הֶדְיוֹט is a Hebraized form of ἰδιώτης, in the sense of a private individual or ordinary citizen rather than one who is a נָשִׂיא or a נָבִיא, etc.

V *Vocabulary*

אֶפִּיטְרֹפּוֹס (ἐπίτροπος) 'administrator, person responsible for something, representative'

אַפִּרְיוֹן 'canopy'

אֵרוּס literally, 'betrothal', the name of a musical instrument used at weddings

חָשַׁשׁ 'take into consideration'

כֵּיוָן שֶׁ- 'as soon as'

לִסְטֵס (λῃστής; plural לִיסְטִים) 'bandit, highwayman'

מָזַג 'mix, pour wine'

מִכָּאן וְאֵילָךְ 'from here onwards'

מֵיצַר (hi. participle of צרר) 'distressed, oppressed'

סְנֵיגוֹר (συνήγορος) 'lawyer for the defence'

סְנֵיגוֹרְיָא (συνηγορία) 'defence'

פֹּלְמוֹס (πόλεμος) 'war'

פַּמַּלְיָא (Latin *familia*) 'household'

פַּרְנָסָה 'sustenance, provisions'

צָלַב 'crucify'

קִיתוֹן (κύαθος, κώθων) 'jug'

קִיטוֹן (κοιτών) 'bedroom'

VI *Exercises*

1. רַבִּי אֱלִיעֶזֶר אוֹמֵר, הָעוֹשֶׂה מִצְוָה אַחַת, קוֹנֶה לוֹ פְרַקְלִית אֶחָד, וְהָעוֹבֵר עֲבֵרָה אַחַת, קוֹנֶה לוֹ קַטֵּיגוֹר אֶחָד.

2. רַבִּי יַעֲקֹב אוֹמֵר, הָעוֹלָם הַזֶּה דּוֹמֶה לַפְּרוֹזְדוֹר בִּפְנֵי הָעוֹלָם הַבָּא, הַתְקֵן עַצְמָךְ בַּפְּרוֹזְדוֹר, כְּדֵי שֶׁתִּכָּנֵס לַטְּרַקְלִין [נ]לִיטְרַקְלִין [K].

3. רַבָּן שִׁמְעוֹן בֶּן גַּמְלִיאֵל אוֹמֵר, שְׁנֵי אַכְסָנָאִין אוֹכְלִין עַל שֻׁלְחָן אֶחָד, זֶה בָּשָׂר, וְזֶה גְבִינָה, וְאֵינָן חוֹשְׁשִׁין.

4. לֹא יְלַמֵּד אָדָם אֶת בְּנוֹ חַמָּר, גַּמָּל, סַפָּר, סַפָּן, רוֹעֶה, וְחֶנְוָנִי, שֶׁאֻמְּנוּתָן אֻמָּנוּת לִסְטִים.

5. שְׁלֹשָׁה מְלָכִים וְאַרְבָּעָה הֶדְיוֹטוֹת אֵין לָהֶם חֵלֶק לָעוֹלָם הַבָּא. שְׁלֹשָׁה מְלָכִים, יָרָבְעָם, אַחְאָב וּמְנַשֶּׁה ... אַרְבָּעָה הֶדְיוֹטוֹת, בִּלְעָם, וְדוֹאֵג, וַאֲחִיתֹפֶל, וְגֵחֲזִי.

6. בַּפֹּלְמוֹס שֶׁלְּאַסְפַּסְיָנוּס גָּזְרוּ עַל עַטְרוֹת חֲתָנִים, וְעַל הָאֵרוּס. בַּפֹּלְמוֹס שֶׁלְּטִיטוֹס גָּזְרוּ עַל עַטְרוֹת כַּלּוֹת, וְשֶׁלֹּא יְלַמֵּד אָדָם אֶת בְּנוֹ יָוְנִית. בַּפֹּלְמוֹס הָאַחֲרוֹן גָּזְרוּ שֶׁלֹּא תֵצֵא הַכַּלָּה בָּאַפִּרְיוֹן בְּתוֹךְ הָעִיר.

7. מָשְׁלוּ מָשָׁל, לְמָה הַדָּבָר דּוֹמֶה? לְעֶבֶד שֶׁבָּא לִמְזוֹג כּוֹס לְרַבּוֹ וְשָׁפַךְ לוֹ הַקִּיתוֹן עַל פָּנָיו.

8. בָּא לוֹ כֹהֵן גָּדוֹל לִקְרוֹת. אִם רָצָה לִקְרוֹת בְּבִגְדֵי בוּץ, קוֹרֵא, וְאִם לֹא,

קוֹרֵא בְּאִצְטְלִ֖ית לָבָן מְשֶׁלּוֹ.

9. והיו מתחננין לספקלטור, זה אומר לו, אני כהן בן כהן גדול, הרגני
תחלה ואל אראה במיתת חבירי, וזה אומר לו, אני נשיא בן נשיא,
הרגני תחלה ואל אראה במיתת חבירי.

10. שהצדקה וגמילות חסדים שלום גדול ופרקליט גדול בין ישראל לאביהם
שבשמים.

11. משל, למה הדבר דומה? ללסטים שנכנסו לפלטין של מלך, בזזו נכסיו
והרגו פמליא של מלך והחריבו פלטרין של מלך. לאחר זמן ישב עליהן
המלך בדין, תפש מהם, הרג מהם, צלב מהם וישב בפלטין שלו. ואחר
כך נתודעה מלכותו בעולם.

12. וארון ברית י"נוסע לפניהם [במדבר י"לני], ... משל, לאנטיקיסר
שהיה מקדים לפני חיילותיו מתקן להם מקום שישרו. כך היתה השכינה
מקדמת לישראל ומתקנת להם מקום שישרו.

13. משל, למה הדבר דומה? למלך בשר ודם שגזר על בנו שלא יכנס לפתח
פלטרין שלו. נכנס לשער והוא אחריו, לחצר והוא אחריו, לטרקלין והוא
אחריו, כיון שבא ליכנס לקיטון אמר לו, בני, מכאן ואילך אתה אסור.

14. משל, למלך שהיו לו נכסים הרבה והיה לו בן קטן, והיה צריך לצאת
למדינת הים. אמר, אם אני מניח נכסי ביד בני הוא עומד ומבזבזם,
אלא הריני ממנה לו אפיטרופוס עד שיגדל. משהגדיל הבן ההוא אמר לו
לאפיטרופוס, תן לי כסף וזהב שהניח לי אבא בידך. עמד ונתן לו
משלו כדי פרנסתו. התחיל אותו הבן מיצר. אמר לו, הרי כל כסף וזהב
שהניח לי אבא בידך. אמר לו, כל מה שנתתי לך לא נתתי לך אלא
משלי, אבל מה שהניח לך אביך הריהו שמור.

15. משל, למלך שמסר את בנו לפידגוג והיה מחזרו ומראה אותו ואומר לו,
כל הגפנים האלו שלך, כל הזיתים האלו שלך. משיגע להראותו אמר
לו, כל מה שאתה רואה שלך הוא.

16. אמר יעקב לרחל, וכי אנטיקיסר של הקדוש ברוך הוא אני?

17. מיכאל וסמאל דומין לסניגור וקטיגור עומדין בדין. זה מדבר וזה
מדבר. גמר זה דבריו, ידע הסניגור שנצח, והתחיל משבח את הדיין
שיוציא איפופסין. בקש אותו קטיגור להוסיף דבר. אמר לו הסניגור,
החרש ונשמע מן הדיין.

18. משל, למלך שהיה דן את בנו, והיה קטיגור עומד ומקטרג. מה עשה
הפדגוג שלבן? כיון שראה אותו מחייב, דחף את הקטיגור ועמד לו
במקומו, מלמד על הבן סניגוריא.

19. בשר ודם משמוציא אפופסין אינו יכול לחזור.

20. אמר הקב"ה לישראל, בניי, אותם הקרבנות שהכתבתי לכם בתורה, היו
זהירין בהן, שאין פרקליט טוב לירידת הגשמים יותר מן הקרבנות.

Sources. 1. Abot 4.11. 2. Abot 4.16. 3. Ḥul 8.2. 4. Qid 4.14. 5. Sanh 10.2.
6. Soṭ 9.14. 7. Suk 2.9. 8. Yom 7.1. 9. ARN 38 (S 114). 10. TosPea 4.21.
11. Mek 15.18 (L 2.78–79). 12. SNm 82.2 (H 78). 13. SNm 134.5 (H 179–
180). 14. SDt 11 (F 19). 15. SDt 19 (F 31). 16. Tanḥuma (Buber) Wa-yeṣe'
19. 17. Exodus Rabbah 18.5. 18. Exodus Rabbah 43.1. 19. PesR 44. 20.
Pesiqta de Rab Kahana 427.

UNIT THIRTEEN

ADJECTIVES

I *Introductory text* (SDt 277 [F 295])

ואם איש עני הוא [דברים כד׳ יב׳] .אין לי אלא עני. עשיר מנין? תלמוד
לומר, ואם איש . אם כן, למה נאמר, עני? ממהר אני ליפרע על ידי עני
יותר מן העשיר.

If he is a poor person [Dt 24.12].

In my opinion, here only the poor person is spoken about. From where can it be deduced that the rich person is spoken about too?

From the text that says, If he is a person.

If that is so, why make mention of 'poor'?

I hasten to see to the cause of the poor before that of the rich.

1. Here is another typical example of rabbinic argumentation. The biblical text says that something given in pledge by a poor person must be returned before sunset. The rabbis understand that the prescription extends to every person, rich or poor, because the Bible says 'person'. The specifying of this person as poor implies that God defends the cause of the poor before that of the rich.

The argument is dramatically developed in the form of a dialogue.

II *Morphology*

2. RH adjectives adhere to the noun patterns used in BH. The most common are as follows:

קָטָל-type: גָּדוֹל 'great';

קָטִיל-type: זָהִיר 'cautious';

קָטוּל-type: passive participles;

קָטִיל-type: active participles;

קַטִּיל-type: צַדִּיק 'righteous';

קַטּוּל-type: חַנּוּן 'compassionate';

Suffixed with ﬢָ- or וֹ-: גַּמְלָן 'mature', אַחֲרוֹן 'latter';

Suffixed with ﬩- or ﬧִ-: gentilics and ordinal numbers.

III *Grammar and usage*

3. Used predicatively, an adjective agrees with its subject in number and gender.

Used attributively, in apposition to a noun, an adjective will agree with the noun in number and gender and will usually also share its determination, although RH is less consistent than BH in this matter (see Unit 3.6–9).

With collectives, adjective agreement is according to semantic sense, so that grammatically singular subjects can be accompanied by attributive or predicative adjectives in the plural. A regular example of this phenomenon is the name Israel, as in

יִשְׂרָאֵל מְשׁוּנִּים בַּמִּצְוֹת

Israel (i.e. the Israelites) are distinguished by (adherence to) the commandments (SNm 99.3 [H 99]).

4. Adjectives of the קְטִיל type often replace verbs, as in

מִי־שֶׁחָבִיב קוֹדֵם אֶת־חֲבֵירוֹ

Whoever is loved has preference over the rest (SDt 37 [F 70]).

This process affects stative verbs in particular and has led to textual inconsistency due to confusion on the part of scribes between such adjectives and participles as טָמֵא and [מְטַמֵּא], קוֹדֶשׁ and קָדֹשׁ, קְדֵשׁ, and טָהֵר and טָהוֹר, etc.

5. There are no special comparative or superlative forms of the adjective.

A. Comparison is usually effected through the preposition מִן, which follows the adjective and precedes the second term in a comparison, for example:

יוֹסֵף זָכָה לִקְבּוֹר אֶת אָבִיו, וְאֵין בְּאֶחָיו גָּדוֹל מִמֶּנּוּ ... מִי לָנוּ גָדוֹל מִיוֹסֵף?

Joseph deserved to bury his father, for there was none among his brothers greater than he .... Whom do we have greater than Joseph? (Soṭ 1.9)

The widespread RH phenomenon of the accumulation of particles has also affected this construction, leading to such forms as עַל מִן, for example

מעשה עגל קשה על מן הכל

The matter of the golden calf was graver than everything else (SDt 1 [F 6]).

B. יוֹתֵר 'more than', used adverbially, can strengthen a comparison, as in a late text, Abot 6.5,

גְּדוֹלָה תוֹרָה יוֹתֵר מִן הַכְּהֻנָּה וּמִן הַמַּלְכוּת

Greater is the Torah than priesthood and royalty,

but also in a tannaitic text like SNm 133.1 (H 176):

בשר ודם, רחמיו על הזכרים יותר מן הנקבות

Flesh and blood loves men more than women.

C. A variant of יוֹתֵר מִן is יְתֵר עַל, where יְתֵר functions as a genuine adjective, taking feminine and plural forms (יְתֵרָה עַל and יְתֵרוֹת עַל). The sense conveyed is always comparative, 'in excess of, more than', for example:

לֹא יֹאכַל פּוֹעֵל יָתֵר עַל שְׂכָרוֹ

The worker will not eat in excess of his wages (BM 7.5)

and

לֹא יִהְיוּ פִּרְצוֹת יְתֵרוֹת עַל הַבִּנְיָן

The empty spaces will be no greater than the built up areas (Erub 1.8).

D. The superlative is expressed through a characteristic construction of RH: adjective followed by -שֶׁבְּ ('the greatest that there is in, the greatest of', etc.), for example:

יוֹסֵף בֶּן יוֹעֶזֶר הָיָה חָסִיד שֶׁבַּכְּהֻנָּה

Joseph ben Joezer was the most pious of the priests (Ḥag 2.7);

שׁוֹטִים/שׁוֹטֶה שֶׁבָּעוֹלָם

The world's greatest fool (SDt 309 [F 348]; Mek 15.14 [L 2.71]);

הַחַלָּשִׁים שֶׁבָּכֶם ... הַגִּבּוֹרִים שֶׁבָּכֶם

The weakest among you ... the most valiant among you (SLv 26.8 [W 111a]);

טוֹב שֶׁבַּגּוֹיִם

The best of the gentiles (Mek 14.7 [L 1.201]).

The construction is often specified as שֶׁבְּיִשְׂרָאֵל 'of Israel', as in

וַאֲפִילוּ עָנִי שֶׁבְּיִשְׂרָאֵל לֹא יֹאכַל עַד שֶׁיֵּסֵב

Even the poorest Israelite will not eat unless he is sitting at table (Pes 10.1).

The same usage, albeit without relative pronoun, is found in LBH, at Ca 6.1, הַיָּפָה בַּנָּשִׁים 'the fairest of women', and, earlier, at Jg 6.15:

הַדַּל בִּמְנַשֶּׁה

The most wretched of Manasseh.

E. For the absolute superlative, מְאֹד 'very' is not employed in the Mishnah with the exception of Abot 4.4,

מְאֹד מְאֹד הֱוֵי שְׁפַל רוּחַ

Be extremely humble,

and Ber 9.5. In the *midrashim*, it only appears in quotations from Scripture.

F. A different way of expressing the superlative is through the repetition of a noun in a construct chain, a formation already known to BH in such phrases as 'holy of holies', 'song of songs', and 'God of gods and Lord of lords' (Dt 10.17), and is seen even in archaic poetry, for example, at Ps 68.34:

לָרֹכֵב בִּשְׁמֵי שְׁמֵי־קֶדֶם

To the one that rides through the remotest skies.

RH examples include the following:

חַמֵּי חַמִּים

Very hot waters (Ber 16a);

מֶלֶךְ מַלְכֵי הַמְּלָכִים הקב״ה

The king of kings of kings, the holy one, blessed be he (Abot 3.1; 4.22; Sanh 4.5),

והקול יורד משמי שמים לבין שני הכרובים

And the voice would descend from the highest heavens between the
two cherubim (SNm 58.1 [H 56]);

משה חכם חכמים גדול גדולים

Moses, the wisest and the greatest (SNm 134.5 [H 180]).

This form of expression is also used without *semikhut* but employing מִן
in a variety of constructions that are difficult to categorize, for example

אפילו נכנס אדם חדר לפנים מן החדר

Even when one entered the most secret of chambers (SNm 83.2 [H
80]).

IV *Phraseology*

6. יוֹתֵר מִכָּאן 'more than this, surpassing this', פָּחוֹת מִכָּאן 'less than this,
below this'; see examples of usage in the exercises and at Kil 4.4; 7.6; Ket
7.1; Kel 29.2,3,7, etc.

V *Vocabulary*

בּוּלִיטוֹס (βουλευτής) 'senator, councillor'
בִּיאָה 'entrance, (sexual) penetration, consummation'
דָּמִים 'price'
הִתְקַדֵּשׁ 'consecrate oneself, become betrothed', קִידּוּשִׁין 'betrothal'
טַבָּח 'butcher'
טִלְטֵל 'move, transfer'
כְּאִלּוּ 'as if'
מְשׁוּנֶּה (pu. participle of שׁנה) 'different, distinct'
פָּסוּק 'verse'
צָהַב 'defy, insult'
קִמְעָא '(a) little'
קִישּׁוּי 'difficulty, problem' (e.g. in labour)
שָׁבוּי (passive participle of שׁבה) 'captive'
שׁוֹטֶה 'foolish, stupid, crazed'
שָׁתַף 'participate in, associate with', שׁוּתָּף 'associate'

VI *Exercises*

‎1. אָמַר רַבִּי עֲקִיבָא, אֲפִלּוּ עֲנִיִּים שֶׁבְּיִשְׂרָאֵל, רוֹאִין אוֹתָם כְּאִלּוּ הֵם בְּנֵי חֹרִין
‎שֶׁיָּרְדוּ מִנִּכְסֵיהֶם, שֶׁהֵם בְּנֵי אַבְרָהָם יִצְחָק וְיַעֲקֹב.
‎2. רַבִּי אֱלִיעֶזֶר אוֹמֵר, אִם הָיָה אָרְכָּהּ יָתֵר עַל רָחְבָּהּ אֲפִלּוּ אַמָּה אַחַת, אֵין
‎מְטַלְטְלִין בְּתוֹכָהּ.

3. אֵין פּוֹדִין אֶת הַשְּׁבוּיִין יוֹתֵר עַל כְּדֵי דְמֵיהֶן, מִפְּנֵי תִקּוּן הָעוֹלָם. וְאֵין
מַבְרִיחִין אֶת הַשְּׁבוּיִין, מִפְּנֵי תִקּוּן הָעוֹלָם. רַבָּן שִׁמְעוֹן בֶּן גַּמְלִיאֵל
אוֹמֵר, מִפְּנֵי תַקָּנַת הַשְּׁבוּיִין. וְאֵין לוֹקְחִים סְפָרִים תְּפִלִּים וּמְזוּזוֹת מִן
הַגּוֹיִם יוֹתֵר עַל כְּדֵי דְמֵיהֶן, מִפְּנֵי תִקּוּן הָעוֹלָם.

4. עַד כַּמָּה הוּא נוֹתֵן לַפּוֹעֲלִים? עַד שְׁלִישׁ. יָתֵר מִכָּאן, קוֹצֵר כְּדַרְכּוֹ וְהוֹלֵךְ,
אֲפִלּוּ לְאַחַר הַמּוֹעֵד.

5. הַקּוֹרֵא בַתּוֹרָה לֹא יִפְחֹת מִשְּׁלֹשָׁה פְסוּקִים. לֹא יִקְרָא לַמְתַרְגְּמָן יוֹתֵר
מִפָּסוּק אֶחָד, וּבַנָּבִיא שְׁלֹשָׁה.

6. שְׁתֵּי הַלֶּחֶם נֶאֱכָלוֹת אֵין פָּחוּת מִשְּׁנַיִם, וְלֹא יָתֵר עַל שְׁלֹשָׁה.

7. כַּמָּה הוּא קִשּׁוּיָהּ? ... רַבִּי יוֹסֵי וְרַבִּי שִׁמְעוֹן אוֹמְרִים, אֵין קִשּׁוּי יוֹתֵר מִשְּׁתֵּי
שַׁבָּתוֹת.

8. בַּת שָׁלֹשׁ שָׁנִים וְיוֹם אֶחָד מִתְקַדֶּשֶׁת בְּבִיאָה, וְאִם בָּא עָלֶיהָ יָבָם, קְנָאָהּ ...
פָּחוּת מִכֵּן כְּנוֹתֵן אֶצְבַּע בָּעַיִן.

9. טוֹב שֶׁבָּרוֹפְאִים לְגֵיהִנָּם, וְהַכָּשֵׁר שֶׁבַּטַּבָּחִים שֻׁתָּפוֹ שֶׁל עֲמָלֵק. רַבִּי נְהוֹרַאי
אוֹמֵר, מַנִּיחַ אֲנִי כָּל אֻמָּנִיּוֹת שֶׁבָּעוֹלָם וְאֵינִי מְלַמֵּד אֶת בְּנִי אֶלָּא תוֹרָה,
שֶׁאָדָם אוֹכֵל מִשְּׂכָרָהּ בָּעוֹלָם הַזֶּה, וְהַקֶּרֶן קַיֶּמֶת לָעוֹלָם הַבָּא.

10. הַגָּדוֹל שֶׁבַּדַּיָּנִים אוֹמֵר, אִישׁ פְּלוֹנִי, אַתָּה זַכַּאי, אִישׁ פְּלוֹנִי, אַתָּה חַיָּב.

11. מֹשֶׁה זָכָה בְּעַצְמוֹת יוֹסֵף, וְאֵין בְּיִשְׂרָאֵל גָּדוֹל מִמֶּנּוּ ... מִי גָדוֹל מִמֹּשֶׁה שֶׁלֹּא
נִתְעַסֵּק בּוֹ אֶלָּא הַמָּקוֹם?

12. אֵיזֶהוּ דָבָר? עִיר הַמּוֹצִיאָה חָמֵשׁ מֵאוֹת רַגְלִי, וְיָצְאוּ מִמֶּנָּה שָׁלֹשׁ מֵתִים
בִּשְׁלֹשָׁה יָמִים זֶה אַחַר זֶה, הֲרֵי זֶה דֶבֶר, פָּחוּת מִכָּאן אֵין זֶה דֶבֶר.

13. וְכֹהֵן גָּדוֹל עוֹמֵד וּמְקַבֵּל וְקוֹרֵא ... וְגוֹלֵל אֶת הַתּוֹרָה וּמַנִּיחָהּ בְּחֵיקוֹ, וְאוֹמֵר,
יוֹתֵר מִמָּה שֶׁקָּרָאתִי לִפְנֵיכֶם כָּתוּב כָּאן.

14. זה הדבר אשר צוה י״י לקטו ממנו ... [שמות טז׳ טז׳]. אמרו, עכשיו
יצא נחשון בן עמינדב וביתו ומלקט הרבה, יצא עני שבישראל ומלקט
קימעא.

15. והכהן המשיח תחתיו מבניו יעשה אתה [ויקרא ו׳ טו׳], מלמד שיהא בן
קודם לכל שבעולם.

16. והלא הלכה עמהם באר במדבר והיתה מעלת להם דגים שמנים יותר
מצרכם?

17. הלא כבני כושיים אתם לי בני ישראל? [עמוס ט׳ ז׳]. וכי כושים היו?
אלא מה כושי משונה בעורו אף ישראל משונים במצוות יותר מכל
אומות העולם.

18. אל תוסף דבר אלי, עלה ראש הפסגה [דברים ג׳ כז׳]. מיכן היה רבי
אליעזר בן יעקב אומר, יפה תפלה אחת יתר ממאה מעשים טובים,
שבכל מעשיו של משה לא נאמר לו, עלה, ובדבר זה נאמר לו, עלה.

19. מנין אתה אומר שאם שמע אדם דבר מפי קטן שבישראל יהא בעיניו
כשומע מפי חכם?

20. משלו משל, למה הדבר דומה? לאחד שהיה עומד וצוהב כנגד בוליוטוס
בשוק. אמרו לו השומעים, שוטה שבעולם, כנגד בוליוטוס אתה עומד
וצוהב.

Sources. 1. BQ 8.6. 2. Erub 2.5. 3. Giṭ 4.6. 4. Kil 7.6. 5. Meg 4.4. 6. Men
11.9. 7. Nid 4.5. 8. Nid 5.4. 9. Qid 4.14. 10. Sanh 3.7. 11. Soṭ 1.9. 12.

Taa 3.4. 13. Yom 7.1. 14. Mek 16.16 (L 2.115). 15. SLv 6.15 (W 31d). 16.
SNm 95.1 (H 95). 17. SNm 99.3 (H 99). 18. SDt 29 (F 47). 19. SDt 41 (F
86). 20. SDt 309 (F 348).

UNIT FOURTEEN

NUMERALS

I *Introductory text* (SDt 329 [F 379])

ראו עתה כי אני אני הוא ואין אלהים עמדי. אני אמית ואחיה [דברים לב׳ לט׳].
זה אחד מארבע הבטחות שניתן להם רמז לתחית המתים, אני אמית ואחיה
[דברים לב׳ לט׳], תמות נפשי מות ישרים [במדמר כג׳ י׳], יחי ראובן ואל
ימות [דברים לג׳ ו׳], יחינו מיומים [הושע ו׳ ב׳].
שומע אני, מיתה באחד וחיים באחד.
תלמוד לומר, מחצתי ואני ארפא [דברים לב׳ לט׳]. כדרך שמכה ורפואה
באחד כך מיתה וחיים באחד.

See now that it is I, I myself, and there is no other God apart from me. I
give death and life [Dt 32.39]. This is one of the four promises in which allu-
sion is made to the resurrection of the dead:
  I give death and life [Dt 32.39];
  May I die the death of the just [Nm 23.10];
  May Reuben live and not die [Dt 33.6];
  In two days he will give us life [and on the third he will resuscitate
    us and we shall be revived in his presence] [Ho 6.2].
  I interpret [I give death and life] to mean that death refers to one and life
to another.
  But the text continues, I harm and I heal [Dt 32.39]. Just as injury and
cure are in reference to the same person, so also death and life apply to the
same person.

1. The resurrection of the dead is a basic tenet of Pharisaic Judaism,
which was opposed in Sadducean circles, where only Scripture was admitted
as authoritative, and by Hellenizers, who regarded the notion as absurd. Our
text presents the four testimonies ('promises' or 'securities' [הַבְּטָחוֹת]) of
Scripture in support of resurrection. And the possible interpretation of 'I give
life and death' as meaning simply that God allows death and birth is coun-
tered by reference to the parallel text: just as 'I harm and I heal' has to do
with the same person who is injured and then cured, so 'I give life and death'
must refer to one person who dies and is then resuscitated.

II *Morphology*

2. The following table displays the cardinal numbers in RH.

Number	Masculine nouns Absolute	Construct	Feminine nouns Absolute	Construct
one	אֶחָד	אַחַד	אַחַת	אַחַת
two	שְׁנַיִם	שְׁנֵי	שְׁתַּיִם	שְׁתֵּי
three	שְׁלֹשָׁה	שְׁלֹשֶׁת	שָׁלֹשׁ	שְׁלֹשׁ
four	אַרְבָּעָה	אַרְבַּעַת	אַרְבַּע	אַרְבַּע
five	חֲמִשָּׁה	חֲמֵשֶׁת	חָמֵשׁ	חֲמֵשׁ
six	שִׁשָּׁה	שֵׁשֶׁת	שֵׁשׁ	שֵׁשׁ
seven	שִׁבְעָה	שִׁבְעַת	שֶׁבַע	שֶׁבַע
eight	שְׁמֹנָה	שְׁמֹנַת	שְׁמֹנֶה	שְׁמֹנֶה
nine	תִּשְׁעָה	תִּשְׁעַת	תֵּשַׁע	תֵּשַׁע
ten	עֲשָׂרָה	עֲשֶׂרֶת	עֶשֶׂר	עֶשֶׂר

3. The numbers one and two are treated as adjectives that agree in gender with the noun being counted.

The numbers three to ten are nouns the gender of which is the opposite of the nouns being counted.

4. Ordinal numbers agree in gender with the noun being itemized. The only difference from BH is that the feminine of שֵׁנִי 'second' is not, as in BH, שֵׁנִית, but שְׁנִיָּה (plural שְׁנִיּוֹת), as at Qin 2.3:

הָרִאשׁוֹנָה וְהַשְּׁנִיָּה אֵין לָהֶם כְּלוּם

The first and the second have nothing.

III *Grammar and usage*

5. Cardinal numbers.

A. אֶחָד and אַחַת generally follow a noun whereas the other cardinal numbers will usually precede it.

B. When preceding a noun, שְׁנַיִם and שְׁתַּיִם usually appear in their construct state (שְׁנֵי and שְׁתֵּי), whereas other numerals can be used either in the construct, determined by the noun being counted (especially in measures, 'two of cors', 'four of logs', etc.), or, more normally, in the absolute state in apposition to the noun being counted:

שְׁנֵי יָמִים טוֹבִים שֶׁלְּרֹאשׁ הַשָּׁנָה

Two feast days of the new year (Shab 19.5);

הַכּוֹתֵב שְׁתֵּי אוֹתִיּוֹת, בֵּין בִּימִינוֹ בֵּין בִּשְׂמֹאלוֹ,
בֵּין מִשֵּׁם אֶחָד בֵּין מִשְּׁנֵי שֵׁמוֹת, בֵּין מִשְּׁנֵי סַמְמָנִיּוֹת בְּכָל לָשׁוֹן, חַיָּב

Whoever writes two letters, be it with the right hand or the left, one name or two, or with two inks, in any language is guilty (Shab 12.3);

שְׁלֹשָׁה אַחִין נְשׂוּאִין שָׁלֹשׁ נָכְרִיּוֹת

Three brothers married to three foreign women (Yeb 3.9);

אֲפִלּוּ בֵית חֲמֵשֶׁת כּוֹרִין, אֲפִלּוּ בֵית עֲשֶׂרֶת כּוֹרִין

Be it a space of five cors; be it a space of ten cors (Erub 2.3).

C. Thus, the noun being counted is to be understood either as determining a numeral in the construct state or as in apposition to a numeral in the absolute state. The noun being counted can also be viewed as an 'accusative of relation'. In this structure, the noun is in the singular if it follows the numeral and in the plural if it precedes the numeral, for example

עִיר הַמּוֹצִיאָה חֲמֵשׁ מֵאוֹת רַגְלִי

The city that provides five hundred foot-soldiers (Taa 3.4).

The following rule of usage is broadly true: the noun being counted is in the plural with the numbers two to nineteen and in the singular with the series twenty, thirty, and so on, up to ninety, and with the series one hundred, two hundred, and so on, up to nine hund d; with compound numbers of the kind twenty-four or two hundred and fou he noun is plural.

D. At times, however, the noun being ounted is singular, either because it denotes something that frequently appears in enumerations (month, year, portion, cubit, etc.) or because it is a generic term:

מְחוֹל הַכֶּרֶם, בֵּית שַׁמַּאי אוֹמְרִין, שֵׁשׁ עֶשְׂרֵה אַמָּה, וּבֵית הִלֵּל אוֹמְרִים, שְׁתֵּים עֶשְׂרֵה אַמָּה

Regarding the space around the vineyard, the school of Shammai say that it is six cubits and the school of Hillel say that it is twelve (Kil 4.1);

שְׁתֵּי הַלֶּחֶם נִלּוֹשׁוֹת אַחַת אַחַת

The two (loaves [חַלּוֹת] of) bread are kneaded on by one (Men 11.1; contrast 11.9).

E. Cardinal numbers can also be used on their own, with he thing being counted understood from context, or can take a pronominal suffix, thus developing a usage known from BH:

ת״ל, וזכרתי את בריתי יעקב ואף בריתי יצחק ואף את בריתי אברהם, מגיד ששלשתן שקולין

The passage teaches, And I shall remember my covenant with Jacob and my covenant with Isaac and my covenant with Abraham, declaring that the three are equal (Mek 12.1 [L 1.3]).

F. In certain contexts, numbers can be used adverbially:

עַד מָתַי חַיָּב לְהַכְרִיז? ... שִׁבְעָה יָמִים, כְּדֵי שֶׁיֵּלֵךְ לְבֵיתוֹ שְׁלֹשָׁה, וְיַחֲזֹר שְׁלֹשָׁה, וְיַכְרִיז יוֹם אֶחָד

How long is it necessary to proclaim [the discovery]? ... For seven days, so that he can go back home in three days, come back in three days, and proclaim it in one day (BM 2.6).

G. When one number is immediately followed by the next, an approximate figure is intended:

אילו היינו שם היינו משיבים לו ארבע וחמש פעמים על כל דבר ודבר

If we had been there we should have responded four or five times to
every issue (SDt 1 [F 3]);

למד שנים שלשה דברים ביום, שנים שלשה פרקים בשבת ...
נמצא מעשיר לאחר זמן

If he studied two or three words a day, two or three chapters a week,
in time he became rich (SDt 48 [F 108]).

6. Ordinal numbers.

A. From 'tenth' onwards, cardinal numbers are used, after the noun. The
following example illustrates the difference between שְׁלֹשִׁים יוֹם 'thirty days'
and יוֹם שְׁלֹשִׁים 'thirtieth day':

מִי שֶׁאָמַר, הֲרֵינִי נָזִיר, מְגַלֵּחַ יוֹם שְׁלֹשִׁים וְאֶחָד. וְאִם גִּלַּח לְיוֹם שְׁלֹשִׁים,
יָצָא. הֲרֵינִי נָזִיר שְׁלֹשִׁים יוֹם, אִם גִּלַּח לְיוֹם שְׁלֹשִׁים, לֹא יָצָא.

Whoever says, I shall be a Nazirite, may cut his hair on the thirty-
first day, but even if he cuts it on the thirtieth day, he has fulfilled
his obligation. [If he says], I shall be a Nazirite for thirty days, if he
cuts his hair on the thirtieth day, he has not fulfilled his obligation
(Naz 3.1).

B. When specifying days of the month in dates, יוֹם is usually omitted, as
occasionally in BH (see Meyer 1992, §61.4). Cardinal numbers are used with
-בְּ, even for the first to ninth days of the month:

זְמַן עֲצֵי כֹהֲנִים וְהָעָם תִּשְׁעָה, בְּאֶחָד בְּנִיסָן, בְּנֵי אָרַח בֶּן יְהוּדָה, בְּעֶשְׂרִים
בְּתַמּוּז, בְּנֵי דָוִד בֶּן יְהוּדָה, בַּחֲמִשָּׁה בְּאָב, בְּנֵי פַרְעשׁ בֶּן יְהוּדָה

There were nine times for the wood offering of the priests and the
people: the first of Nisan was for the descendants of Arah ben Judah, the twentieth of Tammuz was for the descendants of David ben
Judah, and the fifth of Ab for the descendants of Parosh ben Judah
(Taa 4.5).

C. Par 1.1 includes the forms שְׁלִישִׁית 'third' and שְׁלָשִׁית 'three-year old'
and רְבִיעִי 'fourth' and רְבָעִי 'four-year old'.

7. Distributives.

A. 'One each', 'two each', etc. is expressed by repeating the numeral,
usually without intervening -וְ:

שִׁשָּׁה [מִשְׁמָרוֹת] מַקְרִיבִין [כְּבָשִׂים] שְׁנַיִם שְׁנַיִם וְהַשְּׁאָר אֶחָד אֶחָד

Six priestly watches would offer two lambs each and the rest one
each (Suk 5.6).

B. A characteristic way of emphasizing distribution is by prefixing the
repeated numbers with כָּל־: כָּל־אֶחָד וְאֶחָד 'each one', כָּל־שְׁלֹשָׁה וּשְׁלֹשָׁה 'every
three', etc., although in this construction כָּל־ can also convey the sense of
'each and every'. Both usages are illustrated by the the following example
from RS 2.9:

אִם בָּאִין אָנוּ לָדוּן אַחַר בֵּית דִּינוֹ שֶׁלְּרַבָּן גַּמְלִיאֵל, צְרִיכִין אָנוּ לָדוּן אַחַר
כָּל בֵּית דִּין וּבֵית דִּין שֶׁעָמַד מִימוֹת משֶׁה וְעַד עַכְשָׁיו ... וְלָמָּה לֹא

נֶחְפְּרְשׁוּ שְׁמוֹתָן שֶׁל זְקֵנִים? אֶלָּא לְלַמֵּד שֶׁכָּל שְׁלֹשָׁה וּשְׁלֹשָׁה
שֶׁעָמְדוּ בֵית דִּין עַל יִשְׂרָאֵל הֲרֵי הֵם כְּבֵית דִּינוֹ שֶׁל מֹשֶׁה

If we were going to test the tribunal of Rabban Gamaliel, we should
have to test each and every one of the tribunals that have been established from the days of Moses until now .... And why were the
names of the elders not made explicit? It is to teach that any three
who established themselves as a tribunal in Israel were as if they
had re-established the tribunal of Moses.

The formula exemplified by כָּל יוֹם וָיוֹם first appeared in LBH, in contrast to
the classical BH structure of יוֹם יוֹם, and became common in the Dead Sea
Scrolls, Aramaic, and RH (see Qimron 1986, 81).

8. Fractions.

A. As in BH, an ordinal number may be used, with the fractional sense
provided by context: שְׁלִישׁי '(a) third', רְבִיעִי '(a) fourth', etc.

B. RH has also developed a special series of terms for fractions, some already known in BH:

Fraction	RH form
half	מֶחֱצָה, חֵצִי
third	שָׁלִישׁ
quarter	רוֹבַע, רְבִיעַ
fifth	חוֹמֶשׁ
sixth	שְׁתוּת
—	—
eighth	שָׁמִין
ninth	תִּישׁוּעַ
tenth	עִישׂוּר

C. Fractions of less than a tenth are expressed by cardinal numbers preceded by מִן '(out) of', for example אֶחָד מִשְּׁלֹשִׁים 'a thirtieth'.

9. To express repeated or multiple acts, RH employs the cardinal numbers followed by פַּעַם 'time' or פְּעָמִים 'times', as in

וְצָרִיךְ לְכַבֵּס שְׁלֹשָׁה פְעָמִים לְכָל אֶחָד וְאֶחָד

Each one has to be scrubbed three times (Nid 9.7).

פַּעַם and פְּעָמִים can sometimes be omitted but supplied from context, as in

הָיָה מִטַּמֵּא לַמֵּתִים כָּל הַיּוֹם, אֵינוֹ חַיָּב אֶלָּא אַחַת

If he is polluted by a corpse the whole day, he is only guilty the first
time (Naz 6.4).

10. RH also has *Pi'el* denominative verbs based on the numerals: שִׁלֵּשׁ
(in *Hif'il* and *Hitpa'el* as well) 'divide by three, pass three times' (e.g. Mak
1.3); רִבַּע 'square, do for the fourth time' (e.g. SDt 306); חִמֵּשׁ 'divide into
five parts'; תִּשַּׁע 'divide into nine parts'; and עִשֵּׂר 'tithe, take/give tithe' (e.g.
Shab 2.1).

IV *Phraseology*

11. אֶחָד ... וְאֶחָד 'be it like this ... or like that', an expression similar to
בֵּין שֶׁ- ... וּבֵין שֶׁ- 'whether ... or' (see Unit 8.12):

אֶחָד עֲשָׂרָה וְאֶחָד עֶשֶׂר רִבּוֹא

Whether they be ten or they be a hundred thousand (Ber 7.3);

אֶחָד אִילָן סְרָק וְאֶחָד אִילָן מַאֲכָל רוֹאִין אוֹתָן כְּאִלּוּ הֵם תְּאֵנִים

Be it a wild tree or a fruit tree, it is regarded as a fig tree (Shebi 1.3);

אחד עולה נדבה ואחד עולה חובה, זו וזו טעונות סמיכה

The voluntary burnt offering and the obligatory burnt offering are
the same: both require imposition of hands (SLv 1.4 [W 5d]).

12. כְּאֶחָד, כְּאַחַת 'jointly, at the same time, equally':

שְׁלֹשָׁה שֶׁאָכְלוּ כְּאֶחָד, הַיָּבִין לְזַמֵּן

When three eat together, they are obliged to summon another (Ber
7.1);

אבל הקב״ה אמר עשרת הדברות כאחד, מה שאי אפשר לבשר
ודם לעשות כן

The holy one, blessed be he, pronounced the ten commandments all
at once (or, 'by means of only one utterance'), something impossible for flesh and blood (Mek 15.11);

אין משקין שתי סוטות כאחת

One should not force two adulteresses to drink [the bitter waters] at
the same time (TosSoṭ 1.6).

13. הָאַרְבָּעִים 'the forty lashes', in reference to the punishment prescribed
at Dt 25.1–3 (see Mak 1.1; 3.10; Shab 7.2):

וְהָיְתָה שׁוֹתָה בַיַּיִן וּמִטַּמְּאָה לַמֵּתִים, אֵינָה סוֹפֶגֶת אֶת הָאַרְבָּעִים

And [a woman] drinking wine and polluting herself with corpses
does not incur the punishment of the forty lashes (Naz 4.3).

V *Vocabulary*

אַב בֵּית דִּין 'president of the Sanhedrin'

בְּעוּר 'removal, distancing'

הֵזִיד (hi. of זיד) 'act deliberately, with premeditation', as against שָׁגַג 'do by
mistake, inadvertently'

הֵסֵב (participle מֵסֵב; hi. of סָבַב 'surround') 'sit at (table)'

הֶעֱשִׁיר 'become rich'

חָל (root חול) 'occur'

יִסּוּר 'test, correction, (corrective) punishment, suffering that results from
punishment'

לִיתֵּן (infinitive of נתן) 'to give' (BH לָתֵת)

נָשִׂיא 'patriarch'

סִגֵּל 'save, keep'

סָמַךְ 'support, lay hands on'

פְּרַגְמַטְיָא (πραγματεία) 'business'

פֵּרַט 'specify, determine'

פִּרְנֵס 'sustain, provide for'

צֵרַף 'join, transform, change for'

שְׂרָרָה 'power, authority, command'

VI Exercises

1. כָּל הַמְחַלֵּל שֵׁם שָׁמַיִם בַּסֵּתֶר, נִפְרָעִים מִמֶּנּוּ בַּגָּלוּי, אֶחָד שׁוֹגֵג וְאֶחָד מֵזִיד בְּחִלּוּל הַשֵּׁם.

2. הָיוּ יוֹשְׁבִין לֶאֱכוֹל, כָּל אֶחָד וְאֶחָד מְבָרֵךְ לְעַצְמוֹ, הֵסֵבּוּ, אֶחָד מְבָרֵךְ לְכֻלָּן.

3. הָרִאשׁוֹנִים הָיוּ נְשִׂיאִים, וְהַשְּׁנִיִּים לָהֶם אֲבוֹת בֵּית דִּין.

4. כָּל סְאָה שֶׁיֵּשׁ בָּהּ רֹבַע מִמִּין אַחֵר, יְמַעֵט.

5. לֹא מָצְאוּ [אֵפֶר] מִשְּׁבַע [הַפָּרוֹת], עוֹשִׂין מִשֵּׁשׁ, מֵחָמֵשׁ, מֵאַרְבַּע, מִשָּׁלֹשׁ, מִשְׁתַּיִם, וּמֵאַחַת. וּמִי עֲשָׂאָן? הָרִאשׁוֹנָה עָשָׂה מֹשֶׁה, וְהַשְּׁנִיָּה עָשָׂה עֶזְרָא, וְחָמֵשׁ מֵעֶזְרָא וְאֵילָךְ, דִּבְרֵי רַבִּי מֵאִיר. וַחֲכָמִים אוֹמְרִין, שֶׁבַע מֵעֶזְרָא וְאֵילָךְ, וּמִי עֲשָׂאָן? שִׁמְעוֹן הַצַּדִּיק וְיוֹחָנָן כֹּהֵן גָּדוֹל עָשׂוּ שְׁתַּיִם שְׁתַּיִם, אֶלְיְהוֹעֵינַי בֶּן הַקּוֹף וַחֲנַמְאֵל הַמִּצְרִי וְיִשְׁמָעֵאל בֶּן פִּיאָבִי עָשׂוּ אַחַת אֶחָת.

6. כָּל מִצְוֹת הַבֵּן עַל הָאָב, הָאֲנָשִׁים חַיָּבִים, וְהַנָּשִׁים פְּטוּרוֹת, וְכָל מִצְוַת הָאָב עַל הַבֵּן, אֶחָד אֲנָשִׁים וְאֶחָד נָשִׁים חַיָּבִין.

7. וְשָׁלֹשׁ שׁוּרוֹת שֶׁלְּתַלְמִידֵי חֲכָמִים יוֹשְׁבִין לִפְנֵיהֶם, כָּל אֶחָד וְאֶחָד מַכִּיר אֶת מְקוֹמוֹ. הָיוּ צְרִיכִין לִסְמֹךְ, סוֹמְכִין מִן הָרִאשׁוֹנָה, אֶחָד מִן הָשְּׁנִיָּה בָּא לוֹ לָרִאשׁוֹנָה, וְאֶחָד מִן הַשְּׁלִישִׁית בָּא לוֹ לַשְּׁנִיָּה, וּבוֹרְרִין לָהֶן עוֹד אֶחָד מִן הַקָּהָל וּמוֹשִׁיבִין אוֹתוֹ בַּשְּׁלִישִׁית.

8. מִי שֶׁהָיוּ לוֹ פֵּרוֹת שְׁבִיעִית וְהִגִּיעַ שְׁעַת הַבִּעוּר, מְחַלֵּק מָזוֹן שָׁלֹשׁ סְעוּדוֹת לְכָל אֶחָד וְאֶחָד. וַעֲנִיִּים אוֹכְלִין אַחַר הַבִּעוּר, אֲבָל לֹא עֲשִׁירִים, דִּבְרֵי רַבִּי יְהוּדָה. רַבִּי יוֹסֵי אוֹמֵר, אֶחָד עֲנִיִּים וְאֶחָד עֲשִׁירִים אוֹכְלִין אַחַר הַבִּעוּר.

9. יוֹם טוֹב הָרִאשׁוֹן שֶׁלְּחַג שֶׁחָל לִהְיוֹת בַּשַּׁבָּת, כָּל הָעָם מוֹלִיכִין אֶת לוּלְבֵיהֶן לְבֵית הַכְּנֶסֶת. לַמָּחֳרָת מַשְׁכִּימִין וּבָאִין, כָּל אֶחָד וְאֶחָד מַכִּיר אֶת שֶׁלּוֹ, וְנוֹטְלוֹ.

10. נִשְׁתַּיְּרוּ שָׁם אַרְבָּעָה עָשָׂר כְּבָשִׂים לִשְׁמוֹנָה מִשְׁמָרוֹת. בַּיּוֹם הָרִאשׁוֹן, שִׁשָּׁה מַקְרִיבִין שְׁנַיִם שְׁנַיִם, וְהַשְּׁאָר אֶחָד אֶחָד.

11. הָאוֹכֵל תְּרוּמָה שׁוֹגֵג מְשַׁלֵּם קֶרֶן וָחֹמֶשׁ.

12. בראשית ברא אלהים את השמים ואת הארץ [בראשית א' א']. שומע אני, כל הקודם במקרא קודם במעשה. ת"ל, ביום עשות י' אלהים ארץ ושמים [בראשית ב' ד'], מגיד שׁשניהם שקולין כאחד.

13. ומקלל אביו ואמו ... [שמות כא' יז] ... משמע, שניהם כאחת, ומשמע, שניהם אחד אחד בפני עצמו עד שיפרוט לך הכתוב יחדיו.

14. ומנין ליתן את האמור בכולם בכל אחד ואחד?

15. רבי שמעון אומר, מה ת"ל, גמל גמל, שני פעמים? אחד גמל שנולד מן הגמלה ואחד גמל שנולד מן הפרה.

16. שלשה כתרים הם, כתר תורה וכתר כהונה וכתר מלכות ... ואם תאמר, מי

גדול משניהם?, היה רבי שמעון בן אליעזר אומר, מי גדול, הממליך או
המולך? הוי אומר, הממליך, העושה שרים או העושה שררה? הוי אומר
העושה שרים. כל עצמן של שני כתרים הללו אין באים אלא מכחה
של תורה.

17. חביבים יסורים ששלש מתנות נתנו להם לישראל שאומות העולם
מתאוים להן ולא נתנו להם אלא על ידי יסורים, ואלו הם, תורה וארץ
ישראל והעולם הבא.

18. רבי שמעון בן יוחי אומר משל, לשני אחים שהיו מסגלים ממון אחר
אביהם. אחד מצרף דינר ואוכלו, ואחד מצרף דינר ומניחו. זה שהיה
מצרף דינר ואוכלו נמצא אין ביד כלום, וזה שמצרף דינר ומניחו נמצא
מעשיר לאחר זמן. כך תלמידי חכמים, למד שנים שלשה דברים ביום,
שנים שלשה פרקים בשבת, שתים שלש פרשיות בחדש, נמצא מעשיר
לאחר זמן.

19. ויקרא יעקב אל בניו ... [בראשית מט' א'], מאחר שהוכיחם כל אחד
ואחד בפני עצמו, חזר וקראם כולם כאחד.

20. ומשה בן מאה ועשרים שנה [דברים לד' ז']. זה אחד מארבעה שמתו
בן מאה ועשרים שנה, ואלו הם, משה והלל הזקן ורבן יוחנן בן זכיי
ורבי עקיבה. משה היה במצרים ארבעים שנה ובמדין ארבעים שנה,
ופירנס את ישראל ארבעים שנה. הילל הזקן עלה מבבל בן ארבעים
שנה ושימש חכמים ארבעים שנה ופירנס את ישראל ארבעים שנה רבן
יוחנן בן זכיי עסק בפרגמטיא ארבעים שנה ושימש חכמים ארבעים
שנה ופירנס את ישראל ארבעים שנה. רבי עקיבה למד תורה בן
ארבעים שנה ושמש את חכמים ארבעים שנה ופירנס את ישראל
ארבעים שנה. שש זוגות ששנותיהם שוות, רבקה וקהת, לוי ועמרם, יוסף
ויהושע, שמואל ושלמה, משה והלל הזקן, ורבן יוחנן בן זכיי ורבי
עקיבה.

Sources. 1. Abot 4.4. 2. Ber 6.6. 3. Ḥag 2.2. 4. Kil 2.1. 5. Par 3.5. 6. Qid
1.7. 7. Sanh 4.4. 8. Shebi 9.8. 9. Suk 3.13. 10. Suk 5.6. 11. Ter 6.1. 12.
Mek 12.1. 13. Mek 21.17 (L 3.47). 14. SLv 3.5 (W 14c). 15. SLv 11.3. (W
48c). 16. SNm 119.3 (H 144). 17. SDt 32 (F 57). 18. SDt 48 (F 108). 19.
SDt 31 (F 53). 20. SDt 357 (F 429).

PART II

VERBS

UNIT FIFTEEN

CONJUGATIONS (*BINYANIM*)

I *Introductory text* (Ḥag 1.8)

מִקְרָא מְעָט וַהֲלָכוֹת מְרֻבּוֹת.

The biblical text is short but the oral legislation based on it is immense.

1. The text reflects a clear conviction that often the oral law goes well beyond what the Bible says—a freer rendering might be 'so much regulation from so little text'. From the same passage of the Mishnah comes the saying that various rules are 'like mountains hanging by a hair'. Thus, for some elements within rabbinic Judaism the legitimacy of a particular *halakhah* did not depend on its being explicitly mentioned in the Bible.

II *Morphology*

2. The following table displays the major conjugations (or *binyanim*) of the BH verb (rarer forms are omitted).

Simple	*Qal/Pa'al*	**Passive**	*Nif'al*
Causative	*Hif'il*	**Passive**	*Hof'al*
Intensive	*Pi'el*	**Passive**	*Pu'al*
		Reflexive	*Hitpa'el*

Each of these structures has a prefix (imperfect) and suffix (perfect) form, as well as infinitive, participial, imperative, jussive, and cohortative moods, which will be examined in the following units.

3. In comparison, the RH verb exhibits the following features.

A. The *Pu'al* disappears in all but the participle.

B. In the perfect, the *Hitpa'el* is replaced by a *Nitpa'al* conjugation, apart from with certain verbs, such as הִשְׁתַּחֲוָה 'bow down' and הִתְפַּלֵּל 'pray', where the *Hitpa'el* is still found in the perfect. In some instances a *Nittaf'al* form is probably attested (see Mishor 1983a, 205).

C. In *pe-nun* verbs, the *Nuf'al* emerges as the passive of *Qal*, and is regarded by some (for example, M. Moreshet [1980b]) as a special *binyan* of RH. At Soṭ 9.12, some manuscripts read וְנוּטַל טַעַם הַפֵּירוֹת 'the taste of the

fruits has disappeared', and in a liturgical text (the prayer אַתָּה יָצַרְתָּ), we find
וְנוּטַל כָּבוֹד מִבֵּית חַיֵּינוּ 'the glory has been removed from the house of our life'.
Possibly the same conjugation is also to be seen with other verbs, such as
נוּגְאֲלוּ 'they were redeemed' and נוּלְדָה 'she was born', and it may be that
quite often a form pointed as *Nif'al* ought to be corrected to *Nuf'al* (see
Waldman 1989, 121).

D. In certain verbs, the archaic causative conjugations in *Saf'el* and
Shaf'el (see Meyer 1992, §72.1D) reappear, probably under Aramaic influence.

E. Also due to Aramaic influence is the development of intensive
quadriliteral conjugations like *Pi'lel*, *Pilpel*, *Pir'el*, and *Pi'les*, for example
עִרְבֵּב 'mix, confuse' (root ערב), דִּקְדֵּק 'crush, examine in detail, carefully
enunciate' (root דקק), קִרְסֵם 'cut, prune' (root קסם), and פִּרְנֵס 'supply, sustain' (root פנס).

4. Morphologically, the RH *binyanim* coincide with those of BH, with
the following exceptions.

A. *Nif'al*. The loss of intervocalic -ה-, as part of the gradual weakening
of the gutturals, is seen in infinitives preceded by -לְ, so that, for example,
לְהִכָּרֵת 'to be cut off, exterminated' becomes לִיכָּרֵת and לְהִכָּנֵס 'to enter' becomes לִיכָּנֵס:

אני י׳ אלהיכם עתיד ליפרע

I am Y., your God, who will be avenged (SNm 115.5 [H 129]);

שאינן כשרין ליקרב

For they are not fit to be offered (SLv 1.3 [W 5d]).
The same trend is well-represented at Qumran (see Qimron 1986, 48) and
also evidenced in LBH: וּבְכָשְׁלוֹ 'and when he stumbles' (Pr 24.17).

B. *Pi'el*. In *ayin-waw* and *-yod* verbs, we find new forms such as קַיֵּים
'establish, maintain' (already seen in LBH; root קום), בַּיֵּישׁ 'shame, insult'
(root בוש), טַיֵּיב 'do good' (root טוב), etc., as part of a more general trend of
assimilation to the triradical pattern (see Waldman 1989, 120). Similarly, the
root שאר behaves as an *ayin-waw* verb in the formation of the *Pi'el*: שַׁיֵּיר
'leave, reserve' (see Introduction, 9.3).

C. *Pu'al*. In the participle (the only mood RH retains in this *binyan*),
loss of preformative *mem* is common, so that, for example, מְמוּעָט 'reduced'
becomes מוּעָט. The first form is characteristic of the Palestinian branch of
RH (K Ḥag 1.8), whereas the second is typical of Babylonian RH. However,
the Palestinian origins of מוּעָט are clearly evidenced by the appearance of
this form in the Dead Sea Scrolls.

D. *Nitpa'al*. This *binyan* is a fusion of the *Nif'al* and *Hitpa'el*. Its vocalization as *Nitpa'el* is an incorrect composite form of copyists and publishers—the Sefardi and Yemenite traditions have retained the original pronunciation in *a*. As in the BH *Hitpa'el*, the *taw* of the נִת- prefix undergoes
metathesis or assimilation before sibilants and dentals. For example, at Ket
1.8 and 7.6, Jastrow reads מִדַּבֶּרֶת 'becoming intimate with', that is, a

Hitpa'el participle (on the other hand, K [Yalon] has a simple *Pi'el*: מְדַבֶּרֶת 'speaking'). Similarly, at Orl 3.3, manuscripts alternate between מְקַדְּשִׁין 'sanctifying themselves' and מְקַדְּשִׁין 'making holy'. The switch from *Nif'al* to *Nitpa'al*, and vice-versa, was that much easier, and more confusing for copyists, as it did not require alteration of the consonantal text, for example נִמְלַךְ and נִמְלַךְ or נִטְמָא and נִטְמָא.

E. *Hif'il*. As in the *Nif'al* infinitive, so in the *Hif'il*, preformative -ה can disappear after -לְ, so that, for example, לְהַרְבּוֹת 'to increase' becomes לְרַבּוֹת, as in

או אם רצה לרבות ירבה?

Can he increase the number if he prefers? (SNm 107.12 [H 111])

But this feature is not found as consistently in the *Hif'il* as in the *Nif'al*, and there are numerous instances of the retention of *he*, at least in the written form of the language, for example לְהַחְמִיר 'to be rigorous, harden' and לְהָקֵל 'to be tolerant, mitigate', as in

רַבִּי יְהוֹשֻׁעַ וְרַבִּי עֲקִיבָא לֹא זָזוּ מֵאַרְבַּע אַמּוֹת, שֶׁרָצוּ לְהַחְמִיר
עַל עַצְמָן

Rabbi Joshua and Rabbi Akiba did not move more than four cubits, because they wanted to be rigorous with themselves (Erub 4.1).

There is a striking contrast between the text of TosSot 3.2 as it appears in MS Vienna, להראות קלונה 'to show her shame', and in MS Erfurt, לראות את קלנה, which appears to reflect the actual pronunciation. A BH example is provided by Jr 39.7:

לְבִיא אֹתוֹ בָּבֶלָה

To bring him to Babylonia.

F. *Hof'al*. It is a characteristic of RH that the BH *Hof'al* becomes *Huf'al*, with the *u* vowel sometimes written *plene* (-הו, -מו), doubtless because of the association of *u* with the passive (in the BH *Pu'al* and the *Qal* passive participle in קָטוּל). Of particular importance are the frequently-employed הֻתַּר and מֻתָּר '(it was) permitted', the *Hof'al* perfect and participle of נָתַר, as in

בָּשָׂר הַנִּכְנָס לַעֲבוֹדָה זָרָה מוּתָּר

Meat that is introduced into idolatrous worship is permitted (AZ 2.3).

G. The quadriliteral conjugations, usually intensive or causative in function (*Saf'el*, *Shaf'el*, *Pi'lel*, *Pilpel*, *Pir'el*, *Pi'les*) are inflected on the model of the *Pi'el*:

Infinitive	לְפַרְנֵס	לְשַׁחְרֵר
Perfect	פִּרְנֵס	שִׁחְרֵר
Imperfect	יְפַרְנֵס	יְשַׁחְרֵר
Participle	מְפַרְנֵס	מְשַׁחְרֵר
Imperative	פַּרְנֵס	שַׁחְרֵר.

Quadriliterals can also be patterned acording to other conjugations if necessary, for example מְשֻׁחְרָר and מְשֻׁחְרֶרֶת 'freed' (*Pu'al* participle) and נִשְׁתַּחְרָר
'he was freed' (*Nitpa'al* perfect).

III *Grammar and usage*

5. According to E.Y. Kutscher (1971, 1597), 'The exact meanings of the
different conjugations still remain to be clarified'. As a general rule, we may
say that the regular conjugations maintained the values they possessed in BH,
although certain usages specific to RH have to be borne in mind.

6. *Qal.* This is used as in BH, although Kutscher notes that an intransitive form like גָּדַלְתָּ, which could mean in BH either 'you were great' or 'you
became great, you grew', in RH can only have the second meaning ('became
great, grew'), with the stative sense of 'be great' expressed through the
adjective גָּדוֹל:

כָּל יָמַי גָּדַלְתִּי בֵּין הַחֲכָמִים

All my life, I grew up among the wise (Abot 1.17);

יְבָם קָטָן שֶׁבָּא עַל יְבָמָה קְטַנָּה, יִגְדְּלוּ זֶה עִם זֶה

If a levir who is still a minor has sexual relations with his sister-in-
law who is also a minor, they have to wait until both of them grow
up (Yeb 13.12).

SNm 133.2 (H 176) is especially interesting as it clearly exhibits the contrasting meanings:

בא הכתוב ללמדך שכל צדיק שגדל בחיק רשע ולא עשה כמעשיו ...
להודיעך כמה צדקו גדול שגדל בחיק רשע ולא עשה כמעשיו

This passage is intended to teach you that any righteous person who
grows up among the wicked and does not behave according to their
deeds ..., to show you how *great* is that person's righteousness,
who, although having *grown up* among the wicked, does not behave
according to their deeds.

7. *Nif'al.*

A. Passive, as in BH, for example in the common midrashic question
לָמָה נֶאֱמַר 'why was it said?'.

B. Reflexive, for example

בָּרִאשׁוֹנָה הָיָה נִטְמָן יוֹם שְׁנֵים עָשָׂר חֹדֶשׁ

In former times, he (the buyer) would hide himself on the (last) day
of the twelfth month (Arakh 9.4).

Note the striking use of וְנִמְצָא in the sense of 'turn out, end up', for example

מָכַר לוֹ חִטִּים יָפוֹת וְנִמְצְאוּ רָעוֹת

If he sold him wheat as good, but it turned out (to be) bad (BB 5.6),
a common exegetical idiom (see below, §12).

C. To this reflexive usage is added an element of reciprocity in the structure נֶחְלְקוּ 'they were divided, they disputed among one another', a form often found in the context of arguments or discrepancies among different schools, for example

וְאִם נֶחְלְקוּ לֹא נֶחְלְקוּ אֶלָּא עַל קֹהֶלֶת

Although they used to disagree, they would only disagree in respect of Ecclesiastes (Yad 3.5; see also MS 3.6, Erub 1.2, Ket 13.1–2, etc.).

D. Closely related to the reflexive usage is a subtle middle sense that appears in certain verbs, for instance נִזְכַּר 'remember', נִפְרַע 'collect payment, take revenge', נִכְנַס 'enter, get into, meet', and נִשְׁאַל 'consult, ask about, or for, oneself'. The following texts illustrate how these verbs are used:

הָיָה עוֹמֵד בַּתְּפִלָּה וְנִזְכַּר שֶׁהוּא בַעַל קֶרִי

If, when already standing for prayer, he remembers that he had had an involuntary ejaculation (Ber 3.5);

וְהַגַּבָּאִים ... נִפְרָעִים מִן הָאָדָם מִדַּעְתּוֹ וְשֶׁלֹּא מִדַּעְתּוֹ

The tax collectors get their payment whether it is paid willingly or not (Abot 3.16);

מִשָּׁעָה שֶׁהַכֹּהֲנִים נִכְנָסִים לֶאֱכוֹל בִּתְרוּמָתָן

From the moment the priests enter to eat their offerings (Ber 1.1);

מִי שֶׁנָּדַר בְּנָזִיר וְנִשְׁאַל לְחָכָם

Whoever had taken a Nazirite vow and consulted with a sage (Naz 5.3).

8. *Pi'el.*

A. The primarily intensive function of this *binyan* makes it appropriate for conveying repeated action. The distinction between הָלַךְ 'go' and הִלֵּךְ 'walk about, go to and fro' is characteristic of RH (although, surprisingly, N.M. Waldman [1989, 120] claims there is no difference in meaning). הִלֵּךְ, which is occasionally found in the Bible, as well as in Ben Sira and the Dead Sea Scrolls, occurs, for example, in the following passages:

שבשבילם הילכה שכינה בו ביום שלשים וששה מילין כדי שנכנסו ישראל לארץ

For because of them, the Shekhinah had to travel thirty-six miles in a single day so that the Israelites might enter the land (SNm 84.1 [H 80]);

רַבָּן גַּמְלִיאֵל וְרַבִּי אֶלְעָזָר בֶּן עֲזַרְיָה הִלְּכוּ אֶת כֻּלָּה

Rabban Gamaliel and Rabbi Eleazar ben Azariah went through (the boat) from top to bottom (Erub 4.1).

B. The *Pi'el* can also convey an inchoative sense, for example:

יוֹרֵד אָדָם לְתוֹךְ שָׂדֵהוּ וְרוֹאֶה תְּאֵנָה שֶׁבִּכְּרָה, אֶשְׁכּוֹל שֶׁבִּכֵּר, רִמּוֹן שֶׁבִּכֵּר

When someone goes down into his field and observes that the fig, the grape cluster, and the pomegranate have started to ripen (Bik 3.1).

C. Sometimes, however, the creation of a *Pi'el* form does not imply a new meaning but simply replaces a corresponding *Qal* that has lost its expressive power. On other occasions, the *Pi'el* is employed as a denominative, for example, at Shebi 2.2, יָבֵל 'prune', אָבֵק 'spread earth', and עִשֵּׁן 'fumigate, burn incense'.

D. Although often difficult to distinguish in sense from the *Hif'il* used causatively, a typical rabbinic usage of the *Pi'el* is declarative, as in the word-pairs טִיהֵר and טִמֵּא, usually 'declare pure' and 'declare impure' (rather than 'purify' and 'contaminate', the less frequent meanings) and זִכָּה and חִיֵּב, 'declare innocent' and 'declare guilty'. Both pairs are found at Bekh 4.4:

זִכָּה אֶת הַחַיָּב, וְחִיֵּב אֶת הַזַּכַּאי, טִמֵּא אֶת הַטָּהוֹר , וְטִהַר אֶת הַטָּמֵא,
מַה שֶּׁעָשָׂה עָשׂוּי

> If he declares the guilty innocent and the innocent guilty or the pure impure and the impure pure, whatever he has done is done.

Another interesting word-pair is מִיעֵט and רִיבָּה, 'diminish' and 'increase'—the first element is found in the following text from Taa 4.6:

מִשֶּׁנִּכְנַס אָב מְמַעֲטִין בְּשִׂמְחָה

> As soon as the month of Ab comes in, joy is diminished.

9. Hif'il. Apart from conveying its usual causative function, the *Hif'il* sometimes also expresses an inchoative element, as in נָתַן סֶלַע, וְהֶעֱשִׁיר 'he gave a coin and began to be rich' (Arakh 2.1). The *Hif'il* can also be used to express a change of state, for example יַחְכִּים 'make oneself wise'.

10. Hitpa'el, Nitpa'al.

A. Their basic function is to provide a reflexive or passive version of the *Pi'el*. The *Nitpa'al*, a cross between the *Hitpa'el* and *Nif'al*, is a reflection of the language's need to find ever more expressive structures.

B. A reflexive value is found in, for example,

הֱוֵי מִתְאַבֵּק בַּעֲפַר רַגְלֵיהֶם

> Cover yourself in the dust of their feet (Abot 1.4).

In this usage, there is a strong undertone of passivity, toleration, or giving permission ('let yourself be covered'), as at Abot 1.10:

וְאַל תִּתְוַדַּע לָרָשׁוּת

> And don't let yourself know (or, 'become familiar with') power.

C. An inchoative sense, expressing entry into a new condition or situation, can be appreciated in

הַבָּא עַל ... הַשִּׁפְחָה ... וְשֶׁנִּתְגַּיְּירוּ וְשֶׁנִשְׁתַּחֲרְרוּ

> Whoever has sexual relations with a slavegirl ..., whether of those who have become proselytes or who have obtained manumission (Ket 3.1).

D. Related to this inchoative usage is the expression of a middle value by the *Hitpa'el/Nitpa'al*, especially in verbs of thought or emotion such as 'fear', 'propose', 'desire', for example:

פתאום נתירא משה ופתאום נדבר עמו

> All of a sudden Moses was filled with terror and all of a sudden he was spoken to (by God) (SNm 102.1 [H 100]);

לֹא נִתְכַּוְּנוּ לְהַקְרִיב אֶלָּא מַה שֶּׁמָּקוֹם שׂוֹנֵא

They proposed only to offer what the omnipresent one hates (SDt
81 [F 147]);

גֶּזֶל וַעֲרָיוֹת שֶׁנַּפְשׁוֹ שֶׁלְּאָדָם מִתְאַוָּה לָהֶן וּמְחַמְּדָתָן

Robbery and fornication that a person craves and desires (Mak 3.15;
K reads a *Nitpaʿal*: וּמִתְחַמְּדָתָן).

A middle sense is also found in other verbs that appear to us to be active
or transitive, for example:

הִתְקַבַּלְתִּי מִמְּךָ מָנֶה

I have received from you a mina (Ket 5.1);

אַלְמָנָה ... נִתְקַבְּלָה כְּתֻבָּתָהּ

A widow ... who has received her dowry (Ket 11.4).

E. The *Hitpaʿel/Nitpaʿal* also expresses reciprocity, in verbs like נִשְׁתַּתֵּף
'associate with', נִתְעָרֵב 'mix with', or reconciliation, as in

וכשהודה ראובן על המעשה נתרצו לו [אשר] אחיו

When Reuben confessed the deed, his brothers were reconciled with
him (Asher)' (SDt 355 [F 420]).

11. *Safʿel, Shafʿel*. The few verbs that appear in these *binyanim* convey a
causative meaning. The most commonly encountered are שִׁעְבֵּד 'enslave' and
שִׁחְרֵר 'free'. The other quadriliteral *binyanim* also usually function as inten-
sive-causatives.

IV *Phraseology*

12. וְנִמְצָא, וְנִמְצְאוּ 'it turned out', indicating that the conclusion of something was a particular change or result:

מָכַר לוֹ חִטִּים יָפוֹת וְנִמְצְאוּ רָעוֹת ... רָעוֹת וְנִמְצְאוּ יָפוֹת ...
יַיִן וְנִמְצָא חֹמֶץ, חֹמֶץ וְנִמְצָא יַיִן

If he sells him wheat as good, but it turns out to be bad ..., or bad
and it turns out to be good ..., or wine that turns out to be vinegar or
vinegar that turns out to be wine (BB 5.6).

In exegesis, the formula וְנִמְצֵאתָ מְקַיֵּם 'and so you find yourself fulfilling'
usually concludes a successful attempt at harmonizing two apparently contradictory texts (see, for example, SNm 84.2 [H 80]).

13. מִדַּת פּוּרְעָנוּת מְמוּעֶטֶת 'the measure of punishment is restrictive',
מִדַּת הַטּוֹב מְרוּבָּה 'the measure of mercy is expansive' (see SNm 18.1, 115.5
[H 129], 156, 160.13, Mek 12.33 [L 1.103] etc.); these formulas, which al-
lude to the divine attributes (*middot*), are employed in *a fortiori* arguments as
an interpretative axiom—interpretative principles must accord with divine
principles/attributes.

14. נְכָסִים מְשֻׁעְבָּדִים 'mortgaged property', as against נְכָסִים בְּנֵי־חֹרִין 'free,
unmortgaged property':

הַמַּלְוֶה אֶת חֲבֵרוֹ בִּשְׁטָר, גּוֹבֶה מִנְּכָסִים מְשֻׁעְבָּדִים. עַל יְדֵי עֵדִים,

גּוֹבֶה מִנְּכָסִים בְּנֵי חֹרִין

A person who lends to another on the basis of a bond, that person may claim back the loan from mortgaged property. If it was done with witnesses, the lender may claim back the loan from unmortgaged goods (BB 10.8).

V *Vocabulary*

גָּלוּי (passive participle of נִגְלָה) 'revealed'; בַּגָּלוּי–בַּסֵּתֶר 'in secret–in public'

הֵימֶנּוּ (= מִמֶּנּוּ) 'from him'

הִסְתַּכֵּל (htp. of סכל) 'observe, consider'

הָעֶרְיָה 'sexual contact'

זִיבָה 'venereal disease'

כְּלַפֵּי 'towards, against'

מַאֲמָר 'word, command, order'

מָקַק 'perish, decay'

נָדַר 'vow', נָדַר מִן הָעִיר 'vow not to go to the city'

סָבַר 'hope, think, imagine'

עִבּוּר 'city boundary'

עַל אַחַת כַּמָּה וְכַמָּה 'how much more in a similar situation!', an elliptical formula that replaces the conclusion of an *a fortiori* argument

הֶעֱלָה עַל 'impute to'; מַעֲלֶה עָלָיו הַכָּתוּב כְּאִלּוּ 'the passage treats him as though'

פִּרְסֵם 'divulge, make public, publish'

צָעַר 'distress'

רַוָּק 'single, unmarried'

שָׁלַט 'rule'

שִׁמֵּשׁ 'serve'

תְּחוּם 'district, area'

VI *Exercises*

1. הוּא הָיָה אוֹמֵר, כָּל שֶׁמַּעֲשָׂיו מְרֻבִּין מֵחָכְמָתוֹ, חָכְמָתוֹ מִתְקַיֶּמֶת, וְכָל שֶׁחָכְמָתוֹ מְרֻבָּה מִמַּעֲשָׂיו, אֵין חָכְמָתוֹ מִתְקַיֶּמֶת.

2. בַּעֲשָׂרָה מַאֲמָרוֹת נִבְרָא הָעוֹלָם. וּמָה תַלְמוּד לוֹמַר [לוֹמַר K lacks]?! וַהֲלֹא בְמַאֲמָר אֶחָד [הָיָה K +] יָכוֹל לְהִבָּרְאוֹת? אֶלָּא לְהִפָּרַע מִן הָרְשָׁעִים, שֶׁמְּאַבְּדִין [שֶׁהֵן מְאַבְּדִין K] אֶת הָעוֹלָם שֶׁנִּבְרָא בַעֲשָׂרָה מַאֲמָרוֹת, וְלִתֵּן שָׂכָר טוֹב לַצַּדִּיקִים, שֶׁמְּקַיְּמִין [שֶׁהֵן מְקַיְּמִין K] אֶת הָעוֹלָם שֶׁנִּבְרָא בַעֲשָׂרָה מַאֲמָרוֹת.

3. אָמַר רַבִּי יוֹסֵי בֶן קִיסְמָא, פַּעַם אַחַת הָיִיתִי מְהַלֵּךְ בַּדֶּרֶךְ, וּפָגַע בִּי אָדָם אֶחָד, וְנָתַן לִי שָׁלוֹם וְהֶחֱזַרְתִּי לוֹ שָׁלוֹם.

4. הַקּוֹרֵא אֶת שְׁמַע וְלֹא הִשְׁמִיעַ לְאָזְנוֹ, יָצָא ... קָרָא וְלֹא דִקְדֵּק בְּאוֹתִיּוֹתֶיהָ,

רַבִּי יוֹסֵי אוֹמֵר, יָצָא.

5. נִתְגָּרְשָׁה הָאִשָּׁה, נִשְׁתַּחְרֵר הָעֶבֶד, חַיָּבִין לְשַׁלֵּם.

6. עֶבֶד שֶׁנִּשְׁבָּה וּפְדָאוּהוּ, אִם לְשׁוּם [לְשֵׁם K] עֶבֶד, יִשְׁתַּעְבֵּד. אִם לְשׁוּם [לְשֵׁם K] בֶּן חֹרִין, לֹא יִשְׁתַּעְבֵּד. רַבָּן שִׁמְעוֹן בֶּן גַּמְלִיאֵל אוֹמֵר, בֵּין כָּךְ וּבֵין כָּךְ, יִשְׁתַּעְבֵּד.

7. מִי שֶׁיֵּשׁ לוֹ אוֹכְלִים מְרֻבִּים וּנְכָסִים מְעַטִּים [מְמוּעָטִים K], מֵבִיא שְׁלָמִים מְרֻבִּים וְעוֹלוֹת מְעַטּוֹת [מְמוּעָטוֹת K], נְכָסִים מְרֻבִּים וְאוֹכְלִים מְעַטִּין, מֵבִיא עוֹלוֹת מְרֻבּוֹת וּשְׁלָמִים מְעַטִּין.

8. הַנּוֹדֵר מִן הָעִיר, מֻתָּר לִכָּנֵס לַתְּחוּמָהּ שֶׁלָּעִיר, וְאָסוּר לִכָּנֵס לָעִבּוּרָהּ.

9. רַבִּי שִׁמְעוֹן בֶּן אֶלְעָזָר אוֹמֵר, רָאִיתָ מִיָּמֶיךָ חַיָּה וָעוֹף שֶׁיֵּשׁ לָהֶם אֻמָּנוּת? וְהֵן מִתְפַּרְנְסִין שֶׁלֹּא בְצַעַר, וַהֲלֹא לֹא נִבְרְאוּ אֶלָּא לְשַׁמְּשֵׁנִי, וַאֲנִי נִבְרֵאתִי לְשַׁמֵּשׁ אֶת קוֹנִי, אֵינוֹ דִין שֶׁאֶתְפַּרְנֵס שֶׁלֹּא בְצַעַר?

10. וְהָיָה כַּאֲשֶׁר יָרִים מֹשֶׁה יָדוֹ וְגָבַר יִשְׂרָאֵל ... [שמות י״ז י״א]. וְכִי יָדָיו שֶׁלְּמֹשֶׁה עוֹשׂוֹת מִלְחָמָה אוֹ שׁוֹבְרוֹת מִלְחָמָה? אֶלָּא לוֹמַר לָךְ, כָּל זְמַן שֶׁהָיוּ יִשְׂרָאֵל מִסְתַּכְּלִים כְּלַפֵּי מַעְלָה וּמְשַׁעְבְּדִין לִבָּם לַאֲבִיהֶם שֶׁבַּשָּׁמַיִם, הָיוּ מִתְגַּבְּרִים, וְאִם לָאו, הָיוּ נוֹפְלִים.

11. עֲשֵׂה לְךָ שָׂרָף וְשִׂים אֹתוֹ עַל־נֵס, וְהָיָה כָּל־הַנָּשׁוּךְ וְרָאָה אֹתוֹ וָחָי [במדבר כא׳ ה׳]. וְכִי נָחָשׁ מֵמִית, אוֹ נָחָשׁ מְחַיֶּה? אֶלָּא בִּזְמַן שֶׁיִּשְׂרָאֵל מִסְתַּכְּלִים כְּלַפֵּי מַעְלָה וּמְשַׁעְבְּדִין אֶת לִבָּם לַאֲבִיהֶן שֶׁבַּשָּׁמַיִם, הָיוּ מִתְרַפְּאִים, וְאִם לָאו, הָיוּ נִמּוֹקִים.

12. לְפִיכָךְ נִבְרָא אָדָם יְחִידִי, לְלַמֶּדְךָ שֶׁכָּל הַמְאַבֵּד נֶפֶשׁ אַחַת מִיִּשְׂרָאֵל מַעֲלֶה עָלָיו הַכָּתוּב כְּאִלּוּ אִבֵּד עוֹלָם מָלֵא, וְכָל הַמְקַיֵּם נֶפֶשׁ אַחַת מִיִּשְׂרָאֵל מַעֲלֶה עָלָיו הַכָּתוּב כְּאִלּוּ קִיֵּם עוֹלָם מָלֵא.

13. הַכֹּל מִטַּמְּאִין בַּזִּיבָה, אַף הַגֵּרִים. אַף הָעֲבָדִים, בֵּין מְשֻׁחְרָרִין בֵּין שֶׁאֵינָן מְשֻׁחְרָרִין.

14. משה אמר, ומת כל בכור בארץ מצרים [שמות יא׳ ה׳], והיו סבורין שכל מי שיש לו ארבעה או חמישה בנים אין מת אלא הבכור שבהם. והם לא היו יודעין שנשיהם חשודות על העריות והיו כולן בכורות מרווקין אחרים. הן עשו בסתר והמקום פרסמן בגלוי. והרי הדברים קל וחמר, ומה אם מדת הפורענות מעוטה העושה בסתר המקום מפרסמו בגלוי, מדה טובה מרובה על אחת כמה וכמה.

15. שמעון בן יוחי אומר, משלו משל, למה הדבר דומה? לאחד שהיה מהלך בדרך ופגע בו זאב, וניצל ממנו והיה מהלך ומספר מעשה הזאב. פגע בו ארי וניצל הימנו, שכח מעשה זאב והיה מהלך ומספר מעשה ארי. פגע בו נחש וניצל ממנו, שכח מעשה שניהם והיה מהלך ומספר מעשה נחש. כך ישראל, צרות האחרונות משכחות הראשונות.

16. וכן אתה מוצא שכל אומה ולשון שששיעבדה את ישראל, שלטה מסוף העולם ועד סופו בשביל כבודן של ישראל.

17. למה הדבר דומה? למלך בשר ודם שהיה מהלך בדרך ונהג אוהבו עמו. כשהוא נוסע אומר, איני נוסע עד שיבא אוהבי, וכשהוא חונה אומר, איני חונה עד שיבא אוהבי. נמצאת מקיים, על פי משה יחנו, ונמצאת מקיים, על פי י׳ יחנו, ועל פי משה יסעו, ועל פי י׳ יסעו.

18. אני י׳ אלהיכם, אני עתיד לשלם לכם שכר. אני י׳ אלהיכם, עתיד ליפרע.

19. למה נאמר עני ואביון [דברים כד׳ יד׳]? ממהר אני ליפרע על ידי עני

ואביון יותר מכל אדם.

20. והסלים והבכורים ניתנים לכהנים בשביל לרבות מתנה לכהנים.

Sources. 1. Abot 3.9. 2. Abot 5.1. 3. Abot 6.9. 4. Ber 2.3. 5. BQ 8.4. 6. Giṭ
4.4. 7. Ḥag 1.5. 8. Ned 7.5. 9. Qid 4.14. 10. RS 3.8. 11. RS 3.8. 12. Sanh
4.5. 13. Zab 2.1. 14. Mek 12.33 (L 1.103). 15. Mek 13.2 (L 1.133). 16.
Mek 14.5 (L 1.196). 17. SNm 84.2 (H 80). 18. SNm 115.5 (H 129). 19.
SDt 278 (F 296). 20. SDt 300 (F 318).

UNIT SIXTEEN

TENSES AND MOODS

I *Introductory text* (PRE 12)

אמר הקב״ה למלאכי השרת, בואו ונגמול חסד לאדם הראשאן ולעזרו ,
שעל מדת גמילות חסדים העולם עומד. אמר הקב״ה, חביבה גמילות חסדים
מזבחים ועולות שישראל עתידים להקריב לפני על גבי המזבח שנאמר,
כי חסד חפצתי ולא זבח [הושע ו׳ ו׳].

The holy one, blessed be he, said to the ministering angels, Come, let us
exercise mercy towards the first man and his spouse, for the world is founded
on the attribute of deeds of mercy. The holy one, blessed be he, said, Deeds
of mercy are more cherished than the sacrifices and burnt offerings that the
Israelites have to present to me on the altar, as it is written, For I desire
mercy and not sacrifice [Ho 6.6].

1. For the nature of 'deeds of mercy' or 'acts of kindness', see Unit 5.1
and the corresponding introductory text, ARN 4 (S 21). The PRE text above,
which presents God as a model for humans to follow, officiating at, and help-
ing to celebrate, a wedding, continues the prophetic and tannaitic emphasis
on charity. It is significant that in the Gospel of John, Jesus begins his min-
istry by attending a wedding and assisting the newly-weds (Jn 2.1–11).

II *Morphology*

2. Note that in this and the following units, we shall concentrate on the
Qal of the regular, or 'strong', verb.
    BH distinguishes the following tenses and moods:

Prefix conjugation (imperfect), according to the model יִקְטֹל (originally יַקְטֵל);

Suffix conjugation (perfect), according to the model קָטַל;

Cohortative, a lengthened form of the first person imperfect: נִקְטְלָה ,אֶקְטְלָה;

Jussive, an abbreviated form, where possible, of the second and third persons of the imperfect;

Infinitive absolute, according to the underlying model קָטֹל : קָטוֹל;

Imperative;

Infinitive construct, which normally follows the underlying models קְטֹל or קָטֵל, קְטוֹל;

Active participle, according to the underlying model קָטֵיל : כּוֹתֵב;

Stative participle, according to the model קָטֵיל : כָּבֵד;

Passive participle, according to the model קָטוּל : כָּתוּב.

3. In contrast, RH does not use special forms for the cohortative or jussive and does not employ the infinitive absolute.

4. In the morphology of the perfect, RH witnesses to the following changes.

A. Alongside קָטְלָה, the *plene* variant קָטְלָה is common, as in:

הא ותרה כל מה שעשיתה לי, זה קשה עלי יותר מן הכל

See that although there are many things you have done to me, this is much more serious for me than anything else (SDt 1 [F 6]).

The ending חה- is standard at Qumran and is attested in archaic BH:

יָרֵחַ וְכוֹכָבִים אֲשֶׁר כּוֹנָנְתָּה

Moon and stars, which you established (Ps 8.4);

כֹּל שַׁתָּה תַּחַת־רַגְלָיו

Everything you placed beneath his feet (Ps 8.7);

אַתָּה כוֹנַנְתָּה

You established it (Ps 68.10).

We find the same form reading in K, although it has been replaced in printed versions, for example, K Eduy 6.3:

מָה רָאִיתָה לַחֲלוֹק מִידָתָךְ

What is your basis for differentiating your norm (i.e. establishing a different norm)?

Contrast the text of Albeck, quoted at Unit 5.13.

B. In *lamed-he* and *-yod* verbs, the third person feminine singular retains the archaic ending in ת־, thus הָיָת 'she was' (as well as הָיְתָה). The same phenomenon has sometimes escaped copyists' correction in related types of verbs, such as *lamed-alef*, for example

פָּרָה שֶׁשָּׁתָת מֵי חַטָּאת

The cow that has drunk the waters of purification (Par 9.5).

The shift of final *mem* to *nun* (see Unit 10.5A) means that the difference between masculine and feminine versions of the second person plural has disappeared, with קְטַלְתֶּן as the common form. The use of final *mem* in

manuscripts and printed editions often represents correction or deliberate archaizing.

5. In the morphology of the imperfect, the following changes can be
seen in RH.

A. Continuing a process already underway in BH, complete disappearance of the archaic second and third person feminine plural form תִּקְטֹלְנָה,
which is replaced by the corresponding masculine forms תִּקְטְלוּ (second person) and יִקְטְלוּ (third person).

B. Even when their Aramaic counterpart has exactly the same form, BH
forms of the verb with final *nun*, such as the second person feminine singular
תִּקְטְלִין, have almost entirely disappeared from RH, although the second and
third person masculine plural forms תִּקְטְלוּן and יִקְטְלוּן are occasionally employed in addition to the regular structures תִּקְטְלוּ and יִקְטְלוּ.

C. Although there is no linguistic reason for it, the יִקְטֹל conjugation is
usually vocalized *plene*, thus אֶקְטוֹל, a phenomenon also observed at Qumran.

6. Participle.

A. In the active participle, RH prefers the feminine ending *-et*, with the
exception of *ayin-waw* verbs (for example בָּאָה from בוא) and, sometimes,
lamed-yod and *-alef* verbs (see Part II of Unit 19 for more details).

B. In the masculine plural, endings in both *mem* and *nun* are found.

7. Imperative.

The archaic form קְטֹלְנָה has disappeared from RH, leaving only קִטְלוּ
for both the masculine and feminine plural. *Plene* orthography is normally
employed, thus קְטוֹל.

8. Infinitive.

A. Of the two BH infinitives, only the construct is attested in RH, always
with prefixed *lamed*, to which any other relevant preposition (normally מִן) is
prefixed, for example אָסוּר מִלְהַכְנִיס וּמִלְהוֹצִיא 'prohibited from putting in or
taking out' (Erub 2.6). Similarly, negation of an infinitive is expressed by
placing שֶׁלֹּא in front of the *lamed*, as in

מָקוֹם שֶׁנָּהֲגוּ שֶׁלֹּא לַעֲשׂוֹת [מְלָאכָה], אֵין עוֹשִׂים

Where it is not usual to do (work), it is not done (Pes 4.1).

B. As a general rule, the infinitive construct (like the imperative) takes
the form of the imperfect without prefix, thus imperfect אֶקְטוֹל, infinitive
קְטוֹל (with *plene* spelling preferred). The systematic application of this principle has led to the emergence of popular forms considerably different from
those of BH. Below are some examples (see Unit 20.3 for further details).

Perfect	Imperfect	Infinitive	
		RH	BH
נָתַן	יִתֵּן	לִיתֵּן	לָתֵת
יָדַע	יֵדַע	לֵידַע	לָדַעַת
לָקַח	יִקַּח	לִיקַּח	לָקַחַת
אָמַר	יֹאמַר	לוֹמַר	לֵאמֹר

9. Summary paradigm of the *Qal* of the regular verb.

Perfect		Imperfect	
קָטַלְתִּי		אֶקְטוֹל	(אֶקְטְלָה + BH)
קָטַלְתָּה/קָטַלְתָּ		תִּקְטוֹל	
קָטַלְתְּ		תִּקְטְלִי	
קָטַל		יִקְטוֹל	
קָטְלָה/קָטְלָה		תִּקְטוֹל	
קָטַלְנוּ		נִקְטוֹל	(נִקְטְלָה + BH)
קָטַלְתֶּן	(קְטַלְתֶּם + BH)	תִּקְטְלוּן	(תִּקְטֹלְנָה + BH)
קָטְלוּ		יִקְטְלוּן	(תִּקְטֹלְנָה + BH)

Participle	Infinitive	Imperative	
קוֹטֵל, קוֹטֶלֶת	לִקְטוֹל	קְטוֹל	(קִטְלָה + BH)
קוֹטְלִין/ים, קוֹטְלוֹת		קִטְלִי	
		קִטְלוּ	(קְטֹלְנָה + BH)

RH can also employ pausal forms in the perfect, for example אָמָר and אָכְלוּ, and the imperfect, for example תִּקְטוֹלוּ, יִקְטוֹלוּ (see Bar-Asher 1990c).

III *Grammar and usage*

10. Nowadays, scholars prefer to speak of the prefix (imperfect) and suffix (perfect) conjugations of classical BH, and avoid the term 'tenses', since in Hebrew and other Canaanite languages it appears to have been *aspect*—narrative, intensive, durative, jussive, energic, punctual—that predominated in the verbal system. In Hebrew the introduction of the suffix conjugation (in essence, an adjective plus personal pronoun) meant that this structure took on, for example, preterite and narrative aspects, previously expressed through the prefix conjugation. But the earlier system is still visible in structures that employ the so-called *waw*-conversive, a convenient but rather superficial term that disguises the consecutive or narrative function of such forms and the essentially modal and narrative basis of the two conjugations.

11. According to E.Y. Kutscher (1982, 130), '[t]he most revolutionary change between BH and MH [Mishnaic Hebrew] occured in the area of the tenses and moods'. Typical of RH is the culmination of a trend begun in LBH, namely, the disappearance of the *waw*-conversive forms. The narrative mood, as well as other modal aspects such as finality, command, etc., find other means of expression in RH.

12. In RH, we may indeed speak of a system of tenses, although it is an oversimplification to discount the modal aspects that remain. With A. Bendavid (1967, §222), we may say that the forms (*surot*) of the conjugational patterns (*mishqalim*) do not necessarily or exclusively refer to specifications of time (*mashma'im zemanim*), in other words, that it is not possible, even in RH, simply to identify every קָטַל as past (*'avar*), every קָטִיל as present (*howeh*), and every יְקַטֵל as future (*'atid*). However, the following general principles may be stated.

A. The perfect covers the area of past activity. However, M.H. Segal (1927, §306) overstates his claim that forms like יָדַעְתִּי can never have present significance in RH, for, in fact, we find in rabbinic literature certain idiomatic turns of phrase, such as אַתָּה אָמַרְתָּ, in which the present is clearly signified (see Unit 17.9).

B. The participle refers to the present and the future, as in:

עַל שְׁלֹשָׁה דְבָרִים הָעוֹלָם עוֹמֵד

On three things the world rests (Abot 1.2);

רוּחַ הַקֹּדֶשׁ מְבִיאָה לִידֵי תְחִיַּת הַמֵּתִים וּתְחִיַּת הַמֵּתִים בָּאָה עַל יְדֵי
אֵלִיָּהוּ זָכוּר לְטוֹב

The holy spirit *brings about* the resurrection of the dead and the resurrection of the dead *will come* through Elijah, of blessed memory (Soṭ 9.15).

Often, the participle can have an imperative or facultative/jussive significance:

הָאִישׁ מַדִּיר אֶת בְּנוֹ בַּנָּזִיר, וְאֵין הָאִשָּׁה מַדֶּרֶת אֶת בִּנָהּ בַּנָּזִיר

A man may make his son take a Nazirite vow, a woman may not make her daughter take it (Naz 4.6);

מַזְכִּירִין יְצִיאַת מִצְרַיִם בַּלֵּילוֹת

During the nights, the exodus from Egypt should be remembered (Ber 1.5).

For further details about the participle in RH, see Unit 19.

C. The imperfect can refer to the future, especially in subordinate clauses that in other languages might employ a subjunctive form of the verb, and conveys command and intention as aspectual features as well as expressing the jussive mood (see Mishor 1983a and Sharvit 1980). Kutscher (1982, 131) summarizes thus: 'The imperfect denoting the future tense is mainly restricted to the subordinate clause; in the main clause it is chiefly used to indicate desire or command'. Examples include:

וְכֵן לֹא יֹאמְרוּ שְׁנֵיהֶם, הֲרֵי אָנוּ נָזִין אוֹתָהּ כְּאֶחָד

And so neither of them *will be able to say*, We shall provide for her together (Ket 12.1);

הֲרֵינִי מְמַנֶּה לוֹ אֶפִּיטְרוֹפּוֹס עַד שֶׁיִּגְדַּל

I am going to name him a tutor until he *grows up* (SDt 11 [F 19]).

A more detailed treatment can be found in Unit 18.

13. Periphrastic forms.

A. A continuous or repeated action in the past or future (or in the imperative or infinitive mood) can be expressed with the verb הָיָה (in the perfect, imperfect, imperative, or infinitive) followed by the participle of the corresponding verb, for example:

הָיוּ נוֹעֲלִין וּמַנִּיחִין אֶת הַמַּפְתֵּחַ בְּחַלּוֹן שֶׁעַל גַּבֵּי הַפֶּתַח

They used to lock up and leave the key in a window above the door (Erub 10.9);

משה תקן להם לישראל להיות שואלים בענין ודורשים בענין

Moses ordered the Israelites to keep on inquiring into and investigating the matter (SNm 66 [H 62]).

For the formula הוּא הָיָה אוֹמֵר, see Unit 1.12, and for the past conditional (לוּלֵי/אִלּוּ followed by הָיָה and participle), see Unit 28.8D.

B. A clear expression of the future as against the present is provided by the construction עָתִיד לְ- followed by the infinitive. עָתִיד is an adjective, which can be inflected (עֲתִידָה, עֲתִידִים, עֲתִידוֹת) so as to agree in gender and number with its subject, for example:

עֵדַת קֹרַח אֵינָהּ עֲתִידָה לַעֲלוֹת ... עֲשֶׂרֶת הַשְּׁבָטִים אֵינָן עֲתִידִין לַחֲזוֹר

The generation of Korah will not be resurrected ... the ten tribes will not return (Sanh 10.3).

In BH, עָתִיד has the sense of 'prepared, ready' (see Jb 15.24; Est 3.14; 8.13), and it was not difficult for this to shift in RH to 'disposed to, will'. In fact, in RH עָתִיד still occasionally appears with its BH meaning ('ready'), and even when referring to the future can function as an ordinary adjective:

עתידה שעה שיהא אדם מבקש דבר תורה ואיננו מוצא

The time is coming when a person will seek the word of the law but will not find it (TosEduy 1.1).

For M. Mishor (1983a, 124), the difference between the periphrastic structure with עָתִיד and the imperfect is that, although they are sometimes confused or used interchangeably, עָתִיד simply indicates the future whereas the imperfect conveys modal features of desire, prayerfulness, etc.

Perhaps the use of עָתִיד is better illustrated when contrasted with the participle, which indicates the present or near future, whereas עָתִיד לְ- usually points to a distant, often eschatological, future, as, for example, in this text from Abot (3.1), in which the past/present sense of the perfect, present/immediate future sense of the participle, and eschatological future sense of עָתִיד are perfectly laid out:

דַּע מֵאַיִן בָּאתָ וּלְאָן אַתָּה הוֹלֵךְ וְלִפְנֵי מִי אַתָּה עָתִיד לִתֵּן דִּין וְחֶשְׁבּוֹן

Know where you have come from, where you are going to, and before whom you will have to settle up.

(A similar sequence appears in Abot 4.22; for L. Girón [1992], the distinctions are not so clear-cut.)

14. Constructions of the type בְּצֵאתוֹ and כְּצֵאתוֹ, in which the infinitive construct functions as a noun (taking prepositions and suffixes), are replaced in RH by structures of the type כְּשֶׁיָּצָא or by the verbal noun (see Unit 9.9), as at Ber 9.4:

הַנִּכְנָס לַכְּרַךְ מִתְפַּלֵּל שְׁתַּיִם, אַחַת בִּכְנִיסָתוֹ וְאַחַת בִּיצִיאָתוֹ

Whoever enters the city should recite the prayer twice, once on entering and once on leaving.

Compare Ps 68.8, אֱלֹהִים בְּצֵאתְךָ לִפְנֵי עַמֶּךָ 'O God, when you used to go out before your people', with SNm 95.1 (H 95),

הלא כבר נאמר ביציאתם ממצרים, וגם ערב רב עלה אתם וצאן ובקר
[שמות יב' לח']

Was it not already said that when they went out from Egypt, There also went up with them a great crowd and flocks and herds [Ex 12.38]?,

and with AZ 3.4: וּכְשֶׁיָּצָא אָמַר לוֹ 'and on going out, he said to him'.

15. Auxiliary verbs. There are numerous possible constructions employing auxiliary verbs (see Kutscher 1971, 1602–1603), of which we note here only the most common; others will become evident as the different 'tenses' are discussed.

A. Auxiliary verb followed by -לְ (of infinitive) and infinitive, as commonly found in BH but also employed to introduce a final clause ('in order to').

B. Auxiliary verb followed by -שֶׁ, not only to introduce a subordinate clause but also as part of periphrastic imperatives, for example צָרִיךְ שֶׁיֹּאמַר 'it is necessary that he says'.

C. The verb הִתְחִיל 'begin' can be continued by a participle instead of the expected infinitive. M.H. Segal (1929, §328) believed that in such cases the infinitive לִהְיוֹת should be understood before the participle; whether or not this is correct, the construction became widespread and can be rendered with modal force, for example, הִתְחַלְתִּי מֵבִיא לָהֶם רְאָיוֹת 'I began bringing them proofs' (Neg 7.4).

D. The participle of הָלַךְ, וְהוֹלֵךְ (see Unit 19.14), is used with the participle of another verb to convey the modality of continuous or progressive action, as in

מֻתָּר אָדָם לְהַשְׂכִּיר מַשְׁכּוֹנוֹ שֶׁלְּעָנִי לִהְיוֹת פּוֹסֵק עָלָיו וְהוֹלֵךְ

It is permitted to hire out an item given in pledge by a poor person so that one gradually reduces the debt (BM 6.7).

In later usage, וְהוֹלֵךְ, which was usually placed after the main verb, lost the *waw* and, formally speaking, became the main verb, as in:

וְהַיָּם הוֹלֵךְ וְסֹעֵר עֲלֵיהֶם

And the sea continued to rage against them (PRE 10);

הולך ומדבק בעבודה זרה

Becoming ever more attached to idolatry (SDt 46 [F 96]).

The construction is a survival or restoration of the biblical idiom exemplified at 1 S 17.41:

וַיֵּלֶךְ הַפְּלִשְׁתִּי הֹלֵךְ וְקָרֵב אֶל־דָּוִד

Little by little, the Philistine drew nearer to David.

IV *Phraseology*

16. תַּלְמוּד לוֹמַר (ת״ל) is evidently an abbreviated expression of introduction to a biblical text. The meaning is the same as that conveyed by הַכָּתוּב מְלַמֵּד 'the passage teaches', and perhaps the underlying formula was something like יֵשׁ תַּלְמוּד בַּכָּתוּב לוֹמַר 'there is a teaching in the text, which says'. תַּלְמוּד לוֹמַר is usually intended to refute an erroneous interpretation by pointing out biblical teaching on the matter. Similarly, the formula מַה תַּלְמוּד לוֹמַר asks for the relevant biblical teaching. It is usually raised when the literal or obvious sense of a biblical text appears either superfluous or inadmissible for some reason and its real significance needs to be ascertained: 'but in that case, what is this text meant to teach?' (see Pérez Fernández 1987b).

17. לֶעָתִיד לָבוֹא, an expression referring to the future, as against the present (עַכְשָׁיו) and the past (לְשֶׁעָבַר). An eschatological future is not necessarily intended, although at times the expression seems similar to לְעוֹלָם הַבָּא. The following two examples are from the end of SDt 333 [F 383]) and from Ber 9.4:

גדולה שירה זו, שיש בה עכשיו ויש בה לשעבר ויש בה לעתיד
לבוא ויש בה בעולם הזה ויש בה לעולם הבא

Great is this song, for it speaks of the present and the past and the future, of this world and the world to come;

וְנוֹתֵן הוֹדָאָה לְשֶׁעָבַר, וְצוֹעֵק לֶעָתִיד לָבֹא

And he gives thanks for the past, and asks for the future.

V *Vocabulary*

אֵימָתַי 'when?', מֵאֵימָתַי 'from when?'

גַּלְגַּל '(eye)ball

דִּין/דּוּן 'judge' (*Qal* infinitive לָדוּן, ni. infinitiveלִדּוֹן)

הוֹשִׁיט (hi. of יׁשט) 'extend', הוֹשִׁיט יָד 'stretch out the hand'

הקב״ה, abbreviation of הַקָּדוֹשׁ בָּרוּךְ הוּא 'the holy one, blessed be he'

הֶרֶף 'trembling', הֶרֶף עַיִן 'blink of an eye, instant'

וַעַד 'meeting, appointment'

חָתַם 'seal', לַחְתּוֹם (infinitive) 'to conclude, to quote a concluding formula' (cf. לְהַאֲרִיךְ 'to lengthen a form of words, to recite a long prayer'

טִיֵּל (pi. of טול) 'go for a walk'

יִלּוֹד 'born, alive, living being'

מָדוֹר 'dwelling place'

מֶרֶד 'rebelliousness'

מָרָה 'poison'

סְעוּדָה 'banquet, feast'

עִכֵּב 'detain'

רַשַּׁאי 'free, able, 'authorized', empowered', 'with the capacity for'

VI *Exercises*

1. יְהִי בֵיתְךָ בֵּית וַעַד לַחֲכָמִים, וֶהֱוֵי מִתְאַבֵּק בַּעֲפַר רַגְלֵיהֶם, וֶהֱוֵי שׁוֹתֶה בְצָמָא אֶת דִּבְרֵיהֶם.

2. רַבִּי יְהוֹשֻׁעַ אוֹמֵר, עַיִן הָרַע וְיֵצֶר הָרַע וְשִׂנְאַת הַבְּרִיּוֹת מוֹצִיאִין אֶת הָאָדָם מִן הָעוֹלָם.

3. הוּא הָיָה אוֹמֵר, הַיְּלוֹדִים לָמוּת, וְהַמֵּתִים לְהַחֲיוֹת, וְהַחַיִּים לִדּוֹן, לֵידַע לְהוֹדִיעַ וּלְהִוָּדַע שֶׁהוּא אֵל, הוּא הַיּוֹצֵר, הוּא הַבּוֹרֵא, הוּא הַמֵּבִין, הוּא הַדַּיָּן, הוּא עֵד, הוּא בַּעַל דִּין, וְהוּא עָתִיד לָדוּן.

4. מֵאֵימָתַי קוֹרִין אֶת שְׁמַע בַּשַּׁחֲרִית? מִשֶּׁיַּכִּיר בֵּין תְּכֵלֶת לְלָבָן.

5. מָקוֹם שֶׁאָמְרוּ, לְהַאֲרִיךְ, אֵינוֹ רַשַּׁאי לְקַצֵּר, לְקַצֵּר, אֵינוֹ רַשַּׁאי לְהַאֲרִיךְ, לַחְתּוֹם, אֵינוֹ רַשַּׁאי שֶׁלֹּא לַחְתּוֹם, שֶׁלֹּא לַחְתּוֹם, אֵינוֹ רַשַּׁאי לַחְתּוֹם.

6. מֵאֵימָתַי מֻתָּר אָדָם לִקַּח יָרָק בְּמוֹצָאֵי שְׁבִיעִית? ... רַבִּי הִתִּיר לִקַּח יָרָק בְּמוֹצָאֵי שְׁבִיעִית מִיָּד.

7. ליל שמורים הוא לי׳ וגר [שמות י״ב מב׳]. בו נגאלו ובו עתידין להגאל, דברי רבי יהושע ... רבי אליעזר אומר, בו נגאלו אבל לעתיד לבא אינם נגאלים אלא בתשרי, שנאמר, תקעו בחדש שופר וגר׳, מפני מה? כי חק לישראל הוא וגר [תהלים פא׳ ד׳–ה׳]. ומה תלמוד לומר, הוא הלילה הזה לי׳ [שמות י״ב מב׳]? אלא הוא הלילה שאמר המקום לאברהם אבינו, אברהם בלילה הזה אני גואל את בניך, וכשהגיע הקץ לא עיכבן המקום אפילו כהרף עין.

8. ויט משה את ידו על הים [שמות י״ד כא׳]. התחיל הים עומד כנגדו. אמר לו משה בשם הקב״ה שיבקע ולא קבל עליו.

9. עשה פלא [שמות ט״ו יא׳], עשה פלא עם האבות ועתיד לעשות עם הבנים, שנאמר, כימי צאתך מארץ מצרים אראנו נפלאות [מיכה ז׳ טו׳]. אראנו מה שלא הראיתי לאבות, שהרי נסים וגבורות שאני עתיד לעשות עם הבנים יותר הם ממה שעשיתי לאבות.

10. כיון ששמעו אומות העולם שהמקום קרנם של ישראל ומכניסן לארץ התחילו מתרגזין.

11. נמצאת מרבה לו והולך לעולם.

12. [הכתוב] מלמד שתינוק מישראל עתיד להושיט את ידו לתוך גלגל עינו של צפעוני ומוציא מרה מתוך פיו.

13. כך עתיד הקב״ה מטייל עם הצדיקים בגן עדן לעתיד לבוא.

14. כמה גרים ועבדים אתה עתיד להכניס תחת כנפי השכינה.

15. לא במקום אחד ולא בשנים המקום חולק כבוד לזקנים, ובכל מקום שאתה מוצא, זקנים, המקום חולק כבוד לזקנים ... רבי שמעון בן יוחי אומר, מנין שאף לעתיד לבא כן המקום חולק כבוד לזקנים?

16. אני י״ אלהיכם אני עתיד לשלם שכר, אני י״ אלהיכם עתיד ליפרע.

17. התחילו הם בוכים ורבי עקיבה מצחק. אמרו לו, עקיבה, מפני מה אנו בוכים ואתה מצחק?

18. וכיון שמת משה היה יהושע בוכה ומצעק ומתאבל עליו במרד והיה אומר, אבי אבי, רבי רבי, אבי שגדלני, רבי שלמדני תורה. והיה מתאבל עליו ימים רבים עד שאמר לו הקב״ה ליהושע, יהושע, עד כמה אתה מתאבל והולך? וכי לך לבדך מת משה?

‫19. נתקבצו כל ישראל אצל משה. אמרו לו, רבינו משה, אמור לנו מה‬
‫טובה עתיד הקדוש ברוך הוא ליתן לנו לעתיד לבא.‬
‫20. אמר יונה ללויתן, בשבילך ירדתי לראות מקום מדורך, שאני עתיד‬
‫לתן חבל בלשונך ולהעלותך ולזבוח אותך לסעודה הגדולה של צדיקים.‬

Sources. 1. Abot 1.4. 2. Abot 2.11. 3. Abot 4.22. 4. Ber 1.2. 5. Ber 1.4. 6.
Shebi 6.4. 7. Mek 12.42 (L 1.115–116). 8. Mek 14.21 (L 1.227–228). 9.
Mek 15.11 (L 2.66). 10. Mek 15.14 (L 2.71). 11. SLv 14.2 (W 70a–b). 12.
SLv 26.6. (W 111a). 13. SLv 26.12 (W 111b). 14. SNm 80.1 (H 76). 15.
SNm 92.4 (H 92). 16. SNm 115.5 (H 129). 17. SDt 43 (F 94). 18. SDt 305
(F 327). 19. SDt 356 (F 424). 20. PRE 10.

UNIT SEVENTEEN

PERFECT

I *Introductory text* (Naz 3.6)

‫מִי שֶׁנָּזַר נְזִירוּת הַרְבֵּה, וְהִשְׁלִים אֶת נְזִירוּתוֹ, וְאַחַר כָּךְ בָּא לָאָרֶץ, בֵּית שַׁמַּאי‬
‫אוֹמְרִים, נָזִיר שְׁלֹשִׁים יוֹם, וּבֵית הִלֵּל אוֹמְרִים, נָזִיר בַּתְּחִלָּה. מַעֲשֶׂה בְּהִילְנִי‬
‫הַמַּלְכָּה, שֶׁהָלַךְ בְּנָהּ לַמִּלְחָמָה, וְאָמְרָה, אִם יָבֹא בְנִי מִן הַמִּלְחָמָה בְּשָׁלוֹם,‬
‫אֱהֵא נְזִירָה שֶׁבַע שָׁנִים, וּבָא בְנָהּ מִן הַמִּלְחָמָה, וְהָיְתָה נְזִירָה שֶׁבַע שָׁנִים,‬
‫וּבְסוֹף שֶׁבַע שָׁנִים עָלְתָה לָאָרֶץ, וְהוֹרוּהָ בֵית הִלֵּל, שֶׁתְּהֵא נְזִירָה עוֹד שֶׁבַע‬
‫שָׁנִים אֲחֵרוֹת, וּבְסוֹף שֶׁבַע שָׁנִים נִטְמֵאת, וְנִמְצֵאת נְזִירָה עֶשְׂרִים וְאַחַת שָׁנָה.‬

If someone vows to be a Nazirite for a long period, fulfils the vow, and then
enters the land (of Israel), the school of Shammai says, The person will still
be a Nazirite for another thirty days, and the school of Hillel says, The
person must fulfil their Nazirite vow (again) from the beginning. It happened
that Queen Helena, when her son went away to war, said, If my son comes
back from the war safely I shall become a Nazirite for seven years. Now her
son returned from war and she fullfilled her Nazirite vow for seven years. At
the end of the seven years, she went up to the land (of Israel) and the school
of Hillel told her that she would have to fulfil the Nazirite vow another seven
years. When the seven years ended, she contracted an impurity, and so it
turned out that she had to fulfil the Nazirite vow for twenty-one years.

1. The Nazirite vow is an ancient feature of Israelite life, which brought
with it abstinence from wine and spirits, leaving the hair uncut, and avoidance of contamination through contact with a corpse. It was still practised at
a late period, apparently despite some opposition from the rabbis.

The Mishnah, which is basically a corpus of *halakhot*, at times presents important historical material (*ma'asiyyot*), such as we find in this text about Helena of Adiabene, a proselyte of the fifth decade CE. Through this account, we learn of the exceptional piety of Helena, who takes her place alongside other figures of legendary asceticism, as well as of the difference between the schools of Hillel and Shammai—here, contrary to expectation, it is not Shammai who is the stricter.

II *Morphology*

2. Morphological differences between the BH and RH perfect are not especially striking. Those relating to the second person singular masculine (קָטַלְתָּה as well as קָטַלְתְּ), the third person feminine singular (קָטְלָת as well as קָטְלָה), and the second person masculine and feminine plural (קְטַלְתֶּן) have already been outlined in Unit 16.4.

3. In the *Qal* of the regular verb, the perfect follows two models known from BH, קָטַל and קָטֵל, with the choice between them depending in part on whether a given verb is active or stative/intransitive (for example, בָּטֵל 'cease', כָּשֵׁר 'be appropriate', and קָרֵב 'be near'). The BH pattern קָטֹל does not occur in RH in the perfect, with יָכֹל found only as a participle: יְכֹל, יְכוּלָה, יְכוֹלִים/יְכוֹלִין, יְכוֹלוֹת; the BH perfect structures יָכֹלְתִּי and יָכְלָה have been replaced by perfect forms of the verb הָיָה followed by the participle יָכֹל.

4. *Ayin-waw* and -*yod* verbs.

A. In the perfect, all three patterns are known, with *a*, *e*, or *o* (for example, קָם, מֵת, and בּוֹשׁ).

Note the *Nif'al* perfect form נָדוֹן or נִידוֹן.

B. In the intensive conjugations (*Pi'el, Pu'al, Hitpa'el,* and *Nitpa'al*), these verbs tend to double the *yod* or *waw* of the root, giving rise to perfects such as טִיֵּל (טול), נִתְגַּיֵּר (גור), קִיֵּם (קום), and כִּיֵּן (כון).

The verb שאר also forms its *Pi'el* in a similar way: שִׁיֵּר 'leave', which seems to indicate the complete loss of consonantal value for *alef*, to the extent that RH could construct as parallel forms from *qam* a *Pi'el qiyyem* and from *shar* a *Pi'el shiyyer*.

C. *Ayin-waw* and -*yod* verbs also gave rise to secondary conjugations, either through reduplication of the final radical (*Po'lel*), as in עוֹרֵר 'awaken, arouse', from עור, or by repetition of the two 'strong' radicals (*Pilpel*), as in זִגְזֵג 'make clear', from זג.

5. *Lamed-alef* and -*he* verbs.

A. In RH, *lamed-alef* verbs tend to be inflected as though they were *lamed-he*: קָרָאתִי and קָרִיתִי, קָרָאנוּ and קָרִינוּ, מָצָאנוּ and מָצִינוּ, etc. This confusion points to the progressive influence of Aramaic and also, perhaps, scribal negligence. Deterioration in the consonantal value of the gutturals has clearly been a decisive factor.

B. It is in these verbs that we often find the archaic termination -āt in the third person feminine singular, as in הָיָת (alongside הָיְתָה) and שָׁתָת, for example at Par 9.5: פָּרָה שֶׁשָּׁתָת מֵי חַטָּאת 'the cow that has drunk the waters of purification'. Segal 1929, §205 lists other instances of similar variant readings in manuscripts and printed editions.

The same inflection is found in Aramaic and appears at Dt 32.36 (אָזְלַת) and in the *ketiv* of 2 K 9.37 (והית נבלת איזבל 'and the body of Jezebel will remain'); perhaps היה in the Siloam tunnel inscription should be understood in the same way (see Kutscher 1982, 67). Thus, we appear to have here a further example of an early form that has been preserved in a popular dialect (according to Kutscher 1982, 128, the fact that the feature is attested only in *lamed-he* verbs means that Aramaic influence on its own does not provide a sufficient explanation).

C. A similar phenomenon is found in the third person feminine singular of the perfect *Nif'al*, with the BH forms נִגְלְתָה 'was revealed' and נִמְצְאָה 'was found' often being replaced by נִגְלֵית and נִמְצֵאת (forms that are easily confused with the feminine participle, which also prefers a -*t* ending; see Unit 19), for example

וְאִם מִשֶּׁנִּשֵּׂאת בָּאוּ עֵדִים, הֲרֵי זוֹ לֹא תֵצֵא

If witnesses appear after she has married, she must not be dismissed (Ket 2.5)

and שְׁבוּיָה שֶׁנִּפְדֵּית 'the captive who has been ransomed' (Ket 3.2).

D. Frequently, *lamed-he* verbs behave like *lamed-alef* ones when a suffix is attached, as in

נָפְלוּ שְׁנֵיהֶן כְּאַחַת, עֲשָׂאוּהוּ שֵׁנִי

If both fall at the same time, they contaminate it with second-degree impurity (Ṭoh 1.5).

Note also עֲשָׂאָן at Par 3.5.

III *Grammar and usage*

6. In RH, the main function of the perfect is to express an action that took place at some specific point in the past, for example:

ירד על סיחון והרגו, ירד על עוג והרגו

He fell upon Sihon and killed him, he fell upon Og and killed him (SNm 101 [H 99]).

The perfect is not only to be distinguished from forms of the verb that relate to the present or future but also from general or atemporal statements construed with participles. M. Mishor (1983a, 27) cites SNm 136 (H 182):

ניתן כח בעיניו של משה וראה מסוף העולם ועד סופו. וכן אתה מוצא
בצדיקים שרואים מסוף העולם ועד סופו

Power *was given* to the eyes of Moses and he *saw* from one end of the world to the other. Thus, you find that the righteous *can see* from one end of the world to the other.

7. With the disappearance of the BH וַיִּקְטֹל construction, the perfect became the dominant narrative verb-form for expressing events that had occurred in the past:

מֹשֶׁל, למה הדבר דומה? למלך בשר ודם שכעס על בנו, והלך לו הבן
ההוא אצל אוהבו של מלך. אמר לו

A parable: to what may this be compared? To a king of flesh and blood who was annoyed with his son, and then that son went off to a friend of the king and said to him (SNm 86.1 [H 85]).

All *meshalim* begin their narratives in the perfect, according to the pattern 'it is like someone who *did* so-and-so'.

8. In certain contexts the perfect has pluperfect significance, generally in subordinate clauses (introduced by -שֶׁ, -כְּשֶׁ, etc.):

כשירד משה מהר סיני נתקבצו ישראל אצלו. אמרו לו

When Moses had gone down from Mount Sinai, the Israelites gathered and said to him (end of SDt 307 [F 346]);

זה טיטוס הרשע, בן אשתו של אספסיינוס, שנכנס לבית קדש הקדשים
וגדר שתי פרכות בסייף

This is Titus, the impious, the son of Vespasian's wife, the one who had entered the holy of holies and torn down the two curtains with a sword (SDt 328 [F 378–79]).

A sentence with הָיָה followed by a participle or noun and linked by -וֹ to a perfect indicates action prior to that expressed by the perfect:

למלך ששכר פועלין הרבה והיה שם פועל אחד שעשה עמו מלאכה
ימים הרבה

It is like a king who hired many workers when he already had a worker who had worked with him many days (SLv 26.9 [W 111a]);

למלך שיצא לטייל עם אריס בפרדס והיה אותו אריס מיטמר מלפניו

It is like a king who went out to walk in the orchard with his labourer and the labourer had concealed himself from him (SLv 26.12 [W 111b]).

9. In BH, the perfect is often employed with present reference, a function normally taken over in RH by the participle (see Bendavid 1967, §§244ff.). But in certain contexts the usage survived.

A. In dialogues and colloquial speech, notably in the common expression אָמַרְתָּ 'that's what you say' (in rabbinic arguments), or in such formulas as לֹא זָכִיתִי מִן הַדִּין 'I do not arrive at this through deductive reasoning' (see below, §15). Particularly striking is the form of greeting recorded in Bik 3.3:

וְכָל בַּעֲלֵי אֻמָּנִיּוֹת שֶׁבִּירוּשָׁלַיִם עוֹמְדִין לִפְנֵיהֶם וְשׁוֹאֲלִין בִּשְׁלוֹמָם,
אַחֵינוּ אַנְשֵׁי מָקוֹם פְּלוֹנִי, בָּאתֶם לְשָׁלוֹם

All the artisans of Jerusalem arose before them and greeted them, Our brothers of such-and-such a place, you are welcome.

B. When expressing a state or condition that arose in the past but persists in the present, for example

כָּל שֶׁחָבְתִּי בִשְׁמִירָתוֹ, הִכְשַׁרְתִּי אֶת נִזְקוֹ

For everything that I have taken it upon myself to look after, I take
responsibility for any damage (BQ 1.2).

10. The perfect is also used in declarations of general validity, which allow no exception, for example נִכְנַס יַיִן, יָצָא סוֹד 'wine went in, the secret went
out' (Erub 65a). In fact, such sentences amount to conditional clauses,
'if/when/whenever wine enters ...'; compare Pr 18.22:

מָצָא אִשָּׁה מָצָא טוֹב

If you have found a woman, you have found a treasure.

11. Because of that, the perfect is the form normally used when raising a
supposition or condition ('in the case that', 'if', 'when'), generally followed
by a declaration or command ('then', 'in that case', 'one must'):

מָזְגוּ לוֹ אֶת הַכּוֹס, וְאָמַר, הֲרֵינִי נָזִיר מִמֶּנּוּ, הֲרֵי זֶה נָזִיר

If they prepare him a drink and he says, I have to abstain from it,
then he is a Nazirite (Naz 2.3);

מִי שֶׁאָמַר, הֲרֵינִי נָזִיר, מְגַלֵּחַ יוֹם שְׁלֹשִׁים וְאֶחָד

If someone says, I shall be a Nazirite, their hair is cut off on the
thirty-first day (Naz 3.1).

The perfect in the protasis here is equivalent to a real (as against irreal) condition (see Unit 28).

12. This structure is typical of the halakhic-juridical style, and numerous
halakhot begin with a perfect. But the same perfect, with hypothetical or
temporal function, can also be elegantly employed in a narrative sequence,
inserting a sense of liveliness and realism into a series of participles, as at
Bik 3.4:

הֶחָלִיל מַכֶּה לִפְנֵיהֶם, עַד שֶׁמַּגִּיעִים לְהַר הַבַּיִת. הִגִּיעוּ לְהַר הַבַּיִת,
אֲפִילוּ אַגְרִיפַּס הַמֶּלֶךְ נוֹטֵל הַסַּל עַל כְּתֵפוֹ וְנִכְנָס, עַד שֶׁהוּא מַגִּיעַ
לָעֲזָרָה. הִגִּיעַ לָעֲזָרָה, וְדִבְּרוּ הַלְוִיִּם בַּשִּׁיר

The flute is played before them until they reach the Temple Mount.
When they reached the Temple Mount even King Agrippa carries
the basket on his shoulders and goes in as far as the courtyard. *When
he reached* the courtyard, the Levites began to sing.

In a halakhic context, we find the same usage at, for example, Ber 2.3:

הַקּוֹרֵא אֶת שְׁמַע וְלֹא הִשְׁמִיעַ לְאָזְנוֹ, יָצָא

If someone recites the *shema'*, *even though it could not be heard*,
they fulfil their obligation.

M. Mishor (1983a, 27) contrasts narrative set in the past that uses the
perfect with halakhic formulations that use the participle; at Soṭ 7.8, we find
a description of what takes place in the liturgy of a royal ceremony, using
participles (the liturgical atemporal present; see Unit 19.12), but with the
specific historical actions of the king expressed in the perfect:

פָּרָשַׁת הַמֶּלֶךְ כֵּיצַד? ... עוֹשִׂין לוֹ בִּימָה שֶׁלְּעֵץ בָּעֲזָרָה, וְהוּא יוֹשֵׁב
עָלֶיהָ ... חַזַּן הַכְּנֶסֶת נוֹטֵל סֵפֶר תּוֹרָה וְנוֹתְנָהּ לְרֹאשׁ הַכְּנֶסֶת ... וְכֹהֵן

גָּדוֹל נוֹתְנָה לַמֶּלֶךְ, וְהַמֶּלֶךְ עוֹמֵד וּמְקַבֵּל וְקוֹרֵא יוֹשֵׁב. אַגְרִיפַּס הַמֶּלֶךְ
עָמַד וְקִבֵּל וְקָרָא עוֹמֵד וְשִׁבְּחוּהוּ חֲכָמִים

How did the royal liturgy use to unfold? ... They make him (the
king) a platform of wood in the courtyard, and he sits down on it ...
The minister of the synagogue takes the book of the law and passes
it to the leader of the synagogue ... and the high priest passes it to
the king and the king receives it standing up and reads it sitting
down. But King Agrippa *received* it standing up and *read* it
standing up, and the sages *praised* him for it.

(Here, the change of tense helps emphasize the contrast between the expected
and the exceptional; see also Unit 32.4B.)

13. Within a narrative, the perfect can also be incorporated in a series of
imperfects expressing the future (future perfect) to indicate an event that is
regarded as already having taken place (or an inevitable, albeit future,
consequence of that event), for example at Abot 1.11:

חֲכָמִים, הִזָּהֲרוּ בְדִבְרֵיהֶם, שֶׁמָּא תָחוּבוּ חוֹבַת גָּלוּת וְתִגְלוּ לִמְקוֹם מַיִם
הָרָעִים, וְיִשְׁתּוּ הַתַּלְמִידִים הַבָּאִים אַחֲרֵיכֶם וְיָמוּתוּ, וְנִמְצָא שֵׁם שָׁמַיִם
מִתְחַלֵּל

Sages, take care with your words in case you commit an error punishable by exile and are exiled to a place of harmful waters—the
disciples who follow you might drink them and die and the name of
heaven will have been (literally, 'has been found') profaned.

(On וְנִמְצָא, see Unit 15.12.)

14. Expressions of the type מַה־שֶּׁעָשָׂה עָשָׂה or אִם־עָשִׂיתִי עָשִׂיתִי 'what is
done is done', emphasizing the irreversibility of a particular deed (see
Mishor 1983a, 69–71), are common; for example

מה שעשית עשיתה, אבל לא תשנה לעשות כן

What you have done you have done, but don't do it any more
(TosTer 2.13).

The sequence perfect followed by participle is also possible, as in

מַה שֶּׁעָשָׂה עָשׂוּי

What he did is done (Ter 2.2).

IV *Phraseology*

15. לֹא זָכִיתִי מִן הַדִּין 'I do not arrive at this through logical deduction' is
employed when a rabbinic debate is concluded by giving priority to the
meaning of the biblical text over any logical argument (דִּין), as at SNm 153.6
(H 202):

לא זכיתי מן הדין. ת״ל, אלה החקים אשר צוה י׳ את משה [במדמד
ל׳ יז]

But I do not arrive at this through deduction. There is a text that
says, Such are the statutes that Y. prescribed to Moses [Nm 30.17].

16. אָמַרְתָּ, literally, 'you said', is usually found in a concessive or adversative context, replying to a stated opinion, 'all right, but you said', 'that is what you say', 'you just said', with a touch of irony. Almost certainly, this usage underlies the words of Jesus at Mt 26.25,64; 27.11. The following rabbinic example is from SNm 76.2 (H 70):

על הצר הצרר [במדבר י׳ ט׳]. במלחמת גוג ומגוג הכתוב מדבר. אתה
אומר, במלחמת גוג ומגוג הכתוב מדבר, או אינו מדבר אלא בכל
המלחמות שבתורה? ת״ל, ונשעתם מאויביכם [במדבר י׳ ט׳]. אמרת.
צא וראה איזו היא מלחמה שישראל נושעים ממנה ואין אחריה שעבוד.
אין אתה מוצא אלא מלחמת גוג ומגוג. וכן הוא אומר, ויצא י׳ ונלחם
בגוים ההם [זכריה יד׳ ג׳].

Against the enemy that attacks you [Nm 10.9]. This passage refers to the war of Gog and Magog. You argue that this passage refers to the war of Gog and Magog. But could it not refer to any of the wars that are in the Torah? The text teaches, You will be saved from your enemies [Nm 10.9]. *You said it!* Go and see which is the war that Israel comes away from in safety and after which there is no return to servitude; you will find none apart from the war of Gog and Magog. And that is why it says, Then Y. will go out and fight against those peoples [Zc 14.3].

17. יָצָא [לֹא] '(fail to) fulfil one's duty', a juridical expression often found in *halakhot*, for example Ber 6.2:

בֵּרַךְ עַל פֵּרוֹת הָאִילָן, בּוֹרֵא פְּרִי הָאֲדָמָה, יָצָא, וְעַל פֵּרוֹת הָאָרֶץ,
בּוֹרֵא פְּרִי הָעֵץ, לֹא יָצָא

If over the fruits of the tree someone recites the prayer, (Blessed are you, O Lord) creator of the fruits of the earth, they fulfil their duty, but if over the fruits of the earth someone recites, (Blessed are you, O Lord) creator of the fruits of the tree, they do not fulfil their duty.

The longer form of the expression, יָצָא יְדֵי חוֹבָתוֹ, is presented in Unit 22.26.

V Vocabulary

גֵּרֵד 'scrape (clean)'
גִּזְבָּר 'treasurer'
גְּנוּת 'blemish, fault, disgrace'
גְּרוֹגֶרֶת 'dried fig'
דְּיַתִיקִי (διαθήκη) 'pact, testament'
זוּן 'supply, feed'
חִבָּה 'love'
לְמַפְרֵעַ 'irregularly, without order, back to front'
מְצֻפּוֹת (pu. participle plural of צפה) 'covered'
סִימָן 'sign'

סָגָן 'prefect, head'

עִיסָה 'dough'

עֲלִיָּה 'ascent' (especially the ascent to Jerusalem)

פֶּחָה 'noble'

פָּסַק 'agree'

צִימּוּק 'raisin'

רְחִיצָה 'bath'

שָׁוֶה 'equal, equivalent'; בְּשָׁוֶה 'for what is right, for a fair price', בְּפָחוֹת 'for a
lower price'

VI *Exercises*

1. מִי שֶׁמֵּת וְנִמְצֵאת דְּיַתִּיקִי קְשׁוּרָה עַל יְרֵכוֹ, הֲרֵי זוֹ אֵינָהּ כְּלוּם.

2. הִנִּיחַ בָּנוֹת גְּדוֹלוֹת וּקְטַנּוֹת, אֵין הַגְּדוֹלוֹת מְתְפַּרְנְסוֹת עַל הַקְּטַנּוֹת, וְלֹא
קְטַנּוֹת נִזּוֹנוֹת עַל הַגְּדוֹלוֹת, אֶלָּא חוֹלְקוֹת בְּשָׁוֶה.

3. הַקּוֹרֵא אֶת שְׁמַע וְלֹא הִשְׁמִיעַ לְאָזְנוֹ, יָצָא. רַבִּי יוֹסֵי אוֹמֵר, לֹא יָצָא. קָרָא
וְלֹא דִקְדֵּק בְּאוֹתִיּוֹתֶיהָ, רַבִּי יוֹסֵי אוֹמֵר, יָצָא. רַבִּי יְהוּדָה אוֹמֵר, לֹא יָצָא.

4. הַקְּרוֹבִים מְבִיאִים תְּאֵנִים וַעֲנָבִים, וְהָרְחוֹקִים מְבִיאִים גְּרוֹגְרוֹת וְצִמּוּקִים.
וְהַשּׁוֹר הוֹלֵךְ לִפְנֵיהֶם, וְקַרְנָיו מְצֻפּוֹת זָהָב וַעֲטָרָה שֶׁלְזַיִת בְּרֹאשׁוֹ. הֶחָלִיל
מַכֶּה לִפְנֵיהֶם, עַד שֶׁמַּגִּיעִים קָרוֹב לִירוּשָׁלַיִם. הִגִּיעוּ קָרוֹב לִירוּשָׁלַיִם, שָׁלְחוּ
לִפְנֵיהֶם, וְעָטְרוּ אֶת בִּכּוּרֵיהֶם. הַפְּחוֹת, הַסְּגָנִים וְהַגִּזְבָּרִים יוֹצְאִים לִקְרָאתָם.
לְפִי כְבוֹד הַנִּכְנָסִים הָיוּ יוֹצְאִים. וְכָל בַּעֲלֵי אֻמָּנִיּוֹת שֶׁבִּירוּשָׁלַיִם עוֹמְדִין
לִפְנֵיהֶם וְשׁוֹאֲלִין בִּשְׁלוֹמָם, אֲחֵינוּ אַנְשֵׁי מָקוֹם פְּלוֹנִי, בָּאתֶם לְשָׁלוֹם.

5. גֵּר שֶׁנִּתְגַּיֵּר, וְהָיְתָה לוֹ עִיסָה, נַעֲשֵׂת עַד שֶׁלֹּא נִתְגַּיֵּר, פָּטוּר, וּמִשֶּׁנִּתְגַּיֵּר, חַיָּב.

6. הוֹרוּ בֵית דִּין, וְעָשׂוּ כָל הַקָּהָל אוֹ רֻבָּן עַל פִּיהֶן, מְבִיאִין פַּר, וּבַעֲבוֹדָה
זָרָה, מְבִיאִין פַּר וְשָׂעִיר, דִּבְרֵי רַבִּי מֵאִיר.

7. הַקּוֹרֵא אֶת הַמְּגִלָּה לְמַפְרֵעַ, לֹא יָצָא. קְרָאָהּ עַל פֶּה, קְרָאָהּ תַּרְגּוּם, בְּכָל
לָשׁוֹן, לֹא יָצָא.

8. מִי שֶׁאָמַר, הֲרֵינִי נָזִיר, וְשָׁמַע חֲבֵרוֹ וְאָמַר, וַאֲנִי, וַאֲנִי, כֻּלָּם נְזִירִין.

9. מִי שֶׁנָּדַר בְּנָזִיר וְהָלַךְ לְהָבִיא אֶת בְּהֶמְתּוֹ וּמְצָאָהּ שֶׁנִּגְנְבָה, אִם עַד שֶׁלֹּא
נִגְנְבָה בְּהֶמְתּוֹ נָזַר, הֲרֵי זֶה נָזִיר, וְאִם מִשֶּׁנִּגְנְבָה בְּהֶמְתּוֹ נָזַר, אֵינוֹ נָזִיר.

10. מָצִינוּ שֶׁעָשָׂה אַבְרָהָם אָבִינוּ אֶת כָּל הַתּוֹרָה כֻּלָּהּ עַד שֶׁלֹּא נִתְּנָה.

11. פְּעָמִים הַרְבֵּה קָרִיתִי לְפָנָיו בְּדָנִיֵּאל.

12. כֵּיוָן שֶׁשָּׁמְעוּ כְנַעֲנִים שֶׁיִּשְׂרָאֵל נִכְנָסִים לָאָרֶץ עָמְדוּ וְשָׂרְפוּ אֶת הַזְּרָעִים
וְקִצְצוּ אֶת הָאִילָנוֹת וְסָתְרוּ אֶת הַבִּנְיָנִים וְסָתְמוּ אֶת הַמַּעְיָנוֹת.

13. כֵּיוָן שֶׁשָּׁמְעוּ אוּמוֹת הָעוֹלָם שֶׁאָבַד פַּרְעֹה וְחֵילוֹ בַּיָּם וּבָטְלָה מַלְכוּת שֶׁל
מִצְרַיִם וּשְׁפָטִים נַעֲשׂוּ בַּעֲבוֹדָה זָרָה שֶׁלָּהֶן, הִתְחִילוּ מִתְרַגְּזִין.

14. וַיֹּאמֶר אִם שָׁמוֹעַ תִּשְׁמַע [שמות ט"ו כ"ו]. מִכָּאן אָמְרוּ, שָׁמַע אָדָם מִצְוָה
אַחַת, מַשְׁמִיעִין אוֹתוֹ מִצְוֹת הַרְבֵּה, שֶׁנֶּאֱמַר, אִם שָׁמוֹעַ תִּשְׁמַע [שם]. שָׁכַח
אָדָם מִצְוָה אַחַת, מַשְׁכִּחִין לוֹ מִצְוֹת הַרְבֵּה, שֶׁנֶּאֱמַר, וְהָיָה אִם שָׁכֹחַ תִּשְׁכַּח
[דברים ח' י"ט].

15. מָשָׁל, לְמָה הַדָּבָר דּוֹמֶה? לְבַת מְלָכִים שֶׁנִּשֵּׂאת כְּשֶׁהִיא קְטַנָּה, וּפָסְקוּ עִם
אִמָּהּ שֶׁתְּהֵא מְשַׁמֶּשֶׁת עַד שָׁעָה שֶׁתִּלְמַד בָּזֶה. אַף כָּךְ אַהֲרֹן תְּחִלָּה הָיָה

לוי, שנאמר, הלא אהרן אחיך הלוי? [שמות ד' יד'], כשנבחר להיות כהן
גדול אמר לו הקב״ה למשה, אזה תשמשני עד שילמוד אהרן.

16. עכשיו ישראל אומרים, לא נתגייר יתרו מחיבה. כסבור היה יתרו שיש
לגרים חלק בארץ ישראל, עכשיו שראה שאין להם חלק, הניחם והלך לו.

17. מפני מה לא ברא המקום חמים בירושלים כחמי טבריה? כדי שלא יאמר
אדם לחבירו, נלך תעלה לירושלים. הא אם אין אנו עולים אלא בשביל
רחיצה אחת, דיינו. ונמצאית עלייה שלא לשמה.

18. נדפת את כל הקערה כולה ולא שיירתה ממנה כלום.

19. רבי נתן אומר, סימן טוב הוא לאדם שנפרעים ממנו לאחר מיתתו. מת,
לא נספד ולא נקבר, אכלתו חיה או שירדו עליו גשמים, הרי זה סימן
טוב שנפרעים ממנו לאחר מיתתו.

20. עבד י' [דברים לד' ה']. לא בגנותו של משה הכתוב מדבר, אלא
בשבחו, שכך מצינו בנביאים הראשונים שנקראו עבדים.

Sources. 1. BB 8.6. 2. BB 8.8. 3. Ber 2.3. 4. Bik 3.3. 5. Ḥal 3.6. 6. Hor
1.5. 7. Meg 2.1. 8. Naz 4.1. 9. Naz 5.4. 10. Qid 4.14. 11. Yom 1.6. 12.
Mek 13.17 (L 1.172). 13. Mek 15.14 (L 2.71). 14. Mek 15.26 (L 2.95). 15.
SLv 8.15 (W 41c). 16. SNm 80.1 (H 76). 17. SNm 89.5 (H 90). 18. SNm
112.3 (H 120). 19. SNm 112.4 (H 121–22). 20. SDt 357 (F 428).

UNIT EIGHTEEN

IMPERFECT

I *Introductory text* (SDt 41 [F 87])

והיה אם שמע תשמעו אל מצותי אשר אנכי מצוה אתכם היום לאהבה את י'
אלהיכם [דברים יא' יג']. שמא תאמר, הריני למד תורה בשביל
שאעשיר, בשביל שאקרא רבי, בשביל שאקבל שכר לעולם הבא, תלמוד
לומר, לאהבה את י' אלהיכם. כל שאתם עושים לא תהו עושים אלא
מאהבה.

If you obey the commandments that I command you today, loving Y. your
God [Dt 11.13]. So that you cannot say, I'm going to study Torah to get rich,
or to be named a rabbi, or to receive a reward in the next world, the passage
teaches, Loving Y. your God. Everything you do you must do out of love!

1. Three possible motives for studying the law are listed: financial re-
ward, obtaining the title or status of rabbi, ensuring a place in the next world.
The three are perfectly gradated, from the most prosaic to the most spiritual.
In a parallel text, a slightly different formulation is attested:

I am going to study Torah in order to be called wise, to be able to take my seat in the academy [יְשִׁיבָה], to prolong my days in the world to come (SDt 48).

Such texts are significant because of the way they reflect social aspects of Jewish life of the period—compare Mt 23.6–8. More important, though, is the theological message, which unambiguously states that the only valid reason for spending one's life in the study of the Torah is love for God, nothing else.

II *Morphology*

2. As we have already observed (Unit 16.5A), RH sees the disappearance of the second and third person feminine plural form תִּקְטֹלְנָה, which is replaced by the corresponding masculine forms תִּקְטְלוּ (second person) and יִקְטְלוּ (third person). In the Qumran texts studied by E. Qimron (1986, 45), תִּקְטֹלְנָה is only found three times. Also (see Unit 16.5B), despite their similarity to Aramaic, BH forms ending in *nun*, such as the second person feminine singular תִּקְטְלִין, disappear, with the archaizing (perhaps Aramaic-influenced) forms תִּקְטְלוּן and יִקְטְלוּן sometimes being used instead of their regular counterparts תִּקְטְלוּ and יִקְטְלוּ, apparently purely for stylistic reasons. At Qumran, the suffix *-un* is scarcely attested.

3. The lengthened, cohortative, forms of the first person singular, אֶקְטְלָה, and plural, נִקְטְלָה, have also practically disappeared, except in attempts to imitate biblical style.

4. A similar fate has overtaken the shortened, jussive, forms, although in the *Hif'il* a few have survived (probably due to the influence of the Aramaic *Af'el*), for example, at Abot 2.4,

וְאַל תַּאֲמֵן בְּעַצְמָךְ

Don't trust in yourself

(but K reads the non-jussive form תַּאֲמִין), and in other common verbs, clearly under biblical influence, as at Abot 1.8:

אַל תַּעַשׂ עַצְמָךְ כְּעוֹרְכֵי הַדַּיָּנִים

Don't turn yourself into an advocate.

The clustering of such jussives in manuscripts of Abot might suggest that Abot originates in an early stage of literary RH.

5. The verb הָיָה has been especially affected by Aramaic pressure on the one hand and by the persistence of biblical structures on the other, leading, in effect, to two conjugations, biblical and Aramaizing.

Among the biblical forms retained are the jussives יְהִי and תְּהִי, which are employed particularly in proverbial and liturgical contexts, for example

יְהִי מָמוֹן חֲבֵרָךְ חָבִיב עָלֶיךָ כְּשֶׁלָּךְ

May the property of your neighbour be as dear to you as your own (Abot 2.12).

This biblicizing jussive is typical of Abot (see also 1.4,5; 2.10,12,13; 4.3,8,12,15; 5.20), although there is always the possibility that the form יְהִי should be vocalized according to an Aramaizing pattern, יְהֵי.

As well as the biblical forms יְהְיֶה, תִּהְיֶה, אֶהְיֶה, etc., we also find the Aramaizing structures יְהֵא, תְּהֵא, אֶהֵא, etc. (also with final *yod*: יְהִי, תְּהִי, אֶהִי), which gained ground in colloquial usage, for example אֶהֵא נְזִירָה שֶׁבַע שָׁנִים 'I shall be a Nazirite for seven years' (Naz 3.6). The following table displays the two sets of forms.

Biblical		Aramaic		
אֶהְיֶה		אֶהֵא	אֶהִי	
תִּהְיֶה	תְּהִי	תְּהֵא	תְּהִי	
יְהְיֶה	יְהִי	יְהֵא	יְהִי	
נְהְיֶה		נְהֵא	נְהִי	
תִּהְיוּ		תְּהוּ		
יְהְיוּ		יְהוּ	יְהוֹא	

The form תִּהְיֶינָה only occurs in quotations from the Bible.

6. The confusion, already noted (Unit 17.5), between *lamed-alef* and *lamed-he* (or *lamed-yod*) verbs has led to such forms as יְקְרָא for יְקְרֵא and תְּקְרִי for תְּקְרָא; contrast the late text at Abot 6.2,

אַל תִּקְרָא חָרוּת אֶלָּא חֵרוּת

Read not *harut* but *herut*,

with Mek 17.8 (L 2.138): אַל תִּקְרִי שְׁפָטִים אֶלָּא שִׁפּוּטִים 'read not *shefatim* but *shippuṭim*'.

7. The verb הָפַךְ 'turn, go back, change' behaves in the imperfect as though it were a *pe-alef*, evidently as a result of the confusion of *he* and *alef* and through analogy with frequent verbs like אָמַר and אָכַל. Thus, we find in the first and third persons אוֹפַךְ and יוֹפַךְ (like אוֹמַר and יוֹמַר), for example at Kil 2.3:

לֹא יֹאמַר, אֶזְרַע וְאַחַר כָּךְ אוֹפַךְ, אֶלָּא הוֹפַךְ וְאַחַר כָּךְ זוֹרֵעַ

One should not say, I shall sow first and then I shall turn up [the ground]; instead, one should turn up [the ground] first and then sow.

III Grammar and usage

8. With regard to the verb הָיָה, there is no appreciable difference in meaning between the biblical form יְהְיֶה and the standard rabbinic יְהֵא, although the biblical form tends to be employed in more literary contexts or when attempting to imitate biblical style (in prayers, proverbs, etc.); even here, though, choices vary with individual authors and schools of writing. Similar comments apply to the use or non-use of the lengthened and shortened forms of the imperfect.

9. As already said in Unit 16.12C, the imperfect can be used for expressing the future. Through it, an action that has not yet taken place can be represented or a series of future events narrated, as at Abot 1.11:

חֲכָמִים, הִזָּהֲרוּ בְדִבְרֵיהֶם, שֶׁמָּא תָחוּבוּ חוֹבַת גָּלוּת וְתִגְלוּ לִמְקוֹם מַיִם
הָרָעִים, וְיִשְׁתּוּ הַתַּלְמִידִים הַבָּאִים אַחֲרֵיכֶם וְיָמוּתוּ.

Sages, take care with your words in case you are punished by exile
and have to be deported to a place of harmful waters and the disciples who follow you have to drink them and die.

10. In a main, or independent, clause, the imperfect almost inevitably
has a modal aspect, cohortative (expressing volition), optative (expressing a
wish), jussive (expressing a command), for example:

אִם אֱלוֹהַ הוּא, יָבוֹא וְיִמְחֶה

If he is God, let him come and destroy (SDt 328 [F 379]);

מָה אֶעֱשֶׂה

What can I do? (Sanh 3.7);

בִּשְׁלֹשָׁה אוֹמֵר, נְבָרֵךְ

If they are three, he says, Let us bless (Ber 7.3).
(Mishor 1983a and Sharvit 1980 include numerous further examples, classified by mood.)

A typical optative form is that of מִי followed by the imperfect, as in BH.
Compare

מִי יִגְלֶה עָפָר מֵעֵינֶיךָ, רַבָּן יוֹחָנָן בֶּן זַכַּאי

Who could wipe the dust from your eyes, Rabban Johanan ben Zakkai! (Sot 5.2)

with

מִי יַאֲכִלֵנוּ בָּשָׂר

Who would give us meat to eat! (Nm 11.4).

11. The 'persuasive' mood of the imperfect has effectively displaced the
imperative in prayers, petitions, and so on (see Unit 21.7). A prohibition or
negative command or wish is commonly expressed by אַל followed by the
imperfect, as in

אַל תַּרְבֶּה שִׂיחָה עִם הָאִשָּׁה

Don't talk too much with women (Abot 1.5).

In halakhic idiom, the imperfect with לֹא (לֹא יַעֲשֶׂה) is used alongside אֵין
with participle (אֵין עוֹשִׂין) to express a more impersonal form of prohibition.
The first structure is found with singular forms of the verb, the second with
plural forms (see Unit 23.11A).

12. In various proverbial and sapiential contexts, the imperfect has retained one of its earliest functions, namely, expressing durative action (see
Meyer 1992, §100.2A–B), for example

עַל קַן צִפּוֹר יַגִּיעוּ רַחֲמֶיךָ

Unto the nests of the birds your mercy reaches (Meg 4.9).

13. A. Bendavid (1967, §235) notes that many sequences in which BH
employs the imperfect appear in RH with participles, although the difference

in meaning conveyed is not always clear—compare, for example, כֵּיצַד הוּא עוֹשֶׂה 'how must he act?' (Men 5.6) with כֵּיצַד יַעֲשֶׂה 'how will he have to act?' (Men 11.8). It may be true that the imperfect tends to express instruction or command, whereas the participle tends to convey information or news, or that the imperfect relates to the normative and the participle to the commonplace. But the carrying through of such distinctions, even though they might inform a writer's thinking, is subjective, and we can find in the same *halakhah* the simultaneous use of participle and imperfect, apparently in the same sense. For example, in *halakhot* of the type 'where it is the custom' (מְקוֹם שֶׁנָּהֲגוּ), both participle and imperfect are used to express the action to be realized, as at BM 5.5 (see also Shebi 2.5; Pes 4.1; Meg 4.1, etc.):

מְקוֹם שֶׁנָּהֲגוּ לַחֲלוֹק אֶת חֻלְדוֹת מִיָד, חוֹלְקִין, מְקוֹם שֶׁנָּהֲגוּ לְגַדֵּל, יְגַדֵּלוּ

Where it is the custom to share out the offspring immediately, then share them out [participle]; where it is the custom to rear them, then rear them [imperfect].

A striking example of the confusion of participle and imperfect is seen in the following texts from the same *midrash*:

הודיעני אם אכנס לארץ אם לאו ... הודיעני אם ממנה אחה עליהם
פרנסים ואם לאו

Tell me if *I'm going to enter* the land or not ...; tell me if *you're going to assign* them leaders or not (SNm 138 [H 185]);

הודיעני אם אני נכנס לארץ ואם איני נכנס

Tell me if *I'm going to enter* the land or if *I'm not going to enter* (SNm 134.5 [H180]).

As a general rule, nonetheless, in halakhic compositions (Mishnah and Tosefta) the tendency is to formulate impersonally and, thus, to prefer the participle, whereas in midrashic writings, the tendency is towards a more personal and persuasive form of expression, which employs the imperfect.

14. The imperfect is regularly used in subordinate clauses—temporal, final, consecutive, etc.—usually in association with -שֶׁ or a compound of -שֶׁ: שֶׁמָּא 'in case, so as not to', -שֶׁ כְּדֵי 'so that', -שֶׁ בִּשְׁבִיל 'in order to, so that, because', -שֶׁ עַל מְנָת 'on condition that', -שֶׁ לְאַחַר 'after', -שֶׁ לִכְשֶׁ '(for) when', -שֶׁ עַד 'until', etc.—or with the phrases -שֶׁ גּוֹזְרַנִי 'I order that', -שֶׁ שְׁבוּעָה 'I swear that', -שֶׁ צָרִיךְ 'it is necessary that', and -שֶׁ וּבִלְבַד 'provided that, only if'. However, it should be noted that it is also possible to employ the perfect with some of these forms, depending on exactly what meaning is intended (see Bendavid 1967, §233; Mishor 1983a, 125–27). The following examples can be supplemented by the exercises:

שמא תאמר, למדתי חכמת ישראל, אלך ואלמד חכמת האומות

In case you say, I have learned the wisdom of Israel, now I am going to learn the wisdom of the nations (SDt 34 [F 61–62]);

שמא תאמר, הריני למד תורה בשביל שאעשיר

In case you say, I am going to study the Torah to make myself rich (SDt 41 [F 87]);

הֲרֵי זֶה גִּטֵּךְ, עַל מְנָת שֶׁתִּתְּנִי לִי מָאתַיִם זוּז

Here is your document, on condition that you give me two hundred
zuz (Giṭ 7.5);

וּבִלְבַד שֶׁיְּהֵא הַכֶּסֶף מִשֶּׁלַּאֲחֵרִים

Provided that the money comes from others (Qid 1.3).

15. The imperfect following אִם expresses a possible but unfulfilled
condition, an infrequent construction (see Segal, 1927, §486) that is normally
formulated with the temporal conjunctions -לִכְשֶׁ, -כְּשֶׁ, בִּזְמַן שֶׁ, עַד שֶׁ-, etc.:

אִם יִהְיוּ כָל חַכְמֵי יִשְׂרָאֵל בְּכַף מֹאזְנַיִם

If all the sages of Israel were on one balance of a pair of scales
(Abot 2.8).

See as well Unit 28, on conditional clauses.

16. Alongside the construction עָתִיד לְ- followed by the infinitive (see
Units 16.3B and 20.12) is that of עָתִיד שֶׁ- with the imperfect, used to express
an event that could only take place in the future. But it is rare in the tannaitic
literature, occurring not at all in the Mishnah, Sifra, SNm, and Sifre Zuṭṭa,
just once in the Tosefta (TosSoṭ 12.1), three times in SDt 306 (F 329–30),
and twice in Seder Olam Rabbah (3 and 15):

עתידה כנסת ישראל שתעמוד בדין לפני המקום שאומרת

The assembly of Israel will arise before the omnipresent one and
will say (SDt 306 [F 330]; see Girón 1992).

IV *Phraseology*

17. שֶׁמָּא תֹאמַר/תֹאמְרוּ 'in case you interpret, lest you interpret, so that
you do not say' comes after a biblical quotation to introduce an interpretation
regarded as erroneous. To underline that the point of the biblical text is that
such an interpretation be avoided, the text is sometimes reintroduced by
תַּלְמוּד לוֹמַר 'because of that, the text says' (see further, Unit 30.11C). The
formula is widespread in SDt and Sifra, very rare in Mekhilta, and completely absent from SNm:

ושוחד לא תקח [שמות כג' ח']. שמא תאמר, הריני נוטל ממון ואיני מטה
את הדין. ת"ל, כי השוחד יעור עיני חכמים [דברים טז' יט'].

Do not accept a bribe [Ex 23.8]. In case you say, I am going to receive money without it affecting my judgment, the text says, For a
bribe blinds the eyes of the wise [Dt 16.19] (Mek 23.8 [L 3.172]);

שמא תאמרו, הרי מאכל והרי משתה, אם אין שלום אין כלום, ת"ל,
ונתתי שלום בארץ [ויקרא כו' ו'].

[And you will eat your bread to satiety and live securely in your
land (Lv 26.5).] So that you might not say, We have food and drink
but without peace there is nothing, the text says, I shall set peace in
the land [Lv 26.6] (SLv 26.6 [W 111A]);

וירד מצררמה [דברים כו' ה']. שמא תאמר שירד ליטול כתר

מַלְכוּת, תַּלְמוּד לוֹמַר, וַיֵּגֶר שָׁם [שם].

And he went down to Egypt [Dt 26.5]. So that you might not say
that he went down for a royal crown the text says, And he settled
there [ibid.].

V Vocabulary

אָוָה/אָבָה 'desire'

בִּטֵּל 'annul'

בֵּית סְאָה 'space occupied by one seah'

גְּבוּל 'limit', specifically of that which is beyond Jerusalem and the temple

גְּזַר 'decree'

דְּפוּס 'impression, tattoo'

חָגוּן 'worthy (of)'

הִמְתִּין (hi. of מתן), 'keep, leave, postpone. wait'

הִנָּזֵר (ni. of נזר) 'abstain, deprive oneself'

הִתְלִיעַ (hi. of תלע) 'decay, ripen'

נִמְלַךְ (ni. of מלך) 'take advice, reconsider, change one's mind'

עִרְעֵר 'protest'

פָּנָה 'turn', ni. נִפְנָה 'be free, have time'

פְּסִיקְיָא (Latin fascia) 'girdle, brassiere'

קֶבַע 'institution'. i.e. something fixed and established

רְבִיעָה 'autumn rain'

שָׁנָה 'repeat', specifically 'study Mishnah. oral tradition'

חֶלֶם 'furrow'

VI Exercises

1. הוּא הָיָה אוֹמֵר, עֲשֵׂה רְצוֹנוֹ כִּרְצוֹנְךָ, כְּדֵי [כְּדֵי K lacks] שֶׁיַּעֲשֶׂה רְצוֹנְךָ
כִּרְצוֹנוֹ. בַּטֵּל רְצוֹנְךָ מִפְּנֵי רְצוֹנוֹ, כְּדֵי [כְּדֵי K lacks] שֶׁיְּבַטֵּל רְצוֹן
אֲחֵרִים מִפְּנֵי רְצוֹנְךָ. הִלֵּל אוֹמֵר, אַל תִּפְרוֹשׁ מִן הַצִּבּוּר, וְאַל תַּאֲמֵן
[תַּאֲמִין K] בְּעַצְמָךְ עַד יוֹם מוֹתָךְ, וְאַל תָּדִין אֶת חֲבֵרָךְ עַד שֶׁתַּגִּיעַ
לִמְקוֹמוֹ. וְאַל תֹּאמַר דָּבָר שֶׁאִי אֶפְשָׁר לִשְׁמוֹעַ, שֶׁסּוֹפוֹ לְהִשָּׁמַע. וְאַל תֹּאמַר,
לִכְשֶׁאֶפָּנֶה אֶשְׁנֶה, שֶׁמָּא לֹא תִפָּנֶה.

2. וּכְשֶׁאַתָּה מִתְפַּלֵּל, אַל תַּעַשׂ תְּפִלָּתְךָ קֶבַע, אֶלָּא רַחֲמִים וְתַחֲנוּנִים לִפְנֵי
הַמָּקוֹם בָּרוּךְ הוּא ... וְאַל תְּהִי רָשָׁע בִּפְנֵי עַצְמָךְ.

3. מָקוֹם שֶׁנָּהֲגוּ לְהַטִּיל מַיִם בַּיַּיִן, יַטִּילוּ.

4. הָיְתָה שָׂדֵהוּ זְרוּעָה חִטִּים וְנִמְלַךְ לְזָרְעָהּ שְׂעוֹרִים, יַמְתִּין לָהּ עַד שֶׁתַּתְלִיעַ,
וְיוֹפַךְ וְאַחַר כָּךְ יִזְרַע, אִם צָמְחָה. לֹא יֹאמַר, אֶזְרַע וְאַחַר כָּךְ אוֹפַךְ, אֶלָּא
הוֹפֵךְ וְאַחַר כָּךְ זוֹרֵעַ. כַּמָּה יְהֵא חוֹרֵשׁ? כְּתַלְמֵי הָרְבִיעָה. אַבָּא שָׁאוּל אוֹמֵר,
כְּדֵי שֶׁלֹּא יְשַׁיֵּר רֹבַע לְבֵית סְאָה.

5. מָקוֹם שֶׁנָּהֲגוּ לְבָרֵךְ, יְבָרֵךְ, וְשֶׁלֹּא לְבָרֵךְ, לֹא יְבָרֵךְ.

6. הֲרֵינִי נָזִיר עַל מְנָת שֶׁאֱהֵא שׁוֹתֶה יַיִן וּמִטַּמֵּא לַמֵּתִים, הֲרֵי זֶה נָזִיר, וְאָסוּר בְּכֻלָּן.

7. שָׁלַח לוֹ רַבָּן גַּמְלִיאֵל, גּוֹזְרַנִי עָלֶיךָ שֶׁתָּבֹא אֶצְלִי בְּמַקֶּלְךָ וּבְמָעוֹתֶיךָ.

8. וּסְעוּדוֹת גְּדוֹלוֹת עוֹשִׂין לָהֶם [וְלָעֵדִים] בִּשְׁבִיל שֶׁיְּהוּ רְגִילִין לָבֹא.

9. שְׁבוּעָה שֶׁלֹּא אֹכַל, וְאָכַל כָּל שֶׁהוּא, חַיָּב.

10. מַשְׁבִּיעַ אֲנִי עֲלֵיכֶם, כְּשֶׁתֵּדְעוּן לִי עֵדוּת שֶׁתָּבוֹאוּ וּתְעִידוּנִי, הֲרֵי אֵלּוּ פְּטוּרִים, מִפְּנֵי שֶׁקָּדְמָה שְׁבוּעָה לָעֵדוּת.

11. ובני ישראל הלכו ביבשה בתוך הים [והמים להם חֹמָה] [שמות יד׳ כט׳]. והיו מלאכי השרת תמהים לומר, בני אדם עובדי עבודה זרה מהלכין ביבשה בתוך הים. ומנין שאף הים נתמלא עליהם חמה? שנאמר, והמים להם חמה [שם]. אל תקרי חֹמָה אלא חֵמָה.

12. ויוצא משה את העם לקראת האלהים [שמות יט׳ יז׳]. אמר רבי יוסי, יהודה היה דורש, ײ מסיני בא [דברים לג׳ ב׳]. אל תקרא כאן אלא ײ לסיני בא, ליתן תורה לישראל. ואני איני אומר כן אלא, ײ מסני בא, לקבל את ישראל, כחתן זה שהוא יוצא לקראת כלה.

13. אם חבול תחבול וגו׳ [שמות כב׳ כה׳]. רבי ישמעאל אומר, בא הכתוב ללמדך שתהא עושה מצוה ותהא נוטל את שלך.

14. וביום השביעי יהיה לכם קדש וגו׳ [שמות לה׳ ב׳], שלא יהו ישראל אומרים, הואיל ומותרים בעשיית מלאכה בבית המקדש, נהא מותרין לעשות מלאכה בגבולין. ת״ל, וביום השביעי יהיה לכם קדש, לכם קדש ולמקום חול.

15. נבוכדנצר היה הגון שיעשה נס על ידו, אבל אתה מלך רשע אתה ואין אתה הגון שיעשה נס על ידך.

16. אם בחוקתי תלכו [ויקרא כו׳ ג׳]. מלמד שהמקום מתאוה שיהו ישראל עמילים בתורה.

17. משל, למה הדבר דומה? למלך בשר ודם שהיה לו בן בית ונתן לו שדה אחת כמתנה ... בא אחד וערער כנגדו על השדה. אמר לו המלך, כל מי שירצה יבא יערער כנגדך על השדה ...

18. והיא מוציאה דפוס של פעור מתחת פסיקיא שלה ואומרת לו, רבי, רצונך שאשמע לך, השתחוה לזה [...] רצונך שאשמע לך, הנזר מתורתו של משה.

19. כי אם שמור תשמרו את כל המצוה הזאת אשר אנכי מצוה אתכם לעשותה לאהבה את ײ אלהיכם [דברים יא׳ כב׳]. שמא תאמר, הריני למד תורה בשביל שאיקרא חכם, בשביל שאשב בישיבה, בשביל שאאריך ימים לעולם הבא.

20. ולא ירבה לו נשים [דברים יז׳ יז׳], אלא שמנה עשרה. רבי יהודה אומר, מרבה הוא לו ובלבד שלא יהו מסירות את לבו.

Sources. 1. Abot 2.4. 2. Abot 2.13. 3. BM 4.11. 4. Kil 2.3. 5. Meg 4.1. 6. Naz 2.4. 7. RS 2.9. 8. RS 2.5. 9. Shebu 3.1. 10. Shebu 4.9. 11. Mek 14.29 (L 1.246). 12. Mek 19.17 (L 2.218–19). 13. Mek 22.25 (L 3.150). 14. Mek 35.2. (L 3.207). 15. SLv 22.32 (W 99d). 16. SLv 26.3 (W 110c). 17. SNm 117.1 (H 135). 18. SNm 131.1 (H 171). 19. SDt 48 (F 113). 20. SDt 159 (F 210).

UNIT NINETEEN

PARTICIPLE

I *Introductory text* (SDt 329 [F 380])

ואין מידי מציל [דברים לב׳ לט׳], אין אבות מצילין את הבנים, לא אברהם
מציל את ישמעאל ולא יצחק מציל את עשו. אין לי אלא אבות שאין מצילין
את הבנים. אחים את אחים מנין? תלמוד לומר, אח לא פדה יפדה איש
[תהלים מט׳ ח׳]. לא יצחק מציל את ישמעאל ולא יעקב מציל את עשו,
ואפילו נותן אדם לו כל ממון שבעולם, אין נותנין לו כפרו, שנאמר, ואח
לא פדה יפדה איש ... ויקר פדיון נפשם [תהלים מט׳ ח׳-ט׳]. יקרה היא
נפש זו, שכשאדם חוטא בה אין לה תשלומים.

And there is no-one who frees from my hand [Dt 32.39]: fathers cannot rescue sons—Abraham does not free Ishmael nor Isaac Jacob. This only shows
me that fathers cannot free their sons. From where is it deduced that brothers
cannot free brothers either? From the text that teaches, Truly, no-one can redeem a brother [Ps 49.8]: Isaac cannot free Ishmael nor Jacob Esau—even if
someone paid all the money in the world, it would not be sufficient for their
ransom, for it is written, Truly, no-one can redeem a brother ... the redemption of their life is very costly [Ps 49.8–9]. This life is worth much, and when
one sins against it no payment is possible.

1. With regard to the supreme gift of life, a person is completely in the
hands of God—one's personal merits or those of one's parents or siblings
count for nothing; it is entirely a matter of God's grace.

II *Morphology*

2. A characteristic feature of RH is the use of -*t* in the feminine
participle (see Unit 16.6), a result of the search for greater expressivity in the
spoken language. In the plural, the endings -*m* and -*n* alternate.

3. *Qal.*

A. RH retains all three BH models, the active קֹטֵל, and the intransitive
or stative קָטֵל and קָטֹל, as in the following table.

שֹׁמֵר	שֹׁמֶרֶת	שֹׁמְרִין	שֹׁמְרוֹת
בָּטֵל	בְּטֵלָה	בְּטֵלִין	בְּטֵלוֹת
יָכוֹל	יְכוֹלָה	יְכוֹלִין	יְכוֹלוֹת

As well as the feminine in קֹטְלַת, we occasionally find קוֹטְלָה, as at SNm 131.1 (H 170):

וקטנה קוראה ואומרה לו מבפנים

A younger one was calling him and saying to him from inside.

(MS Vatican 32 has אומרת, but note that the structures in the version above could simply be forms of the perfect that have resulted from assimilation: קָרְאָה > קָרְאָה and אָמְרָה > אָמְרָה, i.e. ā > ō before a labial or *resh*.)

The stative participle קָטֵל has the same semantic value as an adjective, and, like an adjective, forms its feminine in -*ah*, for example טָמֵא, טְמֵאָה 'impure'. Sometimes, such structures exist alongside active forms of the participle, for example לָמֵד, לְמֵדָה 'learned' and לָמֵד, לְמֵדָת 'student'. There is a tendency to replace the stative forms by the active, as at Abot 4.20, where the standard text reads

הַלּוֹמֵד מִן הַקְּטַנִּים, לְמָה הוּא דוֹמֶה

A person who learns from little ones, who is such a person like?,

but K has הַלָּמֵד מִן הַקְּטָנִּים (note also SNm 131.1 [H 169]:

כל פרשה שהיא סמוכה לחברתה למֵידָה הֵימֶנה

Any pericope found next to another is illuminated by it).

In these instances, there is a difference in aspect between לוֹמֵד (more active) and לָמֵד (more stative), but in others the difference is more subtle, if there is one at all, giving rise to alternation and confusion of forms. A typical example is at Abot 1.5, where the standard text reads

בּוֹטֵל מִדִּבְרֵי תוֹרָה

Neglecting the study of the law,

but K has בָּטֵל. Other examples relate to דּוֹלֵק and דָּלֵק and אוֹבֵד and אָבֵד. Possibly, the influence of the Aramaic participle in קָטֵל has had a bearing on this matter (as pointed out to me by Dr José Ribera Florit of the University of Barcelona).

The only remnant of the קָטֵל model in RH is יָכוֹל—as seen in Unit 17.3, the perfect and imperfect forms have disappeared. E.Y. Kutscher (1971, 1599) notes the vocalization of the feminine in יְכוֹלָה, for יְכוֹלָה, accentuating its stative character.

B. The first person subject pronoun can be attached as a suffix to the participle, giving rise to the common forms גּוֹזְרַנִי (from גּוֹזֵר אֲנִי 'I decree'), as at Taa 3.8, פּוֹרְטַנִי (from פּוֹרֵט אֲנִי 'I specify'), as at SNm 1.2 (H 1), and שׁוֹמְעַנִי (from שׁוֹמֵעַ אֲנִי 'I interpret'), as at SNm 1.4 (H 2).

C. The passive participle regularly forms the feminine with -*ah*, for example אָמוּר, אֲמוּרָה 'said, mentioned', as at Sot 7.3:

מָה עֲנִיָּה הָאֲמוּרָה לְהַלָּן בִּלְשׁוֹן הַקֹּדֶשׁ, אַף כָּאן בִּלְשׁוֹן הַקֹּדֶשׁ

Just as the response mentioned there was given in the holy tongue, so also here it has to be given in the holy tongue.

Some passive participles have effectively become nominalized adjectives, for example גְּרוּשָׁה 'divorcée'.

D. In *ayin-waw* and *lamed-he* verbs, the BH form of the feminine singular participle, in -ah, is maintained, for example בָּאָה 'coming' and רֹצָה 'desiring'.

Participles of *lamed-alef* verbs can be inflected as though they were *lamed-he*, thus קֹרִין and קֹרָאִין 'calling'. In the feminine singular, the participle can take either -ah or -t: יוֹצְאָה (K יוֹצְאָ) and יוֹצֵאת 'going out':

בַּמֶּה אִשָּׁה יוֹצְאָה וּבַמֶּה אֵינָה יוֹצֵאָה

What may a woman go out with and what may she not go out with? (Shab 6.1);

בֵּית דִּין הַגָּדוֹל ... שֶׁמִּמֶּנּוּ יוֹצֵאת תּוֹרָה לְכָל יִשְׂרָאֵל

The supreme court ... from which teaching extends to all Israel (Sanh 11.2).

Doubtless, יוֹצֵאת is a biblicizing form—at Sanh 11.2 and Yeb 14.1, K reads יוֹצְאָ for, respectively, יוֹצֵאת and יוֹצְאָה. Already in LBH, we find:

כִּשְׁגָגָה שֶׁיֹּצָא מִלִּפְנֵי הַשַּׁלִּיט

Like an error that proceeds from a ruler (Ec 10.5).

E. An active קָטוֹל participle is well-attested in good manuscripts, even though it has been confused with the passive קָטוּל or corrected to the standard קוֹטֵל model. Thus, whereas the standard text of Abot 4.20 reads

הַלּוֹמֵד מִן הַזְּקֵנִים לְמָה הוּא דוֹמֶה? לְאוֹכֵל עֲנָבִים

A person who learns from old people, who is such a person like? (Like) one who eats (ripe) grapes,

K has לאכול, pointed לְאָכוֹל (Mishor 1983a provides a complete list of such participles).

F. The model קְטוֹל for the *Qal* passive participle, alongside the usual קָטוּל, is attested in good manuscripts, but only very rarely, for example שְׁלוּחָה 'her emissary' (K Qid 2.1)—possibly it is this participle that underlies the wordplay with ἀπεσταλμένος at Jn 9.7.

4. *Nif'al*.

In the feminine singular participle, the suffix -t (נִקְטֶלֶת) predominates, as against the BH model in -ah (נִקְטְלָה), for example

ומנין שהארץ עתידה להיות נזרעת ועושה פירות בן יומה

From where is it deduced that in the future the land will be sown and yield fruit in a day? (SLv 26.4 [W 110d])

Even in *ayin-waw*, *lamed-he*, and *lamed-alef* verbs, we find participial forms like נִקְרֵאת, נַעֲשִׂית, etc. An example with בֶּנָה and עָשָׂה is seen at Sanh 10.6:

לְכְמוֹ שֶׁהָיְתָה אֵינָה נִבְנֵית, אֲבָל נַעֲשֵׂית הִיא גַּנּוֹת וּפַרְדֵּסִים

It may not now be rebuilt in the form it used to be, but may be changed into gardens or orchards.

In the masculine singular participle, the forms נַעֲשֶׂה and נֶעֱשָׂה, instead of BH נַעֲשֶׂה, in K and other good manuscripts, result from assimilation of the verb עָשָׂה to the *lamed-alef* model (see Unit 17.5).

For the verb דִּין, we find the *Nif'al* participles נָדוֹן, functioning more as a noun, and נִידּוֹן, which carries more verbal force (see Bar-Asher 1990d).

5. *Pi'el* and *Pu'al.*

A. In the *Pi'el*, the BH paradigm is maintained: מְדַבְּרִין, מְדַבְּרֶת, מְדַבֵּר, מְדַבְּרוֹת. The *Pi'el* participle of הָיָה is attested twice in the Talmud, in two different forms מְהַוֶּה (Ket 40b) and מְהַיֶּה (Qid 18a), but not at all in the Mishnah or tannaitic *midrashim*.

B. Of the *Pu'al*, it is only the participle that survives in RH, and this, again, usually follows the BH model: מְדֻבָּר, מְדֻבֶּרֶת, מְדֻבְּרִין, מְדֻבָּרוֹת. However, in *lamed-he* verbs, the feminine participles take -*h*, for example מְגוּלָה/מְגוּלָּה. As already noted (Unit 15.4C), the preformative *mem* is often omitted in the Babylonian tradition; hence, מְמוּעָט becomes מוּעָט, as at Ḥag 1.8:

מִקְרָא מָעָט וַהֲלָכוֹת מְרֻבּוֹת

Many laws from little Scripture (K מְמוּעָט).

6. *Hitpa'el* and *Nitpa'al.*

As well as the *Hitpa'el* participle in -מִתְ, there is also a *Nitpa'al* participle in -נִתְ. It is often thought that the latter has been corrected by later copyists to the former, perhaps because of the orthographic similarity of נ and מ. In such participles, the assimilation of the -ת- of the preformative is more common than in BH, although in unvocalized texts it is not always possible to distinguish the resulting forms from participles of other conjugations, for example, the *Pu'al.*

7. *Hif'il* and *Hof'al.*

A. In the *Hif'il*, a more colloquial form, מַקְטֶלֶת, is found alongside the BH feminine מַקְטִילָה:

כָּךְ מְטִיבָה, כָּךְ מְרִיעָה

Doing good in this way, doing harm in this way (Sanh 7.10);

הָאִישׁ מַדִּיר אֶת בְּנוֹ בַּנָּזִיר, וְאֵין הָאִשָּׁה מַדֶּרֶת אֶת בְּנָהּ בַּנָּזִיר

A man may impose a Nazirite vow on his son, but a woman may not impose a Nazirite vow on her son (Soṭ 3.8).

The form in -*t* is already encountered in LBH:

אֵין אֶסְתֵּר מַגֶּדֶת מוֹלַדְתָּהּ

Esther did not declare her family background (Est 2.20).

In *lamed-he* verbs, the feminine participle מַעֲלָח is found instead of מַעֲלָה, for example, in the best manuscripts of SNm 95.1 (H 95):

והלא הלכה עמהם באר במדמר והיתה מעלת להם דגים שמנים יותר מצרכם

Did not there accompany them in the desert a well, which brought up for them enormous fishes, beyond their need?

B. The RH *Hof'al* is characterized by the vowel *u* in the preformative, rather than *o*, which tends to highlight the passive character of the conjugation. Thus, the participle follows the model מוּקְדָּם, מוּקְדֶּמֶת. In some *lamed-he* verbs, the feminine participle also ends in -*t*, as in the phrase מוּכַּת עֵץ 'wounded by a piece of wood' (in reference to accidental loss of virginity) at Ket 1.3.

III *Grammar and usage*

8. A participle may be viewed as both noun and verb (see Unit 11.4C), and, as a noun, it can be found in the 'construct' state, for example, in עוֹבְדֵי ע״ז ... עוֹלֵי בָבֶל 'followers of idolatry' (Mek 18.3 [L 2.168]), בָּאֵי הָאָרֶץ 'those who entered the country ... those who went up from Babylonia' (SDt 8 [F 16]), and שׁוֹפְכֵי דָם 'spillers of blood' (Soṭ 9.6)—the same usage is seen in BH, for example כָּל־יוֹרְדֵי עָפָר 'all who go down into the dust' (Ps 22.30).

Nominal and verbal uses can appear alongside each other, as in the well-known wordplay of SLv 26.6 (W 111a):

> אמר ר״ש, אימתי הוא שבחו של מקום? בזמן שאין מזיקים או בזמן שיש
> מזיקים ואין מזיקים?
>> Rabbi Simeon argued, When should one praise a place? When there are no evil powers [מַזִּיקִים]? Or when there are evil powers but they do not cause harm [מַזִּיקִים]?

There are numerous other examples of this sort, intended to have a rhetorical effect, for example הַקּוֹרֵא קוֹרֵא 'the reader reads' (Mak 3.14) or אֵין הַתּוֹרֵם תּוֹרֵם 'the one who collected *terumah* would not collect it (without saying ...)' (Sheq 3.3), etc.

At Abot 5.14, בְּהוֹלְכֵי לְבֵית הַמִּדְרָשׁ 'among those who go to the house of study', there is a degree of grammatical incongruence, with the participle used as noun (governed by a preposition and in the construct state) but with a complement (also governed by a preposition), לְבֵית, more appropriate to a verb. This oddity derives from the ambivalent nature of the participle and can be traced back to the earliest stages of the Hebrew language (see Meyer 1992, §97.3D; note the *ketiv* of 2 S 10.9, בְּחוּרֵי בישראל, corrected by the Masoretes).

9. See Unit 16.12B and 13A for an indication of the way in which the participle relates to the area of the present and future and its imperative, facultative, and iterative moods. See Unit 24.10 for modal (circumstantial/extraposed) noun clauses.

10. An unfolding state or action expressed by a participle is either taking place in the present or has a timeless quality, for example:

> הַתּוֹכֵחָה מְבִיאָה לִידֵי שָׁלוֹם
>> Correction leads to peace (SDt 2 [F 10]);

> הַקּוֹרֵא אֶת הַמְּגִלָּה עוֹמֵד וְיוֹשֵׁב
>> One who reads the scroll can be standing or sitting (Meg 4.1);

> שְׁלוֹשָׁה מִנִים אֲסוּרִין בַּנָּזִיר
>> Three sorts of things are forbidden to the Nazirite (Naz 6.1).

The atemporal nature of the participle is particularly striking in stative verbs, for which the participle can be replaced by an adjective (see Unit 13.4), with the forms קָטֵל, קוֹטֵל, and נִקְטָל alternating among the different manuscripts, or appearing alongside one another in the same text without any apparent difference in meaning (see above, §3A). The virtual equivalence of

זָכוּר, זָכַר‎, and זוֹכֵר‎ is especially striking.

In practice, the participle of the *Qal* passive, קָטוּל‎, and that of the *Nif'al*, נִקְטָל‎, are not always distinguished, although analysis of a good number of texts suggests a certain regularity, namely, that קָטוּל‎ signifies the present result of a past action whereas נִקְטָל‎ indicates the activity itself in process, as seen clearly at SNm 61 (H 59), which says that God showed Moses מנורה עשויה ונעשית‎ 'the lampstand made and being made', that is, not just the finished product but also the process whereby it was made.

11. The participle, especially the plural participle, employed without an explicit subject, is ideal for expressing the impersonal or indefinite nature of a proposition or its general applicability (see Unit 6.13), and for indicating, without actually naming, God as the author of an action, for example:

אִם לָמַדְתָּ תּוֹרָה הַרְבֵּה נוֹתְנִים לָךְ שָׂכָר הַרְבֵּה

If you have studied the Torah a lot, you will be given an abundant reward (Abot 2.16);

הַלּוֹמֵד עַל מְנָת לְלַמֵּד מַסְפִּיקִין בְּיָדוֹ לִלְמוֹד וּלְלַמֵּד

One who studies with the intention of teaching will be enabled to study and to teach (Abot 4.5);

היה ר׳ מאיר אומר, מנין שמידה שאדם מודד, בה מודדין לו

Rabbi Meir used to say, From where is it deduced that people will be measured by the same measure that they themselves use? (TosSoṭ 3.1; cf. Soṭ 1.7; Mt 7.2; Mk 4.24; Lk 6.38).

Parallel to the formula יֵשׁ אוֹמְרִין‎ 'there are those who say, it is said' (see Unit 6.14), are other impersonal constructions like יֵשׁ קוֹרִין‎ 'there are those who read, it is read' or יֵשׁ מְבִיאִין‎ 'there are those who offer, it is offered'.

12. The participle is employed with especially vivid results when used to describe the past as a story unfolding before our eyes, as in this lengthy account from Soṭ 7.8:

פָּרָשַׁת הַמֶּלֶךְ כֵּיצַד? מוֹצָאֵי יוֹם טוֹב הָרִאשׁוֹן שֶׁלְּחָג, בַּשְּׁמִינִי בְּמוֹצָאֵי שְׁבִיעִית, עוֹשִׂין לוֹ בִּימָה שֶׁלְּעֵץ בָּעֲזָרָה, וְהוּא יוֹשֵׁב עָלֶיהָ ... חַזַּן הַכְּנֶסֶת נוֹטֵל סֵפֶר תּוֹרָה וְנוֹתְנָהּ לְרֹאשׁ הַכְּנֶסֶת, וְרֹאשׁ הַכְּנֶסֶת נוֹתְנָהּ לַסְּגָן, וְהַסְּגָן נוֹתְנָהּ לְכֹהֵן גָּדוֹל, וְכֹהֵן גָּדוֹל נוֹתְנָהּ לַמֶּלֶךְ, וְהַמֶּלֶךְ עוֹמֵד וּמְקַבֵּל וְקוֹרֵא יוֹשֵׁב. אַגְרִיפַּס הַמֶּלֶךְ עָמַד וְקִבֵּל וְקָרָא עוֹמֵד וְשִׁבְּחוּהוּ חֲכָמִים

What used to happen in the royal liturgy? At the close of the first festive day of the feast (of Tabernacles), in the eighth year at the end of the sabbatical year, they make him [the king] a platform of wood in the courtyard, and he sits down there ... The minister of the synagogue takes the book of the law and passes it to the leader of the synagogue, the leader of the synagogue hands it to the prefect, the prefect hands it to the high priest, the high priest passes it to the king, and the king receives it standing up and reads it sitting down. But King Agrippa received it standing up and read it standing up, and the sages praised him for this.

In this narrative, it is obvious that the description of habitual actions exactly
as they used to occur and as they should continue to occur (liturgical atemporality) is expressed through participles, whereas the punctual, specific historical, action of Agrippa is related in the perfect. Another example of liturgical
atemporality is the following description from TosSoṭ 2.1:

ממנה רואה וכותב, לא חסר ולא יתר, יוצא ועומד בצד סוטה קורה
ודורש ומדקדק כל דקדוקי פרשה

He carries on looking and writing from it [tablet], without omitting
or adding anything, he goes out and stands at the side of the suspected adulteress, reading, explaining, and enunciating all the letters
of the passage.

Another vivid usage of the participle occurs in the story of the Am-
monite and Moabite women who tempted Israel, at SNm 131.1 (H170):

באותה שעה אדם יוצא לטייל בשוק ומבקש ליטל לו חפץ מן הזקינה
והיתה מוכרת לו בשוה, וקטנה קוראה ואומרת לו מבפנים

Then someone went out to wander through the market and wanted
to buy something from an old woman who was selling it at the right
price, when a younger woman calls to him from inside and says to
him.

13. In the text from Soṭ 7.8 quoted in the preceding section, note the
phrases קוֹרֵא יוֹשֵׁב and קָרָא עוֹמֵד, where יוֹשֵׁב and עוֹמֵד function as adverbial
modifiers of the main verb, 'read standing', 'read sitting down'. Such participles, which act as additional complements to the subject or as verb modifiers,
are widespread, with חָזַר and שָׁנָה especially common in this function:

הָיוּ שׁוֹנִין וְאוֹמְרִין, אָנוּ לְיָהּ וּלְיָהּ עֵינֵינוּ

They continued repeating, We are Y.'s and our eyes are on Y. (Suk
5.4);

יכול משאומרים להם דברי ניחומים חוזרים ואומרים להם דברי
תוכחות

Perhaps after speaking words of consolation to them, they will again
speak words of reproof to them (SDt 342 [F 392]).

Other participles appear to have a purely decorative character, like יוֹשֵׁב
in stereotyped phrases of the kind 'he sat down and said' or עוֹמֵד in the sense
of 'be about to, will':

והוא יושב ומפקדו ואומר לו

He sat down, commanded him, and said to him (SNm 87.2; SDt 43);

והוא יושב ומשקלו ואומר

He sat down, pondered, and said (SLv 26.25 [W 112a]);

היה יושב ומצפה ואומר

He sat down, looked around, and said (SNm 89.5);

אם אני מניח נכסי ביד בני הוא עומד ומבזבזם

If I leave my riches in the hands of my son, he is going to squander
them (SDt 11 [F 19]).

All these examples are taken from parables (*meshalim*), an indication of
their status as literary clichés, a rôle that is especially clear at SNm 88.2 (H
88):

היה יצר הרע יושב ומצעתו כל הלילה ואומר לו

The evil inclination was tormenting him, all the night saying to him.
Another stereotyped formula is הָיָה יוֹשֵׁב וְדוֹרֵשׁ 'he sat down and interpreted, he sat down to interpret' or simply 'he interpreted, he set about interpreting', presented in §23, below.

14. The participle וְהוֹלֵךְ can accompany another participle, this time
having a significant semantic effect by conveying the continuous or
progressive nature of the main activity. To the examples already provided in
Unit 16.15D, may be added:

הוּא מוֹצִיא וְהוֹלֵךְ, עַד שֶׁיּוֹצִיא אֶת כָּל הַכִּיס

He continued spending (literally, 'taking out'), until he had spent
the entire purse (Mei 6.6);

תינוק יונק והולך כל עשרים וארבע חדש ... יונק תינוק והולך אפילו
עד חמש שנים

The child continued suckling for twenty-four months ... The child
continued suckling even up to five years (TosNid 2.3).
Other participles, such as וְיוֹצֵא, וְעוֹלֶה, וְעוֹמֵד, וְיוֹרֵד, וּבָא, and וְיוֹצֵא, can also be
used like וְהוֹלֵךְ:

כל זמן שהיה משה עומד על שפת הבאר, היו המים צפין ועולין
לקראתו

While Moses was waiting at the mouth of the well, the waters kept
on coming up towards him (ARN 20 [S 72]);

היה מצטער ובא עד שהגיע לנמילה של יפו

He became sadder and sadder until he arrived at (or 'as he drew
ever nearer to') the port of Jaffa (TosKippurim 2.4; MS Erfurt reads
ובא for ואוכל);

כָּל הַדּוֹרוֹת הָיוּ מַכְעִיסִין וּבָאִין עַד שֶׁהֵבִיא עֲלֵיהֶם אֶת מֵי הַמַּבּוּל

All the generations were provoking him one after the other until he
brought upon them the waters of the flood (Abot 5.2; K and MS
Parma read וּבָאִין for לְפָנָיו).

מחלחל ויורד

It penetrates, corroding as it passes down (TosSoṭ 1.6).
15. A participle regularly functions as the complement of הִתְחִיל 'begin',
as in

הִתְחִילוּ כָּל הָעָם שׂוֹרְפִין

All the people began burning them (Pes 1.5),
although an infinitive complement is still retained on some occasions, as in
this example from the story of Ḥoni the circle-drawer, where both constructions appear alongside one another:

הִתְחִילוּ הַגְּשָׁמִים מְנַטְּפִין ... הִתְחִילוּ לֵירֵד בְּזַעַף

The rains began dripping ... they began to fall with force (Taa 3.8).

Some other verbs also take a participle as complement:

לֹא נִמְנְעוּ עוֹשִׂין

They are not prevented (from) using (Yeb 1.4);

מה בכור אדם רשיי נותנו לכהן

Just as one is free to give it (redemption fee) to the priest for the firstborn of a human being (SNm 118.2 [H 138]).

The well-known formula דֶּרֶךְ בְּנֵי־אָדָם 'the way of human beings', in reference to habitual behaviour, may be continued by an infinitive or by a participle:

עַד שָׁעָה שֶׁדֶּרֶךְ בְּנֵי אָדָם לֶאֱכוֹל בָּשָׂר

Up to the time that people normally eat meat (Ned 8.6);

מִי שֶׁיֵּשׁ לוֹ בוֹר לִפְנִים מִבֵּיתוֹ שֶׁלַּחֲבֵרוֹ, נִכְנָס בְּשָׁעָה שֶׁדֶּרֶךְ בְּנֵי אָדָם
נִכְנָסִין, וְיוֹצֵא בְּשָׁעָה שֶׁדֶּרֶךְ בְּנֵי אָדָם יוֹצְאִין

If someone owns a well behind a neighbour's house, that person may enter at the time people are accustomed to enter and leave at the time people are accustomed to leave (BB 6.5).

16. The use of the participle with הָיָה is rare in BH, although it starts being employed with some regularity in LBH (see, for example, Ne 2.13, 15; 2 C 24.12; 30.10; 36.16), and in his Qumran corpus, E. Qimron (1986, 70) finds no less than fifty examples of the construction. In RH, it is commonplace as a way of emphasizing the continuous or iterative nature of an action, and is used in reference to both the past and the future, and in the imperative and infinitive moods. The following examples illustrate the different contexts in which the construction is found.

A. Continuous action in the past:

כְּשֶׁהָיָה מִתְפַּלֵּל עַל הַחוֹלִים, הָיָה אוֹמֵר, זֶה חַי וְזֶה מֵת

When he prayed for the sick, he used to say, This one will live, this one will die (Ber 5.5 see Unit 1.12 for the formula הוּא הָיָה אוֹמֵר).

B. Continuous action in the future:

הֲרֵינִי נָזִיר עַל מְנָת שֶׁאֱהֵא שׁוֹתֶה יַיִן וּמִטַּמֵּא לַמֵּתִים

I'll be a Nazirite so long as I can carry on drinking wine and polluting myself with dead bodies (Naz 2.4).

C. Continuous action in the imperative mood:

בְּכָל מִדָּה וּמִדָּה שֶׁהוּא מוֹדֵד לָךְ הֱוֵי מוֹדֶה לוֹ בִּמְאֹד מְאֹד

Whatever the measure he measures out to you, you must continue to thank him without ceasing (Ber 9.5).

D. Continuous action in the infinitive mood:

חָזַר רַבִּי עֲקִיבָא לִהְיוֹת שׁוֹנֶה כְּבֶן עַזַּאי

Rabbi Akiba retracted so as to teach like Ben Azzai (Taa 4.4).

E. הָיָה (perfect) with participle, conjoined (by -וְ) with a perfect, expresses an action prior to another in the past (pluperfect); see Unit 17.8 for examples.

17. Participle with future reference.

A. In idiomatic speech, the participle can designate the immediate

future, or at least an event that seems to the speaker to be on the point of
happening, as in אֲנִי מֵת 'I'm just about to die' (Yeb 16.6) or זֶה מֵת 'this one is
going to die' (Ber 5.5), a usage also found in the Bible: הִנְנִי מֵבִיא אֶת־הַמַּבּוּל
'behold, I am going to cause a flood' (Gn 6.17). In RH, a more distant future
may sometimes also be expressed in the same way:

אבל לעתיד לבא אין נגאלין אלא בתשרי

But in the future, they will be redeemed in Tishri (Mek 12.42 [L
1.116]).

B. In exegetical writing, for example:

ושכבתם ואין מחריד [ויקרא כו' ו']. לא יראים מכל ברייה

You will lie down with none to disturb you [Lv 26.6]. You should
not fear any creature (SLv 26.6 [W 111a]).

C. Often, expressions that employ the imperfect in BH are formulated
with the participle in RH—compare אֲנִי אֶתֵּן at 2 S 21.6 with אֲנִי נוֹתֵן at the beginning of SDt 3, both in the sense of 'I'm going to give' (see Unit 18.13 and
the detailed comparison of BH and RH in Bendavid 1967, §§224–43).

D. The eschatological or inevitable future can be expressed by the formula סוֹף with (-שֶׁ and) the participle (although the infinitive is more usual in
this construction; see Unit 20.12):

אמר לו הקב״ה, אתה רצית לפרוש עצמך מבני אדם, סוף בני אדם
נפרשים ממך

The holy one, blessed be he, said to him (Nebuchadnezzar), You
wanted to separate yourself from humanity, but it will be humanity
that separates itself from you (Mek 15.7 [L 2.46]);

חבלת חבולה אחת, סוף שחובלין בך חבולות הרבה

If you give one loan, you will end up taking out many loans (Mek
15.26 [L 2.97]).

E. A not uncommon construction (especially in the RH of the *amoraim*;
see Girón 1992) is עָתִיד with the participle, a variant of the more usual formula with the infinitive, to express the eschatological future:

כך עתיד הקב״ה מטייל עם הצדיקים בגן עדן לעתיד לבא

In the same way, the holy one, blessed be he, will be walking about
in the garden of Eden with the righteous in the future to come (SLv
26.12 [W 111b]).

18. There tends to be an imperative connotation in expressions of the
immediate or inevitable future:

משישב המלך על כסא י' את מכרית זרע עמלק

After the king has sat down on the throne of Y., you will destroy the
descendants of Amalek (SDt 67 [F 132]).

At SNm 115.5 (H 127), we find a series of imperatives followed by הוֹלֵךְ,

נעול לי ... וטול ... והולך

Help me put on (my sandals), take (my things ahead of me), and go
(to the bath-house),

although here וְהוֹלֵךְ might be interpreted as a modal participle (see above,

§14) or as elliptical for הֱוֵי הוֹלֵךְ (see Unit 21.8).

This imperative use of the participle is standard in halakhic formulations or in statements of principles couched impersonally:

אֵין מַעֲמִידִין בְּהֵמָה בְּפֻנְדְּקָאוֹת שֶׁלַּגּוֹיִם, מִפְּנֵי שֶׁחֲשׁוּדִין עַל הָרְבִיעָה

One must not leave livestock at inns of gentiles, because they are suspected of bestiality (AZ 2.1).

However, when the construction is employed in a positive context, it has to be borne in mind, for interpretative and translational purposes, that it can also have a permissive significance ('one may', not 'one must'), a usage clearly exhibited at Meg 4.1:

הַקּוֹרֵא אֶת הַמְּגִילָּה עוֹמֵד וְיוֹשֵׁב

Whoever reads the scroll may be standing or seated (see also, for example, Ber 1.5 and Naz 4.7).

19. In halakhic formulas of the kind 'if/when/in case ... then', the supposition expressed in the first clause may employ the perfect (see Unit 17.11) or the participle, as in:

הָאוֹמֵר, אֱהֵא, הֲרֵי זֶה נָזִיר

If someone says, I shall be, then they've already become a Nazirite (Naz 1.1);

הַמּוֹצֵא מֵת בַּתְּחִלָּה מֻשְׁכָּב כְּדַרְכּוֹ, נוֹטְלוֹ וְאֶת תְּבוּסָתוֹ

If someone finds a corpse for the first time, lying down in the normal way, they may remove it and the soil around it (Naz 9.3).

20. The passive participle may also be used as a gerundive (see Segal 1927, §334), that is to say, it can express not only a quality or state already acquired ('*amatus*, beloved'), but also one yet to be acquired ('*amandus*, one that must be loved'), or one that has the potential to be acquired ('*amabilis*, lovable'), as, for example, in בדבר הנמחה 'with something that can be erased', not 'with something erased' (SNm 16 [H 21]; see also Qid 2.9 and Yom 6.1).

Thus, the passive participle can be used to indicate the 'destiny' of a subject in such well-established expressions as הַמּוּמָתִים 'those who are to be put to death' (Sanh 6.2) or those well-known because of their biblical allusion; for example, שׁוֹר הַנִּסְקָל is not 'the ox that has been stoned' but 'the ox destined to be stoned', according to the rules prescribed at Ex 21.28; similarly, עֶגְלָה עֲרוּפָה is not 'a calf that has had its neck broken' but 'a calf that is due to have its neck broken', as prescribed at Dt 21.1, and שָׂעִיר הַמִּשְׁתַּלֵּחַ does not refer to 'the goat that has been sent off' but to 'the goat that has been chosen to be sent off' into the desert, in accordance with Lv 16.20–22.

This usage is also attested in the Bible (see Meyer 1992, §104.2A), for example נֶחְמָד 'desirable' (Gn 3.6), לְעַם נוֹלָד 'to a people yet to be born' (Ps 22.32), and הַחַיָּה הַנֶּאֱכֶלֶת 'an animal that may be eaten' (Lv 11.47).

21. When the passive participle expresses a state resulting from an action, such a state will sometimes have an active sense, and the passive par-

tiple will need to be translated accordingly. For example, someone who is
עָסוּק 'occupied' is not occupied by others but by their own concerns, hence,
'busy', זָכוּר can denote not someone who is 'remembered' by others but
someone who has many memories, hence, 'mindful', טָעוּן is something that
is not 'demanded' but 'requiring', מְקַבָּל can designate not the thing
'received' but the 'recipient' of it, סָבוּר is not what is 'thought', but the
person who is 'thinking' it (as in כְּסָבוּר 'as imagining, thinking, convinced
that'), etc. Other participles of this type include שָׁקוּד 'watchful' and תָּלוּי
'depending'. The following examples can be supplemented by the exercises
at the end of this unit (see also Segal 1927, §§333, 336; Kutscher 1982, 131;
Mishor 1983a, 209-11):

מְקַבָּל אֲנִי מֵרַבִּי מְיָאשָׁא, שֶׁקִּבֵּל מֵאַבָּא, שֶׁקִּבֵּל מִן הַזּוּגוֹת,
שֶׁקִּבְּלוּ מִן הַנְּבִיאִים, הֲלָכָה לְמֹשֶׁה מִסִּינַי

I have received from Rabbi Measha, who received from Abba, who
received from the *zugot*, who received from the prophets, a *halakhah* of Moses at Sinai (Pea 2.6)

(here, מְקַבָּל has a special force, as it indicates the final recipient, the reposi-
tory of the tradition that had been handed down);

זָכוּר הָיִיתִי בִּפְלוֹנִית שֶׁיָּצְתָה בְּהִינוּמָא וְרֹאשָׁהּ פָּרוּעַ

I recall a woman going out in her veil with her hair let down (Ket
2.10)

(זָכוּר, as against זוֹכֵר, emphasizes that the memory had persisted in the
speaker's mind);

יוֹדֵעַ אֲנִי שֶׁהַנָּזִיר אָסוּר בְּיַיִן, אֲבָל סָבוּר הָיִיתִי, שֶׁחֲכָמִים מַתִּירִים לִי

I knew that a Nazirite was forbidden wine, but I believed that the
sages would permit me to have it (Naz 2.4);

כָּל הַמֵּסִיךְ אֶת רַגְלָיו טָעוּן טְבִילָה, וְכָל הַמֵּטִיל מַיִם טָעוּן קִדּוּשׁ יָדַיִם
וְרַגְלַיִם

Anyone who defecates requires a ritual bath and anyone who uri-
nates has to purify their hands and feet (Yom 3.2);

כל המנחות שבתורה טעונות שמן ולבונה

All the cereal offerings mentioned in the Torah require oil and
frankincense (TosSot 1.10).

22. The participle, given that it can also function as a noun, may be
negated with אֵין, although לֹא is commonly employed too, and the reason for
choosing the one or the other is not always clear. אַל is never used with the
participle. See Unit 23.11A.

IV *Phraseology*

23. הָיָה יוֹשֵׁב וְדוֹרֵשׁ 'he was sitting down and interpreting, he sat down to
interpret/teach', describes the activity of study or teaching (דָּרַשׁ) of a rabbi;
in the formula, יוֹשֵׁב alludes to the posture adopted while teaching or to the

position held by the rabbi in a יְשִׁיבָה, and, thus, implies instruction that is public or authorized (compare Mt 5.1–2). It is also possible to omit יוֹשֵׁב in translation, where it is clear that it has a purely clichéd or decorative function:

הא כיצד היה יושב ודורש ולא היה יודע מהיכן הוא אוכל ושותה

How could he sit down to interpret not knowing how he would eat or drink? (Mek 16.4 [L 2.104]);

זה אחד משלשה דברים שהיה רבי ישמעאל יושב ודורש כמין משל

This is one of the three things that Rabbi Ishmael used to interpret allegorically (Mek 21.19 [L 3.53]).

See also SNm 112 (H 120), Mek 15.3 (L 2.69), etc.

24. נִמְצֵינוּ לְמֵדִים 'we find ourselves informed', introduces the specific point arising from an exegetical discussion of a biblical text; the formula is sometimes followed by מִן הַתּוֹרָה, emphasizing that the point has been furnished by the Bible itself. For example, in Mek 15.1 (L 2.1), after quoting the biblical text, the author of the *midrash* concludes that the resurrection of the dead is attested in the Torah:

נמצינו למדים תחיית המתים מן תורה

We find ourselves informed about the resurrection of the dead from the Torah.

At SDt 222 (F 255), following the citation of Ex 23.5, the text concludes:

נמצינו למדים שהוא עובר על מצות עשה ועל מצות לא תעשה

We find ourselves learning that this transgresses both the positive and the negative commandments.

See also SNm 116 (H 135), SNm 150 (H 196), etc.

25. בַּמֶּה דְּבָרִים אֲמוּרִים (בד״א) 'what are these things said about?, what does this apply to?, when is this rule applied?', a formula characteristic of the halakhic idiom of the Mishnah, where it occurs no less than fifty times (see BB 3.1, 3; Soṭ 8.7, etc.).

V *Vocabulary*

מַעֲשֶׂה–אֲמִירָה 'saying–deed'

גִּלַּח 'shave, cut one's hair, make the Nazirite hair offering'

הִשְׁפִּיל–הִגְבִּיהַּ 'praise–humble'

יִשּׁוּב 'settled land, civilization', as against מִדְבָּר 'unpopulated land'

מָאַס 'tire of, reject, despise'

וּ[לְ]מַעֲלָה–וּ[לְ]מַטָּה 'below–above'

מִיתָה 'death', סָמוּךְ לַמִּיתָה 'close to death' (סָמַךְ 'support', סָמוּךְ 'near, leaning on')

מַעֲשֵׂה בְרֵאשִׁית 'the work of creation, creation, the order in which creation occurred'

פָּרַע וּפָרַם 'let down (one's hair) and tear (one's clothes)' in mourning (see Lv 10.6)

שִׁנָּה 'change, alter, transform'

תְּחִיַּת הַמֵּתִים 'resurrection of the dead'

עֶלְיוֹנִים–תַּחְתּוֹנִים 'inferiors–superiors, terrestrial beings–celestial beings', etc.

VI *Exercises*

1. רַבִּי נְחוּנְיָא בֶּן הַקָּנָה אוֹמֵר, כָּל הַמְקַבֵּל עָלָיו עֹל תּוֹרָה, מַעֲבִירִין מִמֶּנּוּ עֹל מַלְכוּת וְעֹל דֶּרֶךְ אֶרֶץ, וְכָל הַפּוֹרֵק מִמֶּנּוּ עֹל תּוֹרָה, נוֹתְנִין עָלָיו עֹל מַלְכוּת וְעֹל דֶּרֶךְ אֶרֶץ.

2. רַבִּי יוֹחָנָן בֶּן בְּרוֹקָא אוֹמֵר, כָּל הַמְחַלֵּל שֵׁם שָׁמַיִם בַּסֵּתֶר, נִפְרָעִין מִמֶּנּוּ בַּגָּלוּי. אֶחָד שׁוֹגֵג וְאֶחָד מֵזִיד בְּחִלּוּל הַשֵּׁם.

3. מִי שֶׁיֵּשׁ לוֹ גְּנַאי לִפְנִים מִגִּנְּתוֹ שֶׁלַּחֲבֵרוֹ, נִכְנָס בְּשָׁעָה שֶׁדֶּרֶךְ בְּנֵי אָדָם נִכְנָסִים, וְיוֹצֵא בְּשָׁעָה שֶׁדֶּרֶךְ בְּנֵי אָדָם יוֹצְאִין.

4. מַזְכִּירִין יְצִיאַת מִצְרַיִם בַּלֵּילוֹת.

5. בַּמֶּה דְבָרִים אֲמוּרִים? בְּעָנִי שֶׁבְּיִשְׂרָאֵל, אֲבָל בְּמִכְבָּד, הַכֹּל לְפִי כְבוֹדוֹ.

6. שְׁלֹשָׁה בָתֵּי דִינִין הָיוּ שָׁם, אֶחָד יוֹשֵׁב עַל פֶּתַח הַר הַבַּיִת וְאֶחָד יוֹשֵׁב עַל פֶּתַח הָעֲזָרָה וְאֶחָד יוֹשֵׁב בְּלִשְׁכַּת הַגָּזִית. בָּאִים לָזֶה שֶׁעַל פֶּתַח הַר הַבַּיִת וְאוֹמֵר, כָּךְ דָּרַשְׁתִּי וְכָךְ דָּרְשׁוּ חֲבֵרַי, כָּךְ לִמַּדְתִּי וְכָךְ לִמְדוּ חֲבֵרַי. אִם שָׁמְעוּ, אוֹמְרִים לָהֶם, וְאִם לָאו, בָּאִין לָהֶם לְאוֹתָן שֶׁעַל פֶּתַח הָעֲזָרָה וְאוֹמֵר, כָּךְ דָּרַשְׁתִּי וְכָךְ דָּרְשׁוּ חֲבֵרַי, כָּךְ לִמַּדְתִּי וְכָךְ לִמְדוּ חֲבֵרַי. אִם שָׁמְעוּ, אוֹמְרִים לָהֶם, וְאִם לָאו, אֵלּוּ וְאֵלּוּ בָּאִין לְבֵית דִּין הַגָּדוֹל שֶׁבְּלִשְׁכַּת הַגָּזִית, שֶׁמִּמֶּנּוּ יוֹצֵאת תּוֹרָה לְכָל יִשְׂרָאֵל, שֶׁנֶּאֱמַר, מִן הַמָּקוֹם הַהוּא אֲשֶׁר יִבְחַר ה' [דברים י"ז י']. חָזַר לְעִירוֹ וְשָׁנָה וְלִמֵּד כְּדַרְכּוֹ שֶׁהָיָה לָמֵד, פָּטוּר.

7. מַה בֵּין הָאִישׁ לָאִשָּׁה? הָאִישׁ פּוֹרֵעַ וּפוֹרֵם, וְאֵין הָאִשָּׁה פּוֹרַעַת וּפוֹרֶמֶת, הָאִישׁ מַדִּיר אֶת בְּנוֹ בְּנָזִיר, וְאֵין הָאִשָּׁה מַדֶּרֶת אֶת בְּנָהּ בְּנָזִיר, הָאִישׁ מְגַלֵּחַ עַל נְזִירוּת אָבִיו, וְאֵין הָאִשָּׁה מְגַלַּחַת עַל נְזִירוּת אָבִיהָ, הָאִישׁ מוֹכֵר אֶת בִּתּוֹ, וְאֵין הָאִשָּׁה מוֹכֶרֶת אֶת בִּתָּהּ, הָאִישׁ מְקַדֵּשׁ אֶת בִּתּוֹ, וְאֵין הָאִשָּׁה מְקַדֶּשֶׁת אֶת בִּתָּהּ, הָאִישׁ נִסְקָל עָרֹם, וְאֵין הָאִשָּׁה נִסְקֶלֶת עֲרֻמָּה, הָאִישׁ נִתְלֶה, וְאֵין הָאִשָּׁה נִתְלֵית, הָאִישׁ נִמְכָּר בִּגְנֵבָתוֹ, וְאֵין הָאִשָּׁה נִמְכֶּרֶת בִּגְנֵבָתָהּ.

8. רבי יוסי אומר, רד מטה למעלה, ולמעלה למטה. כל המגביה עצמו על דברי תורה, סוף שמשפילין אותו. וכל המשפיל עצמו על דברי תורה, סוף שמגביהין אותו.

9. רבי אומר, אין כתיב כאן אלא, אז ישיר משה [שמות ט"ו א']. נמצינו למדין תחיית המתים מן התורה.

10. רבן שמעון בן גמליאל אומר, בא וראה כמה חביבין ישראל לפני מי שאמר והיה העולם. ולפי שהם חביבין עליו שנה להם מעשה בראשית, עשה להם עליונים תחתונים ותחתונים עליונים. לשעבר היה הלחם עולה מן הארץ והטל יורד מן השמים .... ועכשיו נתחלפו הדברים, התחיל הלחם יורד מן השמים והטל עולה מן הארץ.

11. רבי יהושע אומר, שונה אדם שתי הלכות בשחרית ושתי הלכות בערבית ועושה במלאכתו כל היום, מעלין עליו כאלו קים כל התורה כולה.

12. נמצאת מרבה לו והולך עד לעולם.

13. וחי אחיך עמך [ויקרא כ"ה ל"ו]. זו דרש בן פטורי, שנים שהיו הולכים

במדבר ואין ביד אחד אלא קיתון של מים, אם שותהו אחד מגיע
ליישוב, ואם שותים אותו שנים שניהם מתים. דרש בן פטורי, ישתו
שתיהם וימותו, שנאמר, וחי אחיך עמך.

14. הא כל שאינו למד ואינו עושה, סוף שהוא מואס באחרים.

15. ויהי בחדש הראשון ... [שמות מ' יז]. נמצינו למדים שבעשרים ושלשה
באדר התחילו אהרן ובניו המשכן וכל הכלים לימשח.

16. עכשיו ישראל אומרים, לא נתגייר יתרו מחיבה. כסבור היה יתרו שיש
לגרים חלק בארץ ישראל, עכשיו שראה שאין להם חלק, הניחם והלך לו.

17. מפני ארבע דברים אין מוכיחים את האדם אלא סמוך למיתה, כדי שלא
יהא מוכיחו וחוזר ומוכיחו, ושלא יהא חבירו רואהו ומתבייש ממנו, ושלא
יהא בלבו עליו, וכדי שיפרש ממנו בשלום.

18. רבי שמעון בן יוחי אומר, משל, למה הדבר דומה? למלך בשר ודם שהיו
לו בנים ועבדים הרבה, והיו נזונים ומתפרנסים מתחת ידו ומפתחות של
אוצר בידו. כשהם עושים רצונו, הוא פותח את האוצר והם אוכלים
ושבעים, וכשאין עושים רצונו, הוא נועל את האוצר והם מתים ברעב.

19. כך אמר להם משה לישראל, אם אי אתם זכורים נסים וגבורות שעשה
לכם הקדוש ברוך הוא במצרים, הזכרו כמה טובות עתיד ליתן לכם
לעולם הבא.

20. אם אמר ליתן ונתן, נותנים לו שכר אמירה כשכר מעשה.

Sources. 1. Abot 3.5. 2. Abot 4.4. 3. BB 6.6. 4. Ber 1.5. 5. Ket 5.9. 6.
Sanh 11.2. 7. Soṭ 3.8. 8. ARN 11 (S 46). 9. Mek 15.1. (L 2.1). 10. Mek
16.4 (L 2.102–103). 11. Mek 16.4 (L 2.103–104). 12. SLv 14.2 (W 70b).
13. SLv 25.36 (W 109c). 14. SLv 26.14 (W 111b). 15. SNm 44.1 (H 49).
16. SNm 80.1 (H 76). 17. SDt 3 (F 10). 18. SDt 40 (F 83). 19. SDt 309 (F
349). 20. SDt 117 (F 176).

UNIT TWENTY

INFINITIVE

I *Introductory text* (SDt 355 [F 418])

ויתא ראשי עם [דברים לג' כא'] ... מלמד שעתיד משה ליכנס בראש כל
חבורה וחבורה, בראש חבורה של בעלי מקרא ובראש חבורה של בעלי
משנה ובראש חבורה של בעלי תלמוד, ונוחל שכר עם כל אחד ואחד, וכן
הוא אומר, לכן אחלק לו ברבים, ואת עצומים יחלק שלל [ישעיה נג' יב'].

And he came with the heads of the people [Dt 33.21] ... This teaches that
Moses will enter at the head of each group, at the head of the group of Bible
scholars, at the head of the group of Mishnah scholars, at the head of the

group of Talmud scholars, and will receive the same reward as each of them. This is why it says, Therefore, I shall give him a portion with the many and with the powerful he will divide spoil [Is 53.12].

1. This representation of Moses receiving the reward with each group of scholars in the written and oral traditions demonstrates an understanding that the entire law, both the written Torah and its immense development in the oral tradition, stems from Moses at Sinai, and is, in some sense, contained in what Moses transmitted.

II *Morphology*

2. RH witnesses the complete disappearance of the infinitive absolute. The infinitive construct prefixed with the prepositions -בְּ and -כְּ is restricted to a few liturgical usages that are imitations, or perhaps genuine remnants, of biblical idiom, at least when they are not the result of mistakes or of correction by copyists. Standard RH knows only the infinitive construct with prefixed -לְ, which can be negated by a preceding שֶׁלֹּא, or prefixed by the preposition מִן (thus, -מִלְּ followed by infinitive construct). In practice, the infinitive construct simply does not occur except with prefixed -לְ.

The development of the negative form of the infinitive may be traced as follows (see Qimron 1986, 78–79): BH לְבִלְתִּי with infinitive; LBH לְאֵין with -לְ and infinitive; Qumran Hebrew לְאֵין with -לְ and infinitive, אֲשֶׁר לֹא with -לְ and infinitive; RH שֶׁלֹּא with -לְ and infinitive (a construction already found in Biblical Aramaic, at Ezr 6.8: דִּי-לָא לְבַטָּלָא 'so as not to stop'):

מְקוֹם שֶׁאָמְרוּ, לְהַאֲרִיךְ, אֵינוֹ רַשַּׁאי לְקַצֵּר, לְקַצֵּר, אֵינוֹ רַשַּׁאי
לְהַאֲרִיךְ, לַחְתּוֹם, אֵינוֹ רַשַּׁאי שֶׁלֹּא לַחְתּוֹם, שֶׁלֹּא לַחְתּוֹם, אֵינוֹ
רַשַּׁאי לַחְתּוֹם

> Where it is established practice to recite the long formula, it is forbidden (here and elsewhere, literally, 'not authorized') to recite the short one, and where the short formula is established, it is forbidden to recite the long one; where it is established practice to recite the concluding formula, it is forbidden not to recite it, and where it is established practice not to recite the concluding formula, it is forbidden to recite it (Ber 1.4);

אַנְשֵׁי חָצֵר שֶׁשָּׁכַח אֶחָד מֵהֶם וְלֹא עֵרֵב, בֵּיתוֹ אָסוּר מִלְּהַכְנִיס
וּמִלְּהוֹצִיא לוֹ, אֲבָל לָהֶם מֻתָּר

> If one of the residents of a courtyard forgets to prepare the *'erub*, that person is not allowed to take anything into or out of their house, but the others are (Erub 2.6).

3. In the *Qal*, even with *pe-nun, pe-yod*, and *pe-alef* verbs, the infinitive has the same form as the imperfect minus preformative. Thus, just as the BH infinitive לְקְטֹל corresponds to the imperfect יִקְטֹל, so in RH לִיתֵּן corresponds to יִתֵּן. This popular standardizing of irregular forms extends to other verbs, like לְקַח and הָלַךְ. The following is a list of those most commonly encountered.

Perfect	Imperfect	Infinitive		Meaning
		RH	BH	
אָכַל	יֹאכַל	לוֹכַל	לֶאֱכֹל	Eat
אָמַר	יֹאמַר	לוֹמַר	לֵאמֹר	Say
יָלַד	יֵלֵד	לֵילֵד	לָלֶדֶת	Give birth
יָרַד	יֵרֵד	לֵירֵד	לָרֶדֶת	Go down
יָשַׁב	יֵשֵׁב	לֵישֵׁב	לָשֶׁבֶת	Dwell
יָדַע	יֵדַע	לֵידַע	לָדַעַת	Know
נָתַן	יִתֵּן	לִיתֵּן	לָתֵת	Give
נָשָׂא	יִשָּׂא	לִישָּׂא	לָשֵׂאת	Raise
לָקַח	יִקַּח	לִיקַּח	לָקַחַת	Take
הָלַךְ	יֵלֵךְ	לֵילֵךְ	לָלֶכֶת	Go

Nonetheless, the occasional verb resists such attempts at regularization, for example יָצָא 'go out', which maintains the biblical form of the infinitive, לָצֵאת, throughout the Mishnah and tannaitic *midrashim*. The verb אָכַל is also very resistant to change, with the new form, לוֹכַל, appearing in very few texts (for example Sifra W 59d; M.H. Segal [1927, §163] only mentions it as occurring in Palestinian texts). However, when they are not written *plene* (לֶאֱמוֹר, לֶאֱכוֹל), it is possible that לֶאכֹל and לֶאמֹר were read *lokal* and *lomar* (Girón 1992). In other verbs too, the biblical form has not completely disappeared, for example לָלֶכֶת (Nid 4.2), לָתֵת (Shab 17.2; Ned 11.1; AZ 2.6–7; Zeb 10.7); a set-phrase like לָשֵׂאת וְלָתֵת 'to trade' is obviously more stable, although this too is found in a non-biblical version, לִישָּׂא וְלִיתֵּן, at Sifra Nedabah *parashah* 13.9 (MS Vatican 66). Of course, we also have to bear in mind the constant attempts of copyists to make rabbinic structures conform more closely to those of the Bible.

Examples of texts containing RH forms of the infinitive include the following:

מִפְּנֵי שֶׁיָּכוֹל לֵילֵךְ לַחוּץ וְלֶאֱכוֹל

Since it is possible to go outside and eat (Erub 3.1);

אל תהי קורא, איש שיבה [דברים לב׳ כה׳] אלא, איש ישיבה, מלמד שכולם ראוים לישב בישיבה

Do not read, Man of grey hairs [שֵׂיבָה; Dt 32.25] but, Man of session [יְשִׁיבָה], teaching that all of them are worthy to take a seat at the session (SDt 321 [F 370]);

אִם תִּזְכּוּ לִשְׁמוֹר אֶת הַשַּׁבָּת, עָתִיד הַקָּבָּ״ה לִיתֵּן לָכֶם שְׁלוֹשָׁה מוֹעֲדוֹת,
פֶּסַח וַעֲצֶרֶת וְסוּכּוֹת

If you succeed in observing the sabbath, the holy one, blessed be he,
will allow you to hold three festivals, Passover, Pentecost, and
Tabernacles (Mek 16.25 [L 2.119]).

M.H. Segal (1927, §169) shrewdly observes that these forms might be at
least as old as their biblical counterparts, with לְחֵתֵּן at 1 K 6.19 a hybrid of
the popular לִיתֵּן and the literary לָחֵת (see also 1 K 17.14).

4. The assimilation of *lamed-alef* to *lamed-he* verbs has led to לִקְרוֹת becoming the normal form of the infinitive of קָרָא instead of לִקְרֹא, and to the
mixed form לְמַלְאוֹת for לְמַלֹּא, as at Ket 1.10:

מַעֲשֶׂה בְּתִינוֹקֶת שֶׁיָּרְדָה לְמַלֹּאות מַיִם מִן הָעַיִן

It happened that a little girl went down to take water from the fountain.

5. As already noted at Unit 15.4A, in the *Nif'al* preformative -ה tends to
be elided after the -ל of the infinitive (a consequence of the general weakening of the gutturals and especially of intervocalic *he*), which gives rise to
such forms as לִכָּנֵס (for לְהִכָּנֵס), לִיבָּטֵל (for לְהִבָּטֵל), לִיכָּרֵת (for לְהִכָּרֵת),
לִינָשֵׂא (for לְהִנָּשֵׂא), לֵיעָשׂוֹת (for לְהֵעָשׂוֹת), etc.

6. The same phenomenon occurs to a lesser extent with the *Hif'il* (see
Unit 15.4E): לַרְבּוֹת (for לְהַרְבּוֹת), etc.

7. The RH infinitive with -ל can only take an object suffix (not one that
functions as subject, as in BH בְּצֵאתִי), for example:

הַמַּשְׂכִּיר בַּיִת לַחֲבֵרוֹ ... אֵינוֹ יָכוֹל לְהוֹצִיאוֹ מִן הֶחָג וְעַד הַפֶּסַח

A person who lets a house to another ... may not turn them out from
Tabernacles to Passover (BM 8.6).

III *Grammar and usage*

8. On RH's abandonment of BH constructions of the type בְּצֵאתוֹ and
כְּצֵאתוֹ, see Units 9.9 and 16.14.

9. In its use, the RH infinitive coincides with that of the BH infinitive
construct with -ל (see Meyer 1992, §102.4): it is like a noun, it may be the
subject or object of a verb, and it can express purpose, as in the exegetical
formulas לְהוֹצִיא 'in order to exclude' and לְהָבִיא 'in order to include' (see
Unit 30.5). The infinitive may also be used in an attributive function,
modifying a noun, for example מָה לַעֲשׂוֹת 'task' (literally, 'what to do'),
תְּבוּאָה
לִקְצֹר 'harvest to be gathered', תִּינוֹק לָמוּל 'child to be circumcised', etc., or
modally, as a gerund, for example לוֹמַר/לֵאמֹר 'saying'.

As the object or complement of a verb, the infinitive is equivalent to -שֶׁ
with the imperfect:

מוּטָב לִי לְהִקָּרֵא שׁוֹטֶה כָּל יָמַי

I should prefer to be called a fool all my life (Eduy 5.6);

מוּטָב לָהֶן לַצִּיבּוּר שֶׁיְּהוּ שׁוֹגְגִין

It is better for the community that they be wrong (TosSot 15.10).
It can sometimes be difficult to decide among manuscript variants in this
matter; for example,

רְאוּיָה הָיְתָה לָבוֹא עָלֶיהָ פּוּרְעָנִיּוֹת

It was predestined (for) punishments to fall upon her,
at TosSot 2.3, has a variant with שֶׁיָּבוֹאוּ.

10. The infinitive לוֹמַר is used to introduce direct speech or a quotation
from a text (in BH, לֵאמֹר can serve the same function, for example, at Jr
7.4), a usage that is sometimes best omitted from translation or rendered as a
gerund:

אֲפִלּוּ עֶבֶד, אֲפִלּוּ שִׁפְחָה, נֶאֱמָנִין לוֹמַר, עַד כָּאן תְּחוּם שַׁבָּת

Even slaves, male and female, deserve credit when they say, The
sabbath limit reaches to this point (Erub 5.5).
On the expression תַּלְמוּד לוֹמַר, see Unit 16.16.

11. With imperative significance, the infinitive is usually found with the
preposition עַל, in reference to the person upon whom an obligation falls:

אָמַר רַבִּי יִשְׁמָעֵאל, אֶלְעָזָר בֶּן עֲזַרְיָה, עָלֶיךָ רְאָיָה לְלַמֵּד, שֶׁאַתָּה
מַחְמִיר, שֶׁכָּל הַמַּחְמִיר עָלָיו רְאָיָה לְלַמֵּד

Rabbi Ishmael said, Eleazar ben Azariah, you have to provide evidence, for you are stricter in your ruling, and anyone who gives
stricter rulings is obliged to furnish evidence (Yad 4.3).
Usually, the formula -עָלַי לְ [הֲרֵין] serves as a cohortative, as at Naz 2.5:

הֲרֵינִי נָזִיר וְעָלַי לְגַלֵּחַ נָזִיר

Now I am a Nazirite, I will make the Nazirite hair offering'.

12. -עָתִיד לְ (see Unit 16.13B) and -סוֹף לְ (see Unit 19.17D) with the infinitive are characteristic RH constructions for expressing events that are regarded as having a secure or inevitable place in the future, especially the eschatological future:

עֲדַת קֹרַח אֵינָהּ עֲתִידָה לַעֲלוֹת ... עֲשֶׂרֶת הַשְּׁבָטִים אֵינָן עֲתִידִין לַחֲזוֹר

The company of Korah will never arise again ... the ten tribes will
never return (Sanh 10.3);

רַבִּי יוֹנָתָן אוֹמֵר, כָּל הַמְקַיֵּם אֶת הַתּוֹרָה מֵעֹנִי, סוֹפוֹ לְקַיְּמָהּ מֵעֹשֶׁר,
וְכָל הַמְבַטֵּל אֶת הַתּוֹרָה מֵעֹשֶׁר, סוֹפוֹ לְבַטְּלָהּ מֵעֹנִי

Rabbi Jonathan says, Anyone who fulfils the Torah in poverty will
surely fulfil it in wealth, and anyone who despises it in wealth will
surely despise it in poverty (Abot 4.9).
Very occasionally in the tannaitic literature, we find -עָתִיד לְ replaced by
-עָתִיד שֶׁ with the imperfect (see Unit 18.16).

The formula -עוֹמֵד לְ 'be about to' is an amoraic idiom which began to
be used in the same way as -עָתִיד לְ. Through the copyists, it has also entered
some tannaitic texts, to which M. Mishor (1983a) has suggested corrections.
Thus, for example, at BQ 9.1, פָּרָה הָעוֹמֶדֶת לֵילֵד 'a cow about to give birth'
might have been פָּרָה מְעֻבֶּרֶת לֵילֵד 'a pregnant cow, for giving birth' and

רָחֵל טְעוּנָה 'a ewe ready for shearing' might have been רָחֵל הָעוֹמֶדֶת לִינָּזֵז or רָחֵל הָעוֹמֶדֶת לִיגָּזֵז 'a ewe that needs to be sheared'.

For the formula לֶעָתִיד לָבוֹא, see Unit 16.17.

13. Another idiomatic RH construction is מָה אֲנִי/אַתָּה/הוּא ... לְ-, meaning 'may I/you/he do so-and-so?', for example:

מָה אֲנִי לְהָבִיא זֶרַע אֶל תַּחַת הַמּוֹתָר

May I plant a seed beneath what remains? (Kil 6.4);

מָה אָנוּ לֵירֵד

May we go down (i.e. 'disembark')? (Erub 4.2).

IV *Phraseology*

14. הָא אֵין עָלֶיךָ לוֹמַר/לָדוּן כַּלָּשׁוֹן הָאַחֲרוֹן אֶלָּא כַלָּשׁוֹן הָרִאשׁוֹן 'Thus, then, you should not interpret/argue according to the first form but according to the last' is a formula typical of the school of Ishmael and especially common in SNm and Mek. Following an exegetical discussion in which two positions are set out, a decision between them is made (see SNm 23.2; 49.2; 55, etc.). In SDt (217, 249, 397), there is a variant, אֵין עָלֶיךָ לָדוּן אֶלָּא כַדִּין הָרִאשׁוֹן 'you should only argue according to the first argument'.

15. לַעֲשׂוֹת ... כְּ- 'to make X like Y, to rank one thing with another' is commonly used when grouping together women with men, or minors with adults. It is an exegetical fomula that, after the quotation of a biblical text, abruptly introduces an interpretation (see further, Unit 26.9)—an introductory expression along the lines of בָּא הַכָּתוּב 'this passage (is intended to make X ...)' is to be understood.

Among other infinitives with exegetical rôles are לְהוֹצִיא 'to exclude' and לְהָבִיא 'to include':

איש או אשה [במדבר ו׳ ב׳], לעשות נשים כאנשים

If a man or a woman [Nm 6.2]: (this is said) in order to rank women the same as men (SNm 22.2 [H 25]);

איש או אשה [במדבר ו׳ ב׳], להוציא את הקטנים

If a man or a woman [Nm 6.2]: (this is said) in order to exclude minors (SNm 22.3 [H 25]).

V *Vocabulary*

אַיְלוֹנִית 'infertile'
חֵפֶץ 'desirable object, trinket'
חָרֵב 'destroyed, in ruins'
כְּנֵסִיָּה 'assembly, meeting'
לִידוֹן (ni. infinitive of דּוּן) 'to be judged'
לָקַח 'take', specifically in RH, 'buy'

לִתֵּן דִּין וְחֶשְׁבּוֹן 'to settle an account'

מַחֲלֹקֶת 'controversy'

פִּקֵּחַ 'intelligent'

VI *Exercises*

1. עֲקַבְיָא בֶּן מַהֲלַלְאֵל אוֹמֵר, הִסְתַּכֵּל בִּשְׁלֹשָׁה דְבָרִים וְאִי אַתָּה בָא לִידֵי עֲבֵרָה, דַּע מֵאַיִן בָּאתָ, וּלְאָן אַתָּה הוֹלֵךְ, וְלִפְנֵי מִי אַתָּה עָתִיד לִתֵּן דִּין וְחֶשְׁבּוֹן.

2. וְאִם עָמַלְתָּ בַתּוֹרָה יֵשׁ לוֹ שָׂכָר הַרְבֵּה לִתֵּן לָךְ.

3. רַבִּי יוֹחָנָן הַסַּנְדְּלָר אוֹמֵר, כָּל כְּנֵסִיָּה שֶׁהִיא לְשֵׁם שָׁמַיִם, סוֹפָהּ לְהִתְקַיֵּם, וְשֶׁאֵינָהּ לְשֵׁם שָׁמַיִם, אֵין סוֹפָהּ לְהִתְקַיֵּם.

4. הוּא הָיָה אוֹמֵר, הַיְלוֹדִים לָמוּת, וְהַמֵּתִים לְהַחֲיוֹת, וְהַחַיִּים לִדּוֹן, לֵידַע לְהוֹדִיעַ וּלְהִוָּדַע שֶׁהוּא אֵל, הוּא הַיּוֹצֵר, הוּא הַבּוֹרֵא, הוּא הַמֵּבִין, הוּא הַדַּיָּן, הוּא עֵד, הוּא בַּעַל דִּין, וְהוּא עָתִיד לָדוּן.

5. כָּל מַחֲלֹקֶת שֶׁהִיא לְשֵׁם שָׁמַיִם, סוֹפָהּ לְהִתְקַיֵּם, וְשֶׁאֵינָהּ לְשֵׁם שָׁמַיִם, אֵין סוֹפָהּ לְהִתְקַיֵּם. אֵיזוֹ הִיא מַחֲלֹקֶת שֶׁהִיא לְשֵׁם שָׁמַיִם? זוֹ מַחֲלֹקֶת הִלֵּל וְשַׁמַּאי. וְשֶׁאֵינָהּ לְשֵׁם שָׁמַיִם? זוֹ מַחֲלֹקֶת קֹרַח וְכָל עֲדָתוֹ.

6. הָיָה רוֹכֵב עַל הַחֲמוֹר [וּבִתְפִלָּה], יֵרֵד, וְאִם אֵינוֹ יָכוֹל לֵירֵד, יַחֲזִיר אֶת פָּנָיו, וְאִם אֵינוֹ יָכוֹל לְהַחֲזִיר אֶת פָּנָיו, יְכַוֵּן אֶת לִבּוֹ כְּנֶגֶד בֵּית קֹדֶשׁ הַקֳּדָשִׁים.

7. מָקוֹם שֶׁנָּהֲגוּ לֶאֱכֹל צָלִי בְּלֵילֵי פְסָחִים, אוֹכְלִין, מָקוֹם שֶׁנָּהֲגוּ שֶׁלֹּא לֶאֱכֹל, אֵין אוֹכְלִין, מָקוֹם שֶׁנָּהֲגוּ לְהַדְלִיק אֶת הַנֵּר בְּלֵילֵי יוֹם הַכִּפּוּרִים, מַדְלִיקִין, מָקוֹם שֶׁנָּהֲגוּ שֶׁלֹּא לְהַדְלִיק, אֵין מַדְלִיקִין.

8. אַיְלוֹנִית וּזְקֵנָה וְשֶׁאֵינָהּ רְאוּיָה לֵילֵד, לֹא שׁוֹתוֹת וְלֹא נוֹטְלוֹת כְּתֻבָּה. רַבִּי אֱלִיעֶזֶר אוֹמֵר, יָכוֹל הוּא לִשָּׂא אִשָּׁה אַחֶרֶת וְלִפְרוֹת וְלִרְבּוֹת הֵימֶנָּה. וּשְׁאָר כָּל הַנָּשִׁים, אוֹ שׁוֹתוֹת, אוֹ לֹא נוֹטְלוֹת כְּתֻבָּה.

9. שֶׁהוּא [הַכֶּלֶב] פִּקֵּחַ, שֶׁאֵין דַּרְכּוֹ לְהַנִּיחַ אֶת הַמָּזוֹן וְלֵילֵךְ לַמַּיִם.

10. בּוֹ בַיּוֹם בָּא יְהוּדָה גֵּר עַמּוֹנִי וְעָמַד לִפְנֵיהֶן בְּבֵית הַמִּדְרָשׁ, אָמַר לָהֶם, מָה אֲנִי לָבוֹא בַקָּהָל? אָמַר לוֹ רַבָּן גַּמְלִיאֵל, אָסוּר אַתָּה. אָמַר לוֹ רַבִּי יְהוֹשֻׁעַ, מֻתָּר אַתָּה.

11. אמרו ישראל למשה, רבינו משה, מה עלינו לעשות? אמר להם, אתם תהיו מרוממים ומפארים ומשבחין ונותנין שיר ושבח וגדולה ותפארת למי שהמלחמות שלו.

12. וזה אחד משלשה דברים שעתיד אליהו להעמיד לישראל, צלוחית של מן וצלוחית של מים וצלוחית של שמן המשחה.

13. ועכשיו גלוי היה לפני מי שאמר והיה העולם שפורענות גדולה עתידה לבא בדורנו.

14. אני הוא שעשיתי לכם ניסים במצרים, אני הוא שעתיד לעשות לכם כל הניסים הללו.

15. והיתה ארצכם שממה ועריכם יהיו חרבה [ויקרא כו' לג']. זו מידה קשה לישראל, שבשעה שאדם גולה מתוך כרמו ומתוך ביתו וסופו לחזור, כאלו אין כרמו וביתו חריבים. אתם אין אתם כן, אלא, והיתה ארצכם שממה ועריכם יהיו חרבה. מפני מה? שאין סופכם לחזור.

16. באותה שעה אדם יוצא לטייל בשוק ומבקש ליקח לו חפץ מן הזקנה
והיתה מוכרת לו בשווי, וקטנה קוראה לו ואומרה לו מבפנים, בוא וקח
לך בפחות, והיה הוא לוקח הימנה ביום הראשון וביום השני.

17. והוא לא אויב לו ולא מבקש רעתו [במדבר לה׳ לג׳], לפסול את
השונאים מלישב בדין.

18. ואת הערים אשר נבוא אליהם [דברים א׳ כב׳], לידע באיזו דרר אנו
באים עליהם.

19. משל למלך שהוו לו שני עבדים וגזר על אחד מהם שלא לשתות יין
שלשים יום. אמר, מה גזר עלי שלא לשתות יין שלשים יום? איני טועמו
אפילו שנה אחת, אפילו שתי שנים.

20. עבר אדם על מצוה קלה, סופו לעבור על מצוה חמורה. עבר על, ואהבת
לרעך כמוך [ויקרא יט׳ יח׳], סופו לעבור על, ... לא תשנא את אחיך,
[ויקרא יט׳ יז׳].

Sources. 1. Abot 3.1. 2. Abot 4.10. 3. Abot 4.11. 4. Abot 4.22. 5. Abot
5.17. 6. Ber 4.5. 7. Pes 4.4. 8. Soṭ 4.3. 9. Ṭoh 3.8. 10. Yad 4.4. 11. Mek
14.14 (L 1.215). 12. Mek 16.33. (L 2.126). 13. Mek 22.22 (L 3.142). 14.
SLv 26.13 (W 111b). 15. SLv 26.33 (W 112b). 16. SNm 131.1 (H 170). 17.
SNm 160.11 (H 219). 18. SDt 20 (F 32). 19. SDt 28 (F 44). 20. SDt 186 (F
226).

UNIT TWENTY-ONE

IMPERATIVE

I *Introductory text* (SDt 49 [F 114])

ללכת בכל דרכיו [דברים יא׳ כב׳]. אלו הן דרכי המקום, י״ אל רחום וחנון
[שמות לד׳ ו׳], ואומר, והיה כל אשר יקרא בשם י״ ימלט [יואל ג׳ ה׳]. וכי
היאך איפשר לו לאדם לקרא בשמו של מקום? אלא נקרא המקום רחום,
אף אתה היה רחום, הקדוש ברוך הוא נקרא חנון, אף אתה היה חנון ...
נקרא המקום צדיק ... אף אתה היה צדיק ... נקרא המקום חסיד ...
אף אתה היה חסיד.

Walking in all his ways [Dt 11.22]. These are the ways of the omnipresent
one: Y, compassionate and gracious God [Ex 34.6], and also, Everyone who
is called by the name of Y. will be saved [Jl 3.5]. How can a person be called
by the name of the omnipresent one? Simply, if the omnipresent one is called
compassionate, you too must be compassionate, if the omnipresent one is
called gracious …, if the omnipresent one is called
righteous [Ps 11.7], you too must be righteous, if the omnipresent one is
called kind [Jr 3.12] …, you too must be kind.

1. This interpretation of Dt 11.22 understands 'ways' as 'conduct', so that to follow the ways of God is to imitate his conduct and to be like him: compassionate, gracious, righteous, kind. A similar formulation is found at Lk 6.36: be merciful, just as your father is merciful.

That a person may receive the names ascribed to God, and, therefore, become like him and be able to imitate him, is demonstrated by reading at Jl 3.5 'everyone who is called (יִקָּרֵא) by the name of Y.' in place of the Masoretic Text, 'everyone who calls [יִקְרָא] upon the name of Y.', employing the interpretative rule of *al tiqra* (see Units 11.1; 18.6; 20.3 [the quotation of SDt 321]).

II *Morphology*

2. 'The imperative survived apparently unchanged', according to E.Y. Kutscher (1971, 1601), a statement that is true, with certain modifications, in respect of both morphology and syntax.

3. The special feminine form of the plural, קְטֹלְנָה, has disappeared in RH, as has the emphatic lengthened form of the masculine singular in -*ah* (קָטְלָה), with a few exceptions in imitation of biblical idiom or for liturgical purposes, for example, הוֹשִׁיעָה נָא 'save'; imitation of biblical style is evident at Mek 18.3 (L 2.168):

תנה לי את ציפורה בתך לאשה

Give me your daughter Zipporah as a wife.

In the *Qal*, then, the paradigm of the imperative is as follows.

2ms	קְטֹול	
2fs	קִטְלִי	
2pc	קִטְלוּ	
	קְטֹולוּ	(pausal)

Note that as in the participle and infinitive, *scriptio plena* with *waw* for the 'o' vowel is normal.

4. In other conjugations and in weak or defective verbs, RH practice generally corresponds with that of BH.

A. In some *pe-yod* verbs, where an original *waw* reappears in certain conjugations, we encounter imperatives like הִתְוַדֵּה 'confess' (from יָדָה), as, for example, at Sanh 6.2:

הָיָה רָחוֹק מִבֵּית הַסְּקִילָה כְּעֶשֶׂר אַמּוֹת, אוֹמְרִים לוֹ, הִתְוַדֵּה

When he was some ten cubits from the place of stoning, they would say to him, Confess.

B. As in BH, in *pe-nun* verbs, the *nun* is usually dropped; thus, תֵּן (from נָתַן) and טוֹל (from נָטַל), etc.

5. The verb הָיָה forms its imperative as though from הֱוֵה/הֱוִי: הֱוֵה/הֱוִי and הֱוּ. Aramaic influence is also seen in the alternative vocalization: הֲוִי/הֲוֵי and הֲווֹ/הֲווֹן (see Kutscher 1971, 1600). The following examples, with somewhat contrasting messages, are from Abot 2.3 and 3.2:

הֱווּ זְהִירִין בָּרָשׁוּת

Be careful with power (K הֲווֹן);

הֱוֵי מִתְפַּלֵּל בִּשְׁלוֹמָהּ שֶׁלַּמַּלְכוּת

Pray for the peace of the empire.

The forms הֱיֵה and הֱיִי are also encountered:

נקרא המקוֹם רחום, אף אתה היה רחום, הקדוֹש ברוך הוא נקרא
חנון, אף אתה היה חנון

If the omnipresent one is called compassionate, you too must be compassionate; if the omnipresent one is called gracious, you too must be gracious (SDt 49 [F114]);

אמר להם, הֱיוּ יודעים שסרבנין וטרחנין הם

He said to them, You should know that they are vexatious and demanding (SNm 91.1 [H 91]).

III *Grammar and usage*

6. As in BH, the imperative is used for positive commands in the second person (see Meyer 1992, §100.4D). Negative commands employ the imperfect, participle, or infinitive with the corresponding negative particle: אַל, אֵין, לֹא, שֶׁלֹּא (see Unit 23.11A).

7. However, even in positive commands, the imperative is little used in RH, as in this function it has been taken over by constructions with the imperfect (see Unit 18.11), the participle (see Unit 19.18), or even the infinitive (see Unit 20.11). In fact, the imperative is practically restricted to positive orders directed to specific individuals, and is not normally used in *halakhot*, legal decrees, or even in prayers. Its presence in the sayings of Abot, then, provides a striking contrast with its absence from the *halakhot* of other tractates.

8. Typical of RH is the periphrastic construction of the imperative of הָיָה followed by participle (or adjective), the effect of which is to emphasize the continuous or repetitive nature of the verb (see Unit 16.13). Within the Mishnah, it is especially characteristic of Abot, which contains 28 of the 33 mishnaic usages of הֱוֵי/הֱוּ with participle/adjective, for example Abot 1.9:

הֱוֵי מַרְבֶּה לַחְקוֹר אֶת הָעֵדִים, וֶהֱוֵי זָהִיר בִּדְבָרֶיךָ, שֶׁמָּא מִתּוֹכָם יִלְמְדוּ
לְשַׁקֵּר

Examine the witnesses at length and be careful of your words in case through them they learn to lie.

(K has הֲוֵי in both instances; see the exercises for further examples.)

IV *Phraseology*

9. הֱוֵי אוֹמֵר 'say, you ought to say, you should recognize', etc. is an expression not found in the Mishnah but occurs in the tannaitic *midrashim* to introduce a piece of evidence, in which context it may sometimes be appropriately rendered as 'evidently', 'obviously', or the like. Usually, it comes in response to alternative possibilities, introduced by either מִי or אֵיזֶה:

איזה מדה מרובה, מדת טובה או מדת פורענות? הוי אומר,
מדת הטובה

> Which measure is the more generous, that of mercy or that of punishment? Evidently, the measure of mercy (SNm 8.8 [H 15]);

מי גדול, האוהבים או המאהיבים? הוי אומר, המאהיבים

> Who are greater, those who love or those who cause others to love? Evidently, those who cause others to love (SDt 47 [F 106]).

That הֱוֵי אוֹמֵר had become a lexicalized expression is evident when the participle אוֹמֵר drops out, leaving just הֱוֵי. In such instances, many understand הֱוֵי to have a similar sense to הֲרֵי (BH הִנֵּה), or they read instead the interjection הוֹי 'alas'. However, הֱוֵי should be regarded as an elliptical form of הֱוֵי אוֹמֵר as a whole:

אל מקום דם האשם [ויקרא יד' כח'], הוי אין הדם גורם אלא
המקום גורם

> Over the place of the blood of the guilt offering [Lv 14.28]: evidently, the place is the cause, not the blood (SLv 14.17 (W 72b).

SDt 342 (F 392) is especially instructive: to the question

יכול משאומרים להם דברי ניחומים חוזרים ואומרים להם דברי
תוכחות

> Perhaps after speaking words of consolation to them, they go back to speaking words of reproach to them?,

the answer given is:

הוי משאומרים להם דברי ניחומים אין אומרים להם דברי תוכחות

> It is obvious that after words of consolation they do not speak words of reproach to them.

Occasionally, the imperative אֱמוֹר is used:

אימתי הוא שבחו של מקום? בזמן שאין מזיקים? או בזמן שיש מזיקים
ואין מזיקים? אמור בזמן שיש מזיקים ואין מזיקים

> When should one praise a place? When there are no evil powers? Or when there are evil powers but they cause no harm? Evidently, when there are evil powers but they cause no harm (SLv 26.6 [W 111a]).

10. הנראה-שׁ is used in the following three passages from SNm:

הנראה שתגיע עמנו אצל מושל עכו

> Do come with us to the governor of Akko (SNm 84.1 [H 80]);

הנראה שתעמידני בשביל שאני הולך ליתן

> Do make me get up, for I am going to give (an inheritance) (SNm 84.2 [H 80]);

הנראה שלא יאכל מאכל רע ואל ישתה משקה רע

Don't eat bad food or drink bad drink (SNm 87.2 [H 87]).

The contexts indicate that הנראה ש- introduces an insistent request, corrre-
sponding to 'I beg you to', 'please', or even to an interjection, 'hey!'.

The structure is usually vocalized as a *Nif'al* with prefixed interrogative,
הֲנִרְאֶה, although it can also be regarded as the first person plural of the imperfect (as in K.G. Kuhn's rendering: 'werden wir es sehen?'). But it seems
likely that the form is compounded of the deictic particle הֵן and the imperative רְאֵה, on the pattern of expressions such as צֵא וּרְאֵה 'go out and see'.
Whatever the exact interpretation, it is clear that הנראה ש- has already become a lexicalized formula.

V *Vocabulary*

אוּמָן 'artisan'

אַיֵּם 'warn'

בִּזָּיוֹן 'scorn, shame'

דִּינֵי מָמוֹנוֹת 'laws concerning financial disputes', דִּינֵי נְפָשׁוֹת 'laws concerning
crimes punishable by death'

זַרְעִית (plural זְרְעִיּוֹת) 'family, descendants'

חָתַךְ 'cut'

מַעֲלָה 'height' (also a designation of God to avoid pronouncing the divine
name)

מַתִּישׁ (hi. participle of תשׁשׁ) 'weaken', לְהַתִּישׁ כֹּחַ שֶׁל מַעֲלָה 'to weaken the
power of (the) height, put God off' (the forms of this verb have been influenced by those of the more common נָתַשׁ)

עֵדֵי נְפָשׁוֹת 'witnesses to crimes punishable by death'

שׁוֹמְרֵי שָׂכָר 'paid custodians', שׁוֹמְרֵי חִנָּם 'unpaid custodians' (in reference to
artisans, creditors, etc. who are entrusted with the property of others)

VI *Exercises*

1. הִלֵּל אוֹמֵר, הֱוֵי תַלְמִידוֹ שֶׁלְּאַהֲרֹן, אוֹהֵב שָׁלוֹם וְרוֹדֵף שָׁלוֹם.

2. הֱוֵי זָהִיר בִּקְרִיַּית שְׁמַע.

3. רַבִּי אֶלְעָזָר אוֹמֵר, הֱוֵי שָׁקוּד לִלְמוֹד תּוֹרָה, וְדַע מָה שֶׁתָּשִׁיב לָאַפִּיקוֹרוֹס,
וְדַע לִפְנֵי מִי אַתָּה עָמֵל.

4. יְהוּדָה בֶּן תֵּימָא אוֹמֵר, הֱוֵי עַז כַּנָּמֵר, וְקַל כַּנֶּשֶׁר, וְרָץ כַּצְּבִי, וְגִבּוֹר כָּאֲרִי
לַעֲשׂוֹת רְצוֹן אָבִיךָ שֶׁבַּשָּׁמַיִם.

5. חַיָּב אָדָם לְבָרֵךְ עַל הָרָעָה כְּשֵׁם שֶׁהוּא מְבָרֵךְ עַל הַטּוֹבָה ... בְּכָל מִדָּה וּמִדָּה
שֶׁהוּא מוֹדֵד לְךָ הֱוֵי מוֹדֶה לוֹ בִּמְאֹד מְאֹד.

6. כָּל הָאֻמָּנִין שׁוֹמְרֵי שָׂכָר הֵן. וְכֻלָּן שֶׁאָמְרוּ, טֹל אֶת שֶׁלְּךָ וְהָבֵא מָעוֹת,
שׁוֹמֵר חִנָּם. שְׁמֹר לִי וְאֶשְׁמוֹר לָךְ, שׁוֹמֵר שָׂכָר. שְׁמֹר לִי וְאָמַר לוֹ, הַנַּח

לְפָנַי, שׁוֹמֵר חִנָּם.

7. כֵּיצַד מְאַיְּמִין [אֶת הָעֵדִים] עַל עֵדֵי נְפָשׁוֹת? ... הֱוֵי יוֹדְעִין, שֶׁלֹּא כְדִינֵי מָמוֹנוֹת דִּינֵי נְפָשׁוֹת. דִּינֵי מָמוֹנוֹת, אָדָם נוֹתֵן מָמוֹן וּמִתְכַּפֵּר לוֹ. דִּינֵי נְפָשׁוֹת, דָּמוֹ וְדַם זַרְעִיּוֹתָיו תְּלוּיִין בּוֹ עַד סוֹף הָעוֹלָם.

8. וְאוֹמְרִים לוֹ, אִישִׁי כֹהֵן גָּדוֹל, קְרָא אַתָּה בְּפִיךָ, שֶׁמָּא שָׁכַחְתָּ אוֹ שֶׁמָּא לֹא לָמַדְתָּ.

9. צא וראה איזה דרך שהיא מביאה את האדם לחיי העולם הבא. הוי אומר, יסורין. רבי נחמיה אומר, חביבין יסורין שכשם שהקרבנות מרצין כך היסורין מרצין.

10. אם עבד יגח השור [שמות כא' לב'], בכנעני הכתוב מדבר, או אינו מדבר אלא בעברי? כשהוא אומר, כסף שלשים שקלים יתן לאדוניו, [שם], הוי בכנעני הכתוב מדבר.

11. רבי שמעון בן יוחי אומר, הרי הוא אומר, ואוהביו כצאת השמש בגבורתו [שופטים ה' לא'], מי גדול, מי שהוא אוהב את המלך או מי שהמלך אוהבו? הוי אומר מי שהמלך אוהבו.

12. כי אני י' אלהיכם והתקדשתם והייתם קדושים כי קדוש אני י', [ויקרא יא' מד'], כשם שאני קדוש כך אתם קדושים, כשם שאני פרוש כך אתם היו פרושים.

13. והייתם לי קדושים כי קדוש אני י' [ויקרא כ' כו'], כשם שאני קדוש כך אתם היו קדושים, כשם שאני פרוש כך אתם היו פרושים.

14. אמר משה לפני המקום, אדוני, כלום הגון להם שתתן להם ותהרגם? אומרים לחמור, טול כור של שעורים ונחתוך ראשך? אומרים לאדם, טול ככר זהב ורד לשאול?

15. רבי שמעון בן אלעזר אומר, מי גדול, הממליך או המולך? הוי אומר הממליך. העושה שרים או העושה שררה? הוי אומר העושה שרים.

16. משל, למה הדבר דומה? למלך שהיתה אשתו נפטרת מן העולם. היתה מפקדתו על בניה. אמרה לו, בבקשה ממך, הזהר לו בבני. אמר לה, עד שאת מפקדתני על בני, פקדי את בניי שלא ימרדו בי ושלא ינהגו בי מנהג בזיון.

17. רבי אליעזר בן יעקב אומר, הרי הוא אומר, כי את אשר יאהב י' יוכיח וכאב את בן ירצה [משלי ג' יב']. מי גרם לבן שירצה לאב? הוי אומר, אלו יסורים ..., אי זה הוא דרך שמביאה האדם לעולם הבא? הוי אומר, אלו יסורים.

18. כך אמר להם הקדוש ברוך הוא לישראל, בני, בראתי לכם יצר הרע שאין רע הימנו ... היו עסוקים בדברי תורה ואינו שולט בכם, ואם פורשים אתם מדברי תורה הרי הוא שולט בכם.

19. בקשתי להיטיב לכם, חזרתם בכם ואמרתם לעגל, אלה אלהיך ישראל, [שמות לב' ד']. הוי כל זמן שאני מבקש להטיב לכם אתם מתישים כח של מעלה.

20. ועדין הדבר תלוי, אין אנו יודעים אם תפילה קודמת לברכה, אם ברכה קודמת לתפילה. כשהוא אומר, וזאת הברכה [דברים לג' א'], הוי תפילה קודמת לברכה, ואין ברכה קודמת לתפילה.

Sources. 1. K Abot 1.12. 2. K Abot 2.13. 3. Abot 2.14. 4. Abot 5.20. 5. Ber 9.5. 6. BM 6.6. 7. Sanh 4.5. 8. Yom 1.3. 9 Mek 20.23 (L 2.280). 10. Mek 21.32 (L 3.89). 11. Mek 22.20 (L 3.138). 12. SLv 11.44 (W 57b). 13. SLv 20.26 (W 93d). 14. SNm 95.1 (H 95). 15. SNm 119.3 (H 144). 16. SNm 142.1 (H 187). 17. SDt 32 (F 56–57). 18. SDt 45 (F 103). 19. SDt 319 (F 365). 20. SDt 342 (F 393).

PART III

PARTICLES

PREPOSITIONS AND CONJUNCTIONS

I *Introductory text* (Soṭ 9.15)

רַבִּי פִּנְחָס בֶּן יָאִיר אוֹמֵר, זְרִיזוּת מְבִיאָה לִידֵי נְקִיּוּת, וּנְקִיּוּת מְבִיאָה לִידֵי
טַהֲרָה, וְטַהֲרָה מְבִיאָה לִידֵי פְרִישׁוּת, וּפְרִישׁוּת מְבִיאָה לִידֵי קְדֻשָּׁה,
וּקְדֻשָּׁה מְבִיאָה לִידֵי עֲנָוָה, וַעֲנָוָה מְבִיאָה לִידֵי יִרְאַת חֵטְא, וְיִרְאַת חֵטְא
מְבִיאָה לִידֵי חֲסִידוּת, וַחֲסִידוּת מְבִיאָה לִידֵי רוּחַ הַקֹּדֶשׁ, וְרוּחַ הַקֹּדֶשׁ
מְבִיאָה לִידֵי תְחִיַּת הַמֵּתִים, וּתְחִיַּת הַמֵּתִים בָּאָה עַל יְדֵי אֵלִיָּהוּ זָכוּר
לְטוֹב, אָמֵן.

Rabbi Phineḥas ben Jair used to say, Asiduous work leads to innocence, innocence leads to purity, purity leads to abstinence, abstinence leads to holiness, holiness leads to humility, humility leads to fear of sin, fear of sin leads
to the spirit of holiness, the spirit of holiness leads to the resurrection of the
dead, and the resurrection of the dead will come through the mediation of
Elijah, of blessed memory. Amen.

1. This long chain of human virtues and divine gifts begins with diligent
work, on the part of human beings, and culminates with the gift of ultimate
resurrection, on the part of God.

II *Morphology*

2. Prepositions and conjunctions are both particles of relation, either
modifying a noun, converting it into the complement of another noun
(prepositions), or connecting clauses by coordination or subordination (conjunctions).

3. It seems that in Proto-Semitic there were no prepositions properly
speaking but rather nouns in the adverbial accusative governing other nouns
in the genitive (Meyer 1992, §87). Such nouns were eventually fossilized to
the point of simply expressing relationship and lost their accent in the process. Thus, we may say, in general, that many prepositions are simply primi-
tive nouns in the construct state, for example בֵּין, בֵּינֵי, תַּחַת, לִפְנֵי, and תּוֹךְ
(לְתוֹךְ, מִתּוֹךְ, בְּתוֹךְ, from the absolute תָּוֶךְ)

4. Viewed carefully, conjunctions of the type לִפְנֵי שֶׁ-, עַד שֶׁ-, and אַחֲרֵי שֶׁ-
are simply prepositions determined by a clause introduced with -שֶׁ. In other

words, the determinant of the noun/preposition is not another noun but an entire clause (see Unit 11.2–3, 7).

5. RH witnesses the disappearance of the biblical particles מוּל, בִּגְלַל, פֶּן, לְמַעַן, and אֵת (in the sense of 'with').

6. The so-called 'inseparable prepositions', -בְּ, -כְּ, and -לְ, are still used, as are אֵת (deictic), בֵּין, עִם, נֶגֶד, אֵצֶל, אֶל (although this is in decline), עַל, עַד, מִן, תַּחַת, אַחֲרֵי, אַחַר, etc.

A. Alongside בְּבֵית, we also find אבית, in the sense of 'in, inside'. This does not represent a new preposition but rather the well-known phenomenon of prosthetic *alef* being added to a word-initial geminated consonant in order to make pronunciation easier (בְּבֵית > *bbet* > *ab-bet*; see Meyer 1992, §29.1). It is a typically Palestinian feature, found in one of the Bar-Kokhba letters (Mur 42.4) and at Qumran (1QpHab 11.6; see Qimron 1986, 39); in Sifra, it is commonly found in the expression אבית הבליעה 'in the stomach', and occurs as well, for example, at SNm 17.1 (H 21): אבית הדשן 'among the ashes, where the ashes are'. The phenomenon is also widespread in the Samaritan tradition, although not always reflected orthographically.

B. -כְּ is attached to pronominal suffixes by means of the lengthened forms כְּמוֹ and כְּמוֹת (see Unit 26.2).

C. Similarly, מִן is still used in the reduplicated form known from BH when attached to pronominal suffixes: מִמֶּנִּי, מִמֶּנּוּ, etc. For the third person singular, RH employs הֵימֶנּוּ and הֵימֶנָּה as well as מִמֶּנּוּ and מִמֶּנָּה. These new forms, unique to RH, were only known through the Babylonian tradition, although they reflected a typically Palestinian pronunciation or dialect, as now evidenced by their presence in the Bar-Kokhba archives from Murabba'at and Naḥal Ḥever.

D. As well as אַחַר and אַחֲרֵי, RH also employs the form אֲחוֹרֵי (dual construct of אֲחוֹר).

7. In BH, there is already a tendency to accumulate particles in the creation of new prepositions (עַל פְּנֵי; מֵחֲמַת, תַּחַת, לְתוֹךְ, מִתּוֹךְ, תּוֹךְ, etc.) and this process is accelerated in RH, where there is an abundance of such combinations, many unknown in BH. Among the most frequent are כְּדֵי, בִּשְׁבִיל, בְּצַד, מֵעֵין, (חֲמָה + מִן) מֵחֲמַת, לְעִנְיַן, (פֶּה + לְ-) לְפִי, לְיַד/לְיָד, (לְאַפֵּי + כְּ-) כְּלַפֵּי, עַל מְנָת, עַל יְדֵי/עַל יַד, עַל גַּב, לְשׁוּם/לְשֵׁם, מִשּׁוּם/מִשֵּׁם, and עַל שֵׁם (the alternation שׁוּם/שֵׁם may be due to assimilation of the vowel to the labial consonant, for example -*em* > -*um*, under Aramaic influence; see Introduction, §9.11).

8. Conjunctions.

The following is a list of conjunctions and clause-connecting particles, indicating where further details of form and use can be found in the following units.

    A. Copulative and disjunctive:

        -וְ (*passim*);

        אוֹ and אוֹ שֶׁ- (24.13; 25.8–9);

        אִם (25.9).

B. Interrogative:

הַ- (25.3, 5);

וְכִי (25.3, 6);

כְּלוּם (25.3, 7);

אִם (25.9);

אוֹ (25.8).

C. Comparative:

כְּמוֹ שֶׁ-, כְּמוֹת שֶׁ- (26.4, 12);

כְּמוֹ כֵן (26.11);

כְּשֵׁם שֶׁ- (26.4, 7);

כְּדֶרֶךְ שֶׁ- (26.4, 7);

כְּעִנְיָן שֶׁ- (26.4, 7);

כְּאִילוּ (26.4; 28.3, 8A);

וּמָה אִם/מָה אִם, מָה (26.8);

בֵּין שֶׁ- ... בֵּין שֶׁ- (8.12; 26.10);

לְ- ... וְשֶׁלֹּא לְ-/בְּ- ... וְשֶׁלֹּא בְּ- (8.12; 26.10).

D. Temporal:

לִכְשֶׁ-, כְּשֶׁ- (27.2–3, 8);

מִשֶּׁ- (27.2–3, 9);

עַד שֶׁ- (27.2–3, 10, 16);

עַד כְּדֵי שֶׁ- (27.2–3, 11);

אַחַר שֶׁ-, קוֹדֶם שֶׁ- (27.3, 12);

כֵּיוָן שֶׁ- (27.3, 13);

אֵימָתַי שֶׁ- (27.3, 14);

כָּל זְמַן שֶׁ-, בִּזְמַן שֶׁ- (27.3, 15);

כָּל שָׁעָה שֶׁ-, בְּשָׁעָה שֶׁ- (27.3, 15).

E. Conditional:

אִם (28.3, 7, 9);

אִלּוּ (28.2–3, 8A);

אִלּוּלֵי (28.2–3, 8B, D);

אִלְמָלֵי (28.3, 8B–C, 10);

הוֹאִיל וְ- (28.5; 29.5, 14).

F. Causal:

שֶׁ- (29.2–4, 6);

מִפְּנֵי שֶׁ- (29.2–4, 7);

מִשּׁוּם שֶׁ- (29.2–4, 8);

עַל שׁוּם שֶׁ-/עַל שֵׁם שֶׁ- (29.2–4, 9);

לְפִי שֶׁ- (29.2–4, 10);

בִּשְׁבִיל שֶׁ- (29.2–4, 11);

מֵאַחַר שֶׁ- (29.2–4, 12);

עַל שֶׁ- (29.2–4, 13);

הוֹאִיל וְ- (28.5; 29.2, 5, 14–15).

G. Final:

לְ- with infinitive (30.2, 5);

שֶׁ- (30.2, 6);

כְּדֵי שֶׁ-, כְּדֵי לְ- (30.2, 8);

עַל מְנָת שֶׁ-, עַל מְנָת לְ- (30.2, 9);

עַל תְּנַאי (30.2, 10);

בִּשְׁבִיל שֶׁ- (29.11; 30.2, 7);

שֶׁמָּא (30.2, 11).

H. Consecutive:

שֶׁ- (30.2–3, 12–13);

כְּדֵי שֶׁ- (30.2–3, 12).

I. Concessive:

אִם (31.2–3);

אֲפִלּוּ (31.2–3, 5);

אַף כְּשֶׁ- (31.6);

אַף עַל פִּי (31.2, 7–8).

J. Adversative:

אֲבָל (32.2–3, 5);

אֶלָּא (32.2–3, 6, 9–10);

וּבִלְבַד שֶׁ- (32.3, 7);

חוּץ מִן (32.3, 8).

III *Grammar and usage*

9. The following observations represent only a tentative presentation of some meanings and uses of certain prepositions, as often texts reveal senses and usages that are difficult to categorize.

10. -בְּ.

A. Apart from its local and instrumental meanings, 'in' and 'by, with', -בְּ can also have an adjectival value, 'as, in the rôle of' (*beth essentiae*):

אִם רָצָה לְהַקְרִיב, מַקְרִיב שֶׁכֹּהֵן גָּדוֹל מַקְרִיב חֵלֶק בָּרֹאשׁ וְנוֹטֵל חֵלֶק בָּרֹאשׁ

If he desires to make an offering he makes it, for as head the high priest offers his portion and as head he takes his portion (Yom 1.2)

(with effectively the same meaning, K reads מֵרֹאשׁ 'in the first place').

B. -בְּ can also mean 'in relation to, with respect to', as in the well-known phrase בַּמֶּה־דְבָרִים־אֲמוּרִים 'what does this apply to?' (BB 3.1,3; Soṭ 8.7, etc.); see Unit 19.25.

C. בְּלֹא 'without':

שֶׁכֵּן מָצִינוּ כְּשֶׁהָיוּ יִשְׂרָאֵל בַּמִּדְבָּר אַרְבָּעִים שָׁנָה קָרְבוּ כְבָשִׂים בְּלֹא לֶחֶם, אַף כָּאן יִקְרְבוּ כְבָשִׂים בְּלֹא לֶחֶם

Just as we found that during the forty years Israel were in the desert they offered lambs without bread, so also now they may offer the lambs without bread (Men 4.3).

בְּלֹא is also employed to negate a participle (in a circumstantial noun clause):

נִכְנַס רַבִּי טַרְפוֹן בְּלֹא מִתְכַּוֵּן

Rabbi Ṭarfon entered (a town) without intending (to spend the sabbath there) (Erub 4.9)

D. The characteristic RH verb זָכָה 'acquire the right to, take possession of' governs its object through the preposition -בְּ, as in BM 1.4:

רָאָה אֶת הַמְּצִיאָה וְנָפַל עָלֶיהָ, וּבָא אַחֵר וְהֶחֱזִיק בָּהּ, זֶה שֶׁהֶחֱזִיק בָּהּ
זָכָה בָּהּ

If someone finds lost property and rushes towards it but someone else arrives and seizes it, the person who seizes it is entitled to keep the property.

In RH, as in BH, this use of -בְּ is also found in connection with other verbs (הֶחֱזִיק בְּ-, בָּחַר בְּ-, etc.).

11. For -כְּ, כְּנֶגֶד, כְּדֶרֶךְ, and -כְּיוֹצֵא בְ, see Unit 26.6,9.

12. -לְ.

In RH, -לְ extends its range of meanings, so that as well as introducing an indirect complement (אָמַר לוֹ), or, with an infinitive, a final clause, and expressing the 'ethic dative' (הָלַךְ לוֹ 'he went away') or 'possessive' relationships of various kinds (for example

סֵפֶר דִּבְרֵי הַיָּמִים לְמַלְכֵי יִשְׂרָאֵל

Chronicle of the kings of Israel),

-לְ also extends into the domain of -בְּ, עַל, and אֶת, and to a great extent replaces אֶל.

A. The formulas אִם לָמַדְתָּ and אִם לָמַדְתִּי (see Unit 28.9) regularly employ -לְ, or occasionally עַל, but never the expected -בְּ, to specify an object:

אם למדתי למנורה שעשה בה את הבנים כאב, אף הקטורת נעשה
בה את הבנים כאב

Seeing that *in connection with* the lampstand sons are treated the same as their father, it follows that in the offering of incense sons are also treated the same as their father (SNm 60.2 [H 58]).

B. Objects of כִּפֶּר 'expiate, forgive' are usually introduced by -לְ, not עַל, the regular BH choice:

אָנָּא הַשֵּׁם, כַּפֶּר נָא לָעֲוֹנוֹת וְלַפְּשָׁעִים וְלַחֲטָאִים, שֶׁעָוִיתִי וְשֶׁפָּשַׁעְתִּי
וְשֶׁחָטָאתִי לְפָנֶיךָ, אֲנִי וּבֵיתִי

O God, forgive the offences, transgressions, and sins with which I have offended, transgressed, and sinned before you, I and my house (Yom 3.8).

C. קִנֵּא אֶת־אִשְׁתוֹ 'he is suspicious of his wife', at Nm 5.14, is reformulated at Soṭ 1.1: הַמְקַנֵּא לְאִשְׁתוֹ 'one who is suspicious of his wife'.

D. In passive sentences, -לְ introduces the agent (as also in BH, e.g. Lv 26.23):

וְנֶאֱכָלִין בְּכָל הָעִיר לְכָל אָדָם

And they (the thanksgiving and Nazirite offerings) can be eaten throughout the city by any person (Zeb 5.6);

חביב בנימין שנקרא ידיד למקום

How beloved is Benjamin, who has been called favourite by the omnipresent one (SDt 352 [F 509]).

13. אֵת.

See Unit 2.3. As distinct from BH, personal object pronouns are usually suffixed directly to personal and infinitive forms of the verb, with אֵת being used much less frequently (a phenomenon already found at Qumran; see Qimron 1986, 75–77). However, the plural participle always employs אֵת to introduce a pronominal object (see Cohen 1982–83).

14. מִן.

מִן is used to express origin, provenance, or separation.

A. A striking usage is of partitive מִן in place of an indefinite pronoun (see Unit 6.11):

תפש מהם, הרג מהם, צלב מהם

Some he seized, others he slaughtered, others he crucified (Mek 15.18 [L 2.80]);

אֲפִלּוּ שָׁמַע מִן הַנָּשִׁים אוֹמְרוֹת ... אֲפִלּוּ שָׁמַע מִן הַתִּינוֹקוֹת אוֹמְרִין

Even though he heard some women saying ... even though he heard some children saying (Yeb 16.5).

The same usage is found in BH: וַיָּמוּתוּ מֵעַבְדֵי הַמֶּלֶךְ 'and some of the king's servants died' (2 S 11.24).

B. הֵימֶנּוּ and הֵימֶנָּה are used exactly the same as the regular constructions מִמֶּנּוּ and מִמֶּנָּה; whereas at Men 8.5, we read

הָרִאשׁוֹן שֶׁבָּרִאשׁוֹן אֵין לְמַעֲלָה מִמֶּנּוּ

The very first (oil) is the best of all,

in SLv 24.2 (W 103c), the same declaration employs הֵימֶנּוּ. Akiba formulated the hermeneutical principle of contiguity in the following terms:

כל פרשה שהיא סמוכה לחברתה למידה הימנה

Every passage that occurs alongside another is explained by the other (SNm 131.2 [H 169]).

15. עַל.

Although the usages attached to עַל in BH are maintained, it can also be used where BH would have -לְ; in comparisons, יָתֵר עַל has the same function as יוֹתֵר מִן (see Unit 13.5C). עַל can also express cause:

עַל שָׁלֹשׁ עֲבֵרוֹת הַנָּשִׁים מֵתוֹת בִּשְׁעַת לֵדָתָן

For three transgressions, women die at childbirth (Shab 2.6).

Construed with an infinitive, עַל designates the one upon whom an obligation is laid (see Unit 20.11), similarly, with a verbal noun:

אין שביתתו עליהן

They are not obliged to uphold the sabbath rest (Shab 16.6).

With personal passive constructions as well, when the agent is introduced by עַל, an element of obligation is conveyed:

הִנִּיחַ בָּנוֹת גְּדוֹלוֹת וּקְטַנּוֹת, אֵין הַגְּדוֹלוֹת מִתְפַּרְנְסוֹת עַל הַקְּטַנּוֹת
וְלֹא הַקְּטַנּוֹת נְזוֹנוֹת עַל הַגְּדוֹלוֹת

If someone leaves older and younger daughters, the older ones do
not have to be maintained by (at the cost of) the younger ones, nor
do the younger ones have to be fed by (at the cost of) the older ones
(BB 8.8).

16. עַל יָד/עַל יַד.

A great variety of meanings is discernible, depending on context.

A. 'Along with': אִם אֵין מִקְדָּשׁ, תִּקָּבֵר עַל יְדֵי עוֹרָהּ 'if the temple no longer
exists, it (the animal) is to be buried along with its skin' (MS 1.6).

B. 'In relation to, as compared with, than', with the verb מָעַט 'diminish,
become less', expressing the relationship between two elements:

אֶלָּא מֵעֵת לָעֵת מְמַעֶטֶת עַל יַד מִפְּקִידָה לִפְקִידָה

Only if the interval of 24 hours is less than the interval between one
inspection and another (Eduy 1.1; cf. Ohol 13.5–6).

C. 'Because of, on account of':

הָאָב גּוֹלֶה עַל יְדֵי הַבֵּן

The parents are exiled on account of the children (Mak 2.2);

עַל יְדֵי כָל הָעֲרָיוֹת מְקַנִּין חוּץ מִן הַקָּטָן וּמִמִּי שֶׁאֵינוֹ אִישׁ

They may become jealous on account of incestuous unions other
than those with minors or with what is not human (Soṭ 4.4).

D. 'For, in favour of, on behalf of, in place of':

מֵבִיא אָדָם עַל יְדֵי בְנוֹ, עַל יְדֵי בִתּוֹ, עַל יְדֵי עַבְדּוֹ וְשִׁפְחָתוֹ קָרְבַּן עָנִי

One may present a poor person's offering on behalf of a son,
daughter, servant, or maidservant (Neg 14.12);

ממהר עני ליפרע על ידי עני יותר מן העשיר

I make greater haste to take revenge on behalf of a poor person than
(I do on behalf of) a rich one' (SDt 277 [F 295]);

E. 'Through, by' (a sense also expressed by בְּיַד/בְּיָד):

וְעָלָיו הוּא מְפוֹרָשׁ עַל יְדֵי יְחֶזְקֵל

And an express statement is made about it by Ezekiel (Tam 3.7; cf.
Mid 4.2);

וְכֵן כָּתוּב בְּסֵפֶר תְּהִלִּים עַל יְדֵי דָוִד מֶלֶךְ יִשְׂרָאֵל

For thus it is written in the Book of Psalms by King David (Abot
6.9 [late]).

F. In certain contexts, עַל יָדוֹ has reflexive significance, 'by oneself, by
one's own endeavours'. But note that in the exercise text 9, (Mek 17.14 [L
2.150]), the meaning of עַל יַד and עַל יְדֵי כֻלָּם is rather *pro*: '(annul a decree)
in place of/overriding (the one who issued it)', that is, to cancel what another
has prescribed.

17. בְּיַד/בְּיָד; לְיַד/לְיָד.

Generally, לְיַד/לְיָד is used with verbs of motion, קָרֵב, יָרַד, and especially בָּא, extending into the territory of אֶל, לְ-, and אֵצֶל:

וְרוּחַ הַקֹּדֶשׁ מְבִיאָהּ לִידֵי תְחִיַּת הַמֵּתִים

And the spirit of holiness leads to the resurrection of the dead (Soṭ 9.15, the introductory text for this unit).

Like בְּיַד/בְּיַד לִיַד/לְיַד can be employed more literally:

אין בידו אלא רשותו

In his hand, means, (In) his possession (Mek 21.16 [L 3.45]);

או כשם שנותנים פדיון למומתים בידי שמים כך יהו נותנים פדיון
למומתים בידי אדם

In the same way that it is possible to pay a ransom for those whose death is in the hands of heaven (i.e. 'God'), so one can pay a ransom for those whose death is in the hands of human beings (SNm 161.1 [H 221]).

18. עַל שֵׁם.

'With regard to, taking into account' (see Unit 29.9 on the conjunction עַל שֵׁם שֶׁ-, the meaning of which casts light on the prepositional usage):

בֵּן סוֹרֵר וּמוֹרֶה נִדּוֹן עַל שֵׁם סוֹפוֹ

An obstinate and rebellious son is to be judged taking into account what would have been his end (i.e. the outcome of his behaviour) (Sanh 8.5);

הַבָּא בַּמַּחְתֶּרֶת נִדּוֹן עַל שֵׁם סוֹפוֹ

Someone (i.e. a thief) who enters surreptitiously will be judged with regard to what they would have done eventually (Sanh 8.6).

Like the related conjunction, עַל שֵׁם is often found in statements of etymology and in wordplays:

נקראו מרים על שם סופן שממררין את הגוף ומערערין את העון

They are called 'bitter' with regard to their end, since they will fill the body with bitterness and expose iniquity (SNm 11.4 [H 117]);

למה נקרא, לחם עוני [דרבים טז׳ ג׳]? אלא על שם עינוי שנתענו
במצרים

Why was it called, Bread of affliction [Dt 16.3]? Simply, because of the affliction with which they were afflicted in Egypt (SDt 130 [F 187]).

19. מִשּׁוּם/מְשֵׁם.

A. Causal, 'on account of, with regard to', widely used when justifying a deed or statement with a text or precept from the Bible or oral tradition (a similar usage attaches to the related conjunction; see Unit 29.8 and Bacher 1899, 121):

וְאֵלּוּ עוֹבְרִין בְּלֹא תַעֲשֶׂה ... עוֹבְרִים מִשּׁוּם, לֹא־תִתֵּן [ויקרא כה׳ לז׳],
וּמִשּׁוּם, בַּל־תִּקַּח מֵאִתּוֹ [ויקרא כה׳ לו׳], וּמִשּׁוּם, לֹא־תִהְיֶה לוֹ כְּנֹשֶׁה
[שמות כב׳ כד׳]

These transgress the negative precept ...; they transgress it with regard to 'you are not to give' [Lv 25.37], with regard to 'you are not to take from him' [Lv 25.36], and with regard to 'you are not to be to him as a creditor' [Ex 22.24] (BM 5.11).

B. 'In the name of', introducing a scholar who has helped transmit a tradition:

רַבָּן שִׁמְעוֹן בֶּן גַּמְלִיאֵל אוֹמֵר מִשּׁוּם רַבִּי יְהוֹשֻׁעַ

Rabban Simeon ben Gamaliel says in the name of Rabbi Joshua (Soṭ 9.12).

20. לְשׁוּם/לְשֵׁם.

A. 'For (the sake of)', signifying the motive or motivation of an action or attitude, as in the characteristic formula לְשֵׁם שָׁמַיִם, which expresses the purest form of motivation (similar to διὰ τὴν βασιλείαν τῶν οὐρανῶν 'for the kingdom of heaven' at Mt 19.12):

כָּל מַחֲלֹקֶת שֶׁהִיא לְשֵׁם שָׁמַיִם, סוֹפָהּ לְהִתְקַיֵּם, וְשֶׁאֵינָהּ לְשֵׁם שָׁמַיִם, אֵין
סוֹפָהּ לְהִתְקַיֵּם. אֵיזוֹ הִיא מַחֲלֹקֶת שֶׁהִיא לְשֵׁם שָׁמַיִם? זוֹ מַחֲלֹקֶת הִלֵּל
וְשַׁמַּאי. וְשֶׁאֵינָהּ לְשֵׁם שָׁמַיִם? זוֹ מַחֲלֹקֶת קֹרַח וְכָל עֲדָתוֹ

Every controversy undertaken for the sake of heaven (i.e. God) will end up successfully, but not if it is not for the sake of heaven. What controversy was for the sake of heaven? The one of Hillel and Shammai. What controversy was not for the sake of heaven? The one of Korah and all his followers (Abot 5.17; see also Abot 2.1,12; 4.11).

B. 'As, in the capacity of, by way of', like עַל שֵׁם, specifying the purpose of an action:

זֶה הַכְּלָל, כָּל שֶׁהוּא בָא לְשֵׁם חַטָּאת וּלְשֵׁם אַשְׁמָה, מוֹתָרָן נְדָבָה

This is the general principle: everything that is offered by way of a sin offering or a guilt offering, the residue is for the freewill offering (Sheq 2.5).

In various manuscripts, מִשּׁוּם/מִשֵּׁם is found in the same sense.

21. בֵּין.

'Between, among', in the formula בֵּין ... לְ- and בֵּין ... וּלְ-; בֵּין is also found in reflexive, reciprocal, and comparative formulas, for example בֵּין ... בֵּינוֹ לְבֵין עַצְמוֹ 'on one's own', בֵּין ... לַחֲבֵרוֹ, and בֵּין ... בֵּין (see Units 7.4C,7C; 8.12; 26.10).

22. בִּשְׁבִיל.

A. Expressing cause, 'because of, on account of', as in Sifra Mekhilta de Millu'im (SLv 9.23 [W 44d]):

בשבילי לא ירדה שכינה לישראל

Because of me, the Shekhinah did not descend on Israel.

B. The dominant sense is, however, of purpose or benefit, 'for (the benefit of, the purpose of), so that':

הַמְכַבֶּה אֶת הַנֵּר מִפְּנֵי שֶׁהוּא מִתְיָרֵא מִפְּנֵי גוֹיִם ... וְאִם בִּשְׁבִיל הַחוֹלֶה
שֶׁיִּישַׁן, פָּטוּר

One who puts out a candle for fear of the gentiles ..., or so that someone ill can sleep, is exempt (Shab 2.5).

See also Shab 16.8 (exercises text 8) and Unit 29.11.

23. כְּדֵי.

'Sufficient for, as much as is required for/appropriate to', in statements of measures and quantities (for an extensive discussion, see Unit 30.8B):

לֹא־יַרְבֶּה־לּוֹ סוּסִים [דברים י׳ טז], אֶלָּא כְדֵי מֶרְכַּבְתּוֹ

He is not to increase his horses [Dt 7.16]: only those required for his chariot (Sanh 2.4);

וְכַמָּה הִיא טֻמְאָה? כְדֵי בִיאָה, וְכַמָּה כְדֵי בִיאָה? כְדֵי הָעֲרָאָה

How much (time is regarded as necessary) for impurity (to be contracted)? As much as is needed for (a completed act of) intercourse (to take place). And how much is needed for intercourse? As much as is needed for contact between genitals (to occur) (TosSoṭ 1.2).

24. מֵחֲמַת.

This construction has lost its etymological sense of 'out of anger' and has become a causal particle:

עָלוּ בוֹ צְמָחִים, אִם מֵחֲמַת הַמַּכָּה, חַיָּב, שֶׁלֹּא מֵחֲמַת הַמַּכָּה, פָּטוּר

If ulcers appear on him because of the blow, he is liable, but if not because of the blow, he is exempt (BQ 8.1).

25. מֵעֵין.

The underlying meaning, 'of the eye of', that is 'as a reflection of, of the same kind as', gives rise to distinct usages.

A. Indicating that one thing is 'of the same type/nature as' another:

הָעוֹשֶׂה מְלָאכוֹת הַרְבֵּה מֵעֵין מְלָאכָה אַחַת, אֵינוֹ חַיָּב אֶלָּא חַטָּאת אַחַת

Someone who carries out many tasks (on the sabbath), but all of the same kind, is only liable to one sin offering (Shab 7.1).

B. Indicating that one thing is like a reflection or synthesis of, or an extract from, another:

רַבָּן גַּמְלִיאֵל אוֹמֵר, בְּכָל יוֹם מִתְפַּלֵּל אָדָם שְׁמוֹנֶה עֶשְׂרֵה. רַבִּי יְהוֹשֻׁעַ אוֹמֵר, מֵעֵין שְׁמוֹנֶה עֶשְׂרֵה. רַבִּי עֲקִיבָא אוֹמֵר, אִם שְׁגוּרָה תְפִלָּתוֹ בְּפִיו, יִתְפַּלֵּל שְׁמוֹנֶה עֶשְׂרֵה, וְאִם לָאו, מֵעֵין שְׁמוֹנֶה עֶשְׂרֵה.

Rabban Gamaliel used to say, Each day, one should recite the eighteen benedictions; Rabbi Joshua said, A summary of the eighteen benedictions; Rabbi Akiba said, If the prayer is fluent on his tongue, he is to recite the eighteen benedictions, if not, just a summary (Ber 4.3).

IV *Phraseology*

26. יָצָא יְדֵי חוֹבָתוֹ, literally, 'he went out from (the power of) his obligation', i.e. he fulfilled his duty:

רַבָּן גַּמְלִיאֵל אוֹמֵר, כָּל שֶׁלֹּא אָמַר שְׁלֹשָׁה דְבָרִים לֹא יָצָא יְדֵי חוֹבָתוֹ, וְאֵלּוּ הֵן, פֶּסַח, מַצָּה, מָרוֹר

Rabban Gamaliel used to say, Anyone who does not explain these three terms during the celebration of passover has not fulfilled their duty; and these are the three terms: passover, unleavened bread, and bitter herbs (Pes 10.5).

See also Suk 2.1; 3.13, etc. As we have already noted at Unit 17.17, the formula is often reduced to just יָצָא.

This use of יְדֵי as preposition is also found in other phrases, as, for example, at Sheq 3.2:

לָצֵאת יְדֵי הַבְּרִיוֹת ... לָצֵאת יְדֵי הַמָּקוֹם

To do what is required by mortals ... to do what is required by God.

V *Vocabulary*

אִיפָּטִיקוֹס (ὑπατικός) 'consul' (i.e. the emperor's consular delegate)

אָרַע 'occur'

דִּיקוּרְיוֹן (Latin *decurio*) '*decurio*, commander'

דֶּשֶׁן '(sacrificial) ashes'

הִתְקִין (hi. of תקן) 'prepare, arrange'

כֶּבֶשׁ 'ramp, grade, bridge'

מָחַק 'crush, dissolve, destroy'

נֶפֶשׁ 'soul', עַל יְדֵי נְפָשׁוֹת 'because of a capital offence'

סִיֵּע 'accompany, attend, support'

סָפַן 'respect', סָפוּן 'distinguished'

פָּסַק 'separate, distribute, assign'

צִבּוּר 'community'

צְהִיבָה 'jealousy, envy, fever'

קְרִיבָה 'approach, coming near'

רֶגֶל (plural רְגָלִים) 'pilgrim festival'

תֵּבֵל '(inhabited) world'

תֶּבֶל 'spice, condiment'

VI *Exercises*

1. וְכָל הָעֲמֵלִים עִם הַצִּבּוּר, יִהְיוּ עֲמֵלִים עִמָּהֶם לְשֵׁם שָׁמַיִם, שֶׁזְּכוּת אֲבוֹתָם מְסַיְעָתָן וְצִדְקָתָן עוֹמֶדֶת לָעַד.

2. רַבִּי יוֹסֵי אוֹמֵר, יְהִי מָמוֹן חֲבֵרְךָ חָבִיב עָלֶיךָ כְּשֶׁלָּךְ, וְהַתְקֵן עַצְמְךָ לִלְמוֹד תּוֹרָה, שֶׁאֵינָה יְרוּשָׁה לָךְ, וְכָל מַעֲשֶׂיךָ יִהְיוּ לְשֵׁם שָׁמַיִם.

3. רַבִּי יוֹחָנָן הַסַּנְדְּלָר אוֹמֵר, כָּל כְּנֵסִיָּה שֶׁהִיא לְשֵׁם שָׁמַיִם, סוֹפָהּ לְהִתְקַיֵּם, וְשֶׁאֵינָה לְשֵׁם שָׁמַיִם, אֵין סוֹפָהּ לְהִתְקַיֵּם.

4. מַעֲשֶׂה בְרַבִּי יוֹחָנָן בֶּן מַתְיָא שֶׁאָמַר לִבְנוֹ, צֵא שְׂכֹר לָנוּ פוֹעֲלִים. הָלַךְ וּפָסַק לָהֶם מְזוֹנוֹת, וּכְשֶׁבָּא אֵצֶל אָבִיו אָמַר לֹו, בְּנִי, אֲפִלּוּ אַתָּה עוֹשֶׂה לָהֶם כִּסְעוּדַת שְׁלֹמֹה בְּשָׁעָתוֹ, לֹא יָצָאתָ יְדֵי חוֹבָתְךָ עִמָּהֶן, שֶׁהֵן בְּנֵי אַבְרָהָם, יִצְחָק וְיַעֲקֹב.

5. הָאִשָּׁה שֶׁנֶּחְבְּשָׁה בִּידֵי גוֹיִם, עַל יְדֵי מָמוֹן, מֻתֶּרֶת לְבַעְלָהּ, עַל יְדֵי נְפָשׁוֹת, אֲסוּרָה לְבַעְלָהּ.

6. הָאָב גּוֹלֶה עַל יְדֵי הַבֵּן, וְהַבֵּן גּוֹלֶה עַל יְדֵי הָאָב. הַכֹּל גּוֹלִין עַל יְדֵי

יִשְׂרָאֵל, וְיִשְׂרָאֵל גּוֹלִין עַל יְדֵיהֶן, חוּץ מֵעַל יְדֵי גֵר תּוֹשָׁב. וְגֵר תּוֹשָׁב אֵינוֹ גוֹלֶה אֶלָּא עַל יְדֵי גֵר תּוֹשָׁב.

7. אֵין הַיָּחִיד נֶאֱמָן עַל יְדֵי עַצְמוֹ.

8. נָכְרִי שֶׁהִדְלִיק אֶת הַנֵּר, מִשְׁתַּמֵּשׁ לְאוֹרוֹ יִשְׂרָאֵל, וְאִם בִּשְׁבִיל יִשְׂרָאֵל, אָסוּר. מִלֵּא מַיִם לְהַשְׁקוֹת בְּהֶמְתּוֹ, מַשְׁקֶה אַחֲרָיו יִשְׂרָאֵל, וְאִם בִּשְׁבִיל יִשְׂרָאֵל, אָסוּר. עָשָׂה גוֹי כֶּבֶשׁ לֵירֵד בּוֹ, יוֹרֵד אַחֲרָיו יִשְׂרָאֵל, וְאִם בִּשְׁבִיל יִשְׂרָאֵל, אָסוּר. מַעֲשֶׂה בְּרַבָּן גַּמְלִיאֵל וּזְקֵנִים, שֶׁהָיוּ בָאִין בִּסְפִינָה, וְעָשָׂה גוֹי כֶּבֶשׁ לֵירֵד בּוֹ, וְיָרְדוּ בּוֹ רַבָּן גַּמְלִיאֵל וְהַזְּקֵנִים.

9. אמר משה לפני הקב״ה, רבונו של עולם, שמא דרכיך כדרכי בשר ודם? אפוטרופוס גוזר גזירה, כליריכוס מבטל על ידו, כליריכוס גוזר גזירה, דיקוריון מבטל על ידו, דיקוריון גוזר גזירה, היגמון מבטל על ידו, היגמון גוזר גזירה, איפרכוס מבטל על ידו, איפרכוס גוזר גזירה, איפיטיקוס מבטל על ידו, איפיטיקוס גוזר גזירה, ובא המושל הגדול ומבטל על ידי כלם, מפני שהן ממונין זה למעלה מזה וזה למעלה מזה.

10. גם את ארי גם הדוב הכה עבדך [שמואל א י״ז ל״ו], אלא אמר דוד, וכי מה אני ספון שהכתי חיות רעות הללו? אלא שמא דבר עתיד לארע את ישראל והם עתידין להינצל על ידי.

11. יחידי שיפול מהם, הרי הוא עלי ככלם. מלמד שאף אחד ממעט עלי ידי כלן. דבר אחר, יחידי שיוטל מהם, הרי הוא עלי כנגד כל מעשה בראשית, שנאמר, כי ל״י עין אדם וכל שבטי ישראל [זכריה ט׳ א׳].

12. ולא ימות ונפל למשכב [שמות כא׳ יח׳]. מגיד שהצהיבה מביאה לידי מיתה.

13. אלעזר בן אחווי אומר, יכול היה מדבר עמו לצורך עצמו? תלמוד לומר, לאמר [ויקרא א׳ א׳], לאמר לישראל. בשביל ישראל היה מדבר עמו ולא היה מדבר עמו לאורך עצמו.

14. מפני מה זכו הכנענים לישב בארצם ארבעים ושבע שנים, שנאמר, וחברון שבע שנים נבנתה לפני צוען מצרים [במדבר יג׳ כב׳]? אלא בשביל שכר, שכבדו את אברהם אבינו שאמרו לו, שמענו, אדוני, נשיא אלהים אתה בתוכינו [בראשית כג׳ ו׳]. בני אדם שכבדו את אברהם אבינו זכו לישב בארצם שבע וארבעים שנה.

15. וידבר י״ אל משה … ואל אהרן … ואל בני ישראל [ויקרא כב׳ א׳-ב׳], הזהיר את אהרן על ידי הבנים ואת הבנים על ידי ישראל ואת הבנים זה על ידי זה.

16. נמחקה המגילה ואמרה [הסוטה], טמאה אני, המים נשפכים והמנחה מתפזרת אבית הדשן, ואין מגילתה כשרה להשקות בה סוטה אחרת.

17. משל, למה הדבר דומה? למלך שנשבה בן אוהבו, וכשפדאו לא פדאו לשום בן חורין אלא לשום עבד, שאם יגזור ולא יהיה מקבל עליו, יאמר לו, עבדי אתה, … כך כשפדא הקב״ה את זרע אברהם אוהבו, לא פדאם לשום בנים אלא לשום עבדים, כשיגזור ולא יהיו מקבלים עליהם יאמר להם, עבדיי אתם.

18. נמצאת אתה אומר שתי קריבות הם, אחת קריבה שהיא לשום שמים ואחת קריבה שאינה לשום שמים. ותקרבון ויעמדון תחת ההר [דברים ד׳ יא׳], זו קריבה לשום שמים, ותקרבון אלי כלכם [דברים א׳ כב׳], זו קריבה שאינו לשום שמים

‫19. עד לא עשה ארץ וחוצות וראש עפרות תבל [משלי ח׳ כו׳]. ארץ,‬
‫אלו שאר ארצות, וחוצות, אלו מדברות, תבל, זו ארץ ישראל. למה‬
‫נקרא שמה תבל? על שם תבל שבתוכה. איזהו תבל שבתוכה? זו תורה,‬
‫שנאמר, בגוים אין תורה [איכה ב׳ ט׳]. מכאן שהתורה בארץ ישראל.‬

‫20. ובאת שמה והבאתם שמה [דברים יב׳ ו׳], לקבעם חובה, שלא יבואו‬
‫אלא ברגל הראשון שפגע בו. יכול אם עבר רגל אחד ולא הביא יהא‬
‫עובר עליו משום, בל תאחר? תלמוד לומר, אלה תעשו לי׳‬
‫במועדיכם [במדבר כט׳ לט׳], הא אין עובר עליו משום, בל תאחר, עד‬
‫שיעברו עליו רגלי שנה כולה.‬

Sources. 1. Abot 2.2. 2. Abot 2.12. 3. Abot 4.11. 4. BM 7.1. 5. Ket 2.9. 6. Mak 2.3. 7. RS 3.1. 8. Shab 16.8. 9. Mek 17.14 (L 2.150). 10. Mek 17.14 (L 2.157). 11. Mek 19.21 (L 2.225). 12. Mek 21.18 (L 3.53). 13. SLv 1.1 (W 4b). 14. SLv 18.3 (W 85c). 15. SLv 22.1 (W 96a). 16. SNm 17.1 (H 21). 17. SNm 115.5 (H 127). 18. SNm 136 (H 182). 19. SDt 37 (F 70–71). 20. SDt 63 (F 130).

UNIT TWENTY-THREE

ADVERBS AND INTERJECTIONS

I *Introductory text* (SNm 84.4)

‫וכן אתה מוצא, כל זמן שישראל משועבדים, כביכול, שכינה משתעבדת‬
‫עמהם, שנאמר, ויראו את אלהי ישראל ותחת רגליו כמעשה לבנת הספיר‬
‫[שמות כד׳ י׳], וכן הוא אומר, בכל צרתם לו צר [ישעיה סג׳ ט׳]‬

And thus you find that whenever Israel is enslaved, the Shekhinah, if one may speak in such a way, is also enslaved with them, as it is said, And they saw the God of Israel and under his feet was a pavement of sapphire [Ex 24.10], and that is why it says, He suffers with them in all their suffering [Is 63.9].

1. This is a key text in which Israel expresses how close it feels to God. The sapphire pavement beneath the throne of glory is throughout Jewish tradition a perennial memorial before God of the people's suffering; the difficult Isaiah text is read in a way that exacts the greatest degree of commitment on the part of God.

II *Morphology*

2. In RH, many BH adverbs have disappeared or are in obvious decline: אוּלַי, אָז, אַיֵּה, אֵיפֹה, אַךְ, רַק, בְּלִי, בִּלְתִּי, טֶרֶם, etc. (see Segal 1927, §294).

3. On the other hand, in RH we find new adverbs, some of them of Aramaic origin. For practical purposes, the following presentation employs a traditional, albeit rather simplistic, classification, with adverbs categorized as being of manner, place, or time, even though there are some that belong to two categories and others which are difficult to classify at all.

4. Adverbs of manner.

A. Affirmatives: הֵן (occasionally written אֵין, easily confusable with the negative אֵין), וַדַּאי/וַדַּי (from the root יָדָה 'confess'), כָּךְ, כֵּן.

B. Negatives: אֵין (or אֵי before words beginning with *alef*), לָאו, לֹא, אַל, בַּל.

C. Interrogatives: הֵיאַךְ/אֵיךְ 'how?', כֵּיצַד, מָה and כַּמָּה, שֶׁמָּא 'perhaps?', יָכוֹל 'is it possible?'.

5. Various words employed as adverbial accusatives, as well as adjectives and participles with modal value (see Unit 19.13–14), also function as adverbs of manner: חֲלִילָה 'in turn, again', לוֹכְסוֹן (λοξόν) 'diagonally, crosswise', כְּלָל 'generally, absolutely', סְתָם 'without comment, implicitly', סֵרוּגִין 'alternately, crosswise', סָפֵק 'doubtfully', יָכוֹל 'possibly', etc.

6. Some frequently-used compound forms with adverbial value are listed below.

A. Compounds with -כְּ: כְּאַחַת/כְּאֶחָד 'jointly, at the same time', כְּגוֹן 'for example', כְּדַרְכּוֹ 'according to usual practice, in its usual way' (see Units 8.10; 11.10; 26.6B), כְּיוֹצֵא ב- 'analogously to' (see Unit 26.6C), כְּלוֹמַר 'that is to say, i.e.'.

B. Compounds with -בְּ: בִּלְבַד 'only', בַּעֲלִיל 'clearly', בְּטוֹבָה 'thankfully, gratefully, with permission', שֶׁלֹּא בְטוֹבָה 'without authorization/permission', בְּפֵירוּשׁ 'distinctly, clearly'.

C. Other: עַל כֹּרַח 'by force, of necessity'.

7. Adverbs of place:

לְכָאן, מִכָּאן, כָּאן/כָּאן 'here';

לְהֵיכָן, מֵהֵיכָן, אֵיכָן/הֵיכָן 'where?';

אֵילַךְ וְאֵילַךְ/הֵילַךְ וְהֵילַךְ 'over here and over there, on both sides' (see, e.g., Mak 3.12);

לְהַלָּן, הַלָּן 'there';

לְאֵין, מִנַּיִן, מֵאַיִן, אַיִן 'where?';

בֵּינְתַיִם 'meanwhile';

לְהוּץ, מִבַּחוּץ, בַּחוּץ, חוּץ 'outside';

לִפְנִים 'inside';

לְמַטָּן, לְמַטָּה, מַטָּה 'below';

לְמַעֲלָן, לְמַעֲלָה, מַעֲלָה 'above';

לְמַפְרֵעַ 'backwards, the other way round, in a disorderly way';

שָׁם 'there', לְשָׁם (in place of BH שָׁמָּה).

8. Adverbs of time.

A. Sometimes, adverbs of place are employed in a temporal sense (or adverbs of time in a locational sense): לְאָחוֹר, כָּאן/כָּאן, בֵּינְתַיִם, אִילָךְ/הֵילָךְ. Note the formula מִכָּאן וְאֵילָךְ 'from now on, from here onwards' (SNm 134.5 [H 180]).

B. BH forms are: עוֹד 'still, again', לְמָחָר/מָחָר 'tomorrow', מֵעוֹלָם/לְעוֹלָם '(from) for ever', כְּבָר 'already, then' (LBH).

C. Forms found for the first time in RH are: אֵימָתַי 'when?', מִיָּד 'immediately', עַל יָד 'gradually', מִכָּאן 'from now on', עֲדַיִן 'still', עַכְשָׁיו 'now', תָּדִיר 'continually, always'.

D. Aramaic influence is obvious in the use of שׁוּב (infinitive: 'to return'), a calque of Aramaic תּוּב in the sense of 'again' and אֶשְׁתָּקַד 'last year', a shortened form of Aramaic שַׁתָּה קַדְמָיָא; from Aramaic אֲתַר 'place' has come the expression עַל אֲתַר 'on the spot, immediately'. All the more surprising, then, is the use of אֶמֶשׁ 'yesterday' in place of BH אֶתְמוֹל, when Aramaic also uses this latter form.

E. Other forms employed as temporal adverbs include בָּרִאשׁוֹנָה 'in the first place' and תְּחִילָּה 'firstly'; for the meaning of מִימֵי, see Unit 10.13.

9. Interjections.

A. Those most commonly used for introducing a discourse are הֲרֵי and הָא/הֲאהֵי, equivalent to BH הִנֵּה 'behold, look':

הֵילָךְ יַיִן וְתֵן לִי שֶׁמֶן

Here you have (literally, 'behold for you') wine, and give me oil (MS 1.1).

שֶׁ-הֲרֵי can carry the sense of 'suppose that' (see Unit 28.6), as at Bik 1.9:

הֲרֵי שֶׁהֵבִיא מִמִּין אֶחָד וְקָרָא, וְחָזַר וְהֵבִיא מִמִּין אַחֵר, אֵינוֹ קוֹרֵא

Suppose that he brought the firstfruits of one kind and performed the recitation, and that he then brought those of another kind—he does not have to perform the recitation.

B. Exclamations of complaint, sadness, joy, or surprise: אִי לִי, אוֹי לִי, הוֹי, אֲלָלַי.

C. אָנָּא is a liturgical interjection, directed to God:

אָנָּא הַשֵּׁם, עָווּ פָּשְׁעוּ חָטְאוּ לְפָנֶיךָ עַמְּךָ בֵּית יִשְׂרָאֵל. אָנָּא הַשֵּׁם, כַּפֶּר נָא לַעֲוֹנוֹת...

O God, your people, the house of Israel, have transgressed, offended, and sinned before you. Forgive, O God, the transgressions ... (Yom 6.2)

D. וְהַלְוַאי expresses desire, 'if only'.

E. For the meaning of הַנְרָאָה, see Unit 21.10.

10. Any word or phrase can be used in exclamation or converted into an interjection, as in the well-known examples of הַמָּעוֹן הַזֶּה 'by this abode' (i.e. the temple), הָעֲבוֹדָה 'by the service (of the temple)', הַשָּׁמַיִם 'by heaven', הַס וְשָׁלוֹם 'heaven forbid', etc. (see Unit 3.4).

III *Grammar and usage*

11. Negative propositions.

A. According to a reasonably long-established classification, negative particles may be categorized in the following way:

לֹא is used in verbal clauses;

אֵין/אַיִן, in keeping with its origins as an adverb of existence ('there is not, there does not exist'), is used in nominal clauses to negate nouns and participles;

אַל is used with the imperfect for prohibitions and negative commands.

This model may be further characterized as follows: in negative halakhic precepts, לֹא plus the imperfect (לֹא תַעֲשֶׂה) and אֵין plus participle (אֵין עוֹשִׂין) have an impersonal character, whereas אַל plus the imperfect (אַל תַּעֲשֶׂה) conveys a more personalized and persuasive mood. This characterization is reflected in the rule, albeit not of universal application, that אֵין עוֹשִׂין and לֹא תַעֲשֶׂה express a permanent prohibition, whereas אַל תַּעֲשֶׂה states a prohibition applicable here and now.

To distinguish the use of אֵין and לֹא in halakhic prohibitions, S. Sharvit (1980) notes that the latter is used with the imperfect in the singular, as in

לֹא יֵשֵׁב אָדָם לִפְנֵי הַסַּפָּר

No-one should sit in front of the barber (Shab 1.2; cf. Shab 6.1; Ber 5.3–4, etc.),

whereas the former is used with the participle in the plural:

אֵין עוֹמְדִין לְהִתְפַּלֵּל

No-one must stand to pray (Ber 5.1; cf. Shab 23.3, etc.).

For further details and examples, see Units 18.11; 19.17–18,22; 21.6; 24.8,10.

B. לָאו is an Aramaic loanword, employed in disjunctive formulas of the kind 'if ... or if not', with the verb not repeated in the negative alternative (see Unit 28.7C). Traces of its colloquial usage can be seen in, for example, Giṭ 7.1:

אִם אָמַר עַל לָאו, לָאו, וְעַל הֵן, הֵן, הֲרֵי אֵלּוּ יִכְתְּבוּ וְיִתְּנוּ

If to 'no', he responds, 'no', and to 'yes', 'yes', they may write (the letter of divorce) and deliver it.

C. בַּל is an early negative particle, found in biblical poetry. In RH, it is only found as part of biblical prohibitions: 'do not kill, do not swear', etc., for example:

עוֹבְרִים מִשּׁוּם, לֹא תִתֵּן [ויקרא כה' לז'], וּמִשּׁוּם, בַּל תִּקַּח מֵאִתּוֹ
[ויקרא כה' לו']

They transgress (the precept) in respect of 'you are not to give' [Lv 25.37] and in respect of 'you are not to take from him' [Lv 25.36] (BM 5.11).

(For the preposition מִשּׁוּם, see Unit 22.19.)

D. שׁוּם and כְּלוּם are used to reinforce a negation, emphasizing its absolute quality: 'absolutely nothing, none whatsoever':

ולבנו אחד לא נתן שום מתנה

But to a son of his, he gave no present whatsoever (SNm 119.2 [H 142]);

אין לו כלום

He has absolutely nothing (ARN 11 [S 47]).

12. Oaths and vows.

These are usually formulated as exclamations, and because of this sometimes include interjections and fossilized expressions like קוֹנָם (see Units 3.4; 8.7B; 28.7E).

13. Wishes.

A. RH has dispensed with the shortened and lengthened forms of imperfect (jussive and cohortative) with which BH formulated wishes and intentions (see Unit 18.3–4). But the imperfect has remained in RH as the mood by which hope, fear, and desire are expressed (see Unit 18.10–11).

B. The interjection וְהַלְוַאי is employed by the *amoraim*, but in the tannaitic *midrashim* וּלְוַאי/לְוַאי/לְוַאי is only found occasionally:

לואי אתה כיוצא בי ולואי כל ישראל כיוצא בך

Would that you were like me and would that all the Israelites were like you (SNm 96.3 [H 96]);

ולואי מתנו בשלשת ימי אפלה במצרים

Would that we had died during the three days of darkness in Egypt (Mek 16.3 [L 2.100]).

C. In tannaitic literature, we encounter various formulas with רָצוֹן 'will, desire', for example שֶׁיְהֵא רָצוֹן- at SNm 89.5 (H 90):

יהי רצון מלפניך שירד ונמצאו הופכים את לבם לשמים

Let it be your will that it (manna) descends, and they found themselves turning their hearts towards heaven.

רָצוֹן can take on a cohortative function, as in רצוננו לשמוע מפי מלכנו 'may we hear it from the very mouth of our king' (Mek 19.9 [L 2.209]).

With second person suffix (רְצוֹנְךָ), רָצוֹן has jussive or desiderative value (see the exercises).

14. יָכוֹל 'possibly' has an interrogative nuance:

יָכוֹל שֶׁכְּבוֹד הָאָב עוֹדֵף עַל כְּבוֹד הָאֵם?

Is it possible that the dignity of the father is superior to that of the mother? (Ker 6.9).

In rabbinic arguments, יָכוֹל can introduce an opinion that is rejected by reference to a biblical quotation (יָכוֹל ... ת"ל):

שטו העם ולקטו [במדבר י"א ח']. יכול מפני שמצטערים עליו בשעת לקיטתו היו מתרעמים? ת"ל, שטו העם, לפתח ביתו היה יוצא ומלקט פרנסתו ופרנסת ביתו

The people dispersed and gathered up (the manna) [Nm 11.8]. Perhaps they rebelled because of what they had to suffer at the time of

gathering it? The text says, The people dispersed: all that was
needed was for a person to go to the door of the house to gather their
own supply and that of their household (SNm 89.1 [H 88–89]).

IV *Phraseology*

15. ‑ש מהן באחד לך הכתוב ופרט סתם, בתורה 'א ונאמר הואיל 'seeing that
in the Torah, ‘A’ is mentioned without any specification, but in a certain
place the text specifies that …', a formula associated with the school of Ishmael (SNm 1.2; 14.1–2; 15.2; 73.1; 107.1; 123.12; 142.5; 153.1) and used to
deduce from an explicitly specified sense (פְּרָט) the general meaning that
should be assigned to other passages in which the sense of the form is not
specified (סְתָם):

אצבעו [במדמד יט' ד'] ימינית שביד ... ת"ל, וטבל הכהן את אצבעו
הימינית [ויקרא יד' טז']. הואיל ונאמרו אצבעות בתורה סתם, ופרט
לך הכתוב באחת מהם שאינה אלא ביד הימינית, אף פורטני בכל
אצבעות שבתורה, שלא יהו אלא ביד הימינית.

> With his finger [Nm 19.4]. It refers to the right finger of the right
> hand …. A text teaches, The priest will moisten the right finger [Lv
> 14.16]. Seeing that in the Torah, fingers are mentioned without fur-
> ther specification, but in one passage of Scripture, it specifies for
> you that the right hand is concerned, I can extend this specification
> to all the fingers mentioned in the Torah: they refer to the finger of
> the right hand (SNm 123.12).

16. כְּבִיָכוֹל (‑כּ + ‑בּ + יָכוֹל), 'if such a thing were possible, as if', usually
employed to mitigate anthropomorphic or anthropophatic expressions (as in
the introductory text of this unit), although sometimes to be interpreted as a
request to excuse an exaggerated statement:

ובזמן שאין עושים רצונו כביכול הוא נלחם בם

> But when they do not carry out his will, he, if one may say so, fights
> against them (SNm 157.8 [H 211]).

V *Vocabulary*

בָּלַע 'swallow, devour, absorb'
בִּשּׁוּל 'cooking'
דָּחַף 'strike'
הִפְטִיר (hi. of פטר) 'do a reading from the prophets, recite the *haftarah*'
לוּלָב 'palm'
מַאֲמָד וּמוֹשָׁב 'standing up and sitting down'
סְקִילָה 'stoning'
רְגִימָה 'stoning'
רִיבּוֹא 'a hundred thousand'

VI *Exercises*

1. וְהִסְתַּכֵּל בִּשְׁלֹשָׁה דְבָרִים וְאִי אַתָּה בָא לִידֵי עֲבֵרָה, דַּע מַה לְמַעֲלָה מִמָּךְ, עַיִן רוֹאָה, וְאֹזֶן שׁוֹמַעַת, וְכָל מַעֲשֶׂיךָ בַּסֵּפֶר נִכְתָּבִין.

2. וְאַל תֹּאמַר דָּבָר שֶׁאִי אֶפְשָׁר לִשְׁמוֹעַ, שֶׁסּוֹפוֹ לְהִשָּׁמֵעַ.

3. יְהִי רָצוֹן מִלְּפָנֶיךָ, יי אֱלֹהֵינוּ, שֶׁתִּבְנֶה עִירְךָ בִּמְהֵרָה בְיָמֵינוּ, וְתֵן חֶלְקֵנוּ בְּתוֹרָתֶךָ.

4. יְהִי רָצוֹן שֶׁתֵּלֵד אִשְׁתִּי זָכָר ... יְהִי רָצוֹן שֶׁלֹּא יִהְיוּ אֵלּוּ בְּנֵי בֵיתִי.

5. אֵין פּוֹרְסִין אֶת שְׁמַע, וְאֵין עוֹבְרִין לִפְנֵי הַתֵּבָה וְאֵין נוֹשְׂאִין אֶת כַּפֵּיהֶם, וְאֵין קוֹרִין בַּתּוֹרָה וְאֵין מַפְטִירִין בַּנָּבִיא וְאֵין עוֹשִׂין מַעֲמָד וּמוֹשָׁב וְאֵין אוֹמְרִין בִּרְכַּת אֲבֵלִים וְתַנְחוּמֵי אֲבֵלִים וּבִרְכַּת חֲתָנִים וְאֵין מְזַמְּנִין בַּשֵּׁם פָּחוֹת מֵעֲשָׂרָה.

6. אִם מָצְאוּ לוֹ זָכוּת, פְּטָרוּהוּ, וְאִם לָאו, מַעֲבִירִין דִּינוֹ לְמָחָר.

7. הַקְּרוֹבִים בָּאִים וְשׁוֹאֲלִין בִּשְׁלוֹם הַדַּיָּנִים וּבִשְׁלוֹם הָעֵדִים, כְּלוֹמַר, שֶׁאֵין בְּלִבֵּנוּ עֲלֵיכֶם כְּלוּם, שֶׁדִּין אֱמֶת דַּנְתֶּם.

8. וּמְלַמְּדִים אוֹתָם לוֹמַר, כָּל מִי שֶׁמַּגִּיעַ לוּלְבִי בְיָדוֹ, הֲרֵי הוּא לוֹ בְמַתָּנָה.

9. וְכֵן חָבִית שֶׁלְּשֶׁמֶן שֶׁנִּשְׁפְּכָה, מֹדָה רַבִּי אֱלִיעֶזֶר וְרַבִּי יְהוֹשֻׁעַ שֶׁאִם יָכוֹל לְהַצִּיל מִמֶּנָּה רְבִיעִית בְּטַהֲרָה, יַצִּיל, וְאִם לָאו, רַבִּי אֱלִיעֶזֶר אוֹמֵר, תֵּרֵד וְתִבָּלַע, וְאַל יְבַלְעֶנָּה בְיָדָיו.

10. אָמַר לָהֶם יוֹסֵף, אֲבִי יָרַד כַּאן לִרְצוֹנוֹ וַאֲנִי הֶעֱלִיתִיו עַל כָּרְחִי, מַשְׁבִּיעַ אֲנִי אֲלֵיכֶם שֶׁמִּמָּקוֹם שֶׁגְּנַבְתּוּנִי לְשָׁם תַּחְזִירוּנִי. וְכֵן עָשׂוּ.

11. רַבִּי אוֹמֵר, דַּבֵּר אֶל בְּנֵי יִשְׂרָאֵל וַיִּסָּעוּ [שמות יד׳ טו׳], יִסִּיעוּ דְבָרִים שֶׁהָיוּ דוֹבְרִים מִלִּבָּן, אֶמֶשׁ הָיוּ אוֹמְרִים, הַמִבְּלִי אֵין קְבָרִים ... [שמות יד׳ יא׳], וְעַכְשָׁיו אַתָּה עוֹמֵד וּמַרְבֶּה בַּתְּפִלָּה?

12. רַבִּי אוֹמֵר, וְכִי מַה אָמַר הַמָּקוֹם לְמֹשֶׁה לֵאמַר לְיִשְׂרָאֵל? אוֹ מַה אָמְרוּ יִשְׂרָאֵל לְמֹשֶׁה לֵאמַר לַמָּקוֹם? אֶלָּא אָמְרוּ, רְצוֹנֵנוּ לִשְׁמוֹעַ מִפִּי מַלְכֵּנוּ, לֹא דוֹמֶה שׁוֹמֵעַ מִפִּי פִרְגוֹד לְשׁוֹמֵעַ מִפִּי הַמֶּלֶךְ. אָמַר הַמָּקוֹם, תֵּן לָהֶם מַה שֶּׁבִּקְשׁוּ ... אָמְרוּ, רְצוֹנֵנוּ לִרְאוֹת אֶת מַלְכֵּנוּ, לֹא דוֹמֶה שׁוֹמֵעַ לְרוֹאֶה. אָמַר הַמָּקוֹם, תֵּן לָהֶם מַה שֶּׁבִּקְשׁוּ.

13. לֹא תְבַשֵּׁל גְּדִי בַּחֲלֵב אִמּוֹ [שמות כג׳ יט׳]. אֵין לִי אֶלָּא שֶׁהוּא אָסוּר בְּבִישׁוּל. וּמִנַּיִן שֶׁהוּא אָסוּר בַּאֲכִילָה? אָמַרְתָּ, קַל וָחֹמֶר, וּמַה אִם הַפֶּסַח, שֶׁאֵין בּוֹ, בַּל תְּבַשֵּׁל, יֵשׁ בּוֹ, בַּל תֹּאכַל, בָּשָׂר בַּחֲלֵב, שֶׁיֵּשׁ לוֹ, בַּל תְּבַשֵּׁל, דִּין הוּא שֶׁיִּהְיֶה בּוֹ, בַּל תֹּאכַל.

14. וְאֶל אִשָּׁה בְּנִדַּת טֻמְאָתָהּ לֹא תִקְרַב לְגַלּוֹת עֶרְוָתָהּ [ויקרא יח׳ יט׳]. אֵין לִי אֶלָּא שֶׁלֹּא יְגַלֶּה. מִנַּיִן שֶׁלֹּא תִקְרַב? תַּלְמוּד לוֹמַר, לֹא תִקְרַב. אֵין לִי אֶלָּא נִדָּה בַּל תִקְרַב בַּל תְּגַלֶּה. מִנַּיִן לְכָל הָעֲרָיוֹת בַּל תִקְרְבוּ וּבַל תְּגַלּוּ? תַּלְמוּד לוֹמַר, לֹא תִקְרְבוּ לְגַלּוֹת.

15. מִיכַּן אָמְרוּ, כָּל הַמּוֹסֵר עַצְמוֹ עַל מְנָת לַעֲשׂוֹת לוֹ נֵס, אֵין עוֹשִׂים לוֹ נֵס, וְשֶׁלֹּא לַעֲשׂוֹת לוֹ נֵס, עוֹשִׂים לוֹ נֵס.

16. [אֵלִיָּהוּ] אָמַר לוֹ, בְּנִי, מֵאֵיזוֹ מִשְׁפָּחָה אַתָּה? אָמַר לוֹ, מִמִּשְׁפָּחָה פְלוֹנִי. אָמַר לוֹ, וְכַמָּה הֱיִיתֶם? אָמַר לוֹ, שְׁלֹשֶׁת אֲלָפִים. וְכַמָּה נִשְׁתַּיֵּיר מִכֶּם? אָמַר לוֹ, אֲנִי. אָמַר לוֹ, רְצוֹנְךָ לוֹמַר דָּבָר אֶחָד וְלִחְיוֹת? אָמַר לוֹ, אֵין [=הֵן]. אָמַר לוֹ, אֱמוֹר, שְׁמַע יִשְׂרָאֵל יי אֱלֹהֶיךָ יי אֶחָד. צָעַק מִיָּד וְאָמַר, חַס כִּי לֹא לְהַזְכִּיר בַּשֵּׁם יי, לֹא לִימְּדַנִי אַבָּא כָךְ.

17. כיצד יתקיימו שני כתובים הללו? [במדבר טו' לה', ויקרא כד' כג]. בית
הסקילה היה גבוה שתי קומות, אחד מן העדים דוחפו על מתניו, נהפך
על לבו הופכו על מתניו. אם מת בה, יצא, ואם לאו, העד השני נוטל
את האבן ונותנה על לבו. אם מת בה, יצא, ואם לאו, רגימתו בכל
ישראל.

18. ויברך אותם משה [שמות לט' מג']. מה ברכה ברכם? אמר להם, יהי
רצון שתשרה שכינה במעשה ידיכם.

19. כי הארץ אשר אתה בא שמה לרשתה לא כארץ מצרים היא [דברים
יא' י]. לרשתה אתם באים, לא להיות עליה מכין שנים שמטים ויובלות,
אלא הפרש בין ביאתה של זו לביאתה של זו. ביאת ארץ מצרים רשות,
ביאת ארץ ישראל חובה. ארץ מצרים בין שעושים רצונו של מקום ובין
שאין עושים רצונו של מקום, הרי לכם ארץ מצרים. ארץ ישראל אינו
כן, אם אתם עושים רצונו של מקום, הרי לכם ארץ כנען, ואם לאו, הרי
אתם גולים מעליה.

20. עמד ומדד לו שמן במאה ריבוא. אמר לו, רצונך שוב? אמר לו, אין לי
מעות. אמר לו, טול ואני אבוא עמך ואטול את מעותי. עמד ומדד לו
שמן בשמונה עשרה ריבוא.

Sources. 1. Abot 2.1. 2 Abot 2.4. 3. Abot 5.20. 4. Ber 9.3. 5. Meg 4.3. 6.
Sanh 5.5. 7. Sanh 6.6. 8. Suk 4.4. 9. Ter 8.10. 10. Mek 13.19 (L 1.181).
11. Mek 14.15 (L 1.219). 12. Mek 19.9 (L 2.209). 13. Mek 23.19 (L 3.190).
14. SLv 16.19 (W 85d). 15. SLv 22.32 (W 99d). 16. SLv 26.25 (W 112a).
17. SNm 114 (H 123; cf. Sanh 6.4). 18. SNm 143.2 (H 191). 19. SDt 38 (F
77). 20. SDt 355 (F 421).

PART IV

CLAUSES

TYPES OF CLAUSE

I *Introductory text* (Mek 13.2 [L 1.133])

רבי שמעון בן יוחי אומר, מושלו משל, למה הדבר דומה? לאחד שהיה
מהלך בדרך ופגע בו זאב וניצל ממנו, והיה הולך ומספר מעשה הזאב.
פגע בו ארי וניצל הימנו, שכח מעשה הזאב, והיה הולך ומספר מעשה
ארי. פגע בו נחש וניצל ממנו, שכח מעשה שניהם והיה הולך ומספר
מעשה נחש. כך ישראל, צרות האחרונות משכחות הראשונות.

Rabbi Simeon ben Yoḥai said, They used to recount a parable. To what may
this be compared? To someone who on a journey was attacked by a wolf but
was rescued from it and continued the journey relating the story of the wolf.
Later, the person was attacked by a lion but was rescued from it and, forget-
ting the story of the wolf, continued the journey relating the story of the lion.
Later, the person was attacked by a snake but was rescued from it and, forget-
ting both the earlier stories, continued the journey relating the story of the
snake. So it is with Israel: their later tribulations make them forget earlier
ones.

1. The parable is introduced to explain Jr 23.7–8, in which vows by Y.
invoke the liberation not from Egypt but from the northern kingdoms. In this
context, it fulfils a typically midrashic function, illuminating the biblical text
by demonstrating an analogy between divine and human action. The argument takes the form of a *kelal*: something that happens later makes what has
happened previously be forgotten. Given the biblical dynamic, there is the
underlying idea not only that the latter replaces the former but also that it is
better, that the second liberation will be superior to the first one.

II *Morphology*

2. Nominal and verbal clauses.
The classification of clauses as nominal or verbal is a traditional first
stage in their grammatical analysis. Grammarians usually understand a verbal
clause as a clause in which the predicate includes a personal form of a verb,
and a nominal clause as a clause in which the predicate is a noun, adjective,
participle, pronoun, or adverbial expression, but never a personal form of a
verb—a common type of nominal clause comprises three members, in which
the third person pronoun or the verb הָיָה functions as copula (see Meyer

1992, §§90–91).

This classification is nowadays regarded as being of only limited value in respect of Hebrew. A more appropriate model would seem to be that of traditional Arabic grammar, which makes a distinction between a clause that begins with a verb and says what the subject does (verbal clause) and one that begins with a noun and says who the subject is (nominal clause). On this understanding, every clause of the type וַיֹּאמֶר 'א is verbal, 'so-and-so said', and every clause of the type אָמַר 'א is nominal, 'so-and-so is the one who said', e.g. 2 S 7.13: הוּא יִבְנֶה־בַּיִת לִשְׁמִי 'he is the one who will build a temple for my name'.

Such distinctions retain some validity in RH—a subject placed before a verb or at the start of a clause has extra emphasis. Indeed, traditional grammar had observed that in nominal clauses the order subject-predicate is the norm, whereas in verbal clauses, the order is reversed, verb-subject, with the different word-orders reflecting differences in emphasis. However, as a linguistic phenomenon, emphasis is extremely difficult to analyse or even to identify, especially when dealing with stylistic variation in a dead language.

In the light of all this, the following general remarks may be made.

Among nominal clauses, a distinction should be made between clauses of identification, in which the subject and the predicate are determined and which usually take the form subject-predicate (אֲנִי י״), and clauses of classification, in which a general or indeterminate predicate is usually placed before the subject (יפה תלמוד תורה).

A distinction should also be made between simple nominal clauses, with the verb 'to be' or a personal pronoun as copula, and complex nominal clauses, which contain a personal form of a finite verb but with the subject, or some other word, preceding it and, therefore, being emphasized. However, it should be noted that not every proposition of the type אָמַר 'א should be automatically interpreted as a complex nominal clause (see Niccacci 1990).

The significance of a nominal clause (who does?) or a verbal clause (what's being done?) should not be viewed solely in the context of an isolated clause, but within that of the various literary genres: narrative, discourse, *halakhah*, prayer, etc. For example, within a narrative framework, such as that provided by the *meshalim* or *ma'aśiyyot*, the word order employed to introduce the words of a character is verb-subject (אמר משה), but in exegetical or halakhic discussions, the order is subject-verb (רבי טרפון אומר). Thus, the identification of genre is indispensable when analysing clause types, as A. Niccacci has shown in respect of biblical prose.

In a so-called verbal clause, given that a personal form of a verb includes reference to a subject by means of affixes, any additional expression of the subject should be viewed as having emphatic value, if placed before the verb, or as in determinative apposition, if placed after. Having said that, the order also depends to a considerable extent on the rhythm of a clause and its accents.

3. Coordination and subordination.

Semitic clause structure frequently evidences the juxtaposing of clauses, with or without *and* (syndetic and asyndetic parataxis), which, nonetheless, conveys logical subordination (hypotaxis):

הָבִיאוּ אֶת־אֲחִיכֶם הַקָּטֹן אֵלַי וְאֵדְעָה

Bring me your younger brother that I might (literally, 'and I shall') know (Gn 42.34).

In BH, we also find more striking instances of logical subordination expressed through the juxtaposition of finite forms of verbs:

לֹא יָדַעְתִּי אֲכַנֶּה

I do not know how to (literally, 'I do not know, I do not') flatter (Jb 32.22):

אָשׁוּבָה אֶרְעֶה

I shall pasture once again (Gn 30.31);

מִי יוֹדֵעַ יְחָנַּנִי י׳

Who knows whether Y. will take pity on me (2 S 12.22).

This phenomenon continued into RH, even though, as we shall see in the following units, there was a considerable increase in the number of conjunctions, often morphologically combined with other particles, which unambiguously express hypotaxis/subordination, as in the following illuminating example. Dt 17.17 states, using coordination,

לֹא יַרְבֶּה־לּוֹ נָשִׁים וְלֹא יָסוּר לְבָבוֹ

He is not to acquire many wives and his heart will not (i.e. 'so that his heart will not') stray,

for which SDt 159 (F 210) places the following interpretation in the mouth of Rabbi Judah:

מרבה הוא לו ובלבד שלא יהו מסירות את לבו

He will be able to acquire more (wives) so long as they do not make his heart stray.

The change from coordination to subordination occurs both as part of language evolution and because of the need for exegetical precision.

4. The two-element syntactic construction.

This is the term that A. Niccacci (1990) employs for the characteristic Hebrew construction of protasis and apodosis, often but not necessarily joined by the so-called *waw apodosis*, which 'serves vividly *to pick up* the train of thought which has been held up or slowed down, and *to link* the two disjointed parts of the statement' (Joüon-Muraoka 1993, §176B). The structure is commonly found with a conditional, temporal, or causal proposition in the protasis, or following a nominal clause, adverbial expression, or *casus pendens*:

יַעַן מָאַסְתָּ אֶת־דְּבַר י׳ וַיִּמְאָסְךָ מִמֶּלֶךְ

Because you rejected the word of Y., he has rejected you as king (1 S 15.23);

בְּמוֹתִי וּקְבַרְתֶּם אֹתִי

When I die, you are to bury me (1 K 13.31);

וַיְהִי בָּעֵת הַהִיא וַיֹּאמֶר

It happened at that time that he said (Gn 21.22).

A comparison of the classical BH text of 1 K 15.13 and its LBH counterpart is illuminating:

וְגַם אֶת־מַעֲכָה אִמּוֹ וַיְסִרֶהָ מִגְּבִירָה

And he even removed his mother, Maacah, from the post of queen mother (1 K 15.13);

וְגַם־מַעֲכָה אֵם אָסָא הַמֶּלֶךְ הֱסִירָהּ מִגְּבִירָה

And even Maacah, (his) mother, Asa the king removed (her) from the post of queen mother (2 C 15.16).

Whereas Kings retains the two-element construction of protasis and apodosis joined by *waw*, Chronicles removes the *waw apodosis* and converts the protasis into a *casus pendens*, which is emphasized because of its position at the beginning of the clause (see below, §11). This process of change would reach its climax in RH, where the *casus pendens* construction abounds and *waw apodosis* is generally absent.

III *Grammar and usage*

5. RH continues to formulate what are in effect subordinate structures through coordination, as in the following example, typically couched as a two-element construction:

נכנסו כל הפרות ואותה הפרה לא נכנסה

When all the other cows came in, that cow did not come in (SLv 26.13 [W 111b]).

In narrative works, it is common to find chains of clauses, sometimes not even linked by the conjunction *waw*, among which a logically subordinate structure is evident, as in the parable from the Mekhilta in the introductory text of this unit (Mek 13.2) or in the parable of the king who ordered that his son be given what he needed day by day, not all at once (SNm 89.5 [H 90]) or of the expert and prudent general (SNm 131.1 [H 170], text 17 in the exercises). The following is a typical example of asyndetic coordination, once again as a two-element construction, expressing simultaneity of action:

התחיל הבן ההוא מנתק, הוציא עליו שטר ואמר

When that son started to protest, he brought the document out to him and said (SNm 115.5 [H 127]).

6. These examples show that RH maintains the two-element syntactic construction, even though *waw apodosis* is generally omitted (sometimes replaced by emphatic הֲרֵי). To this category belong the numerous two-element conditional constructions that appear in *halakhot*, and that are discussed and illustrated in Units 17.11–12, 19.11, and 28.5, for example:

מָזְגוּ לוֹ אֶת הַכּוֹס, וְאָמַר, הֲרֵינִי נָזִיר מִמֶּנּוּ, הֲרֵי זֶה נָזִיר

If they prepare him a drink and he says, I shall abstain from it, that one is a Nazirite (Naz 2.3).

7. A striking construction that is maintained, albeit only as a literary affectation, has two finite verbs asyndetically juxtaposed, with one verb being in reality the main verb and the other an auxiliary:

אמר רבי עקיבה, אני אהיה אבין לפניך

Rabbi Akiba said, I am going to make you understand (literally, 'I shall be, I shall cause to understand') (SDt 60 [F 126]).

More and more, though, logical subordination is achieved through formal subordination based on the use of conjunctions.

8. Negation of verbal clauses is usually effected through לֹא, with אַל regularly used to negate the imperfect expressing a subjunctive sense of desire or exhortation (see Units 18.11; 23.11; Segal 1927, §471).

9. A characteristic feature of RH is the anticipation of an element in a subordinate clause as the object of the main clause:

וְהָעֵדִים מְעִידִין אוֹתוֹ שֶׁגְּנָבוֹ

The witnesses testified (against him) that he had stolen it (Shebu 8.3);

לִימֵד עַל בְּנוֹת יִשְׂרָאֵל שֶׁהֵן מְכַסּוֹת רָאשֵׁיהֶן

Teach (concerning) the daughters of Israel that they are to cover their heads (SNm 11.2 [H 17]).

This kind of anticipation regularly occurs with certain verbs, for example גָּזַר 'decree':

גזר על בנו להיות מפרנסו

He decreed concerning his son to provide for him (i.e. 'he gave a decree to provide for his son') (SNm 89.5 [H 90]).

The anticipated element can also function as a *casus pendens* (see below, §11), as in narratives with מַעֲשֶׂה, for example at Ket 1.10:

מַעֲשֶׂה בְּתִינוֹקֶת שֶׁיָּרְדָה

It happened that a little girl went down.

10. The modal nominal clause.

This is a common BH construction, in which a simple nominal clause (without a finite verb), syndetically or asyndetically juxtaposed to a main clause, conveys a concomitant circumstance. Such a 'circumstantial clause', as it has traditionally been labelled, is found, for example, at Gn 18.1:

וַיֵּרָא אֵלָיו י׳ בְּאֵלֹנֵי מַמְרֵא וְהוּא יֹשֵׁב פֶּתַח־הָאֹהֶל

Y. appeared to him among the terebinths of Mamre while he was sitting at the entrance of his tent.

The construction is continued in RH, especially in narrative style:

וצדיקים רואים אותו ומזדעזעים מלפניו, הריני כיוצא בכם

When the righteous see it and tremble in its presence, (he will say to them) I am like you (SLv 26.12 [W 111n]);

הַמּוֹצֵא כֵלִים וַעֲלֵיהֶם צוּרַת הַחַמָּה

One who finds an object with a figure of the sun engraved (AZ 3.3, a particularly clear example);

מוֹרִידִין לִפְנֵי הַתֵּבָה זָקֵן וְרָגִיל וְיֶשׁ לוֹ בָנִים וּבֵיתוֹ רֵיקָם

They carried before the ark a skilled elder, with sons but with his house already empty (Taa 2.2).

Nominal clauses are usually negated with אֵין (see below, §14, and Unit 23.11).

It should be noted that nominal clauses, as such, are atemporal, with their location in time being given only by context.

11. Nominative absolute or *casus pendens*.

These terms are used to designate a noun, pronoun, or clause that, positioned emphatically at the beginning of a clause, lacks syntactic continuation ('what they're saying, forget it', etc.). As a typically spoken usage, it is especially common in RH, for example

אבל אתם חשבון רב אני עתיד לחשב עמכן

But you, in the future I'm going to agree a large reward for you (SLv 26.9 [W 111a]),

and occurs not only in narrative but also in legal contexts. The effect of this type of construction is to highlight whatever has been made into the first element of the grammatical sequence.

But what to our way of thinking appears to be a *casus pendens* or 'hanging' clause, when carefully considered, may be understood as an instance of asyndetic coordination of clauses, yielding a compound clause in which the nominal subject (which can even be an entire clause) always goes in front, and the predicate forms an independent clause of a verbal or nominal kind (Meyer 1992, §92.4).

The inclusion of *casus pendens* among subjects of nominal clauses is widely contested, with concepts expressed by terms like extraposition, segmentation, isolation, and compound sentence being preferred as more appropriate to the phenomenon concerned, namely, the advance presentation of an element. R. Contini (1982, 56) writes:

> The extraposed element is indeed the 'logical subject' of the sentence, but the latter does not thereby lose its grammatically verbal character, which derives from the morphological nature of the predicate: no-one would consider calling an example such as the ... French *Ce problème, je n'arrive pas à le résoudre* a compound (or 'complex') nominal sentence.

Nonetheless, it seems more correct to view the *casus pendens* structure as a version of the two-element syntactic construction. The following are some of the types found in RH.

Usually, the element brought forward on its own to the beginning of the clause is referred to by a pronoun in the main, or predicative, clause:

הַתְּרוּמָה, מֶה הָיוּ עוֹשִׂין בָּהּ?

The oblation, what is to be done with it? (Sheq 4.1);

מוֹתַר שְׁיָרֵי הַלִּשְׁכָּה, מֶה הָיוּ עוֹשִׂין בָּהֶן?

The remnants of the chamber, what is to be done with them? (Sheq 4.3).

But formal reference may be omitted if there is no possibility of confusion:

הֲרֵי אֵלּוּ חַיָּב לְהַכְרִיז

Note that these are the things one must proclaim (BM 2.2).

This kind of construction is very common in halakhic formulations, especially those commencing with -שֶׁ מִי, which raise in an emphatic manner a particular case to be decided:

מִי שֶׁהָלְכָה אִשְׁתּוֹ לִמְדִינַת הַיָּם, וּבָאוּ וְאָמְרוּ לוֹ, מֵתָה אִשְׁתְּךָ, וְנָשָׂא אֶת אֲחוֹתָהּ, וְאַחַר כָּךְ בָּאת אִשְׁתּוֹ, מֻתֶּרֶת לַחֲזוֹר לוֹ

Someone whose wife left to go to a faraway town, if they come and tell him, Your wife has died, and he then marries her sister, but later it happens that his (first) wife reappears, she may return to him (Yeb 10.4; cf. Yeb 11.6; 13.8–9, etc.).

(On the indefinite or general significance of -שֶׁ מִי and -שֶׁ מָה see Units 5.7 and 6.7.)

Within this group of clauses, a particular type comprises those that begin with הָאִשָּׁה שֶׁהָלְכָה 'when the wife goes away' (Yeb 15.1,6; 16.1, etc.), a further indication that the *casus pendens* is frequently a relative clause with antecedent.

A characteristic feature, especially when the shifted element turns out to be very long or is followed by an extensive digression, is the resumptive use of הֲרֵי followed by a pronoun corresponding to the shifted element:

הָיָה עוֹשֶׂה בְיָדָיו אֲבָל לֹא בְרַגְלָיו, בְּרַגְלָיו אֲבָל לֹא בְיָדָיו, אֲפִילּוּ בִכְתֵפוֹ, הֲרֵי זֶה אוֹכֵל

If someone was working with their hands but not with their feet or with their feet but not with their hands, or even with their shoulder, note that this person may eat (BM 7.3).

Observe that in this example, the *casus pendens* is an extended nominal clause.

Another typical kind of *casus pendens* occurs when the topic of halakhic dispute is left hanging at the beginning of a clause while the competing opinions on the matter are stated—to give just one example:

הֲרֵינִי נָזִיר מִן הַגְּרוֹגְרוֹת וּמִן הַדְּבֵלָה, בֵּית שַׁמַּאי אוֹמְרִים, נָזִיר, וּבֵית הִלֵּל אוֹמְרִים, אֵינוֹ נָזִיר

(If someone says) I shall abstain from dried figs and from fig-cake, the school of Shammai declare that such a person is a Nazirite and the school of Hillel declare that such a person is not (Naz 2.1).

In *meshalim*, or parables, the subject to which the parable applies may appear as the first element, highlighted and syntactically isolated:

כך ישראל, צרות האחרונות משכחות הראשונות

So it is with Israel: their later tribulations make them forget the earlier ones (Mek 13.2 [L 1.133]).

Similarly, in statements of comparison, it is normal to emphasize, by isolation, the object of comparison—סוֹטָה in the following example:

אם למדתי לפרה שעשה בה כל הכלים ככלי חרש, אף סוטה, אינו דין

שנעשה בה כל הכלים ככלי חרש?

Seeing that in the ritual of the red heifer any vessel is treated as an earthen vessel, so also in the ritual of a woman suspected of adultery may we not infer that any vessel is to be treated as an earthen vessel? (SNm 10.2 [H 16])

All the foregoing examples demonstrate that the phenomenon of the nominative absolute or *casus pendens* actually consists of an enunciation of the topic to be discussed, couched as a two-element syntactic construction. At a formal level, it may be regarded as an instance of parataxis; at a logical level there is in practice subordination or hypotaxis (which needs to be translated by means of conditional, temporal or circumstantial clauses: 'if one says', 'when it happens', etc.); at a stylistic or affective level, the structure is an efficient means of conveying emphasis.

The topic, or *casus pendens*, can be given even greater prominence by determining it with the deictic particle אֵת (see Units 2.7 and 8.6F):

אֵת שצריך כפרה, יצא מת שכיפרה לו נפשו

With regard to one who requires expiation, a dead person is excluded as their soul has atoned for them (SNm 4.5 [H 7]).

12. Adjectival clauses.

R. Meyer (1992, §115) perceptively observed that from a syntactic perspective, relative clauses are actually adjectival, as their function is to complete the nominal parts of a main clause.

In RH, אֲשֶׁר has disappeared in favour of -שֶׁ, concerning which, see in particular Unit 8.6.

13. Disjunctive clauses.

These are examined in the context of direct and indirect interrogative, comparative, and conditional clauses (see Units 25–26 and 28). At times a disjunctive structure (either in the Hebrew text or in its translation) is to be understood as merely representing alternative, but not disjunctive, possibilities. RH can indicate such alternative possibilities by means of אוֹ (signifying equivalence), -וְ, or simply by juxtaposition. For example, at Meg 4.1,

הַקּוֹרֵא אֶת הַמְּגִילָה עוֹמֵד וְיוֹשֵׁב

signifies that the reader may be standing or (-וְ) seated, without implying any real disjunction. When a clear disjunction is intended, the forms אוֹ ... אוֹ, אִם ... וְאִם, אוֹ שֶׁ ... אוֹ שֶׁ-, or אִם ... אִם are used:

אֲחוֹתָהּ כְּשֶׁהִיא יְבִמְתָּהּ, אוֹ חוֹלֶצֶת אוֹ מִתְיַבֶּמֶת

If her sister is also her sister-in-law, either she performs *ḥaliṣah* or she marries (Yeb 3.3);

אמר לו בנזירה, שתאכל את הדג או שתלקה מאה מכות או שתתן מאה מנה

He told him sternly, Either you eat the fish, or you receive a hundred lashes, or you pay a hundred minas (Mek 14.5 [L 1.195]);

הודיעני אם אתה מרפא אותה ואם לאו

Tell me if you are going to cure her or not (SDt 26 [F 41]).

IV *Phraseology*

14. וְאֵין אָנוּ, וְאֵין אַתֶּם, וְאֵין אָתֶם, etc., is a common way of beginning a nominal clause that expresses a circumstance with a concomitant, modal, or temporal relationship to the main activity conveyed by the sentence:

ארבע מלכיות מושלות בהם בישראל, ואין בהם חכם ואין בהם נבון

Four empires have ruled over the Israelites, when there was no wise or intelligent person among them (the Israelites). (SDt 304 [F 323]);

ועדין הדבר תלי בדלא תלי, ואין אנו יודעים אם הקדוש ברוך הוא
בחר ביעקוב, אם יעקוב בחר בהקדוש ברוך הוא

But still the matter is not clear, so that we do not know whether it was the holy one, blessed be he, who chose Jacob or whether it was Jacob who chose the holy one, blessed be he (SDt 312 [F 353]).

V *Vocabulary*

אַמָּה 'arm, cubit, channel'

אַרְבָּעָה עָשָׂר [אוֹר] '(the night of) the fourteenth (of Nisan)'

בְּטוֹבָה 'in the expectation of thanks', i.e. 'freely, voluntarily, gratefully'

בָּקִי וּמְיוֹשָׁב 'experienced and serene'

דְּרָקוֹן (δράκων) 'dragon'

זָלַג 'shed (tears)'

חַמָּה 'sun'

טֻמְאָה 'impurity, contamination'; אַב טֻמְאָה 'father of impurity' refers to a primary source of impurity, which can be transmitted to a thing, which, or a person, who, thus becomes a וְלַד טֻמְאָה 'child of impurity', a derived or secondary source of impurity, which can only be transmitted to things.

טָרַד 'expel, throw out'

לְבָנָה 'moon'

נָגֵב 'be dry'

נוֹחַ 'comfortable, good, pleasant'

פִּיתָק 'chit, tablet'

צוּרָה 'shape, figure'

קַלְפִּי (κάλπις) 'urn'

תַּקָּנָה 'ordinance, practical measure'

VI *Exercises*

1. שְׁנַיִם שֶׁיּוֹשְׁבִין וְאֵין בֵּינֵיהֶם דִּבְרֵי תוֹרָה, הֲרֵי זֶה מוֹשַׁב לֵצִים ... אֲבָל שְׁנַיִם שֶׁיּוֹשְׁבִין וְיֵשׁ בֵּינֵיהֶם דִּבְרֵי תוֹרָה, שְׁכִינָה בֵּינֵיהֶם.

2. כָּל הַמְקַבֵּל עָלָיו עֹל תּוֹרָה, מַעֲבִירִין מִמֶּנּוּ עֹל מַלְכוּת וְעֹל דֶּרֶךְ אֶרֶץ, וְכָל הַפּוֹרֵק מִמֶּנּוּ עֹל תּוֹרָה, נוֹתְנִים עָלָיו עֹל מַלְכוּת וְעֹל דֶּרֶךְ אֶרֶץ.

3. הַמּוֹצֵא כֵלִים וַעֲלֵיהֶם צוּרַת הַחַמָּה, צוּרַת הַלְּבָנָה, צוּרַת הַדְּרָקוֹן, יוֹלִיכֵם לְיָם הַמֶּלַח.

4. עֲבוֹדָה זָרָה, שֶׁהָיָה לָהּ גַּנָּה אוֹ מֶרְחָץ, נֶהֱנִין מֵהֶן שֶׁלֹּא בְטוֹבָה, וְאֵין

נֶהֱנִין מֵהֶן בְּטוֹבָה. הָיָה שֶׁלָּהּ וְשֶׁלַּאֲחֵרִים, נֶהֱנִין מֵהֶן בֵּין בְּטוֹבָה וּבֵין שֶׁלֹּא בְּטוֹבָה.

5. בֵּיצָה שֶׁנּוֹלְדָה בְּיוֹם טוֹב, בֵּית שַׁמַּאי אוֹמְרִים, תֵּאָכֵל, וּבֵית הִלֵּל אוֹמְרִים, לֹא תֵאָכֵל.

6. אַמַּת הַמַּיִם שֶׁהִיא עוֹבֶרֶת בֶּחָצֵר, אֵין מְמַלְּאִין הֵימֶנָּה בַּשַּׁבָּת.

7. הָיוּ מְהַלְּכִין בַּדֶּרֶךְ וְאֶחָד בָּא כְנֶגְדָּן, אָמַר אֶחָד מֵהֶן, הֲרֵינִי נָזִיר שֶׁזֶּה פְלוֹנִי, וְאֶחָד אָמַר, הֲרֵינִי נָזִיר שֶׁאֵין זֶה פְלוֹנִי ... בֵּית שַׁמַּאי אוֹמְרִים, כֻּלָּן נְזִירִים ... וְרַבִּי טַרְפוֹן אוֹמֵר, אֵין אֶחָד מֵהֶם נָזִיר.

8. מִי שֶׁנָּזַר וְהוּא בְּבֵית הַקְּבָרוֹת, אֲפִלּוּ הָיָה שָׁם שְׁלֹשִׁים יוֹם, אֵין עוֹלִין לוֹ מִן הַמִּנְיָן, וְאֵינוֹ מֵבִיא קָרְבַּן טֻמְאָה.

9. וַחֲכָמִים אוֹמְרִים, לֹא בָדַק אוֹר אַרְבָּעָה עָשָׂר, יִבְדֹּק בְּאַרְבָּעָה עָשָׂר, לֹא בָדַק בְּאַרְבָּעָה עָשָׂר, יִבְדֹּק בְּתוֹךְ הַמּוֹעֵד, לֹא בָדַק בְּתוֹךְ הַמּוֹעֵד, יִבְדֹּק לְאַחַר הַמּוֹעֵד.

10. כך ישראל, צרות האחרונות משכחות הראשונות.

11. משל, למה הדבר דומה? לאדם שכעס על בנו וטרדו מביתו. נכנס אוהבו לבקש הימנו ולהחזירו לביתו. אמר לו, כלום אתה מבקש ממני אלא מפני בני? כבר נתרצתי לבני.

12. משל, למה הדבר דומה? לאחד שהיה מהלך בדרך והיה מנהיג את בנו לפניו. באו לסטים מלפניו לשבותו, נטלו מלפניו ונתנו לאחריו. בא זאב מאחריו, נטלו מאחריו ונתנו לפניו. באו לסטים מלפניו וזאבים מאחריו, נטלו ונתנו על זרועותיו. התחיל הבן מצטער מפני החמה, פרש עליו אביו בגדו. רעב, האכילו, צמא, השקהו. כך עשה הקב"ה.

13. הלמד שלא לעשות נוח לו שלא נברא.

14. מעשה בימי הורודוס שהיו גשמים יורדים בלילות, בשחרית זרחה חמה ונשבה הרוח ונתנגבה הארץ והפועלים יוצאים למלאכתם ויודעים שמעשיהם לשם שמאים.

15. היו בביתו של אדם חמש זכרים או חמש נקבות. היה יושב ומצפה ואומר, אוי לי, שמא לא ירד המן למחר ונמצינו מתים ברעב, יהי רצון מלפניך שירד.

16. אמר משה, מה אני אעשה? עכשיו כל אחד ואחד אומר, כבר פדאני לוי. עשה משה תקנה, נטל פיתקים וכתב עליהם, לוי, ונטל פיתקים וכתב עליהם, כסף חמשת שקלים, ובללם והטילם בקלפי. אמר להם, באו וטלו פיתקיהם. כל מי שנטל פיתקו וכתוב היה עליו, בן לוי, אומר לו, כבר אתה פדוי. ומי שנטל פיתקו וכתוב עליו, כסף חמשת שקלים, היה משה אומר לו, צא ותן פדיונך.

17. משל, למה הדבר דומה? למדינה שמרדה על המלך. שלח המלך פולימרכוס אחד להחריבה. היה אותו פולימרכוס בקי ומיושב. אמר להם, טלו לכם ימים, ואם לאו, הריני עושה לכם כדרך שעשיתי למדינה פלונית ולחברותיה ולהפרכיא פלונית ולחברותיה.

18. נקרא המקום רחום, אף אתה היה רחום, הקדוש ברוך הוא נקרא חנון, אף אתה היה חנון.

19. מעשה ברבי אלעזר בן שמוע ורבי יוחנן הסנדלר, שהיו הולכים לנציבים אצל רבי יהודה בן בתירה ללמוד ממנו תורה, והגיעו לציידן וזכרו את ארץ ישראל. זקפו עיניהם וזלגו דמעותיהם וקרעו בגדיהם וקראו את המקרא הזה, וירשתם אותה וישבתם בה ושמרת לעשות את

כל החוקים האלה ואת המשפטים [דברים יא' לא'-לב']. אמרו, ישיבת ארץ
ישראל שקולה כנגד כל המצוות שבתורה. הזרו ובאו להם לארץ ישראל.
20. רק אם שמוע תשמע בקול ײ אלהיך [דברים טו' ה']. מיכן אמרו,
שמע אדם קימעה, משמיעים אותו הרבה, שמע אדם דברי תורה,
משמיעים אותו דברי סופרים.

Sources. 1. Abot 3.2. 2. Abot 3.5. 3. AZ 3.3. 4. AZ 4.3. 5. Beṣ 1.1. 6. Erub
8.7. 7. Naz 5.5. 8. Naz 3.5. 9. Pes 1.3. 10. Mek 13.2 (L 1.133). 11. Mek
14.15 (L 1.218). 12. Mek 14.19 (L 1.224–25). 13. SLv 26.3 (W 110c). 14.
SLv 26.4 (W 110d). 15. SNm 89.5 (H 90). 16. SNm 95.2 (H 96). 17. SNm
131.1 (H 170). 18. SDt 49 (F 114). 19. SDt 80 (F 146). 20. SDt 115 (F
174).

UNIT TWENTY-FIVE

INTERROGATIVE CLAUSES

I *Introductory text* (SNm 87.1 [H 86])

זכרנו את הדגה אשר נאכל במצרים חנם [במדבר יא' ה']. וכי יש בענין שהיו
המצריים נותנים להם דגים בחנם? הלא כבר נאמר, ועתה לכו עבדו ותבן
לא ינתן לכם [שמות ה' יח']? אם תבן לא היו נותנים להם בחנם, ודגים היו
נותנים להם בחנם? ומה אני אומר, חנם? מן המצוות.

We remember the fish that we ate without charge in Egypt [Nm 11.5]. Does it
say in the context that the Egyptians had given them fishes without charge?
Rather, is it not said, Now go and work, and you will not even be given straw
[Ex 5.18]? If they didn't even give them straw for nothing, were they going
to give them fishes without charge? In that case, how should I interpret,
Without charge? Without the commandments!

1. Here we see a contrast between grace and commandments that Saint
Paul himself could have put his name to. A detailed and ingenious exegesis
reveals that the Egyptians did not provide fish for free, but rather this was
something that came from God, with 'without charge' indicating that the gift
was not in exchange for merit or for commandments fulfilled, as the Torah
had not yet been promulgated.

II *Morphology*

2. For a presentation of the forms and uses of interrogative pronouns and adverbs, see Units 5 and 23.

3. As well as the BH interrogative particles כִּי, הֲלֹא, הַאִם, and -הֲ, RH employs מָאוּמָה (כָּל + כְּלוּם); see Unit 6.2) and שֶׁמָּא 'perhaps'.

III *Grammar and usage*

4. An interrogative structure may have no formal representation in writing, being detectable only by tone of voice or context. Rhetorical questions of the type 'is it not right that?' are common and easily identified.

In midrashic exposition, a conclusion that is regarded as correct can be formulated with דִּין הוּא 'it is/concerns a deduction' or with a rhetorical question, -שֶׁ אֵינוֹ דִין 'is it not a deduction that?', both forms alternating with no discernible difference in meaning. Such constructions should usually be rendered with a verb rather than a noun 'one deduces, one may infer, it follows' or 'does not one deduce?, may not one infer?, does it not follow?':

אם למדתי לפרה שעשה בה כל הכלים ככלי חרש, אף סוטה, אינו דין
שעשה בה כל הכלים ככלי חרש?

> Seeing that in the ritual of the red heifer any vessel is treated as an earthen vessel, so also in the ritual of a woman suspected of adultery may we not infer that any vessel is to be treated as an earthen vessel? (SNm 10.2 [H 16]).

In the Mishnah, the formula -שֶׁ אֵינוֹ דִין is continually employed as the conclusion in a *qal waḥomer*, or *a fortiori*, argument, following an initial supposition that begins with מָה אִם:

מָה אִם חֲלֵב הָאִשָּׁה, שֶׁאֵינוֹ מְיָחָד אֶלָּא לַקְטָנִים, מְטַמֵּא לִרְצוֹן וְשֶׁלֹּא
לִרְצוֹן, חֲלֵב הַבְּהֵמָה שֶׁהוּא מְיָחָד לַקְטַנִּים וְלַגְּדוֹלִים, אֵינוֹ דִין שֶׁיְּטַמֵּא
לִרְצוֹן וְשֶׁלֹּא לִרְצוֹן?

> If a woman's milk, which is only for infants, contaminates whether it is released voluntarily or involuntarily, does not one deduce that the milk of a beast, which is used for infants and adults, will also cause contamination whether it is released voluntarily or involuntarily? (Makhsh 6.8).

5. The interrogative particle -הֲ is little used in RH. An example is at RS 2.8, where Rabban Gamaliel shows various pictures of the moon to illiterate witnesses and asks them:

הֲכָזֶה רָאִיתָ אוֹ כָזֶה?

> Did it look like this or like this?

More common is הֲלֹא (as in BH), when seeking a response in the affirmative, 'is it not true that', as in the following two examples. At Yom 6.8, in connection with the means of verifying that the scapegoat had reached the desert, R. Judah and R. Ishmael ask:

וַהֲלֹא סִימָן גָּדוֹל הָיָה לָהֶם? ... וַהֲלֹא סִימָן אַחֵר הָיָה לָהֶם?

> Didn't they have a better sign? ... Didn't they have a different sign?

At Sanh 6.4, a question, the answer to which was well-known, is raised:

וַהֲלֹא שִׁמְעוֹן בֶּן שָׁטָח תָּלָה נָשִׁים בְּאַשְׁקְלוֹן?

Did not Simeon ben Shataḥ hang women in Ashkelon?

6. וְכִי is also frequently used: וְכִי כָל הָעֵצִים כְּשֵׁרִים לַמַּעֲרָכָה? 'all the trees are fit for the fire?' (Tam 2.3). It is usually employed in the expectation of a negative response:

וְכִי עַל דַּעְתֵּנוּ עָלְתָה שֶׁזִּקְנֵי בֵית דִּין שׁוֹפְכֵי דָמִים הֵן?

Could it occur to us that the elders of the tribunal were shedders of blood? (Soṭ 9.6);

וכי כושים היו?

Were they (the Israelites) Ethiopians? (SNm 99.3 [H 99]).

Sometimes, וְכִי is employed pleonastically in support of other interrogative particles or expressions, giving rise to structures like וְכִי מָה, וְכִי הֵיאַךְ, וְכִי מִפְּנֵי מָה, וְכִי אֵיזוֹ. Among numerous examples of their use is the following:

וכי איזה מדה מרובה, מדת טובה או מדת פורענות?

Which measure is the more generous, that of mercy or that of punishment? (SNm 8 [H 15]).

7. כְּלוּם is an indefinite particle employed in negative expressions. In later RH, it is also used to introduce questions, but there seems to be only one instance of this usage in the Mishnah, in an apparently colloquial context:

כְּלוּם אָמַרְתָּ אֶלָּא מִפְּנֵי כְבוֹדִי? זֶהוּא כְבוֹדִי

Didn't you say it to give me honour? This is my honour (Ned 8.7).

The usage is also rare in the tannaitic *midrashim*:

אמר משה לפני המקום, אדוני, כלום הגון לדם שתתן להם ותהרגם?

Moses argued before the omnipresent one, My lord, are you giving them something only to kill them afterwards? (SNm 95.1 [H 95]; cf. Mek 20.2 [L 2.229]).

8. Direct disjunctive questions introduce the second part with אוֹ, as at RS 3.8:

וְכִי יָדָיו שֶׁלְמֹשֶׁה עוֹשׂוֹת מִלְחָמָה אוֹ שׁוֹבְרוֹת מִלְחָמָה?

Was it that Moses' hands were able to wage war or perhaps to hinder it? (see Unit 24.13).

9. Indirect questions.

These do not differ at all from direct questions (see Segal 1927, §465; Meyer 1992, §114.4), which means that it is often uncertain which is intended—for example, at Sanh 3.6

אֱמוֹר הֵיאַךְ אַתָּה יוֹדֵעַ

could mean either 'say how you know' or 'say, How do you know?'.

An indirect question may be introduced by אִם (as well as by an interrogative adverb or pronoun, as in the previous example):

וכן לכל אומה ואומה שאל להם אם מקבילים את התורה

And in the same way each of the peoples was asked if they wished to receive the Torah (SDt 343 [F 396]).

A disjunctive indirect question (see Unit 24.13) will usually introduce each part of the question with אִם, as at BQ 10.7:

הָאוֹמֵר לַחֲבֵרוֹ ... אֵינִי יוֹדֵעַ אִם הֶחֱזַרְתִּי לָךְ אִם לֹא הֶחֱזַרְתִּי לָךְ, חַיָּב
לְשַׁלֵּם. אֲבָל אִם אָמַר לוֹ, אֵינִי יוֹדֵעַ אִם גְּזַלְתִּיךָ, אִם הִלְוִיתַנִי, אִם
הִפְקַדְתָּ אֶצְלִי, פָּטוּר מִלְּשַׁלֵּם

If a person says to their companion, But I don't know if I did return
it to you or if I didn't, such a person is obliged to pay. But if they
say, I don't know if I robbed you or if you made me a loan or if you
deposited it with me, they are exempt from repayment.

However, there are other examples in which the alternative possibility is introduced by אוֹ שֶׁ- (see Unit 8.9), for example:

וְאִם אֵינוֹ יָדוּעַ אֵיזֶה מֵהֶם נִשְׁחַט רִאשׁוֹן, אוֹ שֶׁשָּׁחֲטוּ כְּאֶחָד, הוּא אוֹכֵל
מִשֶּׁלּוֹ

And if it is not known which of the two was slaughtered first, or if
the two were slaughtered at the same time, he may start eating his
one (Pes 9.9).

IV *Phraseology*

10. שֶׁ-אֵינוֹ דִין 'is it not a deduction that?'; see above, §4.

11. מָה אֲנִי לְ-, מָה אַתָּה לְ-, מָה אָנוּ לְ-, etc., followed by an infinitive, 'may I
(etc.) do so-and-so?' (see Unit 20.13):

[הַגֵּר] עָמַד לִפְנֵיהֶן בְּבֵית הַמִּדְרָשׁ, אָמַר לָהֶם, מָה אֲנִי לָבֹא בַקָּהָל?
(The proselyte) presented himself to them in the academy and said
to them, May I enter the congregation? (Yad 4.4);

מָה אֲנִי לְהָבִיא זֶרַע אֶל תַּחַת הַמּוֹתָר
May I plant a seed beneath what remains? (Kil 6.4);

אָמְרוּ לוֹ לְרַבָּן גַּמְלִיאֵל, מָה אָנוּ לֵירֵד? אָמַר לָהֶן, מֻתָּר
They asked Rabban Gamaliel, May we go down (i.e. 'disembark')?
He answered them, It is permitted (Erub 4.2).

12. הֲלֹא כְבָר נֶאֱמַר 'has it not already been said?', introducing a scriptural passage regarded as a repetition of the text under discussion; the formula is used when attempting to establish an additional meaning for a
'repeated' text (there can be no throwaway comments in the Torah!), and alternates with a positive variant: הֲרֵי כְבָר נֶאֱמַר 'note that it has already been
said'. The following is a good example:

כי אשה כושית לקח [במדבר יב׳ א׳]. עוד למה נאמר? והלא כבר
נאמר, על אודות האשה הכושית [במדבר יב׳ א׳]? אלא מה ת״ל, כי
אשה כושית לקח? יש לך אשה נאה ביופיה ולא במעשיה,
במעשיה ולא ביופיה ... וזאת נאה בנויה ונאה במעשיה, לכך נאמר,
כי אשה כושית לקח

For he had married an Ethiopian woman [Nm 12.1b]. Why does it
say this again? Was it not already said, On account of the Ethiopian
woman [Nm 12.1a]? So, what teaching is provided by the text, For

he had married an Ethiopian woman. You would have it that a woman can be beautiful because of her looks but not because of her deeds or because of her deeds but not because of her looks ... But this woman was beautiful because of her looks and because of her deeds, and that is why it says, For he had married an Ethiopian woman (SNm 99.4 [H 99]).

V *Vocabulary*

אָכְפַּת (Aramaic) 'burden, preoccupation', מָה אָכְפַּת לְ- 'of what concern is it to?'

בֵּית הַבְּחִירָה 'the house of choice', i.e. the temple

בִּלְבֵּל 'mix'

דָּחָה 'annul, abrogate, expel', דָּחָה הַשַּׁבָּת 'abrogate the sabbath commandment'

דְּלַעַת (plural דְּלוּעִין) 'gourd'

הַזָּאָה 'sprinkling'

זַךְ 'pure'

חִלּוּף 'change, substitution'; used adverbially, 'the other way round'

עַכְבָּר 'mouse'

עֲלִילָה 'pretext'

קָבַל עַל 'accuse, cry out, protest' (as against קִבֵּל 'receive')

קִטְנִית 'pulse' (beans, peas, etc.)

קָלַס 'acclaim, applaud'

רַמַּאי 'fraud, impostor'

VI *Exercises*

1. לֹא יִתֵּן לוֹ ... עַד שֶׁתִּדְרֹשׁ אֶת אָחִיךָ, אִם רַמַּאי הוּא אִם אֵינוֹ רַמַּאי.

2. הַכֹּל לְפִי הַמִּדָּה, הַכֹּל לְפִי הַזְּמַן. אָמַר רַבִּי יוֹחָנָן בֶּן נוּרִי, וְכִי מָה אָכְפַּת לָהֶן לָעֲכְבָּרִין, וַהֲלֹא אוֹכְלִין בֵּין מֵהַרְבֵּה וּבֵין מִקְּמְעָה.

3. אָמַר רַבִּי יוֹסֵי, וְכִי מִי מוֹדִיעֵנִי אֵיזוֹהִי [בֵּיצָא] גְדוֹלָה וְאֵיזוֹהִי קְטַנָּה? אֶלָּא הַכֹּל לְפִי דַעְתּוֹ שֶׁלָּרוֹאֶה.

4. אַף הַמְּנָחוֹת הָיוּ בַדִּין שֶׁיִּטְעֲנוּ שֶׁמֶן זַיִת זָךְ. מָה אִם הַמְּנוֹרָה שֶׁאֵינָה לַאֲכִילָה, טְעוּנָה שֶׁמֶן זַיִת זָךְ, הַמְּנָחוֹת שֶׁהֵן לַאֲכִילָה, אֵינוֹ דִין שֶׁיִּטְעֲנוּ שֶׁמֶן זַיִת זָךְ?

5. הַנּוֹדֵר מִן הַיָּרָק, מֻתָּר בַּדִּלוּעִין, וְרַבִּי עֲקִיבָא אוֹסֵר. אָמְרוּ לוֹ לְרַבִּי עֲקִיבָא, וַהֲלֹא אוֹמֵר אָדָם לִשְׁלוּחוֹ, קַח לִי יָרָק, וְהוּא אוֹמֵר, לֹא מָצָאתִי אֶלָּא דִלוּעִין. אָמַר לָהֶם, כֵּן הַדָּבָר. אוֹ שֶׁמָּא אוֹמֵר הוּא לוֹ, לֹא מָצָאתִי אֶלָּא קִטְנִית? אֶלָּא שֶׁהַדִּלוּעִין בִּכְלָל יָרָק וְאֵין הַקִּטְנִית בִּכְלָל יָרָק.

6. אָמַר לוֹ רַבִּי אֱלִיעֶזֶר, וְעָלֶיהָ אֲנִי דָן. וּמָה אִם שְׁחִיטָה שֶׁהִיא מִשּׁוּם מְלָאכָה דּוֹחָה אֶת הַשַּׁבָּת, הַזָּאָה שֶׁהִיא מִשּׁוּם שְׁבוּת, אֵינוֹ דִין שֶׁדּוֹחָה אֶת הַשַּׁבָּת? אָמַר לוֹ רַבִּי עֲקִיבָא, אוֹ חִלּוּף. מָה אִם הַזָּאָה שֶׁהִיא מִשּׁוּם שְׁבוּת אֵינָה

דּוֹחָה אֶת הַשַּׁבָּת, שְׁחִיטָה שֶׁהִיא מִשּׁוּם מְלָאכָה, אֵינוֹ דִין שֶׁלֹּא תִדְחֶה אֶת הַשַּׁבָּת? אָמַר לוֹ רַבִּי אֱלִיעֶזֶר, עֲקִיבָא, עֲקַרְתָּ מַה שֶׁכָּתוּב בַּתּוֹרָה.

7. עֲשֵׂה לְךָ שָׂרָף וְשִׂים אוֹתוֹ עַל-נֵס, וְהָיָה כָּל-הַנָּשׁוּךְ וְרָאָה אוֹתוֹ וָחָי, [בְּמִדְבָּר כא' ח']. וְכִי נָחָשׁ מֵמִית, אוֹ נָחָשׁ מְחַיֶּה? אֶלָּא בִּזְמַן שֶׁיִּשְׂרָאֵל מִסְתַּכְּלִין כְּלַפֵּי מַעְלָה וּמְשַׁעְבְּדִין אֶת לִבָּם לַאֲבִיהֶן שֶׁבַּשָּׁמַיִם, הָיוּ מִתְרַפְּאִים, וְאִם לָאו, הָיוּ נִמּוֹקִים.

8. בּוֹ בַיּוֹם בָּא יְהוּדָה גֵּר עַמּוֹנִי וְעָמַד לִפְנֵיהֶן בְּבֵית הַמִּדְרָשׁ, אָמַר לָהֶם, מָה אֲנִי לָבֹא בַקָּהָל? אָמַר לוֹ רַבָּן גַּמְלִיאֵל, אָסוּר אַתָּה. אָמַר לוֹ רַבִּי יְהוֹשֻׁעַ, מֻתָּר אַתָּה. אָמַר לוֹ רַבָּן גַּמְלִיאֵל, הַכָּתוּב אוֹמֵר, לֹא יָבֹא עַמּוֹנִי וּמוֹאָבִי בִּקְהַל יְ' גַּם דּוֹר עֲשִׂירִי [דברים כג' ד']. אָמַר לוֹ רַבִּי יְהוֹשֻׁעַ, וְכִי עַמּוֹנִים וּמוֹאָבִים בִּמְקוֹמָן הֵן? כְּבָר עָלָה סַנְחֵרִיב מֶלֶךְ אַשּׁוּר וּבִלְבֵּל אֶת כָּל הָאֻמּוֹת.

9. אוֹמְרִים צַדּוּקִים, קוֹבְלִין אָנוּ עֲלֵיכֶם פְּרוּשִׁים, שֶׁאַתֶּם אוֹמְרִים, כִּתְבֵי הַקֹּדֶשׁ מְטַמְּאִין אֶת הַיָּדַיִם, וְסִפְרֵי הָמֵרָס אֵינָם מְטַמְּאִים אֶת הַיָּדַיִם. אָמַר רַבָּן יוֹחָנָן בֶּן זַכַּאי, וְכִי אֵין לָנוּ עַל הַפְּרוּשִׁים אֶלָּא זוֹ בִלְבָד?

10. אמר משה לפני הקב"ה, רבונו של עולם, שמא דרכיך כדרכי בשר ודם? ... רבונו של עולם, כלום נגזרה גזירה שלא אכנס לה?

11. מפני מה לא נאמרו עשרת הדברות מתחלת התורה? משלו משל, למה הדבר דומה? למלך שנכנס למדינה, אמר להם, אמלוך עליכם, אמרו לו, כלום עשית לנו טובה שתמלוך עלינו?

12. על מה נחלקו? על העושה בתוך היום, שאין יודע אם עשה בשבת אם ביום הכפורים עשה.

13. וכי היאך היה משה יכול להפשיט את בגדיו [של אהרון] כסידרן? ... וכי היאך היה יכול משה להלביש את אלעזר בגדים כסידרן?

14. אמרו ישראל לפני משה, וכי היאך מקלסת מדינה את המלך ואינה רואה פני המלך?

15. ואם אין לאיש גואל [במדבר ה' ח']. רבי ישמעאל אומר, וכי יש לך אדם בישראל שאין לו גואל?

16. ויקריבו הנשיאים את קרבנם לפני המזבח [במדבר ז' י'], ... ועדין לא היה יודע משה כיצד יקריבו אם למסעות אם לתולדות, עד שנאמר לו מפי הקב"ה ... ועדיין לא היה יודע משה כיצד יקריבו נשיאים אם כולן כאחד או כל אחד ואחד יומו, עד שנאמר מפי הקדש.

17. וינוסו משנאיך [במדבר י' לה']. וכי יש שונאים לפני מי שאמר והיה העולם? ... וברוב גאונך תהרוס קמיך [שמות טו' ז']. וכי יש קמים לפני מי שאמר והיה העולם?

18. והלא הלכה עמהם באר במדבר והיתה מעלת להם דגים שמנים יותר מצרכם? אלא שמבקשים עלילה היאך לפרוש מאחרי המקום.

19. זה אחד מן הדברים שאמר משה לפני המקום, הודיעני אם אתה עושה לי אם אי אתה עושה לי. אמר לו הקדוש ברוך הוא, אני עושה.

20. רבי יהודה אומר, שלש מצוות נצטוו ישראל בשעת כניסתם לארץ, למנות להם מלך, לבנות להם בית הבחירה ולהכרית זרע עמלק. איני יודע איזה יקדום, אם למנות להם מלך, אם לבנות להם בית הבחירה, אם להכרית זרע עמלק.

Sources. 1. BM 2.7. 2. BM 3.7. 3. Kel 17.6. 4. Men 8.5. 5. Ned 7.1. 6. Pes 6.2. 7. RS 3.8. 8. Yad 4.4. 9. Yad 4.6. 10. Mek 17.14 (L 2.150–52). 11. Mek 20.2 (L 2.229–30). 12. SLv 4.23 (W 20b). 13. SLv 8.7 (W 41a). 14. SLv 9.4 (W 43d). 15. SNm 4.1 (H 7). 16. SNm 47 (H 52). 17. SNm 84.4 (H 81). 18. SNm 95.1 (H 95). 19. SDt 26 (F 40). 20. SDt 67 (F 132).

UNIT TWENTY-SIX

COMPARATIVE CLAUSES

I *Introductory text* (SDt 8 [F 16])

מה תלמוד לומר, [באו ורשו את הארץ אשר נשבע י' לאבותיכם] לאברהם
ליצחק וליעקב [דברים א' ח]? כדיי אברהם בעצמו, כדיי יצחק בעצמו,
כדיי יעקב בעצמו. משל למלך שנתן לעבדו שדה אחת במתנה, לא
נתנה לו אלא כמות שהיא. עמד העבד ההוא והשביחה ואמר, מה בידי?
לא נתנה לי אלא כמות שהיא. חזר ונטעה כרם ואמר, מה בידי? לא
נתנה לי אלא כמות שהיא. כך כשנתן הקדוש ברוך הוא לאברהם
אבינו את הארץ לא נתנה לו אלא כמות שהיא, שנאמר, קום התהלך
בארץ לארכה ולרחבה כי לך אתננה [בראשית יג' יז]. עמד אברהם
והשביחה, שנאמר, ויטע אשל בבאר שבע [בראשית כא' לג']. עמד
יצחק והשביחה, שנאמר, ויזרע יצחק בארץ ההיא וימצא בשנה ההיא
מאה שערים [בראשית כו' יב']. עמד יעקב והשביחה, שנאמר, ויקן
את חלקת השדה [בראשית לג' יט'].

What instruction is provided by the text, (Come and take possession of the land that I swore to your fathers) to Abraham, Isaac, and Jacob [Dt 1.8]. How worthy was Abraham in his own right, how worthy was Isaac in his own right, and how worthy was Jacob in his own right! A parable—it is like a king who gave a field to his servant—it was given to him just as it was. That servant set about improving it, saying, What should I do? It has been given to me as it is. He came back and planted a vineyard, saying, What should I do? It was given to me just as it is. Thus, in the same way, when the holy one, blessed be he, gave Abraham the land, it was given to him just as it is, as it is said, Arise and go the length and breadth of the land, because I shall give it to you [Gn 13.17]. Abraham set about improving it, as it is said, And he planted a tamarisk at Beer-sheba [Gn 21.33]. Isaac set about improving it, as it is said, And Isaac sowed in that land and reaped a hundredfold that year [Gn 26.12]. Jacob set about improving it, as it is said, And he bought part of the countryside [Gn 33.19].

1. Why is the name of each patriarch expressly mentioned? Would not the generic 'our fathers' have sufficed? The exegesis provided finds the motive for this apparently superfluous form of expression—each one of the patriarchs was worthy in his own right to receive the oath promising the land. The point of the parable is to show that just as the servant was deserving of his lord's gift, so too was each of the patriarchs, for each of them did not rest content with merely maintaining the property in the state it had been given him (כְּמוֹת שֶׁהִיא) but took the risk of working to improve it. (Note the parallel with the parable of the talents in Mt 25.14–30 and Lk 19.12–27.) The midrashic function of the parable is to energize a series of texts describing the work of each patriarch.

The servant's words מָה בְיָדִי are to be interpreted as 'what possibilities are available to me?, what can I do?, as is clear from the parallel text in Midrash Tannaim.

II *Morphology*

2. RH employs the BH comparative particles -כְּ and כְּמוֹ. As in BH, כְּמוֹ is used with personal suffixes, but is also found in a plural or collective form, כְּמוֹת, resulting in a specifically RH paradigm. The following strengthened forms with suffixes are attested in the Mishnah and tannaitic *midrashim*:

1st person	כְּמוֹתִי
2nd person	כְּמוֹתְךָ, כָּמוֹכָה, כָּמוֹךְ
3rd person sing.	כְּמוֹתָהּ, כְּמוֹתוֹ, כָּמוֹהָ, כְּמוֹהוּ
3rd person plur.	כְּמוֹתָם/ן

3. In line with developments in the spoken language, -כְּ is often strengthened by other particles in RH to achieve greater expressivity or to make certain kinds of comparison more explicit:

כְּנֶגֶד 'corresponding to';

כְּדֶרֶךְ 'according to the custom of';

כְּדֵי 'as much as is required for, sufficient for';

כְּיוֹצֵא ב- 'analogously to'.

4. BH's comparative conjunction is כַּאֲשֶׁר (occasionally, just אֲשֶׁר), generally in association with כֵּן:

כַּאֲשֶׁר עָשָׂה כֵּן יֵעָשֶׂה לּוֹ

As he did, so let it be done to him (Lv 24.19).

RH possesses a greater variety of conjunctions for subordinating one clause to another in a relationship of comparison:

כְּמוֹ שֶׁ-;

כְּמוֹת שֶׁ-;

-כְּשֵׁם שֶׁ;

-כְּדֶרֶךְ שֶׁ;

-כְּעִנְיָן שֶׁ;

כְּאִילוּ.

The second term of a comparison may be introduced by modal adverbs like
כְּמוֹ שֶׁ. -אַף כֵּן, כָּךְ or is also found at Qumran.

III *Grammar and usage*

5. Concerning adjectives and comparisons of superiority or inferiority,
see Unit 13.5; on כְּדֵי as a comparative particle, see Unit 30.8B.

6. Some compound prepositions or prepositional phrases convey a meaning that is often difficult to determine precisely.

A. כְּנֶגֶד (-כְּ and נֶגֶד) expresses the idea of corespondence, correlation,
proportion (see Unit 7.1), not opposition or confrontation, as well illustrated
by the late text PRE 12, in which the עֵזֶר כְּנֶגְדּוֹ of Gn 2.18, that is the woman
as help for the man, could be converted into the exact opposite, simply by
reading לְנֶגְדּוֹ:

ר׳ יהודה אומר, אל תקרא, כנגדו, אלא, לנגדו. אם זכה תהיה לו עזר,
ואם לאו, לנגדו להלחם

R. Judah used to say, Do not read כְּנֶגְדּוֹ, but לְנֶגְדּוֹ; if she were righteous, she would be of help to him, but if not, she would be against
him, fighting him.

B. כְּדֶרֶךְ signifies that which is habitual (see Units 8.10 and 11.10).
Hence, we encounter expressions like כְּדַרְכָּה, כְּדַרְכּוֹ, and כְּדַרְכָּן in the sense
of 'as customary, in the habitual manner', or, frequently, 'in his, her, its (etc.)
own way':

וּבֵית הִלֵּל אוֹמְרִים, כָּל אָדָם קוֹרֵא כְּדַרְכּוֹ

The school of Hillel maintains, Each person may read in their own
way (Ber 1.3);

הַבְּהֵמָה מוּעֶדֶת לְהַלֵּךְ כְּדַרְכָּה לְשַׁבֵּר

Livestock has a warning attached to it for going along in its normal
way, causing damage (BQ 2.1);

חַיָּב, שֶׁלֹּא שָׁמַר כְּדֶרֶךְ הַשּׁוֹמְרִים, וְאִם שָׁמַר כְּדֶרֶךְ הַשּׁוֹמְרִים, פָּטוּר

Liable, because he did not look after (the deposit) as guardians normally do, but if he looked after it as guardians normally do, then he
is exempt (BM 3.10).

In the following comparison from Sheq 3.2, the point is not that people
have to carry out their obligations both to mortals and to God but that they
must carry out their obligations to mortals *in the same way* as they carry out
their obligations to God (see below, §7):

לְפִי שֶׁאָדָם צָרִיךְ לָצֵאת יְדֵי הַבְּרִיּוֹת כְּדֶרֶךְ שֶׁצָּרִיךְ לָצֵאת יְדֵי הַמָּקוֹם.

Note also TosSot 1.6:

כדרך שמאיימין עליה בית דין שתחזור בה, כך מאיימין עליה
שלא תחזור בה

In the same way that the tribunal had warned her to repent, so they
used to warn her not to repent.

C. -כְּיוֹצֵא ב literally means 'as it goes out in'. The formula כַּיּוֹצֵא בוֹ is
employed to introduce a list of biblical citations similar to a text just mentioned, conveying the sense of 'analogously, equally, with the same meaning', etc.

But the formula may also simply express identity or similarity, as in the
following striking example from SLv 26.12 (W 111b):

אמר לו המלך ... הריני כיוצא בך ... והקב"ה אומר להם לצדיקים,
הריני כיוצא בכם

The king said to him (his employee) ..., I am like you ... and the
holy one, blessed be he, says to the righteous, I am like you.

7. The new conjunctions -כְּשֵׁם שֶׁ-, כְּדֶרֶךְ שֶׁ, and -כְּעִנְיָן שֶׁ, have a similar
meaning. In origin, they each appear to have had a slightly different sense,
'just as', 'in the same way that', 'corresponding to that which':

לְפִי שֶׁאָדָם צָרִיךְ לָצֵאת יְדֵי הַבְּרִיּוֹת כְּדֶרֶךְ שֶׁצָּרִיךְ לָצֵאת יְדֵי הַמָּקוֹם

For a person must carry out their obligations to mortals in the same
way that they must carry out their obligations to the omnipresent
one (Sheq 3.2);

כענין שאמרו ישראל ליחזקאל

In keeping with what the Israelites said to Ezekiel (SNm 115.5 [H
128]).

The following text from SNm 139.2 (H 185) shows to what extent
-כְּדֶרֶךְ שֶׁ and -כְּשֵׁם שֶׁ had become identical and could be used interchangeably:

אשר יצא לפניהם ואשר יבא לפניהם [במדבר כז' יז], לא כדרך
שאחרים עושים, שהם משלחים חיילות והם באים לבסוף, אלא
כשם שעשה משה

That he might go out at their head and come back at their head [Nm
27.17], not like others do, who send armies out in front while they
come behind, but like Moses did.

8. Formulas expressing analogy.

In both Mishnah and *midrashim*, analogy is fundamental, as it permits,
by means of comparison or contrast, a continual updating in the interpretation
of biblical or halakhic texts. The following three types (*middot*) of comparison are among those to be found in both exegetical and halakhic texts: *gezerah shawah*, *heqqesh*, and *qal wahomer*. A striking grammatical feature is
the use of מָה as a comparative particle (see Unit 5.8), frequently preceded by
-וּ (וּמָה), although without copulative value.

A. *Gezerah shawah* refers to verbal analogy, whereby two or more texts
are elucidated through their use of a common word. The commonest formulation of a *gezerah shawah* analogy is:

נֶאֱמַר כָּאן ... נֶאֱמַר לְהַלָּן, מָה הָאָמוּר כָּאן ... אַף לְהַלָּן

Here it says x and there it says x: if x is y here, then x is also y there.
Invariably, this kind of comparison employs the correlative terms: מָה ... אַף:

נאמר כאן , עפר [במדבר ה' יז'], ונאמר להלן , עפר [במדבר יט' יז'],
מה עפר האמור כאן עפר על פני המים , אף להלן עפר על פני המים

Here [Nm 5.17] it says, Ash, and there [Nm 19.17] it says, Ash: as
the ash mentioned here is (for scattering) over water, so too the ash
mentioned there is (for scattering) over water (SNm 10.4 [H 16]).

B. *Heqqesh* 'comparison' is distinguished from *gezerah shawah* in that it
is concerned more with what the words refer to than the words themselves
(and is thus considered an irrefutable form of argument: אֵין מְשִׁיבִין עַל הַהֶקֵּשׁ
[BQ 106b]). It is not formulated in such a stereotyped way as *gezerah
shawah*, although comparison is, once more, established by means of
מָה ... אַף:

מקיש הרמה לתנופה, מה תנופה מוליך ומביא , אף הרמה כן

You have to match the raising to the waving: as the waving moves
to and fro, so too the raising (SNm 17.2 [H 22]).

C. A *qal wa-homer* or *a fortiori* argument is, from a linguistic perspective, the expression of a relationship between two propositions by means of
the following correlative terms:

מָה אִם ... קַל וָחֹמֶר שֶׁ-;
מָה אִם ... דִּין הוּא;
מָה אִם ... אֵינוֹ דִין שֶׁ-;
מָה אִם ... עַל אַחַת כַּמָּה וְכַמָּה,
etc.

The first proposition corresponds to a protasis and is regularly introduced by
מָה אִם (although sometimes by אִם on its own or מָה on its own). It can normally be rendered as a conditional, 'if this is so'. The apodosis is introduced
by the second part of the forms cited above, and signifies 'how much
more!/less!', 'with greater reason/lesser reason', etc., depending on the supposition expressed by the protasis. The following may be added to the numerous examples of *qal wa-homer* found in the exercises at the end of the unit:

מָה אִם הָעוֹבֵר עֲבֵרָה אַחַת נוֹטֵל נַפְשׁוֹ עָלֶיהָ, הָעוֹשֶׂה מִצְוָה אַחַת, עַל
אַחַת כַּמָּה וְכַמָּה שֶׁתִּנָּתֵן לוֹ נַפְשׁוֹ

If one who commits a transgression pays for it with their life, with
greater reason will one who fulfils a precept have their life restored
to them (Mak 3.15).

Often, the apodosis is understood but not overtly expressed:

אם מדת פורענות ממועטת אבר שהתחיל בעבירה ממנו התחילה
הפורענות, קל וחמר למדת הטוב מרובה

If in accordance with the measure of punishment, which has to be
interpreted restrictively, it is through the member by which the sin
began that punishment begins, with greater reason in accordance
with the measure of mercy, which is interpreted generously (through

the same person who was the first to do good, rewards will begin to flow) (SNm 18.1 [H 22]; cf. SNm 115.5; 156; 160.3).

D. For the formula, אִם לָמַדְתִּי ... אַף/כָּךְ 'considering that ... it follows that', see Unit 28.9.

9. Equalizing comparisons.

The verb עָשָׂה is employed with two objects connected by -כְּ, in the formula עָשָׂה זֶה כָזֶה 'treat this the same as that'. The exegetical formula לַעֲשׂוֹת ... כְּ-, has already been presented in Unit 20.15, with some typical examples expressing equal treatment of men and women or children and adults. The following is a further example:

חומץ יין וחומץ שכר לא ישתה [במדבר ו' ג'], מגיד שעשה בו חומץ כיין

They are not to drink vinegar of wine or vinegar of liquor [Nm 6.3], declaring thereby that vinegar is to be ranked with wine (SNm 23.4 [H 28]).

10. Inclusive formulas of comparison.

These are comparative expressions that exclude any alternative by combining a statement with its exact opposite, as in, 'on foot or seated', 'whether you come or not', etc. RH has various devices of this kind, including the following common structures:

בְּ- ... וְשֶׁלֹּא בְ- (see Unit 8.8);
לְ- ... וְשֶׁלֹּא לְ- (see Unit 8.8);
בֵּין ... בֵּין/בֵּין שֶׁ- ... וּבֵין שֶׁ- (see Unit 8.12);
אֶחָד/אַחַת ... וְאֶחָד/וְאַחַת (see Unit 14.11).

Examples include:

וחכמים אומרים, בחבר עיר ושלא בחבר עיר

The sages say. Either in a congregation or without a congregation (one may recite the *tefillah*) (Ber 4.7);

אֵינוֹ דוֹמֶה הָאִישׁ הַמְּגָרֵשׁ לְאִשָּׁה הַמִּתְגָּרֶשֶׁת, שֶׁהָאִשָּׁה יוֹצְאָה לִרְצוֹנָהּ וְשֶׁלֹּא לִרְצוֹנָהּ, וְהָאִישׁ אֵינוֹ מוֹצִיא אֶלָּא לִרְצוֹנוֹ

There is no similarity between a man who divorces and a woman who is divorced, for a woman has to leave whether she wants to or not, but a man can only dismiss a woman with his own consent (Yeb 14.1).

Mek 23.19 (L 3.189) combines in one sentence constructions with בֵּין, אַחַת, and -שֶׁלֹּא בְ:

אחת בין בארץ בין בחוצה לארץ, ואחת בפני הבית ואחת שלא בפני הבית

In the land and outside the land, while the temple survived and when the temple no longer existed.

IV *Phraseology*

11. כְּמוֹ כֵן 'equally, in the same way' is employed to lend emphasis to the second part of a comparison or to introduce a similar case, as in SLv 11.44 (W 57b):

כשם שאני קדוש, כך אתם קדושים, כשם שאני פרוש כך אתם כמו כן
פרושים

> Just as I am holy, so you must be holy; just as I am set apart, so you too must be set apart.

12. כְּמוֹת שֶׁהוּא/שֶׁהִיא 'as it is …', sometimes in the sense 'simply this, only this', as at BM 2.2:

מָצָא פֵרוֹת בַּכְּלִי, אוֹ כְלִי כְמוֹת שֶׁהוּא, מָעוֹת בַּכִּיס, אוֹ כִיס כְּמוֹת שֶׁהוּא

> If one finds fruit in a fruit basket or simply a fruit basket, or coins inside a purse or simply a purse.

A similar sense is attested in the parable in the introductory text to this unit (SDt 8).

13. בֵּין־כָּךְ וּבֵין־כָּךְ 'as much like this as like that, in either case, whichever way':

בֵּין כָּךְ וּבֵין כָּךְ, נִטָּל בַּשַּׁבָּת

> In either case, it may be moved on the sabbath (Shab 17.3).

With a negative, the sense is 'in no case':

בֵּין כָּךְ וּבֵין כָּךְ, לֹא מָכַר לוֹ אֶת הַמֶּרְחָץ

> In neither case does he sell the bath-house (BB 4.4).

V *Vocabulary*

זְרִיקָה 'sprinkling'
כִּיס 'purse'
כָּרַז 'proclaim, announce'
מַחֲלֹקֶת 'division, separation, dissension, discrepancy'
נֶזֶק 'damage'
נִתֵּז (pi. of נָתַז) 'cut', hi. הִתִּיז רֹאשׁ 'decapitate'
תַּשְׁלוּם 'payment, indemnity'

VI *Exercises*

1. וֶהֱוֵי זָהִיר בְּמִצְוָה קַלָּה כְּבַחֲמוּרָה, שֶׁאֵין אַתָּה יוֹדֵעַ מַתַּן שְׂכָרָן שֶׁלַּמִּצְוֹת.
   וֶהֱוֵי מְחַשֵּׁב הֶפְסֵד מִצְוָה כְּנֶגֶד שְׂכָרָהּ, וּשְׂכַר עֲבֵרָה כְּנֶגֶד הֶפְסֵדָהּ.
2. הַמְחַפֵּל וְטָעָה, סִימָן רַע לוֹ, וְאִם שְׁלִיחַ צִבּוּר הוּא, סִימָן רַע לְשׁוֹלְחָיו,
   מִפְּנֵי שֶׁשְּׁלוּחוֹ שֶׁלְאָדָם כְּמוֹתוֹ.

3. חַיָּב אָדָם לְבָרֵךְ עַל הָרָעָה כְּשֵׁם שֶׁהוּא מְבָרֵךְ עַל הַטּוֹבָה.

4. וְאֵלּוּ חַיָּב לְהַכְרִיז, מָצָא פֵרוֹת בַּכְּלִי אוֹ כְלִי כְּמוֹ שֶׁהוּא, מָעוֹת בַּכִּיס אוֹ כִּיס כְּמוֹ שֶׁהוּא ... הֲרֵי אֵלּוּ חַיָּב לְהַכְרִיז.

5. מִצְוַת הַנֶּהֱרָגִים, הָיוּ מַתִּיזִין אֶת רֹאשׁוֹ בַּסַּיִף, כְּדֶרֶךְ שֶׁהַמַּלְכוּת עוֹשָׂה.

6. וְהַשֵּׁנִי אוֹמֵר, אַף אֲנִי כָּמוֹהוּ, וְהַשְּׁלִישִׁי אוֹמֵר, אַף אֲנִי כָּמוֹהוּ.

7. כָּל הַכֵּלִים הַנִּמְצָאִין בִּירוּשָׁלַם דֶּרֶךְ יְרִידָה לְבֵית הַטְּבִילָה, טְמֵאִין, דֶּרֶךְ עֲלִיָּה, טְהוֹרִין, שֶׁלֹּא כְדַרֵךְ יְרִידָתָן עֲלִיָּתָן.

8. רַבִּי אֱלִיעֶזֶר אוֹמֵר, אֶת שֶׁנִּטְמָא בְאָב הַטֻּמְאָה, בֵּין בִּפְנִים בֵּין בַּחוּץ, יִשָּׂרֵף בַּחוּץ, וְאֶת שֶׁנִּמְצָא בּוֹלַד הַטֻּמְאָה, בֵּין בִּפְנִים בֵּין בַּחוּץ, יִשָּׂרֵף בִּפְנִים.

9. ומה אם מדת הפורענות מעוטה, העושה בסתר המקום מפרסמו בגלוי, מדה טובה מרובה על אחת כמה וכמה.

10. מכה בהמה ישלמנה ומכה אדם יומת [ויקרא כד׳ כא׳]. הקיש הכתוב נזקי אדם לנזקי בהמה ונזקי בהמה לנזקי אדם, ומה נזקי בהמה בתשלומין אף נזקי אדם בתשלומין.

11. עין תחת עין [ויקרא כא׳ כד׳], שומע אני בין מתכוין בין שאינו מתכוין אינו משלם אלא ממון.

12. ומה אם מי שהוא שומע מפי הקב״ה ומדבר ברוח הקודש צריך להתבונן בין פרשה לפרשה ובין ענין לענין, על אחת כמה וכמה הדיוט מן הדיוט.

13. ודין הוא, מה אם הראש שאין טעון תנופה טעון סמיכה, החזה שהוא טעון תנופה אינו דין שיטען סמיכה?

14. רבי אומר, נאמר כאן, בבואכם, ונאמר להלן, בבואם. מה בבואכם אל אהל מועד עשה את היציאה כביאה ואת המזבח כאהל מועד ואינו חיב אלא בשעת עבודה, אף בבואכם אל אהל מועד האמור כאן עשה יציאה כביאה ואת המזבח כאהל מועד ולא יהיה חיב אלא בשעת עבודה.

15. ת״ל, מזכר ועד נקבה תשלחו [במדבר ה׳ ג׳]. בכל אדם הכתוב מדבר אחד גדולים ואחד קטנים במשמע. אתה אומר, אחד גדולים ואחד קטנים במשמע, או אינו אלא כענין שענש? מה מצינו במטמא מקדש שלא ענש אלא גדולים ..., אף כאן לא נזהיר אלא גדולים.

16. ואף י׳ חרה בעם [במדבר יא׳ ג׳]. מלמד ששלח עליהם המקום מכה קשה שלא היה כיוצא בזו מיום שיצאו ממצרים.

17. אמר לה, השמיעי לי. אמרה לו, איני נשמעת אלא לגדול שבכם שהוא כיוצא במשה רבך.

18. ויקרא יעקב אל בניו ... [בראשית מט׳ א׳]. מאחר שהוכיחם כל אחד ואחד בפני עצמו, חזר וקראם כולם כאחד. אמר להם, שמא יש בלבבכם מחלוקת על מי שאמר והיה העולם? אמרו לו, שמע, ישראל אבינו, כשם שאין בלבך מחלוקת, כך אין בלבנו מחלוקת על מי שאמר והיה העולם.

19. וכתבתם [דברים ו׳ ט׳]. שומע אני על גבי אבנים. הרי אתה דן, נאמר כאן, כתב, ונאמר להלן, כתב [דברים כז׳ כח׳]. מה כתב האמור להלן על גבי אבנים, אף כתב האמור כאן על גבי אבנים.

20. ועשית עולותיך הבשר והדם [דברים יב׳ כז׳]. מקיש בשר לדם, מה דם בזריקה אף בשר בזריקה.

Sources. 1. Abot 2.1. 2. Ber 5.5. 3. Ber 9.5. 4. BM 2.2. 5. Sanh 7.3. 6. Sanh 7.5. 7. Sheq 8.2. 8. Sheq 8.7. 9. Mek 12.33 (L 1.103). 10. Mek 21.24 (L 3.67). 11. Mek 21.24 (L 3.68). 12. SLv 1.1 (W 3c). 13. SLv 3.2 (W 13c). 14. SLv 10.9 (W 46c). 15. SNm 1.6 (H 2–3). 16. SNm 98.3 (H 97). 17. SNm 131.2 (H 172). 18. SDt 31 (F 53). 19. SDt 36 (F 66). 20. SDt 78 (F 143).

UNIT TWENTY-SEVEN

TEMPORAL CLAUSES

I *Introductory text* (SNm 58.1 [H 56])

זה מדה בתורה, שני כתובים, זה כנגד זה והרי הם סותרים זה על ידי זה,
יתקיימו במקומם עד שיבוא כתוב אחר ויכריע ביניהם

This is the rule that prevails in the Torah: two texts that contradict one another are fulfilled in their respective places until another text appears that can
decide between them.

1. This is the thirteenth hermeneutical rule of Rabbi Ishmael. Other formulations are found in Baraita de R. Ishmael in Sifra W 3a–b, part of which
may be found in exercise text 13. In the SNm example above, the formal opposition between Lv 1.1 (Y. spoke from the tent of meeting) and Ex 25.22
(Y. spoke from the mercy seat) is resolved in the harmonizing text of Nm
7.89.

II *Morphology*

2. Among the most characteristic temporal conjunctions of BH are כִּי
followed by the imperfect, כַּאֲשֶׁר, טֶרֶם, and בְּטֶרֶם, as well as the compound
forms עַד בִּלְתִּי, עַד אִם, אַחֲרֵי אֲשֶׁר, עַד אֲשֶׁר, and so on.

In RH, בְּטֶרֶם, טֶרֶם, and עַד בִּלְתִּי have disappeared, כַּאֲשֶׁר, אֲשֶׁר and compounds with אֲשֶׁר have been replaced by -שֶׁ, -כְּשֶׁ, and compounds with -שֶׁ.

3. Nearly every RH temporal conjunction is compounded with -שֶׁ:

כְּשֶׁ-, -לִכְשֶׁ 'when';

מִשֶּׁ- 'after';

עַד שֶׁ- 'until, before, while';

עַד כְּדֵי שֶׁ- 'until, before, while';

מֵאַחַר שֶׁ-, לְאַחַר שֶׁ-, אַחַר שֶׁ- 'after';

לְקוֹדֶם שֶׁ-, -קוֹדֶם שֶׁ 'before';

אֵימָתַי שֶׁ- 'when, in the event that';

כֵּיוָן שֶׁ- 'as soon as, immediately after';

בִּזְמַן שֶׁ- 'when';

כָּל זְמַן שֶׁ- 'whenever, all the time that'

בְּשָׁעָה שֶׁ- 'when';

כָּל שָׁעָה שֶׁ- 'whenever, all the time that';

מִשָּׁעָה שֶׁ- 'from the time that, since'.

III *Grammar and usage*

4. As already indicated (see Unit 24.3–5), RH continued using simple juxtaposition of clauses, or parataxis, to convey a relationship of subordination, as at SNm 115.5 (H 127):

התחיל הבן ההוא מנתק, הוציא עליו שטר ואמר

When that son started to protest, he brought the document out to him and said.

5. Furthermore, a clause that is concomitant or simultaneous with the main clause may be elegantly expressed by means of a juxtaposed nominal clause (see Unit 24.10).

6. On the use of the perfect with temporal/conditional significance ('when, if, supposing that, in the event that'), see Unit 17.10–13. As stated there, this usage is not confined to juridical formulations but is also found in wisdom sayings such as נִכְנַס יַיִן, יָצָא סוֹד 'when wine goes in, secrets go out' (Erub 65a) and in narrative.

The participle may also convey temporal value (see Units 19.19 and 28.5).

7. Nonetheless, because of the loss of the consecutive tense forms, RH is less able to formulate temporal relationships simply through parataxis. Because of this, it tends to employ conjunctions and, indeed, to create new conjunctions with an ever more transparently temporal significance (in line with the language's development as a popular idiom), such as בִּזְמַן שֶׁ- 'at the time in which' or מִשָּׁעָה שֶׁ- 'from the moment at which'.

Below are examples of some temporal conjunctions, with brief remarks on their usage.

8. כְּשֶׁ- 'when, if'.

כְּשֶׁ- is used with the perfect as well as the imperfect. The use of לִכְשֶׁ- emphasizes the future or conditional character of the clause that follows (in the imperfect):

הֲרֵינִי נָזִיר לִכְשֶׁיִּהְיֶה לִי בֵן

I shall become a Nazirite when (or, 'only if') I have a son (Naz 2.7).
But one is left with the impression that as the language evolved -לִכְשֶׁ crept in
only as a secondary form in response to the gradual loss of expressive power
of the usual form -כְּשֶׁ: at Naz 2.7, just cited, K reads -כְּשֶׁ instead of -לִכְשֶׁ;
similarly, at Ket 12.1,

לֹא יֹאמַר הָרִאשׁוֹן, לִכְשֶׁתָּבֹא אֶצְלִי אֲזוֹנָה

The first one may not say, When she comes to me, I shall feed her,
K and P have כְּשֶׁתָּבֹא.

SNm 155.5 (H 127) provides an example of -כְּשֶׁ with both past and future:

כך כשפדאה הקב״ה את זרע אברהם אוהבו לא פדאם לשום בנים אלא
לשום עבדים, כשינזור ולא יהיו מקבלים עליהם יאמר להם, עבדיי
אתם

In the same way, when the holy one, blessed be he, freed the descendants of Abraham, his friend, he did not free them as friends but
as servants, so that when he ordered something they did not want, he
could say to them, You are my servants.

With a participle or introducing a nominal clause, -כְּשֶׁ can indicate simultaneity or simply a modality or circumstance:

איפשר שנתן משה את התורה כשהיא חסירה אפילו אות אחת?

Is it possible that Moses would have delivered the Torah with even
one letter missing? (SDt 357 [F 427])

9. -מִשֶּׁ 'after'.

A. -מִשֶּׁ is usually found with the imperfect in reference to a future action:

מוֹכֵר הוּא מִשֶּׁיִּקְצֹר

He can sell (produce) after it has been cut (AZ 1.8).

B. But -מִשֶּׁ is also commonly employed with the perfect, in the sense of
'since, once':

מִשֶּׁרַבּוּ הָרַצְחָנִין ... מִשֶּׁבָּא אֶלְעָזָר בֶּן דִּינַאי ... מִשֶּׁרַבּוּ הַמְנָאֲפִים ...
מִשֶּׁמֵּת יוֹסִי בֶּן יוֹעֶזֶר ...

Since murderers began to multiply ... from the time that Eleazar ben
Dinai came ... after adulterers began to multiply ... once Jose ben
Joezer had died ... (Soṭ 9.9)

C. -מִשֶּׁ is normally followed by the perfect in combination with עַד שֶׁלֹּא,
'before ... after':

שׁוֹר שֶׁנָּגַח אֶת הַפָּרָה וְנִמְצָא עֻבָּרָה בְּצִדָּהּ, וְאֵין יָדוּעַ אִם עַד שֶׁלֹּא נְגָחָהּ
יָלְדָה, אִם מִשֶּׁנְּגָחָהּ יָלְדָה

If an ox has gored a cow and her new-born calf is found beside her,
but it is not known whether she gave birth before it gored her or after it gored her (BQ 5.1);

עד שלא פשטו ידיהם בעבירה לא היה בהם זבים ומצורעים,
ומשפשטו ידיהם בעבירה היו בהם זבים ומצורעים

Before they stretched out their hands to sin, there was among them nobody affected by venereal or skin disease; after they stretched out their hands to sin … (SNm 1.10 [H 4]).

10. -עַד שֶׁ 'until'.

A. -עַד שֶׁ is found with the imperfect, which may also be rendered as a verbal noun:

עַד שֶׁיַּעֲלֶה עַמּוּד הַשַּׁחַר

Until dawn arises/Until the arrival of dawn (Ber 1.1).

-עַד שֶׁ always signifies one point of time in relation to another—in the following sequence from Yom 6.6, it refers to a moment in the past that follows another event, at which the narrator is situated, mentally:

בָּא וְיָשַׁב לוֹ תַּחַת סוּכָּה הָאַחֲרוֹנָה עַד שֶׁתֶּחְשַׁךְ

He came and seated himself under the last booth until it became dark.

But the same sequence of events may be expressed with a perfect if the narrator decides to remain outside the actions described:

שֶׁכָּל הַדּוֹרוֹת הָיוּ מַכְעִיסִין וּבָאִין עַד שֶׁהֵבִיא עֲלֵיהֶם אֶת מֵי הַמַּבּוּל

For all those generations were continually provoking him until he brought upon them the waters of the flood (Abot 5.2).

B. עַד שֶׁלֹּא 'until not' conveys the sense of 'before', and may be construed with a perfect or imperfect, or, in the Mishnah (for example, Kil 9.9), a participle:

אִם יְכוֹלִין לְהַתְחִיל וְלִגְמוֹר עַד שֶׁלֹּא יַגִּיעוּ לַשּׁוּרָה

If they can begin and end (the *shema'*) before reaching the row (Ber 3.2).

Occasionally, -עַד שֶׁ, without the negative particle, bears the same sense, as at Tam 1.4 (see also Ned 9.1 and Makhsh 1.3):

הִזָּהֵר, שֶׁמָּא תִּגַּע בַּכְּלִי עַד שֶׁתְּקַדֵּשׁ יָדֶיךָ וְרַגְלֶיךָ

Take care, in case you touch the vessel before purifying your hands and feet.

C. The temporal value of -עַד שֶׁ becomes modal in sentences where the conjunction is used in the extended sense of 'while, so long as, to the extent that', as at BM 7.2, where R. Jose bar Judah allows the labourers to eat from the field they are working in 'so long as they work with both their hands and their feet':

עַד שֶׁיַּעֲשֶׂה בְיָדָיו וּבְרַגְלָיו.

With the verb רָצָה, this usage is common, 'to the extent that they permit it, while it is permitted, only if permitted', for example, at Kel 1.7: עַד שֶׁיִּרְצוּ 'wherever they will'.

D. The same basic meaning is to be understood in those rabbinic comments on scriptural texts that begin with -עַד שֶׁ: the brief comment thus introduced is intended as a restatement of the biblical passage, with -עַד שֶׁ thus conveying the sense of 'that is to say', 'i.e.', etc:

רַבִּי יְהוּדָה אוֹמֵר, וְעָנְתָה וְאָמְרָה כָּכָה [דְּבָרִים כה׳ ט׳], עַד שֶׁתֹּאמַר בַּלָּשׁוֹן הַזֶּה

Rabbi Judah interprets, She will respond, saying thus [Dt 25.9], that
is to say, she is to respond in this language (BM 2.7).
(Cf. Bik 1.2; Naz 2.7; 3.5, etc.)

11. ‑שֶׁ כְּדֵי עַד.

This innovation of RH coincides in usage with ‑שֶׁ עַד: 'until' (BM 2.6;
4.3); 'to the extent that, while' (Ber 8.7; Meg 4.4). It always refers to a fixed
portion (כְּדֵי), of time—for the meaning and use of כְּדֵי, see Unit 30.8.

12. ‑שֶׁ קוֹדֶם, ‑שֶׁ אַחַר.

These conjunctions are infrequent in tannaitic RH, where one more usually finds the preposition ‑לְ קוֹדֶם or מֵאַחַר/לְאַחַר/אַחַר preceding a noun
(including a verbal noun), although there are exceptions, for example Soṭ 2.6:

לֹא עַל קוֹדֶם שֶׁתִּתְאָרֵס וְלֹא עַל מֵאַחַר שֶׁתִּתְגָּרֵשׁ

Neither concerning the time before becoming engaged nor concerning the time after divorcing.

However, such instances are probably secondary, as indicated by the reading
of K and P (cf. Giṭ 8.4):

קודם לשנתארסה ולא משנתגרשה.

Occasionally, one also encounters an apparently emphatic variant, such
as ‑שֶׁ לְאַחַר, for example, at Ter 5.4, שֶׁהוֹדוּ לְאַחַר 'after they accepted', or
Shab 11.6, מִיָּדוֹ שֶׁיָּצְתָה לְאַחַר 'after it left his hand'.
On the causal value of ‑שֶׁ מֵאַחַר, see Unit 29.12.

13. ‑שֶׁ כֵּיוָן 'as soon as, immediately after'.

This calque from the Aramaic ‑דְּ כֵּיוָן is so common that it eventually
loses its overtone of urgency and often simply means 'when':

כיון שנכנס למדינה אמר לו

As soon as he (the king) entered the city, he (the servant) said to him
(SNm 115.5 [H 127]).

14. ‑שֶׁ אֵימָתַי 'when, in the event that, whenever'.

This conjunction, too, has been developed under Aramaic influence:

אֵימָתַי שֶׁתַּעֲשׂוּ כָּכָה, הַדָּם מִתְכַּפֵּר לָכֶם

Whenever you do accordingly, you atone for yourselves concerning
blood (Soṭ 9.6).

15. Compounds with שָׁעָה and זְמָן: ‑שֶׁ בִּזְמַן, ‑שֶׁ זְמָן כָּל, ‑שֶׁ בְּשָׁעָה,
‑שֶׁ שָׁעָה כָּל, ‑שֶׁ מִשָּׁעָה.

A. The forms with כָּל have a distributive character and should be understood as 'whenever, at any time that':

כָּל זְמָן שֶׁהָיוּ יִשְׂרָאֵל מִסְתַּכְּלִים כְּלַפֵּי מַעְלָה

Whenever the Israelites looked above (RS 3.8).

When a conditional or modal usage is to be emphasized, these forms can
better be rendered as 'provided that, so long as':

רַבִּי יְהוּדָה מַתִּיר כָּל זְמָן שֶׁבִּכְּרוּ עַד שֶׁלֹּא יִכְלֶה הַקַּיִץ

Rabbi Judah declared (the fruits of the sabbatical year) permissible
provided that they were mature before summer (Shebi 9.4).

Sometimes, the forms with כָּל have a predominantly comparative sense, 'to the extent that, so long as', as in:

כָּל זְמַן שֶׁיֵּשׁ לוֹ תַּחְתָּיו, יֵשׁ לוֹ בְּרֹאשׁוֹ

To the extent that (or, 'provided that') what is below it belongs to
him, so too does what is on top of it (Pea 7.2);

זִקְנֵי עַם הָאָרֶץ כָּל זְמַן שֶׁמַּזְקִינִין, דַּעְתָּן מִטָּרֶפֶת עֲלֵיהֶן ... אֲבָל זִקְנֵי
הַתּוֹרָה אֵינָן כֵּן, אֶלָּא כָּל זְמַן שֶׁמַּזְקִינִין, דַּעְתָּן מִתְיַשֶּׁבֶת עֲלֵיהֶן

The older the ignorant aged become, the more they lose their wits,
but the older the elders (in the study) of the Torah become, the more
established in them is knowledge (Qin 3.6).

In LBH, expressions of this type are already found, for example
בְּכָל עֵת אֲשֶׁר:

וְכָל־זֶה אֵינֶנּוּ שֹׁוֶה לִי בְּכָל־עֵת אֲשֶׁר אֲנִי רֹאֶה אֶת־מָרְדֳּכַי הַיְּהוּדִי יוֹשֵׁב
בְּשַׁעַר הַמֶּלֶךְ

But all this means nothing to me as long as I see Mordecai the Jew
sitting in the king's gate (Est 5.13).

B. The semantic values of שָׁעָה 'hour' and זְמָן 'time' would appear to
give more expression to the temporal character of a conjunction, as, for example, at Sanh 6.5:

בְּשָׁעָה שֶׁאָדָם מִצְטַעֵר, שְׁכִינָה מָה הַלָּשׁוֹן אוֹמֶרֶת?

In the hour of a person's suffering, what words does the Shekhinah
say?

But often they are employed without conveying any special extra sense:

מָשׁוּחַ מִלְחָמָה בְּשָׁעָה שֶׁהוּא מְדַבֵּר אֶל הָעָם בִּלְשׁוֹן הַקֹּדֶשׁ הָיָה מְדַבֵּר

When the one anointed for battle spoke to the people, he would do it
in the holy tongue (Soṭ 8.1).

בִּזְמַן שֶׁ- is usually employed in response to the question אֵימָתַי, as at Dem
5.5:

אֵימָתַי? בִּזְמַן שֶׁמַּתָּנָה מְרוּבָּה

When? When the donation has been large.

Further removed from the temporal sphere, בִּזְמַן שֶׁ- is frequently employed in an extended sense of 'so long as, to the extent that':

שֶׁתִּגְלַחַת הַנֶּגַע דּוֹחָה תִּגְלַחַת הַנָּזִיר בִּזְמַן שֶׁהִיא וַדַּאי

For shaving because of leprosy abrogates shaving because of a
Nazirite vow so long as (or, 'provided that') it is certain (Naz 8.2).

IV *Phraseology*

16. עַד שֶׁלֹּא יֹאמַר יֵשׁ לִי בַּדִּין 'before it (Scripture) says, I obtain through
deduction', in other words 'without Scripture needing to have said it, I could
have deduced the same thing through logical argument': the underlying claim
is that the biblical text is superfluous. Midrashic writers will sometimes justify such an apparently superfluous biblical text on the grounds that its presence avoids the need to impose a penalty merely on the basis of logical argument. Among numerous examples, see SNm 23.6 (H 28).

V *Vocabulary*

גָּדַשׁ 'heap up, make a sheaf';

גִּידוּל 'growth, that which grows, produce'

דַּד 'breast, teat, udder'

זָמַם 'plot evil, bear false witness, incite false witness'

יָגַע 'suffer'; htp. 'tire oneself out'

מָלַל 'stitch'

מַלְקוּת 'flagellation, punishment of stripes'

מְשִׁיחָה 'cord'

קַנְקַן 'jug'

רָשַׁל 'be weak'

שָׁבַח 'improve, increase in value' (as also in hi.), pi. 'praise'

VI *Exercises*

1. מֵאֵיזֶה טַעַם אֵינוֹ מֵבִיא? מִשּׁוּם שֶׁנֶּאֱמַר, רֵאשִׁית בִּכּוּרֵי אַדְמָתְךָ [שמות
כג' יט'], עַד שֶׁיִּהְיוּ כָל הַגִּדוּלִין מֵאַדְמָתְךָ.

2. הָיָה עוֹשֶׂה בְיָדָיו אֲבָל לֹא בְרַגְלָיו, בְּרַגְלָיו אֲבָל לֹא בְיָדָיו, אֲפִלּוּ בִכְתֵפוֹ,
הֲרֵי זֶה אוֹכֵל. רַבִּי יוֹסֵי בַּר יְהוּדָה אוֹמֵר, עַד שֶׁיַּעֲשֶׂה בְיָדָיו וּבְרַגְלָיו.

3. עִיסַּת הַכְּלָבִים, בִּזְמַן שֶׁהָרוֹעִים אוֹכְלִין מִמֶּנָּה, חַיֶּבֶת בַּחַלָּה.

4. רַבִּי יוֹסֵי אוֹמֵר, מְשִׁיחוֹת שֶׁלָּאַרְגָּמָן אֲסוּרוֹת, מִפְּנֵי שֶׁהוּא מוֹלֵל עַד שֶׁלֹּא קוֹשֵׁר.

5. מְעִידִין אָנוּ בְּאִישׁ פְּלוֹנִי, שֶׁהוּא חַיָּב מַלְקוּת אַרְבָּעִים, וְנִמְצְאוּ זוֹמְמִים,
לוֹקִים שְׁמוֹנִים.

6. אַנְשֵׁי יְרִיחוֹ קוֹצְרִין בִּרְצוֹן חֲכָמִים, וְגוֹדְשִׁין שֶׁלֹּא בִרְצוֹן חֲכָמִים ... קוֹצֵר
לַשַּׁחַת, וּמַאֲכִיל לַבְּהֵמָה. אָמַר רַבִּי יְהוּדָה, אֵימָתַי? בִּזְמַן שֶׁהִתְחִיל עַד שֶׁלֹּא
הֵבִיאָה שְׁלִישׁ. רַבִּי שִׁמְעוֹן אוֹמֵר, אַף יִקְצֹר וְיַאֲכִיל אַף מִשֶּׁהֵבִיאָה שְׁלִישׁ.

7. מִי שֶׁנָּזַר וְהוּא בְּבֵית הַקְּבָרוֹת, אֲפִלּוּ הָיָה שָׁם שְׁלֹשִׁים יוֹם, אֵין עוֹלִין לוֹ
מִן הַמִּנְיָן, וְאֵינוֹ מֵבִיא קָרְבַּן טֻמְאָה. יָצָא וְנִכְנַס, עוֹלִין לוֹ מִן הַמִּנְיָן,
וּמֵבִיא קָרְבַּן טֻמְאָה. רַבִּי אֱלִיעֶזֶר אוֹמֵר, לֹא בוֹ בַיּוֹם, שֶׁנֶּאֱמַר, וְהַיָּמִים
הָרִאשֹׁנִים יִפְּלוּ [במדבר ו' יב'], עַד שֶׁיִּהְיוּ לוֹ יָמִים רִאשׁוֹנִים.

8. רַבִּי אֱלִיעֶזֶר אוֹמֵר, פּוֹתְחִין לָאָדָם בִּכְבוֹד אָבִיו וְאִמּוֹ, וַחֲכָמִים אוֹסְרִין. אָמַר
רַבִּי צָדוֹק, עַד שֶׁפּוֹתְחִין לוֹ בִּכְבוֹד אָבִיו וְאִמּוֹ, יִפְתְּחוּ לוֹ בִּכְבוֹד הַמָּקוֹם.

9. עֲשֵׂה לְךָ שָׂרָף וְשִׂים אֹתוֹ עַל נֵס, וְהָיָה כָל הַנָּשׁוּךְ וְרָאָה אֹתוֹ וָחָי, [במדבר
כא' ח']. וְכִי נָחָשׁ מֵמִית, אוֹ נָחָשׁ מְחַיֶּה? אֶלָּא בִזְמַן שֶׁיִּשְׂרָאֵל מִסְתַּכְּלִין
כְּלַפֵּי מַעְלָה וּמְשַׁעְבְּדִין אֶת לִבָּם לַאֲבִיהֶם שֶׁבַּשָּׁמַיִם, הָיוּ מִתְרַפְּאִים.

10. וְעַד שֶׁלֹּא נִבְחֲרָה אֶרֶץ יִשְׂרָאֵל, הָיוּ הָאֲרָצוֹת כְּשֵׁרוֹת לַדִּבְּרוֹת. מִשֶּׁנִּבְחֲרָה
אֶרֶץ יִשְׂרָאֵל, יָצְאוּ כָל הָאֲרָצוֹת. עַד שֶׁלֹּא נִבְחֲרָה יְרוּשָׁלַיִם, הָיְתָה כָל אֶרֶץ
יִשְׂרָאֵל כְּשֵׁרָה לַמִּזְבְּחוֹת. מִשֶּׁנִּבְחֲרָה יְרוּשָׁלַיִם, יָצְאָה כָל אֶרֶץ יִשְׂרָאֵל ... עַד
שֶׁלֹּא נִבְחַר בֵּית עוֹלָמִים, הָיְתָה כָל יְרוּשָׁלַיִם רְאוּיָה לַשְּׁכִינָה. מִשֶּׁנִּבְחַר בֵּית
עוֹלָמִים, יָצְאָה כָל יְרוּשָׁלַיִם ... עַד שֶׁלֹּא נִבְחַר אַהֲרֹן, הָיוּ כָל יִשְׂרָאֵל רְאוּיִים
לַכְּהוּנָה. מִשֶּׁנִּבְחַר אַהֲרֹן, יָצְאוּ כָל יִשְׂרָאֵל ... עַד שֶׁלֹּא נִבְחַר דָּוִד, הָיוּ כָל
יִשְׂרָאֵל רְאוּיִים לַמַּלְכוּת. מִשֶּׁנִּבְחַר דָּוִד, יָצְאוּ כָל יִשְׂרָאֵל.

11. וּמַה תַּ"ל, דַּבְּרוּ [שמות יב' ג']? אֶלָּא כֵּיוָן שֶׁהָיָה מֹשֶׁה מְדַבֵּר הָיָה אַהֲרֹן
מֵימִינוֹ וְאֶלְעָזָר מִשְּׂמֹאלוֹ וְאִיתָמָר מִימִינוֹ שֶׁל אַהֲרֹן, וְהָיָה הַדִּבּוּר יוֹצֵא

מביניהם כאילו שניהם מדברים.

12. וי׳ נתן את חן העם וגו׳ [שמות יב׳ לו], כמשמעו, לא הספיק לומר לו
השאילני, עד שהוא מוציא ונותן לו.

13. כתוב אחד אומר, ובבא משה אל אהל מועד לדבר אתו [במדבר ז׳ פט],
וכתוב אחד אומר, ולא יכול משה לבא אל אהל מועד [שמות מ׳ לה].
הכריע, כי שכן עליו הענן [שמות מ׳ לה]. אמור מעתה, כל זמן שהיה
הענן שם, לא היה משה נכנס לשם. נסתלק הענן, היה נכנס ומדבר עמו.

14. משלו משל. למה הדבר דומה? לבני אדם שיוצאים למלחמה, בשעה שהם
יוצאים הם שמחים וכל זמן שהם מתייגעים ידיהם מתרשלות. אבל
ישראל אינו כן, אלא כל זמן שהם מתייגעים הם שמחים ואומרים, נלך
ונירש את ארץ ישראל.

15. מה הדד הזה תינוק מצטער בשעה שפורש ממנו, כך היו ישראל
מצטערים בשעה שפירשו מן המן.

16. ויאמר י׳ אל משה, עלה אל הר העברים הזה, הר נבו [במדבר כז׳
יב׳, דברים לב׳ מט]. זו נחלת בני ראובן ובני גד. בשעה שנכנס משה
לנחלת בני ראובן ובני גד, שמח ואמר, דומה אני שהתיר לי נדרי,
התחיל שופך תחנונים לפני המקום. משל, למה הדבר דומה? למלך בשר
ודם שגזר על בנו שלא יכנס לפתח פלטרין שלו, נכנס לשער והוא
אחריו, לחצר והוא אחריו, לטרקלין והוא אחריו. כיון שבא ליכנס
לקיטון אמר לו, בני, מיכן ואילך אתה אסור. כך בשעה שנכנס משה
לנחלת בני גד ובני ראובן שמח ואמר, דומה אני שהתיר לי נדרי.
התחיל שופך תחנונים לפני המקום ...

17. מה צבי זה קל ברגליו מכל בהמהוחיה, כך פירות ארץ ישראל קלים
לבוא מכל פירות ארצות. דבר אחר, מה צבי זה כשאתה מפשיטו אין
עורו מחזיק את בשרו, כך ארץ ישראל אין מחזקת פירותיה בשעה
שישראל עושים את התורה.

18. מה יין משמח את הלב, כך דברי תורה משמחים את הלב ... מה יין אי
אתה טועם בו טעם מתחלתו וכל זמן שמתישן בקנקן סופו להשביח, כך
דברי תורה כל זמן שמתישנים בגוף סופו להשביח.

19. למען ישוב י׳ מחרון אפו [דברים יג׳ יח]. כל זמן שעבודה זרה
בעולם, חרון אף בעולם. נסתלקה עבודה זרה מן העולם, נסתלק חרון
אף מן העולם. ונתן לך רחמים ורחמך [דברים יג׳ יח], לך רחמים ולא
לאחרים רחמים. מיכן היה רבן גמליאל ברבי אומר, כל זמן שאתה
מרחם על הבריות, מרחמים עליך מן השמים, אין אתה מרחם על
הבריות, אין מרחמים עליך מן השמים.

20. זכור ימות עולם [דברים לב׳ ז]. אמר להם, כל זמן שהקדוש ברוך הוא
מביא עליהם יסורים, הזכרו כמה טובות ונחמות עתיד ליתן להם לעולם הבא.

Sources. 1. Bik 1.2. 2. BM 7.3. 3. Ḥal 1.8. 4. Kil 9.9. 5. Mak 1.3. 6. Men
10.9. 7. Naz 3.5. 8. Ned 9.1. 9. RS 3.8. 10. Mek 12.1 (L 1.4–5). 11. Mek
12.3 (L 1.23). 12. Mek 12.36 (L 1.105). 13. Sifra, Baraita de R. Ishmael (W
3b). 14. SNm 82.1 (H 77–78). 15. SNm 89.4 (H 89). 16. SNm 134.5 (H
179–80). 17. SDt 37 (F 72–73). 18. SDt 48 (F 111). 19. SDt 96 (F 157).
20. SDt 310 (F 351).

UNIT TWENTY-EIGHT

CONDITIONAL CLAUSES

I *Introductory text* (Ned 3.11)

גְּדוֹלָה מִילָה, שֶׁאִילְמָלֵא הִיא לֹא בָרָא הַקָּדוֹשׁ בָּרוּךְ הוּא אֶת עוֹלָמוֹ,
שֶׁנֶּאֱמַר ,כֹּה אָמַר ײ אִם־לֹא בְרִיתִי יוֹמָם וָלַיְלָה חֻקּוֹת שָׁמַיִם וָאָרֶץ לֹא־שָׂמְתִּי
[ירמיה לג׳ כה׳].

Great is circumcision, for except for it the holy one, blessed be he, would not
have created the world, as it is said, Thus says Y., If my covenant did not exist day and night, I should not have ordained the laws of heaven and earth [Jr
33.25].

1. Circumcision is the outward sign of the pact or covenant of God with
his people (Gn 17), a covenant as eternal as day and night and the reason why
the world was created.

II *Morphology*

2. Particles that generally express possible, or 'real', conditions in BH,
are כִּי, אִם, הִנֵּה, and הֵן, all of which may be rendered as 'if', 'in the case that',
'on the assumption that', etc., and in origin have a deictic force.
For impossible, or 'irreal', conditions, BH employs לוּ 'if', לוּלֵי 'if not',
and אִלּוּ (only twice, in LBH: Ec 6.6; Est 7.4).
3. In RH, the use of אִם is widely maintained, although the old forms לוּ
and לוּלֵי are replaced by the compounded structures אִילָה/אִלּוּ (אִם and לוּ),
אִלּוּלֵי/אִלּוּלֵא (לֹא and אִלּוּ), and אִלְמָלֵי/אִלְמָלֵא/אִלְמָלֵא (אִלּוּ and אִם and לֹא).
Comparative force is conveyed by כְּאִלּוּ (-כְּ and אִלּוּ) 'as if' and concessive by אַף (אִלּוּ and אַף) אֲפִילָה/אֲפִלּוּ 'even if', corresponding, respectively, to the
BH forms כְּאִם and גַּם כִּי.
The restrictive particle וּבִלְבַד שֶׁ- 'only when, on condition that' (see Unit
32.7) may also be regarded as having, in effect, conditional value.

III *Grammar and usage*

4. A condition does not have to be formulated by means of a conditional
particle as such.

A. The perfect and participle may be employed without any conjunction to express a supposition or condition (protasis) in legal and sapiential texts (see Units 17.10–11 and 19.19).

B. -שֶׁ רְצוֹנְךָ and רְצוֹנְךָ לְ- are elliptical formulas for expressing 'if you would like':

רצונך שאשמע לך, השתחוה לזה

If you would like me to please you, you will have to prostrate yourself before this (SNm 131.1 [H 171]);

רצונך להכיר את מי שאמר והיה העולם, למוד הגדה

If you would like to know the-one-that-spoke-and-the-world-was, study *haggadah* (SDt 49 [F 115]).

5. The two-member halakhic conditional statement.

This halakhic structure never introduces the supposition or condition with אִם or another conditional particle but with the perfect, participle, or a relative clause of the kind מִי שֶׁאָמַר, אִישׁ שֶׁהָלְכָה, or אִשָּׁה שֶׁהָלְכָה. The apodosis may be a declarative statement (sometimes introduced by הֲרֵי) or a command (generally formulated by means of a participle with jussive or facultative value; see Unit 19.18). The examples that follow are all taken from the Mishah tractate Nazir:

הָאוֹמֵר, אֱהֵא, הֲרֵי זֶה נָזִיר

If someone says, I will be a Nazirite, that person is a Nazirite (Naz 1.1);

נִזְרַק עָלֶיהָ אֶחָד מִן הַדָּמִים, אֵינוֹ יָכוֹל לְהָפֵר

If the blood of one of the sacrifices has been spilt for her, he (the husband) may not annul the vow (Naz 4.5);

מִי שֶׁאָמַר, הֲרֵינִי נָזִיר, מְגַלֵּחַ יוֹם שְׁלֹשִׁים וְאֶחָד

If someone says, I am a Nazirite, that person may cut their hair on (i.e. 'from') the thirty-first day (Naz 3.1).

Although the participle is more usual, the imperative formula in the apodosis may also be expressed by the imperfect. In the protasis, the supposition or condition is not expressed with אִם except when specifying particular cases. Analogously, in the biblical laws, a principal condition is formulated with כִּי while particular cases are introduced by אִם, as at Ex 21.2–3 (see Meyer 1992, §122.3E). The following is a clear example of the phenomenon in RH:

הָאִשָּׁה שֶׁנָּדְרָה בַנָּזִיר וְהִפְרִישָׁה אֶת בְּהֶמְתָּהּ וְאַחַר כָּךְ הֵפֵר לָהּ בַּעֲלָהּ,
אִם שֶׁלּוֹ הָיְתָה בְהֶמְתָּהּ, תֵּצֵא וְתִרְעֶה בָעֵדֶר, וְאִם שֶׁלָּהּ הָיְתָה בְהֶמְתָּהּ,
הַחַטָּאת תָּמוּת

If a woman has taken a Nazirite vow and already set aside the sacrificial beast but afterwards her husband annuls the vow, in the case that (אִם) the beast belongs to him, he is to let it loose to graze with the flock, but in the case that (אִם) the beast belongs to her, it is to die as a sin offering (תָּמוּת) (Naz 4.4).

הוֹאִיל וְ- 'given that, considering that', introduces suppositions or conditions, particularly in rabbinic arguments, where considerations thus expressed correspond to fulfilled real conditions (see Unit 29.14–15).

6. In narrative style, a supposition or condition may also be introduced by the formula -שֶׁ הֲרֵי, equivalent to BH הִנֵּה. It may best be rendered as 'let us suppose that':

הרי שיצאו עמו עשרה בנים ממצרים ובכניסתן לארץ נמצאו חמשה

Let us suppose that one left Egypt with ten children but on entering the land (of Israel) there were only five (SNm 132.2 [H 175]).

7. Uses of אִם.

A. אִם is employed in possible, real, conditions relating to the past or the future. The protasis uses the perfect when the condition is regarded as fulfilled and the participle or, less often, imperfect when the condition is regarded as possible, or real, in the future. Often, the apodosis is introduced with הֲרֵי.

An example with the perfect is

חָתָן פָּטוּר מִקְּרִיאַת שְׁמַע בְּלַיְלָה הָרִאשׁוֹן עַד מוֹצָאֵי שַׁבָּת,
אִם לֹא עָשָׂה מַעֲשֶׂה

The husband is exempted from reciting the *shema'* on the first night (of his being married) until the end of the sabbath if he has not consummated the marriage (Ber 2.5).

אִם with the perfect is also used for indicating the future perfect (or *futurum exactum*) when a condition that might be fulfilled in the future is represented as having already been fulfilled:

אִם אֵחַרְתִּי, צְאוּ וְשַׁחֲטוּ עָלַי

If I am delayed, go out and sacrifice on my behalf (Pes 9.9).

This construction is usual at Qumran (see Qimron 1986, 84–85) as against BH usage: אִם יִקְטֹל.

אִם with the participle is exemplified by

אִם אוכלת בתרומה, לא תאכל במעשר?

If she may eat of the *terumah*, may she not eat of the tithe? (SNm 122.2 [H 150])

In some contexts, אִם has the concessive force of אֲפִלּוּ or -אַף עַל פִּי שֶׁ, as in the late Abot 6.9,

אִם אַתָּה נוֹתֵן לִי כָּל כֶּסֶף וְזָהָב

Though you were to give me all the silver and gold,

but it is more usual to express concessive meaning through the imperfect:

אִם יִהְיוּ כָּל חַכְמֵי יִשְׂרָאֵל בְּכַף מֹאזְנַיִם

Even if all the sages of Israel were on one balance of a pair of scales (Abot 2.8).

(See Unit 31.13.)

In the imperfect, the verb רָצָה 'desire' is commonly used with אִם:

אִם יִרְצֶה הָעֶלְיוֹן לִקַּח אֶת עֲפָרוֹ, אֵין כָּאן יָרָק

If (i.e. 'whenever') the one above wished to collect his earth, there would be no grass (BM 10.6);

אֵין מוֹכְרִין בֵּית הַכְּנֶסֶת, אֶלָּא עַל תְּנַאי שֶׁאִם יִרְצוּ יַחֲזִירוּהוּ

A synagogue may not be sold except on condition that it can be re-
covered when this is desired (Meg 3.2; but K and MS Parma read
אֵמָתַי יִרְצוּ).

Normally, though, future real conditions employ such temporal conjunctions
as -שֶׁ, כְּשֶׁ-, בִּזְמַן שֶׁ, לִכְשֶׁ-, and -עַד שֶׁ (see Unit 27).

B. אִם followed by הָיָה and participle expresses a hypothetical condition
prior to a past event (pluperfect):

אם משה לא היה יודע, אהרן היה יודע?

If Moses had not known, could Aaron have known? (SNm 68.2 [H
63])

C. An alternative negative condition, 'and if not', employs וְאִם לָאו,
without the verb needing to be repeated (see Segal 1927, §489):

אם עובר לפניהם, עוברים, ואם לאו, אינם עוברים

If he passes before them, they will pass, but if not, they will not pass
(SDt 29 [F 48]).

D. אִם is also used in indirect questions (see Unit 25.9), with the particle
repeated for disjunctive questions:

הודיעני אם אתה מרפא אותה ואם לאו

Let me know if you are going to heal her or not (SDt 26 [F 41]).

E. A characteristic usage is represented by oath formulas introduced by
אִם for negative vows (I swear that I shall not) or אִם לֹא for positive vows (I
swear that I shall). These formulas imply an apodosis containing a curse or
imprecation, such that an affirmative condition is to be understood as representing a negative oath and vice-versa, a usage derived from the Bible (see
2 S 11.11; Jr 22.6, etc.). Such conditional oath formulas may also employ an
interjection like קוֹנָם, although usually קוֹנָם introduces an oath with -שֶׁ:

קוֹנָם אִם לֹא רָאִיתִי בַּדֶּרֶךְ הַזֶּה כְּיוֹצְאֵי מִצְרַיִם, אִם לֹא רָאִיתִי
נָחָשׁ כְּקוֹרַת בֵּית הַבַּד

I swear it! Along this road I have seen as many people as in the exodus from Egypt! I have seen a serpent like the beam of an olive-
press! (Ned 3.2).

(For other interjections and oath formulas, see Units 3.4 and 8.7B.)

Often, commands are expressed more forcefully as oaths introduced by
אִם:

מַשְׁבִּיעַ אֲנִי עֲלֵיכֶם אִם לֹא תָבוֹאוּ וּתְעִידוּנִי

I adjure you to come and testify for me without fail (Shebu 4.5).

This usage represents an evolution of the oath formula, which developed
from (1) the expression of a vow that included a condition as part of a curse
to (2) the statement of the condition alone, with the imprecation understood,
and from there to (3) the use of the condition not as a vow but as a command.

F. אִם, or מָה אִם or וּמָה אִם, is also found in qal wa-ḥomer arguments (see
Unit 26.8C).

8. Uses of אִלְמָלֵא, אִלּוּלֵי, (כְּאִלּוּ, אֲפִילוּ/אֲפִלּוּ) אִילוּ/אִלּוּ, and.

All these conjunctions are used to express an irreal condition or one that is impossible to fulfil.

A. אִלּוּ is by far the most widely used, always followed by the perfect:

רַבִּי טַרְפוֹן וְרַבִּי עֲקִיבָא אוֹמְרִים, אִלּוּ הָיִינוּ בְּסַנְהֶדְרִין,
לֹא נֶהֱרַג אָדָם מֵעוֹלָם

Rabbi Ṭarfon and Rabbi Akiba used to say, If we had been in the Sanhedrin, no-one would ever have been executed (Mak 1.10).

B. The compound conjunction אֲפִילוּ/אֲפִלּוּ (אַף and אִלּוּ) has concessive value, 'including, even if, although' (see Unit 31.3), and corresponds to the BH construction כִּי גַּם:

אֲפִלּוּ הַמֶּלֶךְ שׁוֹאֵל בִּשְׁלוֹמוֹ, לֹא יְשִׁיבֶנּוּ, וַאֲפִלּוּ נָחָשׁ כָּרוּךְ עַל עֲקֵבוֹ
לֹא יַפְסִיק

Even if the king greets someone (during prayer), they are not to re-spond, even if a snake is coiled around their feet, they are not to in-terrupt (their prayer) (Ber 5.1).

C. כְּאִלּוּ, compounded of -כְּ and אִלּוּ has lost any irreal conditional value, expressing instead a comparison of equality:

מגיד הכתוב שכל מי ששונא את ישראל כאלו שונא את מי
שאמר והיה העולם

This passage teaches that anyone who hates Israel is as though they hate the-one-that-spoke-and-the-world-was (SNm 84.4 [H 81]).

D. Like אִלּוּלֵי, אִלְמָלֵא has negative force, 'if not', and is frequent in nominal clauses of the type 'if it were not for such-and-such', 'if not', 'had it not been':

אִלְמָלֵא חוֹנִי אַתָּה, גּוֹזְרַנִי עָלֶיךָ נִדּוּי

If you were not Ḥoni, I would decree your excommunication (Taa 3.8);

צָרִיךְ הָיָה הַדָּבָר לְאָמְרוֹ, שֶׁאִלְמָלֵא כֵן יֵשׁ בְּמַשְׁמַע שֶׁאֲפִלּוּ
בְּאֶרֶץ כְּנַעַן לֹא יִנְחָלוּ

It was necessary to say it, for if not, the meaning would have been that they would not even have inherited the land of Canaan (Qid 3.4);

אילמלא אני

Had it not been for me (SDt 346);

אילמלא שבטים

If it had not been for the tribes (SDt 347).

E. אִלּוּלֵי usually begins a clause with -שֶׁ, as at Mek 22.19 (L 3.146):

אחרים אומרים, אלולי ששתפו ישראל שמו של הקדוש ברוך הוא
בעבודה זרה, כלים היו מן העולם

Others said, If the Israelites had not mixed the name of the holy one, blessed be he, with the idols, they would have been extirpated from the world.

On occasions, the negative לֹא is added pleonastically, as at SLv 10.19 (W 47c):

אִילוּלֵי לֹא אֵילוּ בִלְבַד קברתי אלא אפילו אלה קברתי עם אֵילוּ,
לֹא כך הייתי מבזה קוֹדְשֵׁי המקדש

Even if these had not been the only ones I buried but (even if) I had
buried these with others, I would never have treated the holiness of
the sanctuary with disdain.

A usage very similar to that of אִלְמָלֵא can be seen at SLv 26.46 (W
112c):

וְאִילוּלֵי ספר תורה שנשתייר להם, לא היו משנים מאומות העולם כלום

If it had not been for the book of the Torah, which was left for them,
they would not have differed from other peoples in any way.

IV *Phraseology*

9. אִם לָמַדְתָּ 'if you learned', אִם לָמַדְתִּי 'if I learned' are used in rabbinic
arguments to introduce an obvious and universally-accepted fact, which
serves as the basis for the argument. Both formulas should be regarded as expressing a fulfilled or verified condition, 'seeing that you know, having
learnt, considering that', which is followed by a conclusion starting with אַף
or כָּךְ. The thing that has been learnt or is being considered is almost invariably introduced by -שֶׁ ... -לְ or, on a few occasions, by -שֶׁ ... עַל:

אם למדת לישראל שמביאים על שגגת ע״ז, אף הגוים מביאים
על שגגת ע״ז

> Considering that the Israelites have to make an offering for inadver-
> tant sins of idolatry, it is also the case that the gentiles have to make
> an offering for inadvertant sins of idolatry (SNm 123.11 [H 119]).

The conclusion of an אִם לָמַדְתִּי argument begins with אַף or, infre-
quently, כָּךְ; the structure as a whole constituting, in fact, a formula of comparison (see Unit 26.8).

10. אִלְמָלֵא מִקְרָא כָּתוּב 'if it is not a written text' is found at Mek 12.41
(L 1.114); at SNm 84.4 (H 82) and 106.2 (H 105), we find the variant
אִלְמָלֵא מִקְרָא שֶׁכָּתוּב. In each instance, the formula indicates that it would
have been impossible to have accepted an anthropomorphism had it not actually occurred in the biblical text. An example relates to the statement that
God buried Moses with his own hands:

מי לנו גדול ממשה שלא נתעסק בו אלא הקב״ה, שנאמר, ויקבור
אותו בגיא בארץ נבו [דברים לד׳ ו׳]? ר׳ יהודה אומר, אלמלא
מקרא שכתוב, אי אפשר לאמרו

> Whom can we find greater than Moses, for whose sepulchre none
> but the holy one, blessed be he, was responsible, as it is said, And he
> buried him in the valley, in the land of Nebo [Dt 34.6]? R. Judah
> remarked, Were it not for this passage, it would have been impossi-
> ble to say it (SNm 106.2 [H 105]).

V *Vocabulary*

אַסְפַּסְיָנוֹס 'Vespasian'

וְסַח 'conduct'

חָזַק 'be strong', -לְ הַחֲזִיק טוֹבָה לְ 'attribute merit to, praise, show gratitude to'

יָוָן 'Greece'

כִּכָּר וּמַקֵּל 'bread and stick', i.e. 'carrot and stick, 'reward and punishment'

כָּרַךְ 'surround, wrap'

לדיקיא 'Laodicea'

לָוָה 'unite, connect', pi. 'accompany, escort'

עִינּוּי 'harm', עִנּוּי נֶפֶשׁ 'mortification'

פְּדִיָּה 'rescue, redemption, liberation'

פֶּרֶק 'period, chapter', לִפְרָקִים 'periodically'

קָשַׁט 'walk in a straight line', htp. 'adorn oneself, dress up'

VI *Exercises*

1. רַבִּי חֲנַנְיָה סְגַן הַכֹּהֲנִים אוֹמֵר, הֱוֵי מִתְפַּלֵּל בִּשְׁלוֹמָהּ שֶׁל מַלְכוּת, שֶׁאִלְמָלֵא מוֹרָאָהּ אִישׁ אֶת רֵעֵהוּ חַיִּים בָּלָעוֹ.

2. רַבִּי אֶלְעָזָר בֶּן עֲזַרְיָה אוֹמֵר, אִם אֵין תּוֹרָה אֵין דֶּרֶךְ אֶרֶץ, אִם אֵין דֶּרֶךְ אֶרֶץ אֵין תּוֹרָה. אִם אֵין חָכְמָה אֵין יִרְאָה, אִם אֵין יִרְאָה אֵין חָכְמָה. אִם אֵין בִּינָה אֵין דַּעַת, אִם אֵין דַּעַת, אֵין בִּינָה. אִם אֵין קֶמַח אֵין תּוֹרָה, אִם אֵין תּוֹרָה אֵין קֶמַח.

3. רַבִּי אֱלִיעֶזֶר בֶּן יַעֲקֹב אוֹמֵר, אִשָּׁה בַת גֵּרִים לֹא תִנָּשֵׂא לַכְּהֻנָּה, עַד שֶׁתְּהֵא אִמָּהּ מִיִּשְׂרָאֵל, אֶחָד גֵּרִים וְאֶחָד עֲבָדִים מְשֻׁחְרָרִים, וַאֲפִלּוּ עַד עֲשָׂרָה דוֹרוֹת, עַד שֶׁתְּהֵא אִמָּן מִיִּשְׂרָאֵל.

4. הֲרֵי שֶׁהֵבִיא מִמִּין אֶחָד וְקָרָא, וְחָזַר וְהֵבִיא מִמִּין אַחֵר, אֵינוֹ קוֹרֵא.

5. הָאוֹמֵר לִבְנוֹ, קוֹנָם אִי אַתָּה נֶהֱנֶה מִשֶּׁלִּי, אִם מֵת, יִירָשֶׁנּוּ.

6. רַבִּי יוֹסֵי אוֹמֵר, אִם מָתְּרִין לְאוֹתָהּ שַׁבָּת, מָתְּרִין לֶעָתִיד לָבוֹא, וְאִם אֲסוּרִין לֶעָתִיד לָבוֹא, אֲסוּרִין לְאוֹתָהּ שַׁבָּת.

7. הַמָּעוֹן הַזֶּה, אִלּוּ הָיוּ מַנִּיחִים לִי, הָיִיתִי מֵבִיא.

8. פּוֹתְחִים לְאָדָם בִּכְבוֹד עַצְמוֹ וּבִכְבוֹד בָּנָיו. אוֹמְרִים לוֹ, אִלּוּ הָיִיתָ יוֹדֵעַ, שֶׁלְּמָחָר אוֹמְרִין עָלֶיךָ, כָּךְ הִיא וְסִתּוֹ שֶׁלִּפְלוֹנִי, מְגָרֵשׁ אֶת נָשָׁיו, וְעַל בְּנוֹתֶיךָ אוֹמְרִין, בְּנוֹת גְּרוּשׁוֹת הֵן, מָה רָאִיתָ אִמָּן שֶׁלְּאֵלּוּ לְהִתְגָּרֵשׁ? וְאָמַר, אִלּוּ הָיִיתִי יוֹדֵעַ שֶׁכֵּן, לֹא הָיִיתִי נוֹדֵר, הֲרֵי זֶה מֻתָּר.

9. וְאֵלּוּ נְדָרִים שֶׁהוּא מֵפֵר, דְּבָרִים שֶׁיֵּשׁ בָּהֶם עִנּוּי נֶפֶשׁ, אִם אֶרְחַץ וְאִם לֹא אֶרְחַץ, אִם אֶתְקַשֵּׁט וְאִם לֹא אֶתְקַשֵּׁט. אָמַר רַבִּי יוֹסֵי, אֵין אֵלּוּ נִדְרֵי עִנּוּי נֶפֶשׁ.

10. אִם הָיָה חָכָם, דּוֹרֵשׁ, וְאִם לָאו, תַּלְמִידֵי חֲכָמִים דּוֹרְשִׁין לְפָנָיו, וְאִם רָגִיל לִקְרוֹת, קוֹרֵא, וְאִם לָאו, קוֹרִין לְפָנָיו. וּבַמֶּה קוֹרִין לְפָנָיו? בְּאִיּוֹב וּבְעֶזְרָא וּבְדִבְרֵי הַיָּמִים.

11. הֲרֵי שֶׁהָיוּ לְפָנָיו עֲבָדִים עֲרֵלִים, מִנַּיִן אַתָּה אוֹמֵר שֶׁאִם רָצָה לָמוֹלָן וּלְהַאֲכִילָן בְּפֶסַח שֶׁהוּא רַשַּׁאי? תַּלְמוּד לוֹמַר, וּמַלְתָּה אוֹתוֹ אָז יֹאכַל בּוֹ [שמות י"ב מ"ד].

12. רבי יוסי הגלילי אומר, הואיל ואמרה תורה, פדה את בנך ולמד את בנך
תורה, אם למדת על תלמוד תורה שאם לא למדו אביו מלמד הוא את
עצמו, כך אם לא פדאו אביו הוא יפדה את עצמו. לא, אם אמרת
בתלמוד תורה, שהוא שקול כנגד הכל, שאם לא למדו אביו מלמד הוא
את עצמו, תאמר בפדייה, שאינה שקולה כנגד הכל, לפיכך אם לא
פדאו אביו לא יפדה את עצמו.

13. וירדף אחרי בני ישראל [שמות יד׳ ח׳], להודיע שבחן של ישראל, שאלו
היתה אומה אחרת לא היה פרעה רודף אחריה.

14. אבל לא היו יודעים באיזו מיתה ימות, שנאמר, כי לא פורש מה יעשה לו
[במדבר טו׳ לד׳]. וכן הוא אומר, לפרוש להם על פי י׳ [ויקרא כד׳ יב׳],
מלמד שלא היו יודעים אם חייב מיתה אם לאו.

15. לא מאסתים ולא געלתים לכלותם [ויקרא כו׳ מד׳]. וכי מה נשתייר להם
שלא נגעלו ושלא נמאסו? והלא כל נתנות טובות שנתנו להם נטלו מהם?
ואילולי ספר תורה שנשתייר להם, לא היו משנים מאומות העולם כלום.
אלא, לא מאסתים, בימי אספסינוס, ולא געלתים, בימי יון.

16. רבי שמעון בן יוחי אומר, ככר ומקל ירדו כרוכים מן השמים. אמר להם,
אם עשיתם את התורה, הרי ככר לאכול, ואם לאו, הרי מקל ללקות בו.

17. מעשה שבא רבינו מלדיקיא ונכנס רבי יוסי ברבי יהודה ורבי אלעזר בן
יהודה וישבו לפניו. אמר להם, קרבו לכם, אני צריך להחזיק לכם טובה
שתקיימו את התורה אחרי, אף אתם צריכים שתחזיקו טובה לבניכם
שיקיימו את התורה אחריכם. אילו אין משה גדול ואילולא אחרים קבלו
תורה על ידו, לא היתה שוה, [אנן] על אחת כמה וכמה.

18. אש דת למו [דברים לג׳ ב׳], אלולא דת שנתנה עמה, אין אדם יכול לעמוד בה.

19. אליך נשאתי את עיני היושבי בשמים [תהלים קכג׳ א׳], אלמלא אני, כביכול
לא היית יושב בשמים.

20. יחד שבטי ישראל. יחי ראובן ואל ימות [דברים לג׳ ה׳–ו׳]. וכי מה ענין זה
לזה? משל למלך שבא אצל בניו לפרקים. כשהוא נפטר מבניו היו בניו
וקרוביו מלוים אותו. אמר להם, בניי, שמא צורך יש לכם לומר, שמא
דבר יש לכם. אמרו לי. אמרו לו, אבה, אין לנו צורך ואין לנו דבר,
אלא שתתרצה לאחינו הגדול. כך אלמלא שבטים, לא נתרצה המקום
לראובן. לכך נאמר, יחד שבטי ישראל. יחי ראובן ואל ימות.

Sources. 1. Abot 3.2. 2. Abot 3.17. 3. Bik 1.5. 4. Bik 1.9. 5. BQ 9.10. 6.
Erub 9.3. 7. Ker 6.3. 8. Ned 9.9. 9. Ned 11.1. 10. Yom 1.6. 11. Mek 12.44
(L 1.119). 12. Mek 13.13 (L 1.164–65). 13. Mek 14.8 (L 1.203). 14. SLv
24.12 (W 104c). 15. SLv 26.44 (W 112c). 16. SDt 40 (F 83). 17. SDt 335
(F 385). 18. SDt 343 (F 400). 19. SDt 346 (F 404). 20. SDt 347 (F 404).

UNIT TWENTY-NINE

CAUSAL CLAUSES

I *Introductory text* (Pes 10.5)

רַבָּן גַּמְלִיאֵל הָיָה אוֹמֵר, כָּל שֶׁלֹּא אָמַר שְׁלֹשָׁה דְבָרִים אֵלּוּ בַּפֶּסַח לֹא
יָצָא יְדֵי חוֹבָתוֹ. וְאֵלּוּ הֵן, פֶּסַח מַצָּה וּמָרוֹר. פֶּסַח, עַל שׁוּם שֶׁפָּסַח
הַמָּקוֹם עַל בָּתֵּי אֲבוֹתֵינוּ בְמִצְרָיִם. מַצָּה, עַל שׁוּם שֶׁנִּגְאֲלוּ אֲבוֹתֵינוּ
בְמִצְרָיִם. מָרוֹר, עַל שׁוּם שֶׁמֵּרְרוּ הַמִּצְרִיִּים אֶת חַיֵּי אֲבוֹתֵינוּ בְמִצְרָיִם.
בְּכָל דּוֹר וָדוֹר חַיָּב אָדָם לִרְאוֹת אֶת עַצְמוֹ כְּאִלּוּ הוּא יָצָא מִמִּצְרַיִם,
שֶׁנֶּאֱמַר, וְהִגַּדְתָּ לְבִנְךָ בַּיּוֹם הַהוּא לֵאמֹר בַּעֲבוּר זֶה עָשָׂה יְ׳ לִי בְּצֵאתִי
מִמִּצְרָיִם [שְׁמוֹת יג׳ ח׳]. לְפִיכָךְ אֲנַחְנוּ חַיָּבִין לְהוֹדוֹת, לְהַלֵּל, לְשַׁבֵּחַ,
לְפָאֵר, לְרוֹמֵם, לְהַדֵּר, לְבָרֵךְ, לְעַלֵּה וּלְקַלֵּס לְמִי שֶׁעָשָׂה לַאֲבוֹתֵינוּ
וְלָנוּ אֶת כָּל הַנִּסִּים הָאֵלּוּ, הוֹצִיאָנוּ מֵעַבְדוּת לְחֵרוּת, מִיָּגוֹן לְשִׂמְחָה,
וּמֵאֵבֶל לְיוֹם טוֹב, וּמֵאֲפֵלָה לְאוֹר גָּדוֹל, וּמִשִּׁעְבּוּד לִגְאֻלָּה. וְנֹאמַר
לְפָנָיו, הַלְלוּיָה.

Rabban Gamaliel used to say, Whoever has not explained these three terms during the celebration of Passover has not fulfilled their duty: passover, unleavened bread, and bitter herbs. Passover, because the omnipresent one passed high above the houses of our ancestors in Egypt; unleavened bread, because our ancestors were liberated in Egypt; bitter herbs, because the Egyptians embittered the life of our ancestors in Egypt. In each and every generation, a person is obliged to consider themself as though they themself had gone out from Egypt, as it is said, You are to explain to your son that day, saying, It is due to what Y. did for me when I was leaving Egypt [Ex 13.8]. Because of that, we are obliged to give thanks, to praise, to laud, to glorify, to exalt, to honour, to bless, to magnify, and to applaud the one who performed all these marvels for us and for our ancestors: he took us out of slavery into freedom, from sadness to joy, from mourning to festival, from darkness to shining light, and from oppression to redemption. Let us proclaim before him, Hallelujah.

1. Israel's formative experience of the exodus has to be realized anew by each generation. The paschal catachesis presented here has the objective of explaining, by means of popular etymology, how each element in the passover ritual (eating of the paschal lamb, unleavened bread, and bitter herbs) serves as a means of introduction to that essential event. Because of this, the praise of the God of liberation rises up from each new generation of

those who have been truly liberated.

Because of its frequent use and its interplay with liturgical texts, the text of Pesaḥim has tended to be constantly updated, resulting in differences among manuscripts and editions that are more striking than usual.

II *Morphology*

2. Nearly all the causal conjunctions of BH listed by R. Meyer (1992, §120.2) have disappeared in RH, as seen in the table that follows (which also provides examples of passages employing the biblical conjunctions).

BH	Example	RH
כִּי	Gn 3.14	
יַעַן כִּי	Nm 11.20	
עַל כִּי	Jg 3.12	
תַּחַת כִּי	Pr 1.29	
כִּי עַל כֵּן	Gn 18.5	
עֵקֶב כִּי	2 S 12.10	
אֲשֶׁר	Gn 30.18	-שֶׁ
עַל אֲשֶׁר	2 S 3.30	-עַל שֶׁ
מֵאֲשֶׁר	Is 43.4	-מֵאַחַר שֶׁ
בַּאֲשֶׁר	Gn 39.9	-מִפְּנֵי שֶׁ
תַּחַת אֲשֶׁר	1 S 26.21	-לְפִי שֶׁ
עַל דְּבַר אֲשֶׁר	Dt 23.5	-עַל שׁוּם שֶׁ/עַל שֵׁם שֶׁ
עַל כָּל אֹדוֹת אֲשֶׁר	Jr 3.8	-מִשּׁוּם שֶׁ
יַעַן אֲשֶׁר	Gn 22.16	-בִּשְׁבִיל שֶׁ
עֵקֶב אֲשֶׁר	2 S 12.6	
יַעַן	Nm 20.12	-הוֹאִיל וְ
עֵקֶב	Nm 14.24	
עַל	Ps 119.136	
עַל בְּלִי	Gn 31.20	
מִבְּלִי	Dt 28.55	

3. In RH, כִּי and other conjunctions compounded with כִּי no longer have causal force and אֲשֶׁר has been replaced by -שֶׁ (on the origins of which, see Unit 8.2–5). Although -עַל שֶׁ is a calque of BH עַל אֲשֶׁר, the rest of RH's compounds with -שֶׁ do not precisely mirror those of BH in אֲשֶׁר.

4. The table in §2 is a further indication that RH is the result neither simply of evolution from BH nor of rabbinic invention. A structure like -בִּשְׁבִיל שֶׁ (-בְּ plus שְׁבִיל plus -שֶׁ) has no antecedent in BH but, on the other hand, is too far removed from its etymological sense to be regarded as a recent innovation.

5. וְהוֹאִיל- includes a form of the verb יָאַל in the *Hif'il*, 'help', in a fossilized expression that has the sense of 'given that'. On its possible origins, see Bacher 1899, 37–38.

III *Grammar and usage*

6. Causal uses of -שֶׁ.

On the use of -שֶׁ as a conjunction, see Unit 8.5,7.

Instances abound of causal or explicative -שֶׁ:

הַגֵּר מֵבִיא וְאֵינוֹ קוֹרֵא, שֶׁאֵינוֹ יָכוֹל לוֹמַר, אֲשֶׁר נִשְׁבַּע ײ לַאֲבֹתֵינוּ
לָתֶת לָנוּ [וּדְבָרִים כו' ג']

> Proselytes may perform the offering but not the reading *because* they cannot say, That Y. swore to our ancestors to give us [Dt 26.3] (Bik 1.4);

מְאֹד מְאֹד הֱוֵי שְׁפַל רוּחַ, שֶׁתִּקְוַת אֱנוֹשׁ רִמָּה

> You must be extremely humble, *for* the hope of humankind is the worm (Abot 4.4).

שֶׁאִם 'in the case that' introduces a condition as the reason for something:

שֶׁאִם יִרְאֶה בֵית דִּין אֶת דִּבְרֵי הַיָּחִיד

> In the case that the tribunal approves an individual's opinion (Eduy 1.5).

The common construction of שֶׁנֶּאֱמַר introducing a biblical text has a wide and diffuse sense, being found introducing a text as the cause or basis of an affirmation, or merely as an illustration, perhaps as an *a posteriori* confirmation—hence the variety of renderings: 'as it is said', 'for it is said', etc.

Very often, compounds with -שֶׁ are used for greater expressivity and to indicate a certain nuance in the causal relationship being expressed. Although differences among the conjunctions relate more to style than to semantic content (in the exercises to this unit, it can be seen how -שֶׁ, שֶׁ-, מִפְּנֵי, and other forms are used without distinction), it is still possible to outline a number of regular features in their use.

7. מִפְּנֵי שֶׁ-.

This combination, the most frequent compound of causal -שֶׁ, possesses an unequivocally causal sense. It can be followed by a participle or perfect verb but is also commonly found as part of a nominal clause:

הַמִּתְפַּלֵּל וְטָעָה, סִימָן רַע לוֹ, וְאִם שְׁלִיחַ צִבּוּר הוּא, סִימָן רַע לְשׁוֹלְחָיו,
מִפְּנֵי שֶׁשְּׁלוּחוֹ שֶׁלְאָדָם כְּמוֹתוֹ

> If someone makes a mistake in reciting prayers, it is a bad sign for them; if they are sent by (i.e. reciting prayers on behalf of) the community, it is a bad sign for the ones commissioning, *for* the envoy of a person is like the person themself (Ber 5.5);

מִפְּנֵי מָה זֶה תָּלוּי? מִפְּנֵי שֶׁבֵּרַךְ אֶת הַשֵּׁם וְנִמְצָא שֵׁם שָׁמַיִם מִתְחַלֵּל

Why was this person hanged? *Because* they blasphemed the name
(of God) and the heavenly name ended up being profaned (Sanh
6.4).

8. מִשּׁוּם שֶׁ-/מִשֶּׁם שֶׁ-.

Concerning the different vocalizations, see Introduction, §§8.3; 9.11;
10.2.

Normally this conjunction is employed to confirm a statement with a
biblical text, usually in the formula מִשּׁוּם שֶׁנֶּאֱמַר, which leaves no room for
doubt concerning the causal force of שֶׁנֶּאֱמַר. Thus, at Par 3.7, the saying of R.
Jose,

לֹא מִשּׁוּם זֶה, אֶלָּא מִשּׁוּם שֶׁנֶּאֱמַר

It is not because of this, but *because it is said*

(K and MS Parma have מִשֶּׁם), it is obvious that here a biblical text is presented as the clear and immediate basis of a statement. It is not much used in
the tannaitic *midrashim* (see SNm 123.9 [H 153]; SDt 112 [F 172]). At
TosSot 1.6, we can see the development of the construction from מִן הַשֵּׁם to
מִשֶּׁם:

לא מן השם הוא זה אלא משם שנאמר

It is not for that reason but because it is said.

9. עַל שׁוּם שֶׁ-/עַל שֵׁם שֶׁ-.

Meaning 'inasmuch as', the conjunction is always employed in (popular)
etymologizing explanations, such as that found in the introductory text:

פֶּסַח, עַל שׁוּם שֶׁפָּסַח הַמָּקוֹם עַל בָּתֵּי אֲבוֹתֵינוּ בְּמִצְרַיִם. מַצָּה, עַל שׁוּם
שֶׁנִּגְאֲלוּ אֲבוֹתֵינוּ בְּמִצְרַיִם. מָרוֹר, עַל שׁוּם שֶׁמֵּרְרוּ הַמִּצְרִיִּים אֶת חַיֵּי
אֲבוֹתֵינוּ בְּמִצְרַיִם

Passover, because the omnipresent one passed high above the
houses of our ancestors in Egypt; unleavened bread, because our ancestors were liberated in Egypt; bitter herbs, because the Egyptians
embittered the life of our ancestors in Egypt (Pes 10.5).

Another characteristic example is found at SNm 78.1 (H 72–73):

ר׳ שמעון בן יוחי אומר, שני שמות היו לו, חובב ויתרו . יתרו, על שם
שיתר פרשה אחת בתורה ... חובב, על שם שחיבב את התורה שלא
מצינו בכל הגרים שחיבבו את התורה כיתרו

R. Simeon ben Yohai taught, He had two names, Hobab and
Jethro—Jethro, inasmuch as he added (יְתֵּר) a pericope to the Torah;
Hobab, inasmuch as he loved (חִבֵּב) the Torah to the extent that we
have never found any proselyte who loved it as much as Jethro did.

10. לְפִי שֶׁ-.

This has a basically explicative function, 'since, given that', although
when introducing a biblical text it has a comparative force, 'according to,
conforming to':

לְפִי שֶׁאָדָם צָרִיךְ לָצֵאת יְדֵי הַבְּרִיּוֹת כְּדֶרֶךְ שֶׁצָּרִיךְ לָצֵאת יְדֵי הַמָּקוֹם

Seeing that people have to do what is required by mortals in the same way as they do what is required by God (Sheq 3.2; see Unit 26.6B).

Although in the Mishnah לְפִי שֶׁ- is never found introducing a biblical text, in the tannaitic *midrashim* of the school of R. Ishmael (SNm and Mek), the formula לְפִי שֶׁהוּא אוֹמֵר commonly introduces a biblical text, which is then followed by אֵין לִי אֶלָּא or אוֹ or יָכוֹל or שׁוֹמֵעַ אֲנִי: 'given that/in accordance with what it (i.e. the biblical text) says ... I could understand':

ר׳ יאשיה אומר, איש או אשה [במדבר ה׳ ו], למה נאמר? לפי שהוא

אומר, וכי יפתח איש בור או כי יכרה איש בור [שמות כא׳ לג׳], אין לי

אלא איש, אשה מנין?

R. Josiah said, Why does it say, A man or a woman [Nm 5.6]? (Because) *in accordance with what it says* (at Ex 21.33), When a man opens a pit or a man digs a pit, I might conclude that it only refers to the man. From where may it be deduced that it refers also to the woman?

11. בִּשְׁבִיל שֶׁ-.

A. Followed by an imperfect, בִּשְׁבִיל שֶׁ- usually expresses final purpose, and is, therefore, most often to be rendered as a simple final conjunction, 'for, so that, in order that':

וְאִם מִתְּחִלָּה נְטָלָן בִּשְׁבִיל שֶׁלֹּא יֹאבְדוּ

And if from the beginning one took them (fruits) so that they would not go bad (Dem 3.3).

At RH 2.6, the correspondence between בִּשְׁבִיל שֶׁ- and the final conjunction כְּדֵי שֶׁ- is very clear:

לֹא שֶׁהָיוּ צְרִיכִין לָהֶן, אֶלָּא כְּדֵי שֶׁלֹּא יֵצְאוּ בְּפַחֵי נֶפֶשׁ, בִּשְׁבִיל שֶׁיְּהוּ רְגִילִים לָבֹא

Not because they neeeded them (witnesses) but so that they would not go away frustrated and so that they would get used to coming.

B. In contrast, the properly causal use of בִּשְׁבִיל שֶׁ- becomes apparent when followed by a participial or nominal construction:

בשביל שהמלך כשר ... עכשיו יאמרו עלי בשביל שאין בו כח

להכניסנו לארץ

Because the king is very capable ... Now they will say of me, Because he lacks the force to get us into the land (SDt 3 [F 11]).

12. מֵאַחַר שֶׁ-.

This conjunction has a primarily temporal sense (see Unit 27.12), 'after', and from this easily developed causal significance:

אָמַר רַבִּי מֵאִיר, מֵאַחַר שֶׁשְּׁנֵיהֶן יְכוֹלִין לְמַחוֹת זֶה עַל זֶה, רוֹאִין מֵהֵיכָן יָרָק זֶה חַי

Rabbi Meir said, *Since* each can impede the other, it has to be observed from which part the grass is able to grow (BM 10.6).

In Sifra, the formula מֵאַחַר שֶׁלָּמַדְנוּ 'since we already know' precedes מָה תַּלְמוּד לוֹמַר, commonly used to ask what additional meaning a text might have (see SLv 15.11 [W 77a]).

13. -שֶׁ עַל.

Not widely used in the Mishnah, -שֶׁ עַל also appears in combination with the preposition עַל, as at Shab 2.6:

עַל שָׁלֹשׁ עֲבֵרוֹת הַנָּשִׁים מֵתוֹת בִּשְׁעַת לֵדָתָן, עַל שֶׁאֵינָן זְהִירוֹת בַּנִּדָּה
וּבַחַלָּה וּבְהַדְלָקַת הַנֵּר

For three transgressions women die when giving birth: for not being careful about (the laws concerning) menstruation, about the dough offering, and about the lighting of the (sabbath) lamp.

-שֶׁ עַל always seems to relate to an act (מַעֲשֶׂה) as the basis/cause of a particular consequence:

מַעֲשֶׂה שֶׁיָּרְדוּ זְקֵנִים מִירוּשָׁלַיִם לְעָרֵיהֶם וְגָזְרוּ תַעֲנִית עַל שֶׁנִּרְאָה
כִמְלֹא פִי תַנּוּר שְׁדָפוֹן בְּאַשְׁקְלוֹן. וְעוֹד גָּזְרוּ תַעֲנִית עַל שֶׁאָכְלוּ זְאֵבִים שְׁנֵי
תִינוֹקוֹת בְּעֵבֶר הַיַּרְדֵּן. רַבִּי יוֹסֵי אוֹמֵר, לֹא עַל שֶׁאָכְלוּ אֶלָּא עַל שֶׁנִּרְאוּ

It happened that when the elders went down from Jerusalem to their towns they decreed a fast *due to the fact that* in Ashkelon there appeared a blight large enough to fill the mouth of an oven. They also decreed a fast *due to the fact that* across the Jordan wolves had devoured two children. Rabbi Jose explained, It was not *due to the fact that* they devoured them but simply *due to the fact that* they appeared (Taa 3.6).

In line with RH's tendency to turn the subject of a secondary clause into the object of a main clause (see Unit 24.9), a subordinate clause introduced by -שֶׁ עַל also frequently appears with an object after the עַל, for example

עַל אֵלּוּ מַתְרִיעִים בַּשַּׁבָּת, עַל עִיר שֶׁהִקִּיפוּהָ גוֹיִם אוֹ נָהָר

For these things the *shophar* is sounded on the sabbath: for a river's, or the gentiles', encircling of a town (literally, 'for a town that gentiles or a river have surrounded') (Taa 3.7).

14. -וְ הוֹאִיל 'since, given that, it being the case that'.

A. Equivalent to a fulfilled real condition: at Eduy 1.5, it is asked why an isolated opinion should be mentioned '*it being the case that* the halakhah is determined by the majority':

הוֹאִיל וְאֵין הֲלָכָה אֶלָּא כְדִבְרֵי הַמְרֻבִּין.

B. Marking the protasis in a comparison, the apodosis usually having a correlative אַף ,כָּךְ, or הֲרֵי:

רַבִּי מֵאִיר אוֹמֵר, הוֹאִיל וְהוּא נִרְאֶה כְּתַבְנִית הַכְּרָמִים, הֲרֵי זֶה כֶרֶם

Rabbi Meir used to say, Since it has the appearance of a vineyard, it is regarded as a vineyard (Kil 5.1).

C. Very frequently in rabbinic arguments, introducing a consideration:

היה ר׳ ישמעאל אומר, הואיל ונאמרו צוואות בתורה סתם, ופרט לך
הכתוב באחת מהן שאינה אלא מיד בשעת מעשה ובדורות, אף פורטני
בכל הצוואות שבתורה, שלא יהו אלא מיד בשעת מעשה ולדורות

R. Ishmael used to argue, *Considering that* the Torah contains commandments that are mentioned without any further specification but that in some of them Scripture specifies for you that they are valid the moment they are decreed and for all time, I can specify concerning all the commandments that are in the Torah that they must be valid the moment they are decreed and for all time (SNm 1.2 [H 1]).

IV *Phraseology*

15. הוֹאִיל וְאָמְרָה תוֹרָה 'considering that the Torah says' is a formula with which Mekhilta introduces a biblical text that is cited not literally but with the contents freely expressed (see Bacher 1899, 38); in the following example, the biblical reference is to Dt 6.8 (see also Mek 13.3; 21.11,17,26, etc.):

הואיל ואמרה תורה, תן תפילין בראש, תן תפילין ביד. מה בראש ארבע
טוטפות אף ביד ארבע טוטפות

Considering that the Torah says you are to place phylacteries on your head and you are to place phylacteries on your arm, since the four sections are on the head, the four sections are also to be on the arm (Mek 13.9 [L 1.150]).

V *Vocabulary*

אָרִיס 'tenant'
גַּזְלָן 'violent, robber, one who takes something by violence'
דְּבֵילָה 'fig cake, fig bread'
זוּן 'feed'
חָכוּר/חָכִיר 'labourer, sharecropper'
חָרוּב 'carob'
סִיקָרִיקוֹן (σικαρικόν) 'confiscated property' (confiscated by Rome),
    'confiscator' or 'usurper' of such property
(עַל אַחַת כַּמָּה וְכַמָּה) עאכ"ו 'how much more!'
עִרְעֵר 'strip'
פָּשַׁל 'twist, knot, tie'
פָּרַח 'fly'
קְמִיצָה 'fistful'
שָׁאַל עַל פְּתָחִים 'call door to door, begging'
תַּרְנְגוֹל 'cock'

VI *Exercises*

1. מִי שֶׁמֵּת וְהִנִּיחַ בָּנִים וּבָנוֹת, בִּזְמַן שֶׁהַנְּכָסִים מְרֻבִּים, הַבָּנִים יִירְשׁוּ וְהַבָּנוֹת
יְזוֹנוּ. הַנְּכָסִים מֻעָטִין, הַבָּנוֹת יְזוֹנוּ וְהַבָּנִים יִשְׁאֲלוּ עַל הַפְּתָחִים. אַדְמוֹן
אוֹמֵר, בִּשְׁבִיל שֶׁאֲנִי זָכָר הִפְסַדְתִּי? אָמַר רַבָּן גַּמְלִיאֵל, רוֹאֶה אֲנִי אֶת

דִּבְרֵי אַדְמוֹן.

2. מֵאֵיזֶה טַעַם אֵינוֹ מֵבִיא? מִשּׁוּם שֶׁנֶּאֱמַר, רֵאשִׁית בִּכּוּרֵי אַדְמָתְךָ [שמות כג'
יט'], עַד שֶׁיִּהְיוּ כָל הַגִּדּוּלִין מֵאַדְמָתְךָ. הָאֲרִיסִין וְהֶחָכוֹרוֹת וְהַסִּקְרִיקוֹן
וְהַגַּזְלָן אֵין מְבִיאִין מֵאוֹתוֹ הַטַּעַם, מִשּׁוּם שֶׁנֶּאֱמַר, רֵאשִׁית בִּכּוּרֵי אַדְמָתְךָ.

3. הַמַּפְקִיד מָעוֹת אֵצֶל חֲבֵרוֹ, צְרָרָן וְהִפְשִׁילָן לַאֲחוֹרָיו, אוֹ שֶׁמְּסָרָן לִבְנוֹ
וּלְבִתּוֹ הַקְּטַנִּים, וְנָעַל בִּפְנֵיהֶם שֶׁלֹּא כָרָאוּי, חַיָּב, שֶׁלֹּא שָׁמַר כְּדֶרֶךְ
הַשּׁוֹמְרִים, וְאִם שָׁמַר כְּדֶרֶךְ הַשּׁוֹמְרִים, פָּטוּר.

4. רַבִּי יְהוּדָה אוֹמֵר, שׁוֹר הַמִּדְבָּר, שׁוֹר הַהֶקְדֵּשׁ, שׁוֹר הַגֵּר שֶׁמֵּת, פְּטוּרִים מִן
הַמִּיתָה, לְפִי שֶׁאֵין לָהֶם בְּעָלִים.

5. וְלָמָּה מַזְכִּירִין דִּבְרֵי הַיָּחִיד בֵּין הַמְרֻבִּין, הוֹאִיל וְאֵין הֲלָכָה אֶלָּא כְדִבְרֵי
הַמְרֻבִּין? שֶׁאִם יִרְאֶה בֵית דִּין אֶת דִּבְרֵי הַיָּחִיד וְיִסְמֹךְ עָלָיו, שֶׁאֵין בֵּית
דִּין יָכוֹל לְבַטֵּל דִּבְרֵי בֵית דִּין חֲבֵרוֹ עַד שֶׁיִּהְיֶה גָדוֹל מִמֶּנּוּ בְּחָכְמָה וּבְמִנְיָן.

6. רַבִּי יְהוּדָה בֶן בָּבָא הֵעִיד חֲמִשָּׁה דְבָרִים, שֶׁמְמַאֲנִים אֶת הַקְּטַנּוֹת,
וְשֶׁמַּשִּׂיאִין אֶת הָאִשָּׁה עַל פִּי עֵד אֶחָד, וְשֶׁנִּסְקַל תַּרְנְגוֹל בִּירוּשָׁלַיִם עַל
שֶׁהָרַג אֶת הַנֶּפֶשׁ, עַל הַיַּיִן בֶּן אַרְבָּעִים יוֹם, שֶׁנִּתְנַסַּךְ עַל גַּב הַמִּזְבֵּחַ, וְעַל
תָּמִיד שֶׁלְּשַׁחַר, שֶׁקָּרֵב בְּאַרְבַּע שָׁעוֹת.

7. רַבִּי שִׁמְעוֹן אוֹמֵר, כְּבָשִׂים קוֹדְמִין לְעִזִּים בְּכָל מָקוֹם. יָכוֹל מִפְּנֵי שֶׁהֵן
מֻבְחָרִין מֵהֶן? תַּלְמוּד לוֹמַר, וְאִם כֶּבֶשׂ יָבִיא קָרְבָּנוֹ לְחַטָּאת [ויקרא ד' לב'].
מְלַמֵּד שֶׁשְּׁנֵיהֶם שְׁקוּלִין ... הָאָב קוֹדֵם לָאֵם בְּכָל מָקוֹם. יָכוֹל שֶׁכְּבוֹד הָאָב
עוֹדֵף עַל כְּבוֹד הָאֵם? תַּלְמוּד לוֹמַר, אִישׁ אִמּוֹ וְאָבִיו תִּירָאוּ [שם ט' ג'],
מְלַמֵּד שֶׁשְּׁנֵיהֶם שְׁקוּלִים, אֲבָל אָמְרוּ חֲכָמִים, הָאָב קוֹדֵם לָאֵם בְּכָל מָקוֹם,
מִפְּנֵי שֶׁהוּא וְאִמּוֹ חַיָּבִין בִּכְבוֹד אָבִיו. וְכֵן בְּתַלְמוּד תּוֹרָה, אִם זָכָה הַבֵּן לִפְנֵי
הָרַב, הָרַב קוֹדֵם אֶת הָאָב בְּכָל מָקוֹם, מִפְּנֵי שֶׁהוּא וְאָבִיו חַיָּבִין בִּכְבוֹד רַבּוֹ.

8. חָצֵר גְּדוֹלָה הָיְתָה בִירוּשָׁלַיִם, וּבֵית יַעֲזֵק הָיְתָה נִקְרֵאת, וּלְשָׁם כָּל הָעֵדִים
מִתְכַּנְּסִים, וּבֵית דִּין בּוֹדְקִין אוֹתָם שָׁם. וּסְעוּדוֹת גְּדוֹלוֹת עוֹשִׂין לָהֶם בִּשְׁבִיל
שֶׁיְּהוּ רְגִילִין לָבֹא.

9. מֵאֵימָתַי מַזְכִּירִין גְּבוּרוֹת גְּשָׁמִים? רַבִּי אֱלִיעֶזֶר אוֹמֵר, מִיּוֹם טוֹב הָרִאשׁוֹן
שֶׁלֶּחָג. רַבִּי יְהוֹשֻׁעַ אוֹמֵר, מִיּוֹם טוֹב הָאַחֲרוֹן שֶׁלֶּחָג. אָמַר לוֹ רַבִּי יְהוֹשֻׁעַ,
הוֹאִיל וְאֵין הַגְּשָׁמִים אֶלָּא סִימַן קְלָלָה בֶּחָג, לָמָּה הוּא מַזְכִּיר?

10. וַיֹּאמֶר מֹשֶׁה, אִכְלֻהוּ הַיּוֹם כִּי שַׁבָּת הַיּוֹם לַה', הַיּוֹם לֹא תִמְצָאֻהוּ בַּשָּׂדֶה
[שמות טז' כה']. רַבִּי זְרִיקָה אוֹמֵר מִכַּאן שָׁלֹשׁ סְעֻדוֹת בַּשַּׁבָּת. לְפִי שֶׁהָיוּ
יִשְׂרָאֵל רְגִילִין לָצֵאת בַּשַּׁחֲרִית, אָמְרוּ לוֹ, רַבֵּינוּ מֹשֶׁה, נֵצֵא בַשַּׁחֲרִית? אָמַר
לָהֶם, אֵינוּ הַיּוֹם. אָמְרוּ לוֹ, הוֹאִיל וְלֹא יָצָאנוּ שַׁחֲרִית נֵצֵא בֵּין הָעַרְבַּיִם? אָמַר
לָהֶם, כִּי שַׁבָּת הַיּוֹם לַה'.

11. וָאֶשָּׂא אֶתְכֶם עַל כַּנְפֵי נְשָׁרִים [שמות יט' ד'], מַה נִּשְׁתַּנָּה הַנֶּשֶׁר הַזֶּה מִכָּל
הָעוֹפוֹת כֻּלָּם? שֶׁכָּל הָעוֹפוֹת כֻּלָּן נוֹתְנִין אֶת בְּנֵיהֶם בֵּין רַגְלֵיהֶם מִפְּנֵי שֶׁהֵן
מִתְיָרְאִין מֵעוֹף אַחֵר שֶׁהוּא פּוֹרֵחַ עַל גַּבֵּיהֶם, אֲבָל הַנֶּשֶׁר הַזֶּה אֵינוֹ מִתְיָרֵא
אֶלָּא מֵאָדָם בִּלְבַד. שֶׁמָּא יָזְרֹק בּוֹ חֵץ, אוֹמֵר מוּטָב שֶׁיִּכָּנֵס בּוֹ וְלֹא בְּבָנָיו.

12. רַבִּי נָתָן אוֹמֵר, הוֹאִיל וְאָמְרָה תוֹרָה, תֵּן כֶּסֶף, וּ, בַּל תִּתֵּן כֶּסֶף, מַה, תֵּן
כֶּסֶף, עַד שֶׁלֹּא בָאוּ בָהּ סִימָנִין, אַף, בַּל תִּתֵּן כֶּסֶף, מִשֶּׁבָּאוּ בָהּ סִימָנִין.

13. הוֹאִיל וּמָצִינוּ שֶׁאֵין כַּפָּרָה אֶלָּא בַדָּם, מַה תַּלְמוּד לוֹמַר, וְסָמַךְ ... וְנִרְצָה,
[ויקרא א' ד']?

14. רַבִּי אֱלִיעֶזֶר אוֹמֵר, לֹא נִתְחַיְּבוּ אֶלָּא עַל שֶׁהוֹרוּ הֲלָכָה בִּפְנֵי מֹשֶׁה רַבָּן,
וְכָל הַמּוֹרֶה הֲלָכָה בִּפְנֵי רַבּוֹ, חַיָּב מִיתָה.

‫15. אז תרצה הארץ את שבתותיה [ויקרא כו' לד']. אני אמרתי לכם שתהו‬
‫זורעים שש ומשמטים לי אחת, בשביל שתדעו שהארץ שלי היא, ואתם לא‬
‫עשיתם כן.‬

‫16. וביד הכהן יהיו מי המרים המאררים [במדבר ה' יח'] ... נקראו מרים על‬
‫שם סופן שממררין את הגוף ומערערין את העון.‬

‫17. ומה אלו [= הגרים] שקירבו את עצמן כך קירבם המקום, ישראל שעושים‬
‫את התורה עאכ"ו.‬

‫18. משל. אומרים לאדם, מפני מה אתה אוכל פת שעורים? אמר להם, מפני‬
‫שאין לי פת חטים. מפני מה אתה אוכל חרובים? אמר להם, מפני שאין לי‬
‫דבילה. כך אלו היתה בידן של ישראל מאותה קמיצה שקמצו ביום שמת‬
‫בו משה, שאכלו ממנו כל ארבעים יום, לא רצו לאכול מתבואת ארץ כנען.‬

‫19. וכן אתה מוצא בדרכי מקום, שכל מי שחביב קודם את חבירו. תורה,‬
‫לפי שחביבה מכל, נבראת קודם לכל ... בית המקדש, לפי שחביב מכל,‬
‫נברא לפני כל ... ארץ ישראל, שחביבה מכל, נבראת לפני כל.‬

‫20. דבר אחר, האזינו השמים ואדברה [דברים לב' א'], על שם שניתנה תורה‬
‫מן השמים, שנאמר, אתם ראיתם כי מן השמים דברתי עמכם [שמות כ' כב'].‬

Sources. 1. BB 9.1. 2. Bik 1.2. 3. BB 3.10. 4. BQ 4.7. 5. Eduy 1.5. 6.
Eduy 6.1. 7. Ker 6.9. 8. RS 2.5. 9. Taa 1.1. 10. Mek 16.25 (L 2.119). 11.
Mek 19.4 (L 2.202–203). 12. Mek 21.11 (L 3.31). 13. SLv 1.4 (W 6a). 14.
Sifra, Mek of Millu'im (SLv 10.2 [W 45c]). 15. SLv 26.34 (W 112b). 16.
SNm 11.4 (H 17). 17. SNm 78.1 (H 73). 18. SNm 89.4 (H 90). 19. SDt 37
(F 70). 20. SDt 306 (F 334).

UNIT THIRTY

FINAL AND CONSECUTIVE CLAUSES

I *Introductory text* (K Sanh 4.5)

‫לְפִיכָךְ נִבְרָא אָדָם יָחִיד בָּעוֹלָם.‬
‫—לְלַמֵּד שֶׁכָּל הַמְאַבֵּד נֶפֶשׁ אַחַת מַעֲלִין עָלָיו כִּילוּ אִבֵּד עוֹלָם מָלֵא‬
‫וְכָל חֲמַקְיֵם נֶפֶשׁ אַחַת מַעֲלִין עָלָיו כִּילוּ קִיֵם עוֹלָם מָלֵא.‬
‫—מִפְּנֵי שְׁלוֹם הַבְּרִיּוֹת, שֶׁלֹּא יֹאמַר אָדָם לַחֲבֵרוֹ, אַבָּא גָדוֹל מֵאָבִיךְ.‬
‫—שֶׁלֹּא יְהוּ הַמִּינִין אוֹמְרִים, רְשׁוּיוֹת הַרְבֵּה בַּשָּׁמָיִם.‬
‫—לְהַגִּיד גְּדֻלָּתוֹ שֶׁלְמֶלֶךְ מַלְכֵי הַמְּלָכִים הַקָּדוֹשׁ בָּרוּךְ הוּא, שֶׁאָדָם טוֹבֵעַ‬
‫מֵאָה מַטְבְּעוֹת בְּחוֹתָם אֶחָד וְכוּלָן דּוֹמִין זֶה לָזֶה, וּמֶלֶךְ מַלְכֵי הַמְּלָכִים‬
‫הַקָּדוֹשׁ בָּרוּךְ הוּא טָבַע אֶת כָּל הָאָדָם בְּחוֹתָמוֹ שֶׁלְאָדָם הָרִאשׁוֹן וְאֵין‬
‫אֶחָד מֵהֶן דּוֹמֶה לַחֲבֵירוֹ. לְפִיכָךְ כָּל אֶחָד וְאֶחָד חַיָּיב לוֹמַר,‬
‫בִּשְׁבִילִי נִבְרָא הָעוֹלָם.‬
‫—שֶׁמָּא תֹאמְרוּ, מַה לָּנוּ וְלַצָּרָה הַזֹאת? וַהֲלֹא כְבָר נֶאֱמַר,‬
‫וְהוּא עֵד אוֹ רָאָה אוֹ יָדָע [אִם־לוֹא יַגִּיד] וְגוֹ' [וַיִּקְרָא ה' א']? אוֹ שֶׁמָּא‬
‫תֹאמְרוּ, מַה לָּנוּ לְחַיֵּיב בְּדָמוֹ שֶׁלָּזֶה. וַהֲלֹא כְבָר נֶאֱמַר, [וּבַאֲבֹד‬
‫רְשָׁעִים רִנָּה [מִשְׁלֵי יא' י'].‬

Because of this, only a single person was created in the world.

—To teach that anyone who destroys a single life is regarded as having destroyed an entire world and anyone who saves a single life is regarded as having saved an entire world.

—With regard to social peace, so that no-one might say to another, My father is greater than yours.

—So that the heretics [erased in K] cannot say, There are many powers in heaven.

—To proclaim the greatness of the king of kings of kings, the holy one, blessed be he: for a person makes a hundred coins with the same seal and all look alike, but the king of kings of kings, the holy one, blessed be he, has coined every person with the seal of the first human being and nobody looks like another. Therefore, each and every one is obliged to say, The world has been created for me.

—So that you do not (or 'may you not') dare to say, What is such and such a problem to do with us, is it not already said, A witness who has seen or heard (but does not give evidence, incurs guilt) [Lv 5.1]? So that you do not (or 'may you not') dare to say, What is our responsibility for the blood of this person, is it not already said, When the wicked perish, there is joy (in the city) [Pr 11.10]?

1. The text is important in the context of this unit, as it displays several ways of constructing a final clause. But above all, it is important from a theological perspective: all Israel and humankind are found in the unique (יָחִיד) person of Adam, a uniqueness that causes a person to share in the uniqueness of God, the divine seal upon the first human being ('like *one* of us' [Gn 3.22]). This seal is the basis of a person's dignity, as a creature sealed by God, and of a person's solidarity with every other human being, which does not allow one to remain unaffected by another's pain or happiness.

A comparison of K with standard printed versions of this text demonstrates striking and significant differences of both a linguistic and a theological nature.

II *Morphology*

2. Virtually all the final conjunctions of BH have disappeared from, or been altered in, RH. As an example of the developments taking place, we may note the rare use of final/consecutive -שֶׁ in LBH—

וְהָאֱלֹהִים עָשָׂה שֶׁיִּרְאוּ מִלְּפָנָיו

And God acted so that they would fear him (Ec 3.14)—

which became commonplace in RH.

Similarly, at Ec 7.14, in a statement akin to the one just quoted, we find -עַל דִּבְרַת שֶׁ, an early version of RH's -עַל מְנָת שֶׁ:

גַּם אֶת־זֶה לְעֻמַּת־זֶה עָשָׂה הָאֱלֹהִים עַל־דִּבְרַת שֶׁלֹּא יִמְצָא הָאָדָם
אַחֲרָיו מְאוּמָה

God made the one thing and the other so that no-one might find
fault.

The following is a table of final conjunctions in BH and RH.

BH	RH
-לְ + infinitive	-לְ + infinitive
לְבִלְתִּי + infinitive	שֶׁלֹּא + infinitive
	-כְּדֵי לְ + infinitive
	-עַל מְנָת לְ + infinitive
אֲשֶׁר + imperfect	
-שֶׁ + imperfect (LBH)	-שֶׁ + imperfect
לְמַעַן	
לְמַעַן אֲשֶׁר	
בַּעֲבוּר	
בַּעֲבוּר אֲשֶׁר	
	-כְּדֵי שֶׁ
	כְּדֵי שֶׁלֹּא
	-בִּשְׁבִיל שֶׁ
	בִּשְׁבִיל שֶׁלֹּא
-עַל דִּבְרַת שֶׁ	-עַל מְנָת שֶׁ
	-עַל תְּנַאי שֶׁ
פֶּן	שֶׁמָּא + imperfect
אֲשֶׁר לֹא	שֶׁלֹּא + imperfect

שֶׁמָּא probably derives from -שֶׁ and לָמָה, with LBH representing an intermediate stage:

שַׁלָּמָה אֶהְיֶה כְּעֹטְיָה

Why do I have to go about as a stray? (Ca 1.7)

The Aramaic equivalent דִּילְמָא is perhaps a calque from RH, but in any
case the אָ- in שֶׁמָּא is a clear sign of Aramaic influence. In K, the normal vocalization is שֶׁמָא.

3. There are no specifically consecutive particles in BH or RH, with the
following forms being used instead.

BH	RH
כִּי	-שֶׁ
אֲשֶׁר	-כְּדֵי שֶׁ
אֲשֶׁר לֹא	כְּדֵי שֶׁלֹּא

III *Grammar and usage*

4. BH usually expresses finality through the simple coordination of
clauses with -וְ, especially common in the sequence imperative followed by
וְקָטַלְתָּ or וְיִקְטֹל. In RH, such simple coordination tends to be replaced by the
use of the infinitive with -לְ or of final conjunctions. Nonetheless, some examples remain:

וְהִסְתַּכֵּל בִּשְׁלֹשָׁה דְבָרִים וְאִי אַתָּה בָא לִידֵי עֲבֵרָה

Consider three things so as not to fall into the hands of sin (Abot
3.1).

5. -לְ + infinitive.

A. The use of this construction in final clauses is widespread:

נתקבצו כולן זו על זו ליטול עצה

They joined up, this one with that one, to take counsel (SNm 133.1
[H 176]).

B. The negative form of the construction employs שֶׁלֹּא:

לֹא הָיוּ יָמִים טוֹבִים לְיִשְׂרָאֵל כַּחֲמִשָּׁה עָשָׂר בְּאָב וּכְיוֹם הַכִּפּוּרִים, שֶׁבָּהֶן
בְּנוֹת יְרוּשָׁלַם יוֹצְאוֹת בִּכְלֵי לָבָן שְׁאוּלִין, שֶׁלֹּא לְבַיֵּשׁ אֶת מִי שֶׁאֵין לוֹ

There were no happier days in Israel than the fifteenth of Ab and the
day of atonement, when the girls of Jerusalem would go out in white
clothes, borrowed, so as not to offend those who did not have any
(Taa 4.8).

C. A so-called exegetical infinitive can begin the explanation of a biblical passage, '(this is said) in order' לְהוֹצִיא 'to exclude', לְהָבִיא 'to include',
לְהוֹדִיעַ 'to proclaim', לְלַמֶּדְךָ 'to teach you', etc., and may be regarded as responding to an implied question of the kind לָמָּה נֶאֱמַר:

וכי יזיד איש על רעהו להרגו [שמות כא׳ יד׳] ... וכי יזיד, להוציא את
השוגג, איש, להוציא את הקטן, איש, להביא את האחרים, רעהו,
להוציא את האחרים

When a man becomes enraged enough against his companion to kill
them [Ex 21.14] ... When a man becomes enraged: (this is said) in
order to exclude someone acting unintentionally; a man: in order to
exclude minors; a man: to include the others; against his companion:
to include minors; against his companion: to exclude the others.
(Mek 21.14 [L 3.36–37]);

ויעש כן אהרן, [במדבר ח׳ ג׳]. להודיע שבחו של אהרן,
שכשם שאמר לו משה כן עשה

And thus Aaron did [Nm 8.3]. (This is said) to proclaim the praise
of Aaron, who acted as Moses had ordered him (SNm 60.1 [H 57]).

6. Final and exegetical -שֶׁ.

Followed by the imperfect and with final value, this construction has the
same function as an exegetical infinitive (see Units 8.7C and 20.9):

ונקה האיש מעון [במדבר ה׳ לא׳]. שלא יאמר, אוי לי שהרגתי בת ישראל

He will be clear of sin [Nm 5.31]. (This is said) so that no-one has to say, Woe is me, for I have killed a daughter of Israel (SNm 21.3 [H 24]).

(Note how final and consecutive values might easily be confused.)

7. -‎שֶׁ בִּשְׁבִיל.

That the reason why and the reason for are near neighbours is clearly seen in this conjunction, which can refer to both cause and end. See Unit 29.11 for instances of ‎שֶׁ- בִּשְׁבִיל with the imperfect expressing finality or final cause and of the same conjunction followed by a participle or noun to express merely cause. There is a further example at Taa 3.8:

צְאוּ וְהַכְנִיסוּ תַנּוּרֵי פְסָחִים, בִּשְׁבִיל שֶׁלֹּא יִמּוֹקוּ

Go and fetch the paschal ovens so that they don't fall apart.

8. -‎שֶׁ כְּדֵי and -‎ל כְּדֵי.

A. Any difference, beyond the purely stylistic, that exists between the use of the imperfect with -‎שֶׁ כְּדֵי and of the infinitive with -‎ל כְּדֵי lies in the more subjective, personal, and persuasive mood of the imperfect as against the more impersonal nature of the infinitive:

לָמָּה אָמְרוּ חֲכָמִים, עַל חֲצוֹת? כְּדֵי לְהַרְחִיק אֶת הָאָדָם מִן הָעֲבֵרָה

Why did the sages say, Up to midnight (one must recite the *shema'*)? So as to distance people from sin (Ber 1.1);

לָמָּה קָדְמָה ,שְׁמַע, ל, וְהָיָה אִם שָׁמֹעַ? אֶלָּא כְּדֵי שֶׁיְּקַבֵּל עָלָיו עֹל מַלְכוּת שָׁמַיִם תְּחִלָּה, וְאַחַר כָּךְ יְקַבֵּל עָלָיו עֹל מִצְוֹת

Why does, Hear (O Israel), precede, And it will be, if you listen? It is simply so that first one might take upon oneself the yoke of the kingdom of heaven and only afterwards the yoke of the commandments (Ber 2.2);

ומשמיע בכל לשון ששומעת, כדי שתהא יודעת על מה היתה שותה

It is said in any language she can understand, so that she will know why she is drinking (the bitter waters) (TosSoṭ 2.1).

It should be noted that in the two examples from Berakhot, K reads להרחיק and אלא יקבל, without ‎כְּדֵי (K also lacks ‎כְּדֵי at Abot 2.4: see text 3 in the exercises). It seems, then, that the use of ‎כְּדֵי to introduce a simple final clause did not become generalized in a uniform way and might represent a later stage of the language, when ‎כְּדֵי no longer carried the connotation of 'quantity'.

B. But in virtue of its etymological force, 'as much as is sufficient', ‎כְּדֵי can also introduce an attributive or adjectival clause in order to determine, quantitatively, a noun, expressing thereby not so much the final intention of the subject of the main clause as something of the end use or nature of the object referred to by the noun being thus determined. In Shab 8, there are many examples of -‎ל כְּדֵי specifying the quantitative value of an object. For example,

הַמּוֹצִיא ... דְּבַשׁ כְּדֵי לִתֵּן עַל הַכָּתִית

(Shab 8.1) does not refer to the person carrying honey to put it on a wound but to 'whoever carries *enough* honey to put on a wound'; similarly,

שֶׁמֶן כְּדֵי לָסוּךְ אֵבֶר קָטָן

is 'oil enough to anoint the smallest member',

חֶבֶל כְּדֵי לַעֲשׂוֹת אֹזֶן

is 'enough rope to make a handle' (Shab 8.2),

נְיָר כְּדֵי לִכְתּוֹב עָלָיו קֶשֶׁר מוֹכְסִין

is 'enough paper for writing a taxcollector's note', and

דְּיוֹ כְּדֵי לִכְתּוֹב שְׁתֵּי אוֹתִיוֹת

is 'ink in sufficient quantity to write two letters' (Shab 8.3). The adjectival value of final clauses like these is decisive in preventing them from being understood as clauses expressing the final intention of the subject of the main clause.

In fact, in every example I have been able to check, כְּדֵי functions as an indeclinable adjective ('sufficient, enough') that can introduce either an infinitive with -ל or the corresponding verbal noun. Thus, at Hul 11.2, we find that to the question

וְכַמָּה נוֹתְנִים לוֹ?

How much (wool) must one give him?

the answer given is כְּדֵי לַעֲשׂוֹת מִמֶּנּוּ בֶּגֶד קָטָן 'enough for a small garment to be made from it' and כְּדֵי מַתָּנָה 'enough for a present'. In both cases, what is expressed is not the intention of the person who wants the wool but the quantity of wool that is needed.

9. עַל מְנָת ל- and עַל מְנָת שֶׁ-.

עַל מְנָת שֶׁ- occurs with the imperfect, and, depending on vocalization, the participle. On the difference between imperfect and infinitive constructions, see above, §8A.

The use of עַל מְנָת underlines the interest or intention of the subject; in line with its original sense of '(laying a bet) on the (corresponding) portion', it is usually rendered as 'on condition that', as in the well-known statement of Antigonus of Socoh:

אַל תִּהְיוּ כַעֲבָדִים הַמְשַׁמְּשִׁין אֶת הָרַב עַל מְנָת לְקַבֵּל פְּרָס, אֶלָּא הֱווּ
כַעֲבָדִים הַמְשַׁמְּשִׁין אֶת הָרַב שֶׁלֹּא עַל מְנָת לְקַבֵּל פְּרָס

Do not be like servants who work for their master on condition that they receive a salary, but like servants who work for their master without the intention of receiving remuneration (Abot 1.3).

At Ma'aśrot 2.7, the labourer accepts his contract עַל מְנָת שֶׁאוֹכַל תְּאֵנִים 'on condition that I may eat figs'. (In this instance, some prefer to read a participle, עַל מְנָת שֶׁאוֹכֵל.)

10. עַל תְּנַאי שֶׁ-.

This has a similar function, but because it is not of itself a conjunction, it can still be employed independently of any following clause, as an adverbial modifier of the clause that precedes:

אַף עַל פִּי שֶׁנְּתָנוֹ לָהּ עַל תְּנַאי וְלֹא נַעֲשָׂה הַתְּנַאי

Even though he gave it to her conditionally, but the condition was not fulfilled (Git 8.8).

Its use as a conjunction is exemplified by Meg 3.2:

אֵין מוֹכְרִין בֵּית הַכְּנֶסֶת, אֶלָּא עַל תְּנַאי שֶׁאִם יִרְצוּ יַחֲזִירוּהוּ

A synagogue may only be sold on the condition that, whenever it is so wished, it can be returned.

11. שֶׁמָּא/שְׁמָא.

This form has both adverbial and conjunctional value, 'perhaps, maybe' and 'in case, lest'; when compared with the conjunction שֶׁלֹא, שֶׁמָּא can be seen to add a note of fear or insecurity, and is associated in RH with the verbs of fear (יָרֵא) and caution (הִזְהִיר). It replaces BH פֶּן, as can be seen in the following exegetical text (SDt 43 [F 92] on Dt 11.16):

השמרו לכם פן יפתה לבבכם. אמר להם, תזהרו שמא תמרדו במקום

Be careful that your heart is not beguiled. It was trying to say to them, Take care not to rebel against the omnipresent one.

At Sanh 4.5, a wide variety of senses is attested.

A. Negative final conjunction:

מְאַיְּמִין עֲלֵיהֶן, שֶׁמָּא תֹאמְרוּ מֵאֹמֶד וּמִשְּׁמוּעָה

They warned them, So that you do not utter suppositions or hearsay.

B. Adverb:

שֶׁמָּא אִי אַתֶּם יוֹדְעִין שֶׁסּוֹפֵנוּ לִבְדּוֹק אֶתְכֶם?

Perhaps you do not know that in the last resort we shall have to investigate you.

C. Preventive final conjunction.

In the meaning 'lest, in case', שֶׁמָּא is usually found in justification of a biblical text. In the tannaitic *midrashim*, it appears in the standard formula שֶׁמָּא תֹאמַר/תֹאמְרוּ ... ת"ל 'lest you say (i.e. 'so that you do not argue' in such and such a way) ... the biblical text says' (see Unit 18.17). A similar usage is to be seen in the final part of the introductory text to this unit (Sanh 4.5), where Lv 5.1 and Pr 11.10 are cited in order that no-one might argue (שֶׁמָּא תֹאמַר) against solidarity.

The expression of preventive purpose is not found only in connection with biblical interpretation. שֶׁמָּא can also be used to prevent, or to express fear about, any event:

אַף אִשָּׁה אַחֶרֶת מַתְקִינִין לוֹ, שֶׁמָּא תָמוּת אִשְׁתּוֹ

Another woman had to be assigned to him in case his wife were to die (Yom 1.1).

Compare the version of this *halakhah* in SLv 16.32 (W 83b):

כך מקדישים לו אשה אחרת על תנאי שמא יארע דבר באשתו

... in case something were to happen to his wife.

Note that in these two examples it is especially clear that the negative final ('so that not') and preventive final ('in case') values of שֶׁמָּא cannot be used interchangeably.

12. Consecutive clauses.

A. As in BH (see Meyer 1992, §118), a consecutive clause can be connected to its main clause by -וְ:

כַּמָּה יְהֵא בַזַּיִת וְלֹא יְקָצֵֽנּוּ?

How much must there be in an olive tree so that it may not be
pruned? (Shebi 4.10)

B. The similarity of consecutive and final constructions enables the use
of conjunctions like כְּדֵי שֶׁ- with consecutive value:

מוֹרִידִין לִפְנֵי הַתֵּבָה זָקֵן וְרָגִיל וְיֵשׁ לוֹ בָנִים וּבֵיתוֹ רֵיקָם, כְּדֵי שֶׁיְּהֵא
לִבּוֹ שָׁלֵם בַּתְּפִלָּה

They placed before the ark a well-versed elder, with children but
with his house already empty, so that he might pray with all his
heart (Taa 2.2).

C. Typical are consecutive clauses introduced by שֶׁ- or שֶׁלֹּא following an
exclamation or emphatic adjective:

חביב בנימין שנקרא ידיד למקום

How beloved is Benjamin, such that he has been called, Favourite,
by the omnipresent one! (SDt 352 [F 409]);

מה כח עבירה קשה שעד שלא פשטו ידיהם בעבירה לא היה
בהם זבים ומצורעים

How terrible is the power of sin, such that before they stretched out
their hands to sin none of them had been affected by venereal or
skin disease! (SNm 1.10 [H 4]);

אוי לי שאני ערום מן המצוות

Woe is me, such that I have become stripped of precepts! (SDt 36 [F
68]).

גדול שלום שאפילו מתים צריכים שלום

How great is peace, such that even the dead need peace! (SDt 199 [F
237]);

וכי מה אני ספון, שהכתי חיות רעות הללו?

Why have I been distinguished to the extent that I can kill these wild
beasts? (Mek 17.14 [L 2.157]);

וְנֶאֱמָן הוּא בַּעַל מְלַאכְתָּךְ, שֶׁיְשַׁלֵּם לָךְ שְׂכַר פְּעוּלָתָךְ

Your employer is faithful, such as to pay you for your work (Abot
2.16).

(Note that K replaces the relative/consecutive clause here with a simple final
infinitive structure: לשלם.)

IV *Phraseology*

13. חֲבִיבִין יִשְׂרָאֵל שֶׁ- 'how beloved are the Israelites, such that ...'; the
clause dependent on the exclamation should be understood as a consequence
rather than a cause (although it is indeed possible for a causal relationship to
be formulated in the same exclamatory fashion). Numerous examples include:

חֲבִיבִין יִשְׂרָאֵל, שֶׁנִּקְרְאוּ בָנִים לַמָּקוֹם

How beloved are the Israelites, such that they have been called children of the omnipresent one (Abot 3.14);

חביבין ישראל, שסבבם הכתוב במצות, תפילין בראשיהם ותפילין
בזרועותיהם, מזוזה בפתחיהם, ציצית בבגדיהם

How beloved are the Israelites, such that Scripture surrounds them with precepts: phylacteries on their heads and phylacteries on their arms, a *mezuzah* on their doors, and a tassel on their garments (SDt 36 [F 67–68]).

See also Mek 21.30 (L 3.87–88); SNm 1.10 (H 4); 161.3 (H 222), etc.

V *Vocabulary*

אָפְסַנְיָא/אַסְפַּנְיָא (ὀψώνιον) '(soldier's) pay, rations'

הִסְפִּיק (hi. of סָפַק) 'grant, authorize, supply'

כַּף 'ladle'

לֵבֶס (λέβης) '(cooking) pot'

לִיפְתָּן 'condiment'

מַחְתָּה 'brazier'

מָתוּן 'careful, considered'

פְּרָס 'piece (of bread)'

פְּרוּטָה '*peruṭah*' (a small coin), in plural, 'small change, coppers'

קָמְקוּם 'cauldron'

הִשְׁתַּקַע (htp. of שָׁקַע) 'sink down, be submerged', i.e. 'live permanently', as against גּוּר 'pass through, wander'

VI *Exercises*

1. שִׁמְעוֹן בֶּן שָׁטַח אוֹמֵר, הֱוֵי מַרְבֶּה לַחְקוֹר אֶת הָעֵדִים, וֶהֱוֵי זָהִיר בִּדְבָרֶיךָ,
שֶׁמָּא מִתּוֹכָם יִלְמְדוּ לְשַׁקֵּר.

2. אַבְטַלְיוֹן אוֹמֵר, חֲכָמִים, הִזָּהֲרוּ בְדִבְרֵיכֶם, שֶׁמָּא תָחוּבוּ חוֹבַת גָּלוּת וְתִגְלוּ
לִמְקוֹם מַיִם הָרָעִים, וְיִשְׁתּוּ הַתַּלְמִידִים הַבָּאִים אַחֲרֵיכֶם וְיָמוּתוּ, וְנִמְצָא שֵׁם
שָׁמַיִם מִתְחַלֵּל.

3. הוּא [רַבָּן גַּמְלִיאֵל] הָיָה אוֹמֵר, עֲשֵׂה רְצוֹנוֹ כִּרְצוֹנָךְ, כְּדֵי [כְּדֵי lacks K]
שֶׁיַּעֲשֶׂה רְצוֹנָךְ כִּרְצוֹנוֹ. בַּטֵּל רְצוֹנָךְ מִפְּנֵי רְצוֹנוֹ, כְּדֵי [כְּדֵי lacks K]
שֶׁיְּבַטֵּל רְצוֹן אֲחֵרִים מִפְּנֵי רְצוֹנָךְ. הִלֵּל אוֹמֵר, אַל תִּפְרשׁ מִן הַצִּבּוּר, וְאַל
תַּאֲמֵן בְּעַצְמָךְ עַד יוֹם מוֹתָךְ, וְאַל תָּדִין אֶת חֲבֵרָךְ עַד שֶׁתַּגִּיעַ לִמְקוֹמוֹ.
וְאַל תֹּאמַר דָּבָר שֶׁאִי אֶפְשָׁר לִשְׁמוֹעַ, שֶׁסּוֹפוֹ לְהִשָּׁמַע. וְאַל תֹּאמַר,
לִכְשֶׁאֶפָּנֶה אֶשְׁנֶה, שֶׁמָּא לֹא תִפָּנֶה.

4. רַבִּי יִשְׁמָעֵאל בְּנוֹ אוֹמֵר, הַלּוֹמֵד עַל מְנָת לְלַמֵּד, מַסְפִּיקִין בְּיָדוֹ לִלְמוֹד
וּלְלַמֵּד, וְהַלּוֹמֵד עַל מְנָת לַעֲשׂוֹת, מַסְפִּיקִין בְּיָדוֹ לִלְמוֹד וּלְלַמֵּד, לִשְׁמוֹר
וְלַעֲשׂוֹת. רַבִּי צָדוֹק אוֹמֵר, אַל תַּעֲשֵׂם עֲטָרָה לְהִתְגַּדֵּל בָּהֶם, וְלֹא קַרְדֹּם
לַחְפּוֹר בָּהֶם.

5. הוּא הָיָה אוֹמֵר, הַיְלוֹדִים לָמוּת, וְהַמֵּתִים לְהַחֲיוֹת, וְהַחַיִּים לִדּוֹן, לֵידַע, לְהוֹדִיעַ וּלְהִוָּדַע שֶׁהוּא אֵל, הוּא הַיּוֹצֵר, הוּא הַבּוֹרֵא, הוּא הַמֵּבִין, הוּא הַדַּיָּן, הוּא עֵד, הוּא בַּעַל דִּין, וְהוּא עָתִיד לָדוּן.

6. עֲשָׂרָה דוֹרוֹת מֵאָדָם עַד נֹחַ, לְהוֹדִיעַ כַּמָּה אֶרֶךְ אַפַּיִם לְפָנָיו, שֶׁכָּל הַדּוֹרוֹת הָיוּ מַכְעִיסִין וּבָאִין עַד שֶׁהֵבִיא עֲלֵיהֶם אֶת מֵי הַמַּבּוּל. עֲשָׂרָה דוֹרוֹת מִנֹּחַ עַד אַבְרָהָם, לְהוֹדִיעַ כַּמָּה אֶרֶךְ אַפַּיִם לְפָנָיו, שֶׁכָּל הַדּוֹרוֹת הָיוּ מַכְעִיסִין וּבָאִין עַד שֶׁבָּא אַבְרָהָם וְקִבֵּל עָלָיו שְׂכַר כֻּלָּם.

7. כְּלֵי מַתָּכוֹת כַּמָּה הוּא שִׁעוּרָן? הַדְּלִי, כְּדֵי לְמַלֹּאות בּוֹ. קְמְקוּם, כְּדֵי לָחֵם בּוֹ. מֵחַם, כְּדֵי לְקַבֵּל סְלָעִים. הַלֶּבֶס, כְּדֵי לְקַבֵּל קִיתוֹנוֹת. קִיתוֹנוֹת, כְּדֵי לְקַבֵּל פְּרוּטוֹת. מְדוֹת יַיִן, בַּיַּיִן, מְדוֹת שֶׁמֶן, בַּשֶּׁמֶן.

8. לֹא יַרְבֶּה־לּוֹ סוּסִים [דברים י׳ ט״ז], אֶלָּא כְדֵי מֶרְכַּבְתּוֹ. וְכֶסֶף וְזָהָב לֹא יַרְבֶּה־לּוֹ מְאֹד [דברים י׳ ט׳], אֶלָּא כְדֵי לִתֵּן אַסְפַּנְיָא.

9. וְלָמָּה אָמְרוּ חֲכָמִים, עַד חֲצוֹת? לְהַרְחִיק מִן הָעֲבֵירָה וְלַעֲשׂוֹת סְיָג לַתּוֹרָה וּלְקַיֵּם דִּבְרֵי אַנְשֵׁי כְּנֶסֶת הַגְּדוֹלָה, שֶׁהָיוּ אוֹמְרִים שְׁלֹשָׁה דְבָרִים, הֱווּ מְתוּנִין בַּדִּין וְהַעֲמִידוּ תַלְמִידִים הַרְבֵּה וַעֲשׂוּ סְיָג לַתּוֹרָה.

10. וְשַׁלִּשִׁים עַל כֻּלּוֹ [שמות יד׳ ז׳], עַל מְנָת לְכַלּוֹת. לְשֶׁעָבַר, כָּל הַבֵּן הַיִּלּוֹד וְגו׳ [שמות א׳ כב׳], אֲבָל כָּאן, וְשַׁלִּשִׁים עַל כֻּלּוֹ, עַל מְנָת לְכַלּוֹת, שֶׁנֶּאֱמַר, אָרִיק חַרְבִּי תּוֹרִשִׁימוֹ יָדִי [שמות טו׳ ט׳].

11. שָׁאַל אַנְטוֹנִינוֹס אֶת רַבֵּנוּ הַקָּדוֹשׁ, אֲנִי מְבַקֵּשׁ לֵילֵךְ לְאָלֶכְּסַנְדְּרִיָּא, שֶׁמָּא תַּעֲמִיד עָלַי מֶלֶךְ וִינַצְּחֵנִי? אָמַר לוֹ, אֵינִי יוֹדֵעַ. מִכָּל מָקוֹם כָּתוּב לָנוּ שֶׁאֵין אֶרֶץ מִצְרַיִם יְכוֹלָה לְהַעֲמִיד לֹא מֶשֶׁל וְלֹא שַׂר, שֶׁנֶּאֱמַר, וְנָשִׂיא מֵאֶרֶץ מִצְרַיִם לֹא יִהְיֶה עוֹד [יחזקאל ל׳ יג׳].

12. אִם סוֹפֵינוּ לְרַבּוֹת אֶת כָּל הָאוֹכֶל אע״פ שֶׁאֵינוּ שׁוֹכֵב, מַה תַּלְמוּד לוֹמַר, הָאוֹכֵל ... וְהַשּׁוֹכֵב [ויקרא יד׳ מז׳]? אֶלָּא כְּדֵי לִתֵּן שִׁעוּר לַשּׁוֹכֵב כְּדֵי שֶׁיֹּאכַל. וְכַמָּה הִיא שִׁעוּר אֲכִילָה? כְּדֵי אֲכִילַת פְּרָס פַּת חִטִּים וְלֹא פַת שְׂעוֹרִים מֵיסֵב וְאוֹכְלוֹ בְּלִפְתָּן.

13. וּבָא אַהֲרֹן אֶל־אֹהֶל מוֹעֵד [ויקרא טז׳ כג׳]. כָּל הַפָּרָשָׁה כֻּלָּהּ אֲמוּרָה עַל הַסֵּדֶר חוּץ מִן הַפָּסוּק הַזֶּה, וּבָא אַהֲרֹן אֶל־אֹהֶל מוֹעֵד. וְלָמָּה בָּא? כְּדֵי לְהוֹצִיא אֶת הַכַּף וְאֶת הַמַּחְתָּה.

14. כְּמַרְאֶה אֲשֶׁר הֶרְאָה יְ׳ אֶת מֹשֶׁה כֵּן עָשָׂה [במדבר ח׳ ד׳], לְהוֹדִיעַ שִׁבְחוֹ שֶׁל מֹשֶׁה, שֶׁכְּשֵׁם שֶׁאָמַר לוֹ הַמָּקוֹם כֵּן עָשָׂה.

15. כְּכֹל אֲשֶׁר צִוָּה יְ׳ אֶת מֹשֶׁה כֵּן עָשׂוּ בְּנֵי יִשְׂרָאֵל [במדבר ט׳ ה׳], לְהוֹדִיעַ שִׁבְחָן שֶׁל יִשְׂרָאֵל, שֶׁכְּשֵׁם שֶׁאָמַר לָהֶם מֹשֶׁה, כֵּן עָשׂוּ.

16. וַתִּקְרַבְנָה בְּנוֹת צְלָפְחָד [במדבר כז׳ א׳]. כֵּיוָן שֶׁשָּׁמְעוּ בְּנוֹת צְלָפְחָד שֶׁהָאָרֶץ מִתְחַלֶּקֶת לַשְּׁבָטִים לַזְּכָרִים וְלֹא לַנְּקֵבוֹת, נִתְקַבְּצוּ כֻּלָּן זוֹ עַל זוֹ לִטּוֹל עֵצָה. אָמְרוּ, לֹא כְרַחֲמֵי בָשָׂר וָדָם רַחֲמֵי הַמָּקוֹם. בָּשָׂר וָדָם רַחֲמָיו עַל הַזְּכָרִים יוֹתֵר מִן הַנְּקֵבוֹת, אֲבָל מִי שֶׁאָמַר וְהָיָה הָעוֹלָם אֵינוֹ כֵן, אֶלָּא רַחֲמָיו עַל הַזְּכָרִים וְעַל הַנְּקֵבוֹת, רַחֲמָיו עַל הַכֹּל, שֶׁנֶּאֱמַר, נוֹתֵן לֶחֶם לְכָל בָּשָׂר ... [תהלים קלו׳ כה׳].

17. אֲשֶׁר אֲנִי שׁוֹכֵן בְּתוֹכָם [במדבר ה׳ ג׳]. חֲבִיבִים הֵם יִשְׂרָאֵל, שֶׁאע״פ שֶׁהֵם טְמֵאִים, שְׁכִינָה בֵּינֵיהֶם, וְכֵן הוּא אוֹמֵר, הַשּׁוֹכֵן אִתָּם בְּתוֹךְ טֻמְאֹתָם [ויקרא טז׳ טז׳] ... ר׳ יוֹסֵי הַגְּלִילִי אוֹמֵר, בּוֹא וּרְאֵה מַה כֹּחַ עֲבֵירָה קָשֶׁה שֶׁעַד שֶׁלֹּא פָשְׁטוּ יְדֵיהֶם בַּעֲבֵירָה לֹא הָיָה בָהֶם זָבִים וּמְצוֹרָעִים, וּמִשֶּׁפָּשְׁטוּ יְדֵיהֶם בַּעֲבֵירָה הָיוּ בָהֶם זָבִים וּמְצוֹרָעִים.

18. ‏ואכלח ושבעת. השמרו לכם [דברים יא׳ טו׳-טז׳]. אמר להם, הזהרו שמא
‏יטעה אתכם יצר הרע ותפרשו מן התורה, שכיון שאדם פורש מן התורה
‏הולך ומדבק בעבודה זרה.

19. ‏ואמרת, אוכלה בשר כי תאוה נפשך לאכול בשר [דברים יב׳ כ׳], ... רבי
‏אלעזר בן עזריה אומר, לא בא הכתוב אלא ללמדך דרך ארץ, שלא
‏יאכל אדם בשר אלא לחיאבון.

20. ‏ואמרת לפני י׳ אלהיך ארמי אובד אבי [דברים כו׳ ה׳], מלמד שלא
‏ירד אבינו יעקב לארם אלא על מנת לאבד, ומעלה על לבן הארמי
‏כאילו איבדו. וירד מצרימה [דברים כו׳ ה׳], מלמד שלא ירד להשתקע
‏אלא לגור שם. שמא תאמר שירד ליטול כתר מלכות, תלמוד לומר,
‏ויגור שם [שם].

Sources. 1. Abot 1.9. 2. Abot 1.11. 3. Abot 2.4. 4. Abot 4.5. 5. Abot 4.22.
6. Abot 5.2. 7. Kel 14.1. 8. Sanh 2.4. 9. Mek 12.8 (L 1.46). 10. Mek 14.7
(L 1.203). 11. Mek 15.7 (L 2.50). 12. SLv 14.47 (W 74c). 13. SLv 16.23
(W 82b). 14. SNm 61 (H 59). 15. SNm 67.2 (H 63). 16. SNm 133.1 (H
176). 17. SNm 1.10 (H 4). 18. SDt 43 (F 96). 19. SDt 75 (F 139–40). 20.
SDt 301 (F 319).

UNIT THIRTY-ONE

CONCESSIVE CLAUSES

I *Introductory text* (SNm 119.2 [H 142])

‏ויאמר י׳ אל אהרן ... אני חלקך ונחלתך [במדבר יח׳ כ׳]. על שולחני
‏אתה אוכל ועל שולחני אתה שותה. משל, למה הדבר דומה?
‏למלך בשר ודם שנתן לבניו מתנות ולבנו אחד לא נתן שום מתנה.
‏אמר לו, בני, אע״פ שלא נתתי לך מתנה, על שולחני אתה אוכל
‏ועל שולחני אתה שותה. וכך הוא אומר, חלקם נתתי אותה מאשי
‏[ויקרא ו׳ י׳], אשי י׳ ונחלתו יאכלון [דברים יח׳ א׳].

And Y. said to Aaron ..., I am your portion and your inheritance [Nm 18.20].
You eat at my table and drink at my table. A parable: to what may this be
compared? To a king of flesh and blood who gave presents to his sons and to
only one son gave no present but said to him, My son, although I have not
given you a present, you eat at my table and drink at my table. That is why it
says, It is the portion that I give them of my offerings by fire [Lv 6.10], They
are to eat of Y.'s offerings by fire and of his patrimony [Dt 18.1].

1. The parable restates the traditional explanation of why, remarkably, the tribe of Levi was allotted no territory. This model of a praiseworthy tribe, sustained from outside so as to be free of the normal duties of life, has passed into other religions.

II *Morphology*

2. In BH, the following particles are used with concessive value: כִּי (Is 54.10), אִם (Nm 22.18; Jb 9.15), גַּם (Is 49.15), גַּם כִּי (Is 1.15), and עַל with noun (Jb 16.17) and with infinitive (Jr 2.35).

In RH, various combinations with the particle אַף are employed, אֲפִילוּ (אִילוּ and אַף), אַף עַל פִּי, אַף כְּשֶׁ-, as well as אִם.

III *Grammar and usage*

3. Concession is a type of conditional relationship, and it can be seen that many formally conditional clauses may be understood concessively. This is particularly common with אִם and כִּי in BH, and the same is found in RH (see also Unit 28.7A):

אִם לָמַדְתָּ תוֹרָה הַרְבֵּה ... אִם יִהְיוּ כָל חַכְמֵי יִשְׂרָאֵל בְּכַף מֹאזְנַיִם

Even though you had studied Torah a lot ... even if all the sages of Israel were on one balance of a pair of scales (Abot 2.8);

אִם אַתָּה נוֹתֵן לִי כָל כֶּסֶף ... אֵינִי דָר אֶלָּא בִּמְקוֹם תּוֹרָה

Although you were to give me all the silver (in the world) ..., I would not live except in a place where there was Torah (Abot 6.9).

The reverse is also true, so that אֲפִילוּ can be used to indicate a simple condition:

אֲפִילוּ מָצָא חָבִית, וְהִיא מְלֵאָה פֵּרוֹת, וְכָתוּב עָלֶיהָ, תְּרוּמָה, הֲרֵי אֵלּוּ חֻלִּין

If one finds a vessel full of fruit, with *terumah* written on it, they are regarded as profane (MS 4.11).

Here, the irreal value of אִילוּ (see Unit 28.8A) has been lost and it expresses instead a straightforward hypothesis concerning something that, while exceptional, is quite possible.

4. A concessive aspect can even be signalled by -וְ joining two clauses, usually according to the pattern (concessive) verbal clause followed by -וְ and a nominal clause:

שְׁתֵּי נָשִׁים שֶׁנִּשְׁבּוּ, זֹאת אוֹמֶרֶת, נִשְׁבֵּיתִי וּטְהוֹרָה אֲנִי

Let us imagine two women who have been taken captive, one of whom says, *Although I was taken captive*, I remain pure (Ket 2.6).

Concession may also be expressed in RH by simple parataxis, without -וְ:

הֵא וְתֵרָה כל מה שעשיתם, מעשה עגל קשה עלי מן הכל

Although there are many things you have done to me, the incident of the golden calf takes precedence over all (SDt 1 [F 6]).

It should be noted that in this example, the concessive clause is in reality a nominal clause emphasized with the particle הֵא.

5. אֲפִלּוּ.

Although, as we have just seen, אֲפִלּוּ can have purely conditional value, in its concessive function it signals an exceptional circumstance. It is quite normal for אֲפִלּוּ to introduce a nominal or participial clause; between the main clause and the concessive clause, a real and formal subordination can be seen:

אֲפִילוּ הֵן בִּשְׁתֵּי עֲיָרוֹת, מַעֲלוֹת זוֹ אֶת זוֹ

Even though they are in two different towns, the one (grain) neutralizes the other (Ter 4.12);

אֲפִלּוּ הַמֶּלֶךְ שׁוֹאֵל בִּשְׁלוֹמוֹ, לֹא יְשִׁיבֶנּוּ, וַאֲפִלּוּ נָחָשׁ כָּרוּךְ עַל עֲקֵבוֹ לֹא יַפְסִיק

Even if the king greets someone (during prayer), they are not to respond, even if a snake is coiled around their feet, they are not to interrupt (their prayer) (Ber 5.1).

But the fact that there are also instances of אֲפִלּוּ with personal forms of the verb suggests that it is the unusualness of a condition or circumstance that predominates rather than its concessive aspect:

אֲפִלּוּ הִנִּיחַ אֶת בֵּיתוֹ וְהָלַךְ לִשְׁבּוֹת אֵצֶל בִּתּוֹ בְּאוֹתָהּ הָעִיר, אֵינוֹ אוֹסֵר

Even if he leaves his house and goes to spend the sabbath with his
daughter in the same city, it does not create a prohibition (Erub 8.5).

See also Yeb 16.5, etc.

6. אַף כְּשֶׁ-.

There are three examples in the Mishnah, followed by participle, perfect, and imperfect, respectively:

קְדֻשָּׁתָן אַף כְּשֶׁהֵן שׁוֹמְמִין

Their holiness (remains) even though they are in ruins (Meg 3.3);

אַף כְּשֶׁאָמְרוּ בֵית שַׁמַּאי

Although the school of Shammai said (Naz 2.1–2);

אַף כְּשֶׁיֹּאמַר, רַגְלָהּ שֶׁלָּזוֹ תַּחַת זוֹ

Even if one were to say, This one's leg for that one's (Tem 1.3).

7. אַף עַל פִּי.

A. אַף עַל פִּי שֶׁ-:

הַמְחַלֵּל אֶת הַקֳּדָשִׁים וְהַמְבַזֶּה אֶת הַמּוֹעֲדוֹת וְהַמַּלְבִּין פְּנֵי חֲבֵרוֹ בָּרַבִּים וְהַמֵּפֵר בְּרִיתוֹ שֶׁלְּאַבְרָהָם אָבִינוּ, עָלָיו הַשָּׁלוֹם, וְהַמְגַלֶּה פָנִים בַּתּוֹרָה שֶׁלֹּא כַהֲלָכָה, אַף עַל פִּי שֶׁיֵּשׁ בְּיָדוֹ תּוֹרָה וּמַעֲשִׂים טוֹבִים, אֵין לוֹ חֵלֶק לָעוֹלָם הַבָּא

A person who profanes the holy things, who despises the festival days, who humiliates another in public, who breaks the covenant of Abraham our father (peace be upon him), who discovers in the Torah meanings that are not in agreement with the *halakhah*, even if such a person has (learning in) Torah and good deeds, they will have no part in the world to come (Abot 3.11).

Before a participle, the -שֶׁ can be omitted:

אַף עַל פִּי כְּפוּפִין, אַף עַל פִּי מְקַבְּלִין

Even if they (earthenware vessels) are bent, even if they are receptacles (Kel 2.3).

B. אַף עַל פִּי כֵן, which constitutes a clause in its own right, 'though it be so, despite that, nonetheless', following a concessive clause serves to contrast with the main clause that follows. In the following text from Qid 2.3, both אַף עַל פִּי variants are present:

וּבְכֻלָּם, אַף עַל פִּי שֶׁאָמְרָה, בְּלִבִּי הָיָה לְהִתְקַדֵּשׁ לוֹ, אַף עַל פִּי כֵן,
אֵינָה מְקֻדֶּשֶׁת

Even though she said, It was in my heart to become engaged to him, in spite of everything, she has not become engaged.

IV *Phraseology*

8. אַף עַל פִּי שֶׁאֵין רְאָיָה לַדָּבָר, זֵכֶר לַדָּבָר שֶׁנֶּאֱמַר 'although there is no evidence in its favour, there is an allusion to it in the text that says ...' contrasts strict proof (רְאָיָה) with an indication or an allusion (זֵכֶר) and is used to introduce texts that have only an indirect bearing on a matter of dispute. In the Mishnah, the formula appears at Shab 8.7 and 9.4 and Sanh 8.2 (Bacher 1899, 51–55 has a list of biblical texts adduced with this formula in the tannaitic literature).

V *Vocabulary*

הִסִּיעַ אֶת לִבּוֹ מִן 'distance the heart from, decide against'

יִחֵד (pi.) 'unite, confer an honour or a name'

כֹּבֶד רֹאשׁ 'inclination of the head', indicating respect or honour

כְּדָא/כְּדַי 'worthy, appropriate, sufficient'

מָנַע 'hold back, refuse'

מְצֻיָּין (ptc. of צִיֵּן [pi.]) 'noted, distinguished'

רַחֲמִים 'compassion, mercy', מָנַע עַצְמוֹ מִן הָרַחֲמִים 'refuse mercy', i.e. despair of mercy, cease praying

שָׁהָה 'be slow, delay'

VI *Exercises*

1. אֵין עוֹמְדִין לְהִתְפַּלֵּל אֶלָּא מִתּוֹךְ כֹּבֶד רֹאשׁ. חֲסִידִים הָרִאשׁוֹנִים הָיוּ שׁוֹהִים שָׁעָה אַחַת וּמִתְפַּלְּלִים, כְּדֵי שֶׁיְּכַוְּנוּ אֶת לִבָּם לַמָּקוֹם. אֲפִלּוּ הַמֶּלֶךְ שׁוֹאֵל בִּשְׁלוֹמוֹ, לֹא יְשִׁיבֶנּוּ, וַאֲפִלּוּ נָחָשׁ כָּרוּךְ עַל עֲקֵבוֹ, לֹא יַפְסִיק.

2. חַיָּב אָדָם לְבָרֵךְ עַל הָרָעָה כְּשֵׁם שֶׁהוּא מְבָרֵךְ עַל הַטּוֹבָה, שֶׁנֶּאֱמַר, וְאָהַבְתָּ

אֶת יְיָ אֱלֹהֶיךָ בְּכָל לְבָבְךָ וּבְכָל נַפְשְׁךָ וּבְכָל מְאֹדֶךָ [דברים ו' ה']. בְּכָל לְבָבְךָ, בִּשְׁנֵי יְצָרֶיךָ, בְּיֵצֶר טוֹב וּבְיֵצֶר רָע. וּבְכָל נַפְשְׁךָ, אֲפִלּוּ הוּא נוֹטֵל אֶת נַפְשֶׁךָ. וּבְכָל מְאֹדֶךָ, בְּכָל מָמוֹנֶךָ.

3. אֵיזוֹ הִיא בְתוּלָה? כָּל שֶׁלֹּא רָאֲתָה דַם מִיָּמֶיהָ, אַף עַל פִּי שֶׁנְּשׂוּאָה.

4. אֵין שׁוֹחֲטִין אֶת הַפֶּסַח עַל הַיָּחִיד, דִּבְרֵי רַבִּי יְהוּדָה. וְרַבִּי יוֹסֵי מַתִּיר. אֲפִלּוּ חֲבוּרָה שֶׁלְּמֵאָה שֶׁאֵין יְכוֹלִין לֶאֱכֹל כַּזַּיִת, אֵין שׁוֹחֲטִין עֲלֵיהֶן. וְאֵין עוֹשִׂין חֲבוּרַת נָשִׁים וַעֲבָדִים וּקְטַנִּים.

5. הָיוּ יָדָיו טְהוֹרוֹת, וְהִסִּיעַ אֶת לִבּוֹ מִלֶּאֱכֹל, אַף עַל פִּי שֶׁאָמַר, יוֹדֵעַ אֲנִי שֶׁלֹּא נִטְמְאוּ יָדַי, יָדָיו טְמֵאוֹת, שֶׁהַיָּדַיִם עַסְקָנִיּוֹת.

6. אֲפִלּוּ שָׁמַע מִן הַנָּשִׁים אוֹמְרוֹת, מֵת אִישׁ פְּלוֹנִי, דַּיּוֹ.

7. ועד שלא נבחרה ארץ ישראל היו כל הארצות כשרות לדברות, משנבחרה ארץ ישראל יצאו כל הארצות ... ואם תאמר, דן אני את הנביאים שנדבר עמהם בחוצא לארץ, אף על פי שנדבר עמהם בחוצה לארץ, לא נדבר עמהם אלא בזכות אבות.

8. ומפני מה שרתה שכינה בחלקו של בנימין? שכל השבטים היו שותפים במכירתו של יוסף ובנימין לא היה שותף עמהם, וכל השבטים נולדו בחוץ לארץ ובנימין נולד בארץ ישראל. אף על פי כן, ההר [סיני] חמד אלהים לשבתו [תהלים סח' יז'].

9. אלהים אני לכל באי עולם. אף על פי כן לא ייחדתי שמי אלא על עמי ישראל.

10. ויאמר אל אהרן, קח לך עגל בן בקר לחטאת [ויקרא ט' ב'], מלמד שאמר לו משה לאהרן, אהרן אחי, אף על פי שנתרצה המקום לכפר על עונותיך, צריך אתה ליתן לתוך פי של שטן.

11. ונתתי גשמיכם בעתם [ויקרא כה' ד'], ברביעיות. אתה אומר, ברביעיות, או אינו אלא בערבי שבתות? אמרו, אפילו שנים כשני אליהו ונגשמים יורדים בערבי שבתות, אינו אלא סימן קללה. הא מה אני מקים, ונתתי גשמיכם בעתם? ברביעיות.

12. ר' יוסי בן דורמסקית אומר משל, ביד אדם איסר ופרוטה והוא יושב ומשקלו. ואומר, אקח בו פת, אוכל אני ולא שבע, אקח בו תמרים, שמא אוכל אני ושבע. אף על פי כן, אוכל ולא שבע, שנאמר, ואכלתם ולא תשבעו [ויקרא כו' כו'].

13. גדל פרע שער ראשו [במדבר ו' ה'], למה נאמר? לפי שהוא אומר, והיה ביום השביעי יגלח את כל שערו, את ראשו את זקנו ואת גבות עיניו, [ויקרא יד' ט'], אף הנזיר במשמע, ומה אני מקים, גדל פרע שער ראשו? בשאר כל הנזירים חוץ מן המנוגע? או אף על פי מנוגע? ומה אני מקים, יגלח את כל שערו? בשאר כל המנוגעים חוץ מן הנזיר? או אף הנזיר? ת"ל, יגלח, אע"פ הנזיר.

14. ר' אלעזר בנו של רבי אלעזר הקפר אומר, גדול השלום, שאפילו ישראל עובדין עבודה זרה ושלום ביניהם, כביכול אמר המקום, אין השטן נוגע בהם, שנאמר, חבור עצבים אפרים הנח לו [הושע ד' יז'], אבל משנחלקו מה נאמר בהם? חלק לבם עתה יאשמו [הושע י' ב']. הא גדול השלום ושנואה מחלוקת.

15. וידבר יְיָ אל משה לאמר, עשה לך שתי חצוצרות כסף [במדבר י' א'– ב']. למה נאמרה פרשה זו? לפי שהוא אומר, על פי יְיָ יחנו ועל פי יְיָ יסעו [במדבר ט' כג'], שומע אני, הואיל ונוסעים על פי הדיבר וחונים על

פי הדיבר, לא יהיו צריכים חצוצרות. ת״ל, עשה לך שתי חצוצרות כסף. מגיד הכתוב שאף על פי שנוסעים על פי ״ וחונים על פי ״, צריכים היו חצוצרות.

16. מכאן אמר רבי אלעזר המודעי, המחלל את הקדשים והמבזה את המועדות והמפר בריתו של אברהם אבינו, אע״פ שיש בידו מצות הרבה כדיי הוא לדחותו מן העולם.

17. ומה אם משה, חכם חכמים, גדול גדולים, אבי דנביאים, אע״פ שידע שנגזרה עליו גזירה לא מנע עצמו מן הרחמים, קל וחומר לשאר בני אדם.

18. ואבדתם מהרה. ושמתם את דברי אלה ... [דברים יא' יז']. אף על פי שאני מגלה אתכם מן הארץ לחוצה לארץ, הֱיו מצויינים במצות שכשתחזרו לא יהו עליכם חדשים.

19. המוציא אתכם מארץ מצרים [דברים יג' ו']. אפילו אין לו עליך אלא שהוציאך מארץ מצרים, די.

20. וקראת אליה לשלום [דברים כ' י']. גדול שלום, שאפילו מתים צריכים שלום. גדול שלום, שאפילו במלחמתם של ישראל צריכים שלום. גדול שלום, שדרי רום צריכים שלום, שנאמר, עוש שלום במרומיו [איוב כה' א']. גדול שלום, שחותמים בו ברכת כהנים. ואף משה היה אוהב שלום, ואשלח מלאכים ממדבר קדמות אל סיחון מלך חשבון דברי שלום [דברים ב' כו'].

Sources. 1. Ber 5.1. 2. Ber 9.5. 3. Nid 1.4. 4. Pes 8.7. 5. Ṭoh 7.8. 6. Yeb 16.5. 7. Mek 12.1 (L 1.4–5). 8. Mek 19.16 (L 2.222). 9. Mek 23.17 (L 3.185). 10. SLv 9.2 (W 43c). 11. SLv 26.4 (W 110b). 12. SLv 26.26 (W 112a). 13. SNm 25.6 (H 31). 14. SNm 42.2 (H 46). 15. SNm 72.1 (H 67). 16. SNm 112.4 (H 121). 17. SNm 134.5 (H 180). 18. SDt 43 (F 102). 19. SDt 86 (F 150–51). 20. SDt 199 (F 237).

UNIT THIRTY-TWO

ADVERSATIVE CLAUSES

I *Introductory text* (SDt 313 [F 355])

יצרנהו כאישון עינו [דברים לב' י']. אפילו בקש הקדוש ברוך הוא מאברהם אבינו גלגל עינו היה נותן לו, ולא גלגל עינו בלבד אלא אף נפשו שחביבה עליו מן הכל, שנאמר, קח נא את בנך את יחידך ... את יצחק [בראשית כב' ב']. והלא ידוע שהוא בנו יחידו? אלא זו נפש שנקראת יחידה, שנאמר, הצילה מחרב נפשי מיד כלב יחידתי [תהילים כב' כא'].

He cares for him like the pupil of his eye [Dt 32.10]. Even if the holy one, blessed be he, had asked our father Abraham for his eyeball, he would have given it to him, and not only the eyeball but his very soul, which was dearer to him than anything, as it is said, Take your son, your beloved ..., Isaac [Gn 22.2]. Is it not known that this refers to his beloved son? No, rather it refers to the soul, which is called, Beloved, as it is said, Free my soul from the sword, my beloved from the claws of the dog [Ps 22.21].

1. To God's loving care, Abraham responds with a love so great that not only does he hand over to God his son but his very soul, according to an interpretation that, in the light of Ps 22.21, equates יְחִיד with 'soul'.

Note that in this interpretation, the meaning of a highly anthropomorphic expression has been reversed, so that it is no longer God who holds Israel as dear as the pupils of his eyes, but Abraham who is prepared to deliver even more than the pupils of his eyes.

II *Morphology*

2. The only exclusively adversative particle in BH is אוּלָם (Gn 28.19), although -וְ, אַךְ, and כִּי אִם (in antithetic relationship to a preceding negative) can also be used adversatively; as a restrictive, BH employs אַךְ and in earlier texts also אֲבָל (Gn 17.19). In LBH, אֲבָל reappears as an adversative conjunction, 'but' (Ezr 10.13).

3. In RH, אֲבָל has become a full adversative and a new particle has developed under the influence of Aramaic: אֶלָּא (אִן and לָא). אוּלָם has disappeared.

New restrictive or exceptive compounds are בִּלְבַד שֶׁ- and חוּץ מִשֶּׁ-.

III *Grammar and usage*

4. RH, like BH (see Lv 2.12), evidences widespread use of copulative -וְ with adversative value:

נתן לבניו מתנות ולבנו אחד לא נתן שום מתנה

He gave presents to his sons but to one he gave nothing (SNm 119.2 [H 142]).

A. The value of -וְ is made clear by the flow of thought, when it joins two opposing terms or concepts:

זָקֵן וְרָגִיל וְיֶשׁ לוֹ בָּנִים וּבֵיתוֹ רֵיקָם

A well-versed elder, with children but with his house already empty (Taa 2.2).

B. Sometimes, a difference in tense between coordinated clauses (see Unit 17.12 with its quotation of Soṭ 7.8) underlines the adversative context:

אָדָם טוֹבֵע כַּמָּה מַטְבְּעוֹת בְּחוֹתָם אֶחָד וְכֻלָּן דּוֹמִין זֶה לָזֶה, וּמֶלֶךְ מַלְכֵי

הַמֶּלֶךְ הַקָּדוֹשׁ בָּרוּךְ הוּא טָבַע כָּל הָאָדָם בְּחוֹתָמוֹ שֶׁלְאָדָם הָרִאשׁוֹן
וְאֵין אֶחָד מֵהֶן דּוֹמֶה לַחֲבֵירוֹ

A person *makes* various coins with the same seal and all look alike,
but the king of kings of kings, the holy one, blessed be he, *has
coined* every person with the seal of the first human being and nobody looks like another (Sanh 4.5).

C. Given that in RH the personal pronoun already has a particularly emphatic rôle (see Unit 1.7), when it is also introduced by -וֹ, the resulting form,
for example וְהוּא, usually implies a contrast:

הַמְזַמִּין אֶת חֲבֵרוֹ שֶׁיֹּאכַל אֶצְלוֹ וְהוּא אֵינוֹ מַאֲמִינוֹ עַל הַמַּעַשְׂרוֹת

If someone invites another for a meal, but the latter is not sure that
the former can be trusted with regard to tithes (Dem 7.1).

Such a contrast is even more patent with the vernacular construction וְהוּא שֶׁ-
introducing a verb that contradicts a preceding claim, as amply demonstrated
by the following example:

הֵיכָן שׁוֹרִי? אָמַר לוֹ, מֵת, וְהוּא שֶׁנִּשְׁבַּר ..., נִשְׁבַּר, וְהוּא שֶׁמֵּת ..., נִשְׁבָּה,
וְהוּא שֶׁמֵּת ..., נִגְנַב, וְהוּא שֶׁמֵּת ..., אָבַד וְהוּא שֶׁמֵּת

(If he asked) Where is my ox?, and he answered, It's dead, when in
fact it was only lame ..., or, It's lame, when in fact it was dead ...,
or, It's been captured, when in fact it was dead ..., or, It's lost, when
in fact it was dead (Shebu 8.2).

5. אֲבָל.

'אֲבָל introduces a co-ordinated sentence which contains a new case in
opposition to the foregoing' (Segal 1927, §503). In Abot, there is a rich display of parallel but opposing sentences coordinated with אֲבָל:

שְׁנַיִם שֶׁיּוֹשְׁבִין וְאֵין בֵּינֵיהֶם דִּבְרֵי תוֹרָה, הֲרֵי זֶה מוֹשַׁב לֵצִים ...
אֲבָל שְׁנַיִם שֶׁיּוֹשְׁבִין וְיֵשׁ בֵּינֵיהֶם דִּבְרֵי תוֹרָה, שְׁכִינָה בֵינֵיהֶם

When two people sit together and do not exchange words of Torah,
then this is a meeting of cynics ... but when two people sit together
and exchange words of Torah, the Shekhinah stays between them
(Abot 3.2).

(See Abot 3.3,17; 5.17 for the same structure.)

Frequently, contrasting positive and negative statements are coordinated
with אֲבָל לֹא:

יָרְדוּ לַצְּמָחִין אֲבָל לֹא יָרְדוּ לָאִילָן

If (enough rain) came down for the plants but not enough came
down for the trees (Taa 3.2).

When the order is negative followed by positive, the meaning of
לֹאאַיִן ... אֲבָל should be carefully distinguished from that of אֵין ... אֶלָּא (see
below, §6). Whereas the former coordinates two clauses ('he didn't do that,
but [אֲבָל] he did this') the latter restricts the meaning of a single sentence
('he only did/he did nothing but [אֶלָּא] that); see Sanh 1.5, etc.

אֲבָל אִם and -אֲבָל בְּ introduce new hypothetical statements ('but if, but in
such a case'):

בְּנֵי הָעִיר שֶׁמָּכְרוּ רְחוֹבָה שֶׁלָּעִיר, לוֹקְחִין בְּדָמָיו בֵּית הַכְּנֶסֶת ...
אֲבָל אִם מָכְרוּ תוֹרָה, לֹא יִקְחוּ סְפָרִים

If the people living in a city sell a square, with the proceeds they may buy a synagogue ... but if they sell a Torah scroll, they will not be able to buy books (Meg 3.1).

(See as well Ket 5.9.)

6. אֶלָּא.

This particle has a basically restrictive or exceptive value.

A. אֶלָּא ... אֵין/לֹא ('not ... but rather') corresponds to BH לֹא ... כִּי אִם and usually expresses the lack of alternative actions available to a subject: 'he did not do anything but', that is to say, 'he only did', such and such. This exclusive/restrictive force can be made yet stronger by adding בִּלְבַד 'only' at the end of a clause:

כָּל מָה שֶׁבָּרָא הַקָּדוֹשׁ בָּרוּךְ הוּא בְּעוֹלָמוֹ לֹא בָרָא אֶלָּא לִכְבוֹדוֹ

All that the holy one, blessed be he, created in his world, he created exclusively for his glory (Abot 6.11);

שֶׁכֵּן מָצִינוּ בְּדָוִד מֶלֶךְ יִשְׂרָאֵל, שֶׁלֹּא לָמַד מֵאֲחִיתֹפֶל אֶלָּא שְׁנֵי דְבָרִים
בִּלְבַד, וּקְרָאוֹ רַבּוֹ

For thus we found it with David, king of Israel, that he learned no more than two things from Ahithophel, and then he called him his teacher (Abot 6.3).

There is also an isolated example of אֶלָּא following כְּלוּם, in which the latter has an interrogative negative force (see Unit 25.7).

B. אֶלָּא כִי לֹא 'it is not so, but rather; that is not true, instead' is a colloquial formula that mixes BH and Aramaic:

זֶה אוֹמֵר, שׁוֹרְךָ הִזִּיק, וְזֶה אוֹמֵר, לֹא כִי אֶלָּא בַסֶּלַע לָקָה

One said. Your ox has injured (another ox), and the other said, It's not true; rather, it hurt itself on a stone (BQ 3.11);

הַלֶּחֶם מְעַכֵּב אֶת הַכְּבָשִׂים ... אָמַר שִׁמְעוֹן בֶּן נַנָּס, לֹא כִי אֶלָּא
הַכְּבָשִׂין מְעַכְּבִין אֶת הַלֶּחֶם

The bread invalidates the lambs ... R. Simeon ben Nannas said, It is not so, rather, the lambs invalidate the bread (Men 4.3).

C. אֶלָּא ... אֵין in exegetical idiom expresses the equivalence of two terms: A is B, A means B, A is understood as B, etc. Abot 6.3, though late, is a superb example of its use and the rabbinic thinking that it embodies—in order to prove that כָּבוֹד is to be identified with תּוֹרָה, Pr 3.35 and 28.10 are cited; from these it is deduced that כָּבוֹד is identified with טוֹב; then, Pr 4.2 is adduced to show that טוֹב is identified with תּוֹרָה; hence, if כָּבוֹד is the same as טוֹב and טוֹב is the same as תּוֹרָה, it follows that כָּבוֹד and תּוֹרָה must also be the same:

וְאֵין כָּבוֹד אֶלָּא תוֹרָה, שֶׁנֶּאֱמַר, כָּבוֹד חֲכָמִים יִנְחָלוּ [מִשְׁלֵי ג׳ לה׳],
וּתְמִימִים יִנְחֲלוּ־טוֹב [מִשְׁלֵי כח׳ י׳], וְאֵין טוֹב אֶלָּא תוֹרָה, שֶׁנֶּאֱמַר,
כִּי לֶקַח טוֹב נָתַתִּי לָכֶם תּוֹרָתִי אַל־תַּעֲזֹבוּ [מִשְׁלֵי ד׳ ב׳]

Honour is Torah, as it is said, The wise will inherit honour [Pr 3.35],

And the blameless will inherit good [Pr 28.10], and 'good' is Torah,
as it is said, I give you teaching of good, do not abandon my Torah
[Pr 4.2].

Examples of such reasoning are widespread in the tannaitic *midrashim*:

אין מעילה בכל מקום אלא שיקור

Offence always means Infidelity (SNm 7.5 [H 11]);

ואין ברית אלא תורה

Covenant means Torah (SNm 111.1 [H 116]);

אין פלילים אלא דיינים

Pelilim [Dt 32.31] are the judges (Mek 21.22 [L 3.66]);

אין נזירה אלא הפרשה

Abstinence implies separation (SLv 15.31 [W 79b]).

אֵין תַּלְמוּד לוֹמַר ... אֶלָּא, a common formula associated with the school of
Rabbi Ishmael, has to be understood in the same way. It does not reject the
text introduced by ת״ל, but assigns it a new meaning; generally speaking, the
formula may be rendered as 'this text only signifies that', 'it only teaches
that', etc.:

אין ת״ל, לאמר. אלא שאמר לו, השיבני אם אתה גואלם אם לאו

Saying only means that he said to him, Tell me if you are going to
free them or not (SNm 105.5 [H 104]).

(Other examples from SNm are 103.6 [H 102]; 118.12 [H 141]; 125.3 [H
160]; 138 [H 185].)

A contrast can be made even more striking by interposing the question
מָה ת״ל between אֵין ת״ל and אֶלָּא, resulting in the somewhat overloaded sequence אֵין ת״ל, א׳. מָה ת״ל, א׳? אֶלָּא, the point being to emphasize that the
meaning of a particular biblical text is not apparent: *a* makes no sense; what,
then, is the meaning of *a*?; *a* can only mean that. This formula is applied
when *a* is a term regarded as superfluous, for example, according to the text
quoted in the last paragraph (SNm 105.5), לאמר; in another version of this
passage, at SNm 138 (H 184–85), the longer form of the formula is employed. In the following example, it is a superfluous הוא that is the object of
interpretation:

טמא הוא [במדבר יט׳ טו׳]. אין ת״ל, טמא הוא. מה ת״ל, טמא הוא?
אלא הוא שיציל על עצמו צמיד פתיל באהל המת, יציל על עצמו צמיד
פתיל באהל השרץ

He will be impure [Nm 19.15]. 'He will be impure' makes no sense,
so what is it that 'He will be impure' teaches? That he who can by
himself prevent contamination in a hermetically-sealed tent containing a corpse is the same as he who can by himself prevent contamination in a hermetically-sealed tent containing a (dead) insect (SNm
126.10 [H 164]).

The same terminology is also to be found in the Mishnah, as in the following passage:

בּוֹ בַּיּוֹם דָּרַשׁ רַבִּי עֲקִיבָא, אָז יָשִׁיר־מֹשֶׁה וּבְנֵי יִשְׂרָאֵל אֶת־הַשִּׁירָה

הַזֹּאת לַי׳ וַיֹּאמְרוּ לֵאמֹר [שְׁמוֹת טו׳ א׳]. שֶׁאֵין תַּלְמוּד לוֹמַר, לֵאמֹר.
וּמָה תַּלְמוּד לוֹמַר, לֵאמֹר? מְלַמֵּד שֶׁהָיוּ יִשְׂרָאֵל עוֹנִין אַחֲרָיו
שֶׁלְּמֹשֶׁה עַל כָּל דָּבָר וְדָבָר

That same day, Rabbi Akiba explained, Then Moses and the people
of Israel sang this song to Y., saying [Ex 15.1]. 'Saying' offers no
teaching. What meaning, then, could 'Saying' have? It teaches that
the Israelites were responding to each of the words that Moses said
(Soṭ 5.4).

D. אֶלָּא does not always have to follow a negative. Thus, אֶלָּא, or -אֶלָּא שֶׁ,
even without a preceding negative, still has an obviously restrictive function,
'except that, in contrast, however, in fact', attested in both Mishnah and
midrashim:

אָמַר רַבִּי אֱלִיעֶזֶר, שָׁמַעְתִּי כְּשֶׁהָיוּ בוֹנִים בַּהֵיכָל עוֹשִׂים קְלָעִים לַהֵיכָל
וּקְלָעִים לָעֲזָרוֹת, אֶלָּא שֶׁבַּהֵיכָל בּוֹנִים מִבַּחוּץ וּבָעֲזָרָה בּוֹנִים מִבִּפְנִים

Rabbi Eliezer said, I heard that when they were building the temple
they made curtains for the temple and curtains for the courtyards,
except that for the temple they built outside and for the courtyards
they built inside (Eduy 8.6);

וירשתם גוים גדולים ועצומים מכם [דברים יא׳ כג׳]. אף אתם
גדולים ועצומים, אלא שהם גדולים ועצומים מכם

You will dispossess peoples greater and stronger than you [Dt
11.23]. You too are great and strong, but, nonetheless, they are
greater and stronger than you (SDt 50 [F 115]);

וחכמים אומרים, מן היה משתנה להם לישראל לכל דבר שרוצים,
אלא שלא היו רואים בעיניהם אלא מן

The sages interpreted thus: manna transformed itself into anything
the Israelites desired, except that what they saw with their eyes was
only manna (SNm 87.2 [H 87]),

a striking example of this construction.

In the tannaitic *midrashim*, אֶלָּא and -אֶלָּא שֶׁ may begin an interpretation
immediately after a text has been cited, as at SDt 159 (F 210):

ולא ירבה לו נשים [דברים יז׳ יז׳], אלא שמונה עשרה

He is not to obtain for himself many wives [Dt 17.17], only eighteen.
Here, an ellipsis of the complete formula ('not ... but rather') should be understood or perhaps an undertone of polemic against another, more pre-
dictable, interpretation, present in some form in the mind of the midrashic
writer—this is clear when אֶלָּא is used in response to the explicitly-presented
question לָמָה נֶאֱמַר or מָה תַּלְמוּד לוֹמַר:

ומה תלמוד לומר, במועדו [במדבר כח׳ ב׳]? אלא מופנה להקיש ולדון
ממנו גזירה שוה

What teaching is provided by 'At its appointed time' [Nm 28.2]? In
fact, this is a redundant term used so that a comparison can be established and an argument from analogy can be made (SNm 65.1 [H
61]).

In any case, the use of אֶלָּא at the beginning of an answer to a question always marks a contrast that is more or less amenable to translation:

מָה בֵּין נְדָרִים לִנְדָבוֹת? אֶלָּא שֶׁהַנְּדָרִים, מֵתוּ אוֹ נִגְנְבוּ, חַיָּבִים בְּאַחֲרָיוּתָם, וּנְדָבוֹת, מֵתוּ אוֹ נִגְנְבוּ, אֵין חַיָּבִים בְּאַחֲרָיוּתָן

What difference is there between vows and voluntary offerings. It is that in vows, if they (the birds) die or are stolen, the obligation (to replace them) remains, and in voluntary offerings, if they die or are stolen, then there is no such obligation (Qin 1.1).

7. ‏וּבִלְבַד שֶׁ-.

Always with restrictive force, 'only if, in the case that, provided that', the *waw* has lost all conjunctive value. The construction is, in effect, equivalent to a conditional particle, and is generally employed with the imperfect:

הֲרֵי הַמָּעוֹת הָאֵלּוּ נְתוּנִים לָךְ בְּמַתָּנָה וּבִלְבַד שֶׁלֹּא יְהֵא לְבַעֲלִיךְ רְשׁוּת בָּהֶן

Look, this money is given to you as a gift provided that your husband cannot use it (Ned 11.8);

רבי יהודה אומר, מרבה הוא לו [נשים] ובלבד שלא יהו מסירות את לבו

Rabbi Judah interpreted thus: He will be able to obtain more (wives) for himself so long as they do not lead his heart astray (SDt 159 [F 210]).

8. ‏חוּץ מִן.

This expression introduces an exception:

מפני מה המן משתנה להם לכל דבר שהיו רוצים חוץ מחמשת מינים הללו?

Why did the manna use to transform itself into whatever they desired apart from those five things? (SNm 87.2 [H 86–87])

Following a negative statement, it can have the same sense as אֶלָּא:

אֵין מְבִיאִין בִּכּוּרִים חוּץ מִשִּׁבְעַת הַמִּנִים

One may only bring firstfruits from the seven kinds (Bik 1.3).

In general, חוּץ מִן comes before a noun and is not, therefore, strictly speaking, a conjunction (which joins clauses together). However, occasionally we find חוּץ מִשֶּׁ- introducing an adjectival or relative clause:

הַכֹּל יִפָּדֶה וְיֵאָכֵל בִּפְנִים חוּץ מִשֶּׁנִּטְמָא בְּאַב הַטֻּמְאָה בַּחוּץ

Everything can be redeemed and consumed within (the city walls) except whatever has been contaminated outside by a primary source of impurity (MS 3.9).

IV *Phraseology*

9. אֵין לִי אֶלָּא is a formula from rabbinic dialectic, with the לְ signalling a personal view, 'for me, in my opinion', which goes against the tone of the biblical text. The most frequently found context is

אֵין לִי אֶלָּא א'. ב' מְנַיִן? תַּלְמוּד לוֹמַר ...,

where א and ב are the two possible interpretations:

ואם באבן יד אשר ימות בה הכהו וימות רוצח הוא מות יומת הרוצח

[במדבר לה' יז'] ... אין לי אלא שהרגו באבן שיהא חייב. גלגל עליו
סלעים ועמודים מניך? ת"ל, רוצח הוא מות יומת הרוצח, מכל מקום

If he injured him with a stone in his hand so badly that he could die,
and he did die, he is a murderer, he must be put to death [Nm 35.17]
... In my opinion, only if he kills him with a stone is he to be condemned to death; from where may it be deduced that this is also true
if he kills him by rolling boulders or pillars over him? From the text
that says, He is a murderer, he must be put to death, in whatever circumstance (SNm 160.6 [H 217]);

לא יתיצב איש בפניכם [דברים יא' כה']. אין לי אלא איש. אומה
ומשפחה אשה בכשפיה מניך? תלמוד לומר, לא יתיצב איש, מכל
מקום. אם כן, למה נאמר, איש? אפילו כעוג מלך הבשן ...

No man will be able to stand against you [Dt 11.25]. In my opinion,
it only refers to a man; from where may it be deduced that it also
applies to a people or a family or a woman with her enchantments?
From the text that says, No man (i.e. 'no-one') will be able to stand
against you. And if so, why does it say, Man? Because, even if he
were like Og, king of Bashan ... (SDt 52 [F 118]).

The second text here is developed in a manner that is frequently attested—if the first interpretation, which is literal and more restrictive, is not
correct, why does the text say what it does say literally? A perfect opportunity is offered to look for a further meaning, which transcends the merely literal.

10. ... אֶלָא ? ... -שֶׁ אִיפְשַׁר 'but is it possible that...? In fact, ...', expresses a reaction to a biblical text that is, if taken literally, absurd or scan-
dalous (for example, the text referred to at SDt 359 [F 427] that might be
taken to imply that Moses wrote all the Torah, including the account of his
own death), with אֶלָא introducing a more appropriate interpretation:

בשנאת י' אתנו [דברים א' כז']. איפשר שהמקום שונא את ישראל?
והלא כבר נאמר, אהבתי אתכם אמר י' [מלאכי א' ב']? אלא הם
שונאים את המקום

Because Y. hates us [Dt 1.27]. But is it possible that the omnipresent
one hates Israel? For is it not said, I have loved you, says Y. [Ml
1.2]? It is they who are are the ones that hate Y.! (SDt 24 [F 34]).
(Further examples, including SDt 359, can be found in the exercise texts.)

V *Vocabulary*

אוֹבְדָן 'destruction'
הֵגִּיז (hi. of גּוּז [BH גָּזַז]) 'bring, drag'
מָדַי 'Media'
מַמָּשׁ 'reality'; used adverbially, 'in reality'
מִשְׁנֵה הַתּוֹרָה 'copy of the law'; in rabbinic idiom, מִשְׁנֶה תּוֹרָה means

'Deuteronomy' (the 'second law')

פְּטִירָה 'exit, farewell, death'

ר״ע, abbreviation of רַבִּי עֲקִיבָא 'Rabbi Akiba'

שְׁבִיתָה 'sabbath rest'

שָׁמַע 'listen, obey'; in halakhic idiom, also 'interpret, permit'

VI *Exercises*

1. רַבִּי שִׁמְעוֹן אוֹמֵר, שְׁלֹשָׁה שֶׁאָכְלוּ עַל שֻׁלְחָן אֶחָד וְלֹא אָמְרוּ עָלָיו דִּבְרֵי תוֹרָה, כְּאִלּוּ אָכְלוּ מִזִּבְחֵי מֵתִים, שֶׁנֶּאֱמַר, כִּי כָּל־שֻׁלְחָנוֹת מָלְאוּ קִיא צֹאָה בְּלִי מָקוֹם [ישעיה כח׳ ח׳], אֲבָל שְׁלֹשָׁה שֶׁאָכְלוּ עַל שֻׁלְחָן אֶחָד וְאָמְרוּ עָלָיו דִּבְרֵי תוֹרָה, כְּאִלּוּ אָכְלוּ מִשֻּׁלְחָנוֹ שֶׁלַּמָּקוֹם בָּרוּךְ הוּא, שֶׁנֶּאֱמַר, וַיְדַבֵּר אֵלַי זֶה הַשֻּׁלְחָן אֲשֶׁר לִפְנֵי י״י [יחזקאל מא׳ כב׳].

2. אָמַר רַבִּי יוֹסֵי בֶּן קִיסְמָא, פַּעַם אַחַת הָיִיתִי מְהַלֵּךְ בַּדֶּרֶךְ, וּפָגַע בִּי אָדָם אֶחָד וְנָתַן לִי שָׁלוֹם וְהֶחֱזַרְתִּי לוֹ שָׁלוֹם. אָמַר לִי, רַבִּי, מֵאֵיזֶה מָקוֹם אַתָּה? אָמַרְתִּי לוֹ, מֵעִיר גְּדוֹלָה שֶׁלַּחֲכָמִים וְשֶׁלְּסוֹפְרִים אֲנִי. אָמַר לִי, רַבִּי, רְצוֹנְךָ שֶׁתָּדוּר עִמָּנוּ בִּמְקוֹמֵנוּ, וַאֲנִי אֶתֵּן לְךָ אֶלֶף אֲלָפִים דִּינְרֵי זָהָב וַאֲבָנִים טוֹבוֹת וּמַרְגָּלִיּוֹת. אָמַרְתִּי לוֹ, בְּנִי, אִם אַתָּה נוֹתֵן לִי כָּל כֶּסֶף וְזָהָב וַאֲבָנִים טוֹבוֹת וּמַרְגָּלִיּוֹת שֶׁבָּעוֹלָם, אֵינִי דָר אֶלָּא בִּמְקוֹם תּוֹרָה, לְפִי שֶׁבִּשְׁעַת פְּטִירָתוֹ שֶׁלָּאָדָם אֵין מְלַוִּין לוֹ לָאָדָם לֹא כֶסֶף וְלֹא זָהָב וְלֹא אֲבָנִים טוֹבוֹת וּמַרְגָּלִיּוֹת, אֶלָּא תוֹרָה וּמַעֲשִׂים טוֹבִים בִּלְבַד.

3. רַבִּי אֱלִיעֶזֶר בֶּן יַעֲקֹב אוֹמֵר, מוֹשְׁכִים אֶת הַמַּיִם מֵאִילָן לְאִילָן, וּבִלְבַד שֶׁלֹּא יַשְׁקֶה אֶת כָּל הַשָּׂדֶה.

4. הַכֹּל מִטַּמְּאִין בַּנְּגָעִים, חוּץ מִן הַגּוֹיִם וְגֵר תּוֹשָׁב. הַכֹּל כְּשֵׁרִים לִרְאוֹת אֶת הַנְּגָעִים, אֶלָּא שֶׁהַטֻּמְאָה וְהַטָּהֳרָה בִּידֵי כֹהֵן.

5. נָכְרִי שֶׁבָּא לְכַבּוֹת, אֵין אוֹמְרִים לוֹ, כַּבֵּה, וְ, אַל תְּכַבֶּה, מִפְּנֵי שֶׁאֵין שְׁבִיתָתוֹ עֲלֵיהֶן, אֲבָל קָטָן שֶׁבָּא לְכַבּוֹת, אֵין שׁוֹמְעִין לוֹ, מִפְּנֵי שֶׁשְּׁבִיתָתוֹ עֲלֵיהֶן.

6. אָמַר לְאֶחָד בַּשּׁוּק, הֵיכָן שׁוֹרִי שֶׁגְּנַבְתָּ? וְהוּא אוֹמֵר, לֹא גָנַבְתִּי, וְהָעֵדִים מְעִידִין אוֹתוֹ שֶׁגְּנָבוֹ, מְשַׁלֵּם תַּשְׁלוּמֵי כֶפֶל.

7. שָׁלַח לוֹ שִׁמְעוֹן בֶּן שָׁטָח, אִלְמָלֵא חוֹנִי אַתָּה, גּוֹזְרַנִי עָלֶיךָ נִדּוּי. אֲבָל מָה אֶעֱשֶׂה לָךְ, שֶׁאַתָּה מִתְחַטֵּא לִפְנֵי הַמָּקוֹם וְעוֹשֶׂה לָךְ רְצוֹנְךָ כְּבֵן שֶׁהוּא מִתְחַטֵּא עַל אָבִיו וְעוֹשֶׂה לוֹ רְצוֹנוֹ.

8. וירדו כל עבדיך אלה ... [שמות יא׳ ח׳], שאין תלמוד לומר, אלה, אלא שסופך עתיד לירד בראשם. אלא שמשה חלק כבוד למלכות.

9. היום אתם יוצאים בחדש האביב [שמות יג׳ ד׳]. שאין תלמוד לומר, חדש האביב, אלא, חדש שהוא כשר לכם, לא חמה קשה ולא גשמים, וכן הוא אומר, אלהים מושיב יחידים ביתה, מוציא אסירים בכושרות [תהלים סח׳ ז׳]. שאין תלמוד לומר, בכושרות, אלא, חדש שהוא כשר לכם, לא חמה קשה ולא גשמים.

10. בידון [שמות כא׳ טז׳]. אין בידו אלא רשותו, ואף על פי שאין ראיה לדבר, זכר לדבר, ויקח כל ארצו מידו [במדבר כא׳ כו׳], ואומר, ויקח העבד עשרה גמלים מגמלי אדוניו וילך וכל טוב אדוניו בידו [בראשית כד׳ י׳], הא אין ידו בכל מקום אלא רשותו.

11. רבי דוסא אומר, הרי הוא אומר, כי לא יראני האדם וחי [שמות לג׳ כ׳], בחייהן אינן רואים, אבל רואין במיתתן.

12. בני ישראל מניפין ואין בנות ישראל מניפות. ואין לי אלא בני ישראל. מנין לרבות הגרים, העבדים, המשוחררים? תלמוד לומר. המקריב [ויקרא ז׳ כט׳].

13. ואבדתם בגוים [ויקרא כו׳ לח׳]. ר״ע אומר, אילו י׳ שבטים שגלו למדי. אחרים אומרים, ואבדתם בגוים, אין אובדן אלא גולה. יכול אובדן ממש? כשהוא אומר, ואכלה אתכם ארץ איביכם [ויקרא כו׳ לח׳], הרי אובדן ממש אמור. הא מה אני מקים, ואבדתם בגוים? אין אובדן אלא גולה.

14. ואין שופר אלא של חירות, שנאמר, והיה ביום ההוא יתקע בשופר גדול ... [ישעיה כז׳ יג׳]. אבל איני יודע מי תוקעו. ת״ל, וי׳ אלהים בשופר יתקע [זכריה ט׳ יד׳].

15. ויהי העם [במדבר יא׳ א׳]. אין העם אלא הרשעים, שנאמר, מה אעשה לעם הזה? [שמות יז׳ ד׳], עד אנא ינאצוני העם הזה [במדבר יד׳ יא׳] ... וכשקוראן, עמי, אין עמי אלא כשרים, שנאמר, שלח עמי ויעבדני [שמות ז׳ טז׳] ...

16. ומדוע לא יראתם לדבר בעבדי במשה? [במדבר יב׳ ח׳]. אין ת״ל, בעבדי במשה, אלא שתחת שדברתם בי דברתם בעבדי משה. משל, למה הדבר דומה? למלך בשר ודם שהיה לו אפוטרופוס במדינה והיו בני המדינה מדברים בפניו. אמר להם המלך, לא בעבדי דברתם אלא בי דברתם, ואם תאמרו, איני מכיר במעשיו, זו קשה מן הראשונה.

17. לא אוכל לבדי שאת אתכם [דברים א׳ ט׳]. איפשר שלא היה משה יכול לדון את ישראל, אדם שהוציאם ממצרים וקרע להם את הים והוריד להם את המן והגיז להם את השליו ועשה להם נסים וגבורות, ולא היה יכול לדונם? אלא כך אמר להם, י׳ אלהיכם הרבה אתכם על גבי דייניכם.

18. וכתב לו את משנה התורה [דברים יז׳ יח׳]. אין לי אלא משנה תורה, שאר דברי תורה מנין? תלמוד לומר, לשמור את כל דברי התורה הזאת ואת החקים האלה לעשתם [דברים יז׳ יט׳]. אם כן, למה נאמר, משנה התורה? שעתידה להשתנות. אחרים אומרים, אין קוראים ביום הקהל אלא משנה תורה בלבד.

19. ואם איש עני הוא [דברים כד׳ יב׳]. אין לי אלא עני, עשיר מנין? תלמוד לומר, ואם איש. אם כן, למה נאמר, עני? ממהר אני ליפרע על ידי עני יותר מן העשיר.

20. וימת שם משה [דברים לד׳ ה׳], איפשר שמת משה וכותב, וימת שם משה? אלא עד כאן כתב משה, מיכן ואילך כתב יהושע. רבי מאיר אומר, הרי הוא אומר, ויכתוב משה את התורה הזאת [דברים לא׳ ט׳], איפשר שנתן משה את התורה כשהיא חסירה אפילו אות אחת? אלא מלמד שהיה משה כותב מה שאמר לו הקדוש ברוך הוא כתוב.

Sources. 1. Abot 3.3. 2. Abot 6.9. 3. MQ 1.3. 4. Neg 3.1. 5. Shab 16.6. 6. Shebu 8.4. 7. Taa 3.8. 8. Mek 12.31 (L 1.101). 9. Mek 13.4 (L 1.140). 10. Mek 21.16 (L 3.45). 11. SLv 1.1 (W 4a). 12. SLv 7.29–30 (W 39b). 13. SLv 26.38 (W 112b). 14. SNm 77.4 (H 72). 15. SNm 85.2 (H 84). 16. SNm 103.6 (H 102). 17. SDt 9 (F 17). 18. SDt 160 (F 211). 19. SDt 277 (F 295). 20. SDt 357 (F 427).

BIBLIOGRAPHY

Abbreviations

ANDRL1, ANDRL2=Archive of the new dictionary of rabbinical literature, 1 (ed. by E.Y. Kutscher; Ramat-Gan, 1972), 2 (ed. by M.Z. Kaddari; Ramat-Gan, 1974); *BI=Bar-Ilan*; *CBQ=The Catholic Biblical Quarterly*; *ET=The Expository Times*; *HDSSBS*=T. Muraoka and J.F. Elwolde (eds.), *The Hebrew of the Dead Sea Scrolls and Ben Sira: proceedings of a symposium held at Leiden University, 11-14 December 1995* (Leiden, 1997); *HLSZBH*=M. Bar-Asher, A. Dotan, G.B. Ṣarfatti, and D. Téné (eds.), *Hebrew language studies presented to Professor Zeev Ben-Ḥayyim* (Jerusalem, 1983); *HUCA =Hebrew Union College Annual*; *HYMV*=E.Y. Kutscher, S. Lieberman, and M.Z. Kaddari (eds.), *Ḥenoch Yalon memorial volume* (Bar-Ilan Departmental Researches, 2; Ramat-Gan, 1974); *JBL=Journal of Biblical Literature*; *JQR=Jewish Quarterly Review*; *JSS=Journal of Semitic Studies*; *Lᵉš.= Lᵉšonénu*; *LS1, LS2-3, LS4, LS5-6*=M. Bar-Asher (ed.), *Language studies [Meḥqarim ba-lashon]*, 1, 2-3, 4, 5-6 (Jerusalem, 1985, 1987, 1990, 1992); *MEAH =Miscelánea de Estudios Arabes y Hebraicos*; *P9WCJS=Proceedings of the Ninth World Congress of Jewish Studies. Jerusalem, August 4-12, 1985* (Jerusalem, 1986, 1988); *RB=Revue Biblique*; *REJ=Revue des Etudes Juives*; *SHJLSM*=M. Bar-Asher (ed.), *Studies in Hebrew and Jewish languages presented to Shelomo Morag* (Jerusalem, 1996); *SHSLEYK*=G.B. Ṣarfatti, P. Artzi, J.C. Greenfield, and M.Z. Kaddari (eds.), *Studies in Hebrew and Semitic languages dedicated to the memory of Prof. E.Y. Kutscher* (Ramat-Gan, 1980); *SYHA*=S. Lieberman (ed.), *Sefer ha-yovel le-Rabbi Ḥanokh Albeck* (Jerusalem, 1963); *ZNW=Zeitschrift für die neutestamentliche Wissenschaft*.

Doct. diss. = Doctoral dissertation; H. (at the end of a reference) = (written in) Hebrew; repr. = reprinted; * indicates pages within a separately paginated Hebrew section.

Abbot, W.G.M., 1944–45: 'Did Jesus speak Aramaic?', *ET* 56, 305.
Abramson, S., 1956–57: 'Mi-leshon ḥakhamim', *Lᵉš.* 21, 94–103.
Academy of the Hebrew Language, 1988: *The historical dictionary of the Hebrew language. Material for the dictionary. Series I: 200 B.C.E.–300 C.E. Guides and indices to the microfiche.* Jerusalem.
Albeck, C., 1971: *Einführung in die Mischna.* Berlin/New York.
Albrecht, K., 1911: 'Še- in der Mischnah', *Zeitschrift für die alttestamentliche Wissenschaft* 31, 205–17.
    1913: *Neuhebräische Grammatik auf Grund der Mishna.* Munich.
Alexander, P.S., 1990: '*Quid Athenis et Hierosolymis?* Rabbinic midrash and

hermeneutics in the Greco-Roman world', in P.R. Davies and R.T. White (eds.), *A tribute to Geza Vermes: essays on Jewish and Christian Literature and history*, Sheffield, pp. 101–24.

Allony, N., 1963: 'Qeṭaʿ Mishnah 'im niqqud Ereṣ-Yisra'el', in *SYHA*, pp. 30–40.

1973–74: *Qiṭʿe Genizah shel Mishnah, Talmud, u-midrash menuqqadim be-niqqud Ereṣ-Yisre'eli*. Jerusalem.

Andersen, F.I., 1970: *The Hebrew verbless clause in the Pentateuch*. Nashville/New York.

1974: *The sentence in Biblical Hebrew*. The Hague.

Argyle, A.W., 1955–56: 'Did Jesus speak Greek?', *ET* 67, 92–93.

Azar, M., 1983: 'Pseudo-"casus pendens" in the Mishnah', *Lᵉš.* 47, 264–71. H.

1990: 'The elliptical sentence in the Mishna: syntactical conditions', in *LS4*, pp. 5–25. H.

1995: *Taḥbir leshon ha-Mishnah*. Jerusalem.

Bacher, W., 1899 (repr. 1965): *Die exegetische Terminologie der jüdischen Traditionsliteratur*, 1. Leipzig.

Bar-Asher, M., 1971: *Mishna codex Parma 'B', Seder Ṭeharot*. Jerualem.

1972–80 (ed.): *Qoveṣ ma'amarim bi-lshon HaZaL*. 2 vols. Jerusalem.

1976: 'Ṣurot nedirot bi-lshon ha-tanna'im', *Lᵉš.* 41, 83–102.

1980: *The tradition of Mishnaic Hebrew in the communities of Italy (according to MS Paris 328–329)*. Jerusalem. H.

1983: 'Nishkaḥot bi-lshon ha-tanna'im: ben ha-sofer la-naqdan shel Ketav-yad Kaufmann shel ha-Mishnah (berur rishon)', in *HLSZBH*, pp. 83–110.

1984a: 'Ha-ṭipusim ha-shonim shel leshon ha-Mishnah', *Tarbiẓ* 53, 187–220.

1984b: 'On vocalization errors in Codex Kaufmann of the Mishna', in *Massorot: studies in language traditions*, I, Jerusalem, pp. 1–17. H.

1985: 'The historical unity of Hebrew and Mishnaic Hebrew research', in *LS1*, pp. 75–99. H.

1986a: 'La langue de la Mishna d'après les traditions des communautés juives d'Italie', *REJ* 145, 267–78.

1986b: 'Linguistic studies in the manuscripts of the Mishnah', *Proceedings of the Israeli National Academy of Sciences* 7.7, Jerusalem, pp. 183–210. H.

1987: 'The different traditions of Mishnaic Hebrew', in D.M. Golomb and S.T. Hollis (eds.), *Working with no data: Semitic and Egyptian studies presented to Thomas O. Lambdin*, Winona Lake, pp. 1–38.

1988: 'The study of Mishnaic Hebrew grammar—achievements, problems and goals', in *P9WCJS*, Panel sessions: Hebrew and Aramaic, pp. *3–37. H.

1990a: 'L'hébreu mishnique: esquisse d'une description', in *Académie des Inscriptions et Belles-Lettres: comptes rendus des séances de l'année 1990*, 1, Paris, pp. 200–37.

1990b: 'L'hébreu mishnique et la tradition samaritaine de l'hébreu', in *Proceedings of the First International Congress of Samaritan Studies*, Tel Aviv.

1990c: 'Contextual forms and pausal forms in Mishnaic Hebrew according to MS Parma B', in *LS4*, pp. 51–100. H.

1990d: 'Quelques phénomènes grammaticaux en hébreu mishnique', *REJ* 149, 351–67.

1990e: 'hmn (= mn) in a fragment from Qumran', *Lᵉš.* 55, 75. H.

Barr, J., 1970: 'Which language did Jesus speak? Some remarks of a Semitist',

Bulletin of the John Rylands Library 53, 9–29.

Beit-Arié, M., 1980: 'Ketav-yad Kaufmann shel ha-Mishnah, moṣa'o u-zemano', in Bar-Asher 1972–80, II, pp. 84–92.

van Bekkum, W.J., 1983a: 'Observations on stem formations (*binyanim*) in rabbinical Hebrew', *Orientalia Lovaniensia Periodica* 14, 167–98.

1983b: 'The origins of the infinitive in rabbinical Hebrew', *JSS* 28, 247–72.

Bendavid, A., 1967: *Biblical Hebrew and Mishnaic Hebrew*. Tel-Aviv. H.

Ben-Ḥayyim, Z., 1957–77: *The literary and oral tradition of Hebrew and Aramaic amongst the Samaritans*. 5 vols. Jerusalem. H.

1958: 'The Samaritan tradition and its ties with the linguistic tradition of the Dead Sea Scrolls and with Mishnaic Hebrew', *Lᵉš.* 22, 223–45. H.

1985: 'The historical unity of the Hebrew language and its divisions into periods', in *LS1*, pp. 3–25. H.

Berggrün, N., 1974: 'Berurim bi-lshon hakhamim', in *HYMV*, pp. 59–63.

Birkeland, H., 1954: *The language of Jesus*. Oslo.

Birnbaum, G., 1986: 'The noun determination in Mishnaic Hebrew', in *P9WCJS*, Divison D, pp. 39–43. H.

A phonological and morphological description of Geniza fragments T-S E1 43— Mishna Shabbat 9–17, in *LS4*, pp. 27–50. H.

Black, M., 1956–57: 'The recovery of the language of Jesus', *New Testament studies* 3, 305–13.

1957: 'Die Erforschung der Muttersprache Jesu', *Theologische Literaturzeitung* 82, 653–68.

Blau, J., 1953: 'Benoni *pa'ul* be-hora'ah 'aqṭivit', *Lᵉš.* 18, 67–81.

1957: '*O she*- bi-lshon hakhamim', *Lᵉš.* 21, 7–14.

1983a: 'Are Rabbinical Hebrew forms like hâyât archaic?', *Lᵉš.* 47, 158–59. H.

1996: 'On the border between Mishnaic Hebrew and Aramaic (a possible abstract grammatical borrowing)', in *SHJLSM*, pp. *73–78. H.

Brauerman, N., 1986: 'Concerning the language of the Mishnah and the Tosephta', in *P9WCJS*, Division D, pp. *31–38. H.

Brody, R., 1983: 'Two lexical notes on Mishnaic Hebrew', *Lᵉš.* 47, 295–97. H.

Bruce, F.F., 1944–45: 'Did Jesus speak Aramaic?', *ET* 56, 328.

Buber, S., 1885 (repr. 1964): *Midrasch Tanḥuma*. Wilna.

Cantineau, J., 1955: 'Quelle langue parlait le peuple en Palestine au prémier siècle de notre ère?', *Semitica* 5, 99–101.

Cavalletti, S., 1957: 'Ebraico biblico ed ebraico mishnico'. *Sefarad* 17, 122–29.

Chomsky, W., 1951–52: 'What was the Jewish vernacular during the Second Commonwealth?', *JQR*, n.s., 42, 193–212.

Cohen, Ḥ, 1982–83: 'Expressing the pronominal object in Mishnaic Hebrew', *Lᵉš.* 47, 208–18. H.

1990: 'Compound nouns with the possessive pronoun in Tannaitic Hebrew', in *LS4*, pp. 205–18.

Contini, R., 1982: *Tipologia della frase nominale nel semitico nordoccidentale del I millennio a.C.* Pisa.

Dalman, G.H., 1902: *The words of Jesus considered in the light of post-biblical Jewish writings and the Aramaic language*. I: *Introduction and Fundamental ideas*. Edinburgh.

1929: *Jesus-Jeshua: studies in the Gospels*. London.

1938 (repr. 1987): *Aramäisch-neuhebräisches Handwörterbuch zu Targum, Talmud und Midrasch*. 3rd ed. Göttingen.

Draper, H.M., 1955–56: 'Did Jesus speak Greek?', *ET* 67, 317.

Duensing, H., 1960: *Verzeichnis der Personennamen und geographischen Namen in der Mischna*. Stuttgart.

Elwolde, J.F., 1997: 'Developments in Hebrew vocabulary between Bible and Mishnah', in *HDSSBS*, pp. 17–55.

Emerton, J.A., 1973: 'The problem of vernacular Hebrew in the first century A.D. and the language of Jesus', *The Journal of Theological Studies*, n.s., 24, 1–23.

Epstein, J.N.,1957: *Introduction to tannaitic literature: Mishna, Tosephta and halakhic midrashim*. Ed. by E.Z. Melamed. Jerusalem/Tel-Aviv. H.

1964: *Mavo le-nosah ha-Mishnah*. 2nd ed. Jerusalem.

Fellman, J., 1977: 'The linguistic status of Mishnaic Hebrew', *Journal of Northwest Semitic Languages* 5, 21–22.

Fellman, K., 1982: *Variations of a nominal pattern in the traditions of Hebrew: the pattern* qṓṭel *in Mishnaic Hebrew*. Jerusalem.

Finkelstein, L., 1939 (repr. 1969): *Siphre ad Deuteronomium H.S. Horovitzii schedis usus cum variis lectionibus et adnotationibus*. Berlin

Fitzmyer, J.A., 1970: 'The languages of Palestine in the first century A.D.', *CBQ* 32, 501–31.

Friedman, S, 1995: 'An ancient scroll fragment (B. Hullin 101a–105a) and the rediscovery of the Babylonian branch of Tannaitic Hebrew', *JQR*, n.s., 86, 9–50

1996: 'The manuscripts of the Babylonian Talmud: a typology based upon orthographic and linguistic features', in *SHJLSM*, pp. *163–90. H.

Friedmann, C.B., 1927: *Zur Geschichte der ältesten Mischna-Überlieferung*. Frankfurt am Main.

Friedmann, M., 1880 (repr. 1963): *Pesikta Rabbati: Midrasch für den Fest-Cyclus und die ausgezeichneten Sabbathe*. Vienna.

Geiger, A., 1845: *Lehr- und Lesebuch zur Sprache der Mischnah*. Breslau.

Girón Blanc, L., 1988–89: 'Aproximación a la lengua del Šir ha-širim Rabbah y modelo de edición', *MEAH* 37–38, 249–72.

1989: *Midrás Exodo Rabbah*, I. Valencia.

1990: 'A preliminary description of the language of Canticles Rabbah: sample edition', in *LS4*, pp. 129–60. H.

1991: *Midrás Cantar de los Cantares Rabbá*. Estella.

1992: 'The use of *'atid* and *sof* in the language of the Palestinian *amoraim*', in *LS5–6*, pp. 215–24. H.

Gluska, I., 1980–81: 'Nouns of the *maqṭel* pattern in Biblical and Mishnaic Hebrew and their meanings', *Lᵉš.* 45, 280–98. H.

1983: 'The gender of *śade* in Mishnaic Hebrew', *BI* 20–21, 43–66. H.

1987: 'The influences of Aramaic on Mishnaic Hebrew'. Doct. diss., Bar-Ilan University, Ramat-Gan. H.

Goldberg, A., 1962–77: 'Le-ṭiv leshon ha-Mishnah', *Lᵉš.* 26, 104–17; 41, 6–20.

Gordis, R., 1945: 'Studies in the relationship of Biblical and Rabbinic Hebrew', in S. Lieberman *et al.* (eds.), *Louis Ginzberg jubilee volume on ... his seventieth birthday*, New York, pp. 173–99.

Griffiths, J.G., 1944–45: 'Did Jesus speak Aramaic?', *ET* 56, 327–28.

Grintz, J.M., 1960: 'Hebrew as the spoken and written language in the last days of the

Second Temple', *JBL* 79, 32–47.

Gundry, R.H., 1964: 'The language milieu of first-century Palestine: its bearing on the authenticity of the Gospel tradition', *JBL* 83, 404–408.

Gwilliam, G.H., 1890–91: 'The vernacular of Palestine in the time of Our Lord and the remains of it in St. Mark', *ET* 2, 133–34.

Hadas-Lebel, Mireille, 1995: *Histoire de la langue hébraïque, des origines à l'époque de la Mishna.* 4th ed. Paris/Leeuven.

Haneman, G., 1974: 'Uniformization and differentiation in the history of two Hebrew verbs', in *ANDRL2*, pp. 24–30. H.

1974a: 'Le-masoret ha-ketiv shel Ketav-yad ha-Sifra ha-menuqqad (Ketav-yad Romi 66)', in *HYMV*, pp. 84–98.

1976: '''Al millat-ha-yaḥas *ben* ba-Mishnah u-va-Miqra', *Lᵉš.* 40, 33–53.

1980a: *A morphology of Mishnaic Hebrew according to the tradition of the Parma Manuscript (De Rossi 138).* Tel-Aviv. H.

1980b: 'Mi-meḥqar leshon ha-Mishnah', in *SHSLEYK*, pp. 19-23.

Hillel, F., 1891: *Die Nominalbildung in der Mischna.* Frankfurt am Main.

Horovitz, H.S., 1917 (repr. 1966): *Siphre d'be Rab,* Fasciculus primus: *Siphre ad Numeros adjecto Siphre Zutta.* Leipzig.

Hurvitz, A., 1997: 'The linguistic status of Ben Sira as a link between Biblical and Mishnaic Hebrew: lexicographical aspects', in *HDSSBS,* pp. 72–86.

Jastrow, M., 1886–1903 (repr. 1989): *A dictionary of the Targumim, the Talmud Babli and Yerushalmi, and the midrashic literature.* 2 vols. London/New York.

Joüon, P. and Muraoka, T. 1993: *A grammar of Biblical Hebrew.* Corrected ed. 2 vols. Rome.

Kaddari, M.Z., 1972: 'Grammatical notes on Saul Lieberman's *Tosefta Kifshutah* (Zeraʿim)', in *ANDRL1,* pp. 163–73. H.

1974: '''Mah le-'' + N(oun) P(hrase) preceeding clauses in Mishnaic Hebrew', in *ANDRL2,* pp. 85–95. H.

1977–78: '*Nitpaʿal* ke-benoni ba-lashon ha-rabbanit (ha-Š. u-T.)–mah ṭivo?', *Lᵉš.* 42, 190–202.

1978–79: '''Al ha-poʿal *HYH* bi-lshon ha-Miqra', *BI* 16–17, 112–25.

1981: 'Homonymy and polysemy of *Nitpaʿel* forms in the language of the *responsa* literature', *BI* 18–19, 233–47. H.

1990: 'Syntax of *harbe* in Mishnaic Hebrew', in *LS4,* pp. 311–34. H.

1991–94 (ed.): *Postbiblical Hebrew syntax and semantics: studies in diachronic Hebrew.* 2 vols. Ramat-Gan. H.

Kahana, M., 1995: *Manuscripts of the halakhic midrashim: an annotated catalogue.* Jerusalem. H.

Kara, Y., 1996: 'Yemenite traditions of Mishnaic Hebrew according to the oral traditions in the tractate Kelim', in *SHJLSM,* pp. *405–26.

Kessar, T, 1996; 'The Mishnaic pattern *pᵉʿal* in the Yemenite tradition', in *SHJLSM,* pp. *427–39. H.

Kosovsky, B., 1965–69: *Otsar leschon ha-tannaim: concordantiae verborum quae in Mechilta d'Rabbi Ismael reperiuntur.* 4 vols. Jerusalem.

1967–69: *Otsar leschon ha-tannaim: Sifra.* 4 vols. New York/Jerusalem.

1971–74: *Thesaurus Sifrei: concordantiae verborum quae in Sifrei Numeri et Deuteronium reperiuntur.* 5 vols. Jerusalem.

Kosovsky, H.J., 1957–61: *Concordantiae verborum quae in sex Mishnae ordinibus reperiuntur*. 4 vols. Jerusalem.

Kosovsky, H.J. and B., 1932–61: *Concordantiae verborum quae in sex Tosephtae ordinibus reperiuntur*. 6 vols. Jerusalem.

Krauss, S., 1898–1900: *Griechische und lateinische Lehnwörter im Talmud, Midrasch und Targum*. 2 vols. Berlin.

Kutscher, E.Y., 1956: 'Leshon ḥakhamim, mah ṭivah?', *Ha-aretz*, 22 June; 29 July.

— 1960: 'Das zur Zeit Jesu gesprochene Aramäisch', *ZNW* 5, 46–54.

— 1961: *Words and their history*. Jerusalem. H.

— 1961–62: 'The Hebrew and Aramaic letters of Bar Koseba and his contemporaries', *Lᵉš.* 25, 117–33; 26, 7–23. Repr. in 1977, pp. *36–70. H.

— 1963: 'Mishnaic Hebrew', in *SYHA*, pp. 246–80. Repr. in 1977, pp. *73–107. H.

— 1963–64: 'Aramaic calque in Hebrew', *Tarbiẓ* 33, 118–30. Repr. in 1977, pp. *394–406. H.

— 1964: 'Mišnisches Hebräisch', *Rocznik orientalistyczny* 28, 35–48.

— 1967: 'Mittelhebräisch und Jüdisch-Aramäisch im neuen Köhler-Baumgartner', in B. Hartmann (ed.), *Hebräische Wortforschung, W. Baumgartner Festschrift* (Supplements to Vetus Testamentum, 16), Leiden, pp. 158–175. Repr. in 1977, pp. 156–73.

— 1969a: 'Articulation of the vowels *u*, *i* in [Greek and Latin] transcriptions of Biblical Hebrew, in Galilean Aramaic and in Mishnaic Hebrew', in E.Z. Melamed (ed.), *Sefer zikkaron le-Benjamin de Vries*, Jerusalem, pp. 218–51. Repr. in 1977, pp. *135–68. H.

— 1969b: 'Studies in the grammar of Mishnaic Hebrew according to MS Kaufmann', in M.Z. Kaddari (ed.), *Bar-Ilan volume in humanities and social sciences*, Decennial volume, 2 (Jerusalem), pp. 51–77. Repr. in 1977, pp. *108–34. H.

— 1971: 'Hebrew language, Mishnaic', in *Encyclopaedia Judaica* (New York), Vol. XVI, pp. 1590–1607.

— 1972a: 'The present state of research into Mishnaic Hebrew (especially lexicography) and its tasks', in *ANDRLI*, pp. 3–28. H.

— 1972b: 'Some problems of the lexicography of Mishnaic Hebrew and its comparisons with Biblical Hebrew', in *ANDRLI*, pp. 29–82. H.

— 1972c: 'Addenda to the lexicographical section', in *ANDRLI*, pp. 83–94. H.

— 1972d: 'Trivia', in *ANDRLI*, pp. 95–105. H.

— 1974: *The language and linguistic background of the complete Isaiah Scroll (1QIsaᵃ)*. Leiden.

— 1977: *Hebrew and Aramaic studies*. Ed. by Z. Ben-Ḥayyim, A. Dotan, and G.B. Ṣarfatti. Jerusalem.

— 1982: *A history of the Hebrew language*. Ed. by R. Kutscher. Leiden/Jerusalem.

Lapide, P., 1972–75: 'Insights from Qumran into the languages of Jesus', *Revue de Qumran* 8, 483–501.

Lauterbach, J.Z., 1933–35 (repr. 1976): *Mekilta de-Rabbi Ishmael: a critical edition ... with an English translation, introduction and notes*. 3 vols. Philadelphia.

Levy, J., 1924: *Wörterbuch über die* Talmudim *und* Midraschim. 2nd ed. Berlin/Vienna.

Lieberman, S., 1942: *Greek in Jewish Palestine*. New York.

— 1950: *Hellenism in Jewish Palestine*. New York.

— 1955: *The Tosefta*. 5 vols. New York.

Lifschitz, E.M., 1917: 'Ha-diqduq ha-miqra'it we-ha-diqduq ha-mishnati', in

Sefatenu, I, Jerusalem/Berlin, pp. 39–42.

Luzzatto, S.D., 1846–47: 'Über die Sprache der Mischnah', *Literatur-Blatt des Orients* 7, 829–32; 8, 1–5, 46–48, 55–57.

Maman, A., 1984: 'The reading tradition of the Jews of Tetouan: phonology of Biblical and Mishnaic Hebrew', in M. Bar-Asher (ed.), *Massorot: studies in language traditions*, I, Jerusalem, pp. 120–51. H.

Mannes, S., 1899: *Über den Einfluss des Aramäischen auf den Wortschatz der Mischna*. Berlin.

Margaliot, E., 962–63. "Ivrit wa-'Aramit ba-Talmud u-va-midrash', *Lᵉš.* 27–28, 20–33.

Melamed, E.Z., 1982–83: 'Taboos in Mishnaic Hebrew', *Lᵉš.* 47, 3–16. H.

Meyer, A., 1896: *Jesu Muttersprache*. Leipzig.

Meyer, R., 1992: *Hebräische Grammatik*. 3rd rev. ed. 4 vols. in 1. Berlin.

Mieses, J., 1919: *Neuhebräisches Wörterbuch: ein Supplement*. Vienna.

Milik, J.T., 1953: 'Une lettre de Siméon Bar Kokheba', *RB* 60, 276–94.

   1962: 'Le rouleau de cuivre provenant de la grotte 3Q (3Q15)', in M. Baillet, J.T. Milik, and R. de Vaux, *Les 'Petites grottes' de Qumrân* (Discoveries in the Judaean Desert of Jordan, III), Oxford, pp. 200–302.

Mishor, M., 1979–80: 'Le-habba'at ha-modaliut bi-lshon ḥakhamim', *Lᵉš.* 44, 76–79.

   1983a: 'The tense system in Tannaitic Hebrew'. Doct. diss., Hebrew University, Jerusalem. H.

   1983b: 'Ha-zeman ba-mashlim ha-pesuqi bi-lshon ha-tanna'im', in *HLSZBH*, pp. 407–18.

   1985–86: 'On the style of mishnaic-talmudic literature: the imperfect with indicative meaning', *Tarbiẓ* 55, 345–58.

   1989: '*Iggeret 'Ivrit* Oxford MS Heb. d. 69(p): a new publication', *Lᵉš.* 53, 215–64. H.

   1990: 'Talmudic Hebrew in the light of epigraphy', in *LS4*, pp. 253–70. H.

   1991: 'Le-gibbush ha-niggud *–ym/–yn* be-siyyumat ha-ribbui', in *Sugyot bi-lshon ḥakhamim*, Institute for Advanced Studies of the Hebrew University of Jerusalem, Jerusalem, pp. 80–85.

Mittwoch, E., 1943: 'Some observations on the language of the prayers, the benedictions and the Mishnah', in I. Epstein, E. Levine, and C. Roth (eds.), *Essays in honour of J.H. Hertz*, London, pp. 325–30.

Morag, S., 1956–57a: 'Le-meḥqar mesorot ha-'edot bi-lshon ḥakhamim', *Tarbiẓ* 26, 4–16.

   1956–57a: 'The *Pa'el* and *Nithpa'el* verbal systems', *Tarbiẓ* 26, 349–56. H.

   1957–58: 'More on the subject of *Pa'el* and *Nithpa'el*', *Tarbiẓ* 27, 556. H.

   1963: *The Hebrew language tradition of the Yemenite Jews*. Jerusalem. H.

   1966–67: "'Ad ematay dibberu 'Ivrit?', *Lᵉšonénu la-'am* 67–68, 3–10.

   1970 (ed.): *The Mishnah tractates Neziqin, Qodashin, Ṭeharoth: Codex Jerusalem Heb. 4° 1336*. Jerusalem.

   1977: *The Hebrew language tradition of the Baghdadi community: the phonology*. (Edah we-lashon, I.) Jerusalem.

   1988: 'The study of Mishnaic Hebrew—the oral evidence, its nature and evaluation', in *P9WCJS*, Panel sessions: Hebrew and Aramaic, pp *39–54. H.

Moreshet, M., 1976: '*Hif'il* le-lo' hevdel min ha-*Qal* bi-lshon HaZaL (be-hashwa'ah li-lshon ha-Miqra)', *BI* 13, 249–81.

1979: 'The present participle with enclitic nominative pronoun in Mishnaic Hebrew', *BI* 16–17, 126–48. H.

1980a: *A lexicon of the new verbs in Tannaitic Hebrew*. Ramat-Gan. H.

1980b: 'On the *Nuf'al* stem in Post-Biblical Hebrew', in *SHSLEYK*, pp. 126–39. H.

1981: '*Polel/Hitpolel* in Mishnaic Hebrew and Aramaic dialects', *BI* 18–19, 248– 69. H.

Muraoka, T., 1990: 'The nominal clause in Late Biblical Hebrew and Mishnaic Hebrew', in *LS4*, pp. 219–52. H.

1993: see Joüon and Muraoka.

Mussies, G., 1976: 'Greek in Palestine and the diaspora', in S. Safrai and M. Stern (eds.), *The Jewish people in the first century*, II, Assen/Amsterdam, pp. 1040–60.

Naeh, M, 1990: 'Notes to Tannaitic Hebrew based on Codex Vat. 66 of the Sifra', in *LS4*, pp. 271–95. H.

Nathan, H, 1984: 'Did Mishnaic Hebrew lose the distinction between the pronominal suffixes of the third person feminine singular and plural?', in *HLSZBH*, pp. 121– 34. H.

1986: 'Some juridical terms in Tannaitic Hebrew'. in *P9WCJS*, Division D, pp. *23–29. H.

Navarro Peiró, Mᵃ Angeles, 1987: *Abot de Rabbí Natán*. Valencia.

Naveh, J., 1978: *On stone and papyrus: the Aramaic and Hebrew inscriptions from ancient synagogues*. Jerusalem. H.

1981: 'Ancient synagogue inscriptions', in L.I. Levine (ed.), *Ancient synagogues revealed*, Jerusalem, pp. 133–39.

Nebe, G.W., 1997: 'Die hebräische Sprache der Naḥal Ḥever Dokumente 5/6Ḥev 44– 46', in *HDSSBS*, pp. 150–57.

Netzer, N., 1983: 'Mishnaic Hebrew in the works of medieval Hebrew grammarians'. Doct. diss., Hebrew University, Jerusalem. H.

1988: 'Biblical Hebrew in the light of Mishnaic Hebrew: the contribution of R. Shelomo Parḥon, the author of *Maḥberet he-'Aruch*', *Lᵉš.* 52, 26–67. H.

Niccacci, A, 1990: *The syntax of the verb in Classical Hebrew prose*. Sheffield.

Ott, H., 1967: 'Um die Muttersprache Jesu: Forschungen seit Gustaf Dalman', *Novum Testamentum* 9, 1–25.

Ouellette, J., 1980: 'An unnoticed device for expressing the future in Middle Hebrew', *Hebrew Annual Review* 4, 127–29.

Pérez Fernández, M., 1984: *Los capítulos de Rabbí Eliezer (Pirqê Rabbí 'Eli'ezer)*, Valencia.

1986: 'Hermenéutica de los tannaítas: la exégesis introducida por *lammah ne'e- mar*', *Sefarad* 46, 391–96.

1987a: 'Fórmulas con *'amar* y *din* en la exégesis de los tannaítas', in *II Simposio Bíblico Nacional, Córdoba 1985*, Valencia, pp. 581–90.

1987b: 'Modelos de argumentación en la exégesis de los tannaítas: las series *talmud lomar* y *mah talmud lomar*', *Sefarad* 47, 363–81.

1989: *Midrás Sifre Números: versión crítica, introducción y notas*. Valencia.

1990: 'Reinterpretación de palabras bíblicas con *'amar*: un procedimiento hermen- éutico de los tannaítas', *MEAH* 39, 31–38.

1992: 'Oraciones finales en hebreo rabínico', *Sefarad* 52, 193–99.

1994: '*Din* versus *talmud lomar* en los *midrashim* tannaíticos', in *Proceedings of the Eleventh World Congress of Jewish Studies, Jerusalem, 1993* (Jerusalem),

Division C, Vol. I, pp. 9–16.

1997: *Midrás Sifra: el comentario rabínico al Levítico*. Vol. I. Estella.

Porath, E., 1938: *Mishnaic Hebrew as vocalized in the early manuscripts of the Babylonian Jews*. Jerusalem. H.

Prijs, L., 1967: 'Ergänzungen zum talmudisch-aramäischen Wörterbuch', *Zeitschrift der Deutschen Morgenländischen Gesellschaft* 117, 266–86.

Qimron, E., 1977: '*Nitpa'al* benoni', *Lᵉš*. 41, 144–57.

1986: *The Hebrew of the Dead Sea Scrolls*. Atlanta.

1988: 'The origins of the *Nuf'al* conjugation', *Lᵉš*. 52, 178–79. H

1990: 'Considerations on modal tenses in Mishnaic Hebrew', *Lᵉš*. 55, 89–96.

Qimron, E. and Strugnell, J., 1994: *Qumran Cave 4*, Vol. V: *Miqṣat ma'aśé ha-Torah*. (Discoveries in the Judaean Desert, X.). Oxford.

Rabin, C., 1970: 'Hebrew', in T.A. Sebeok (ed.), *Linguistics in South West Asia and North Africa* (Current Trends in Linguistics, VI), The Hague/Paris, pp. 304–46.

1976: 'Hebrew and Aramaic in the first century', in S. Safrai and M. Stern (eds.), *The Jewish people in the first century*, II, Assen/Amsterdam, pp. 1007–39.

Rabinowitz, I., 1962: '*Be opened = effatha* (Mark 7, 34): did Jesus speak Hebrew?', *ZNW* 53, 229–38.

1971a: '*Effatha* (Mark vii 34): certainly Hebrew, not Aramaic', *JSS* 16, 151–56.

Richter, A, 1925: *Das Neuhebräische in babylonischer Überlieferung*. I: *Handschriften und Akzente*. Giessen.

Ridzewski, Beate, 1992: *Neuhebräische Grammatik auf Grund der ältesten Handschriften und Inschriften*. Frankfurt am Main.

Roberts, A., 1877: 'That Christ spoke Greek', *The expositor*, first series, 6, 81–96, 161–76, 285–99, 367–83.

1878: 'That Christ spoke Greek—a reply', *The expositor*, first series, 7, 278–95.

Rosén, H.B., 1963: 'Palestinian *koinê* in rabbinic illustration', *JSS* 8, 55–72.

Rosenthal, D., 1981: 'Mishna Aboda Zara: a critical edition with introduction'. Doct. diss., Hebrew University, Jerusalem. H.

Russell, J.K., 1955–56: 'Did Jesus speak Greek?', *ET* 67, 246.

Sachs, H., 1897: *Die Partikeln der Mischna*. Berlin.

Sáenz-Badillos, A., 1975: 'El hebreo del s. II d.C. a la luz de las transcripciones griegas de Aquila, Símmaco y Teodoción', *Sefarad* 35, 107–30.

1996: *A history of the Hebrew language*. Corrected first ed., Cambridge.

Sanday, W., 1878: 'The language spoken in Palestine at the time of Our Lord', *The Expositor*, first series, 7, 81–99.

1878: 'Did Christ speak Greek?—a rejoinder', *The Expositor*, first series, 7, 368–88.

Sarfatti, G.B, 1964–66: ''Iyyunim ba-semanṭiqah shel leshon HaZaL u-bi-drashotehen', *Lᵉš*. 29, 238–44; 30, 29–40.

1979–80: 'Ha-tafqid ha-prosodi shel *he* ha-yedi'ah bi-lshon hakhamim', *Lᵉš*. 44, 185–201.

1980: ''Al odot ha-yadua' shel ṣerufe ha-semikhut ha-kevulim bi-lshon hakhamim', in *SHSLEYK*, pp. 140–54.

1983: 'Masoret leshon hakhamim—masoret shel *lashon sifrutit hayah*', in *HLSZBH*, pp. 451–58.

1984: 'L'uso dell'articolo determinativo in espressioni del tipo *keneset ha-gedolah*', *Annuario di studi ebraici* 10, 219–28.

1985: 'Ṣimmude millim be-seder qavua' bi-lishon ḥakhamim', in B.Z. Luria (ed.), *Sefer Avraham Even-Shoshan*, Jerusalem, pp. 301–13.

Schechter, S, 1887 (repr. 1979): *Aboth de Rabbi Nathan: edited from manuscripts with an introduction, notes and appendices*. Vienna. H.

Schürer, E., 1979: The history of the Jewish people in the age of Jesus Christ 175 B.C.–A.D. 135. Revised ed. by G. Vermes, F. Millar, and M. Black, Vol. II, Edinburgh.

Schürmann, H., 1958: 'Die Sprache des Christus', *Biblische Zeitschrift*, n.s., 2, 54–84.

Segal, M.H., 1908–1909: 'Mishnaic Hebrew and its relation to Biblical Hebrew and to Aramaic', *JQR* 20, 647–737.

1910: 'Hebrew in the period of the Second Temple', *International Journal of Apocrypha* 11, 79–82.

1927: *A grammar of Mishnaic Hebrew*. Oxford.

1936: *Diqduq leshon ha-Mishnah*. Tel-Aviv.

1939: 'Ḥalom—ḥalomot—ḥᵃlomot', *Lᵉš.* 10, 154–56.

Segert, S., 1957: 'Aramäische Studien, ii: Zur Verbreitung des Aramäischen in Palästina zur Zeit Jesu', *Archiv Orientální* 25, 21–37.

Sevenster, J.N., 1968: *Do you know Greek? How much Greek could the first Jewish Christians have known?* Leiden.

Sharvit, S., 1974: 'Studies in the lexicography and grammar of Mishnaic Hebrew based on the *Introductions* of J.N. Epstein', in *ANDRL2*, pp. 112–24.

1977: 'Textual variants and language of the treatise Abot'. Doct. diss., Bar-Ilan University, Ramat-Gan. H.

1980: 'The "tense system" of Mishnaic Hebrew', in *SHSLEYK*, pp. 110–25. H.

1981: 'The crystallization of Mishnaic Hebrew research', *BI* 18–19, 221–32. H.

1983: 'Ha-'aplologiah bi-lshon ḥakhamim', in *HLSZBH*, pp. 557–68.

1988a: 'Shte tofa'ot fonologiot bi-lshon ḥakhamim', in *Mehqarim be-'Ivrit u-va-'Aravit: sefer zikkaron le-D. 'Iron*, Tel Aviv, pp. 43–61.

1988b: 'The study of Mishnaic Hebrew—accomplishments and tasks', in *P9WCJS*, Panel sessions: Hebrew and Aramaic, pp. *61–75. H.

1990: 'Nouns with double formation in the plural in Tannaitic Hebrew', in *LS4*, pp. 335–73.

1996: 'Three-place verbs in Tannaitic Hebrew', in *SHJLSM*, pp. *223–35. H.

Shivtiel, I., 1937–39 (repr. 1963): 'Mesorot ha-Temanim be-diqduq leshon ḥakhamim', in Ḥ Yalon, (ed.), *Qunṭeresim le-'inyene ha-lashon ha-'Ivrit*, Jerusalem, I, pp. 8–15; II, pp. 61–69.

1963: 'Yemenite traditions relating to the grammar of the language of the Mishnah', in *SYHA*, pp. 338–59. H.

Siegfried, C., 1897: 'Beiträge zur Lehre von den zusammengesetzten Satze im Neuhebräischen', in G.A. Kohut (ed.), *Semitic studies in memory of Rev. Dr. Alexander Kohut*, Berlin, pp. 543–56.

Siegfried, C. and Strack, H.L., 1884: *Lehrbuch der neuhebräischen Sprache und Literatur*. 2 vols. Karlsruhe/Leipzig.

Sokoloff, M., 1969: 'The Hebrew of Berēšit Rabba according to MS Vat. Ebr. 30', *Lᵉš.* 33, 25–42, 135–49, 270–79. H.

Sokolow, N., 1937: 'The living Hebrew language in the foundation of the Mishnah', in *J. Klausner jubilee volume*, Tel Aviv, pp. 109–31.

Sperber, A., 1929: 'Das Alphabet der Septuaginta-Vorlage', *Orientalistische*

Literaturzeitung 32, 533–40.

Sperber, D., 1974: 'Etymological studies in Rabbinic Hebrew', in *ANDRL2*, pp. 102–111. H.

1975: 'Studies in Greek and Latin loan-words in rabbinic literature', *Scripta classica israelica* 2, 163–74.

1977–79: 'Greek and Latin words in rabbinic literature. Prolegomena to a new dictionary of classical words in rabbinic literature', *BI* 14–15, 9–60; 16–17, 9–30.

1982: *Essays on Greek and Latin in the Mishnah, Talmud and midrashic literature.* Jerusalem. H.

1984: *A dictionary of Greek and Latin legal terms in rabbinic literature.* Leiden/Ramat-Gan.

1986: *Nautica talmudica.* Leiden/Ramat-Gan.

1988–89: 'Etymological studies in Rabbinic Hebrew', *Lᵉš.* 53, 60–66.

Stein, S., 1888: *Das Verbum der Mischnasprache.* Berlin.

Stemberger, G., 1996: *Introduction to the Talmud and midrash.* 2nd [English] ed., ed. by M. Bockmuehl. Edinburgh.

1997: 'Historia de la redacción de Sifra', in Pérez Fernández 1997, pp. 17–65.

Sussman, J., 1974: 'A halakhic inscription from the Beth-Shean valley', *Tarbiz* 43, 88–158.

Sznol, S., 1990: 'Jefe o supremo: estudio lexicográfico de los compuestos con *'archi* en fuentes judías de la *koine* oriental', *MEAH* 40, 55–70.

Talshir, D., 1987: 'The autonomic status of Late Biblical Hebrew', in *LS2–3*, pp. 161–72. H.

1996: 'Ha-'Ivrit ba-meah ha-sheniyyah la-sefirah: leshon ha-'epigrafiyah be-hashwa'ah li-lshon ha-tanna'im', in M. Bar-Asher (ed.), *'Iyyunim bi-lshon hakhamim*, Institute for Advanced Studies of the Hebrew University of Jerusalem. Jerusalem, pp. 42–49.

Taylor, R.O.P., 1944–45: 'Did Jesus speak Aramaic?', *ET* 56, 95–97.

Ṭur-Sinai, N.H., 1937: 'Millim she'ulot bi-lshonenu', *Lᵉš.* 8, 99–109, 259–78.

de Vaux, R., 1953: 'Quelques textes hébreux de Murabba'at', *RB* 60, 268–75.

Waldman, N.M., 1972: 'Akkadian loanwords and parallels in Mishnaic Hebrew'. Doct. diss., Dropsie College, Philadelphia.

1989: *The recent study of Hebrew: a survey of the literature with selected bibliography.* Cincinnati/Winona Lake.

Wartsky, I., 1970: *Leshon ha-midrashim.* Jerusalem.

Weinberg, W., 1985: 'Observations about the pronunciation of Hebrew in rabbinic sources', *HUCA* 56, 117–43.

Weisberg, D., 1968: 'Some observations on late Babylonian texts and rabbinic literature', *HUCA* 39, 71–80.

Weiss, I.H., 1862 (repr. 1947): *Sifra. Commentar zu Leviticus aus der Anfange des III. Jahrhunderts.* Vienna.

1867: *Mishpaṭ leshon ha-Mishnah.* Vienna.

Wiesenberg, E.J., 1976: 'Rabbinic Hebrew as an aid in the study of Biblical Hebrew, illustrated in the exposition of the rare words *rḥt* and *mzrh*', *HUCA* 47, 143–80.

Wilson, R.M., 1956–57: 'Did Jesus speak Greek?', *ET* 68, 121–22.

Yalon, Ḥ, 1959–60: 'Nimmuqim le-mishnayot menuqqadot', *Lᵉš.* 24, 15–39, 157–66, 253.

1960–61a: 'Mishnahs and their pointing', *Sinai* 48, 89–105. H.

1960–61b: 'Versions and forms of language in various Mishnahs', *Sinai* 48, 254–60. H.

1963–64: *Introduction to the vocalization of the Mishnah.* Jerusalem. H

1964–65: 'He'arot we-tiqqunim', *L^{e}š.* 29, 59–62.

1967: *Studies in the Dead Sea Scrolls: philological essays 1949–1952.* Jerusalem. H.

1967–68: 'Gleanings on Mishnaic Hebrew', *Tarbiẓ* 37, 133–34. H.

1971: *Pirqe lashon.* Jerusalem.

Yeivin, I., 1974 (ed.): *Osef qiṭ'e ha-Genizah shel ha-Mishnah be-niqqud Bavli.* Jerusalem.

1990: 'Interchange of roots in the language of the Mishna and *piyyuṭ*', in *LS4*, pp. 161–204. H.

Zuckermandel, M.S., 1880 (repr. 1970): *Tosephta.* Pasewalk.

Zuntz, G., 1956: 'Greek words in the Talmud', *JSS* 1, 129–40.

INDICES

Texts

(Bible, Ben Sira, Inscriptions, Dead Sea Scrolls, Mishnah, Tosephta, Talmud,
ARN, Pesiqta de Rab Kahana, PesR, Mek, SLv, SNm, SDt, Seder Olam
Rabbah, Tanḥuma, PRE, Midrash Rabbah, Targums)

Hebrew and Aramaic forms

Verb conjugations (binyanim)

Types of verbal root

Forms of the paradigm verb קָטַל

Noun patterns (mishqalim)

Forms from other Semitic languages

Greek forms

Latin forms

English glosses